SIMPSON

The publisher and the University of California Press Foundation gratefully acknowledge the generous support of the Simpson Imprint in Humanities.

The publisher also gratefully acknowledges the generous support of the Chairman's Circle of the University of California Press Foundation, whose members are: Elizabeth and David Birka-White, Harriett Gold, Maria and David Hayes-Bautista, Michael Hindus, Gary Kraut, Susan McClatchy, Lisa See, and Lynne Withey.

Savage Journey

Savage Journey

Hunter S. Thompson and the
Weird Road to Gonzo

PETER RICHARDSON

University of California Press

University of California Press
Oakland, California

Library of Congress Cataloging-in-Publication Data

Names: Richardson, Peter, 1959– author.
Title: Savage journey : Hunter S. Thompson and the weird road to
    Gonzo / Peter Richardson.
Description: Oakland, California : University of California Press, 2022. |
    Includes bibliographical references and index.
Identifiers: LCCN 2021025600 (print) | LCCN 2021025601 (ebook) |
    ISBN 9780520304925 (hardback) | ISBN 9780520973244 (ebook)
Subjects: LCSH: Thompson, Hunter S.—Criticism and interpretation. |
    Thompson, Hunter S.—Influence. | Journalists—United States—
    Biography. | American literature—20th century—History and
    criticism. | BISAC: BIOGRAPHY & AUTOBIOGRAPHY / Literary
    Figures | LANGUAGE ARTS & DISCIPLINES / Journalism
Classification: LCC PS3570.H62 Z86 2022 (print) | LCC PS3570.H62 (ebook) |
    DDC 818/.5409—dc23
LC record available at https://lccn.loc.gov/2021025600
LC ebook record available at https://lccn.loc.gov/2021025601

Manufactured in the United States of America

31 30 29 28 27 26 25 24 23 22
10 9 8 7 6 5 4 3 2 1

All this stuff avoids coming to the point that matters, which is what I turn out. Funny, I almost never get questioned about writing.

HUNTER S. THOMPSON, 1987

Contents

INTRODUCTION   1

1. BROODING   7

2. THE STORM OF LIFE   15

3. ROUGHING IT   25

4. OBSERVER   36

5. NEW JOURNALIST   52

6. HASHBURY   78

7. TOTALLY GONZO   99

8. ROLLING STONE   116

9. LAS VEGAS   133

10. CAMPAIGN TRAIL   159

11. AFTER NIXON   179

12. LEGACY   203

   Acknowledgments   215

   Notes   217

   Bibliography   239

   Index   251

   Illustrations follow page 98.

Introduction

More than five decades after the publication of his first bestselling book, Hunter S. Thompson remains a cultural icon. A steady stream of publications and films have told his remarkable story, several in detail. Most of these accounts—which feature his drug and alcohol consumption, gun fetish, and "fortified compound"—are centered in Woody Creek, Colorado, where Thompson lived from 1966 until his suicide in 2005.

Although Thompson's books still find large audiences, his literary executor maintains that his greatest achievement was "the collective work, and the fact that he created this one persona—the Hunter Figure—which is one of the great artistic creations of the 20th century." Douglas Brinkley is certainly correct that Thompson's outlaw persona ensured his celebrity from the 1970s on. It also eclipsed his work and private identity. "I'm really in the way as a person," Thompson said in 1978. "The myth has taken over." Perhaps for this reason, his writing has received surprisingly little critical attention. Readers must consult various sources of uneven quality to learn about his influences, trademark style, and critical reception. In this sense, *New York Times* writer David Streitfeld observed, Thompson "stands in front of his work, often obscuring it."

Studies of Thompson's literary formation are especially thin on the ground. What little commentary we have is split over how, when, and where he became the author who wrote the works. Although his literary formation was a lengthy process, the evidence suggests that it was largely a San Francisco story. Like Mark Twain a century earlier, Thompson arrived in the city as an obscure journalist, thrived on its anarchic energy, and left as a national figure. Raoul Duke, Thompson's narrator in *Fear and Loathing in Las Vegas* (1972), famously reflects on that time and place. "You could strike sparks anywhere," Duke says. "There was a fantastic universal sense that whatever we were doing was *right,* that we were winning." Five years later, Duke notes, that feeling was gone, but Thompson had finally arrived.

Toward the end of his life, Thompson confirmed that Raoul Duke spoke for him. In his introduction to the 2003 edition of Timothy Crouse's *The Boys on the Bus,* Thompson detoured from the topic at hand—the 1972 presidential campaign—to reflect on his stint in San Francisco. At that time, he was surrounded by flower children with little interest in politics; even so, they presumed they would inherit the earth.

> Exactly *how* they were going to take over the world without knowing, or wanting to know, anything about politics seemed like a pipe dream to me, but I didn't mind dreaming it from time and time, and I also lived right in the middle of it for four years, and I definitely liked the neighborhood. These were my people—along with the Hell's Angels, Ken Kesey, Bill Graham and the Fillmore Auditorium, the Golden Gate Bridge, Big Sur and all those who have ever lived there. The list is long, and I love it. San Francisco was clearly the best place in the world to be living in those years—1960–70, to be specific—and my memories of life in that purest of tornadoes still cause me to babble and jabber and dance.

Here and elsewhere, Thompson depicted his years in San Francisco, that purest of tornadoes, as a peak period. He rode with the Hell's Angels, listened to Jefferson Airplane at The Matrix, and participated enthusiastically in the city's drug culture. He read *Ramparts* magazine, the legendary San Francisco muckraker, and wrote about Haight-Ashbury for the *New York Times Magazine.* His subsequent work for *Rolling Stone* magazine, which was founded in San Francisco after the Summer of Love, vaulted him to celebrity status.

The fact that Thompson identified "his people" in Crouse's book is also notable. Although he is associated with Tom Wolfe, Joan Didion, and other paragons of New Journalism, he rarely presented himself as a member of any group. (The NRA was a notable exception.) And though he was a skillful literary networker, he also took care to distinguish himself from his colleagues. "A good writer stands above movements, neither a leader nor a follower, but a bright white golf ball in a fairway of wind-blown daisies," he wrote to a friend in 1958. As a young man, Thompson even singled out Ayn Rand's *The Fountainhead* for praise. Few critics hold that novel in high regard, but he thought its libertarian thrust affirmed "a freedom and mobility of thought that few people are able—or even have the courage—to achieve."

As that remark suggests, Thompson prized independence above all, but he needed help to achieve it. Like his idols, he lived far from the nation's publishing capitals, and he used his correspondence to build and maintain his literary network. Taken as a whole, his letters demonstrate an extraordinary ability to charm, amuse, ingratiate, importune, threaten, and attack. That talent was not lost on editors, who frequently ran his missives in their magazines. Unspoiled by deadlines and editorial overreach, his letters to government officials, local television stations, and customer service departments rose to the level of art. One might even argue, as Thompson suggested more than once, that his correspondence was his most important work. Although his published letters represent a small fraction of that output, they also provide crucial insights into his literary formation and model of authorship.

Several assumptions inform what follows. The first has to do with Thompson's collaborators. Although he was a rare talent, skilled editors shaped his output and career at virtually every stage. Carey McWilliams, the only editor whom Thompson unhesitatingly admired, gave Thompson the story idea for his first bestselling book. Warren Hinckle, whom Thompson called the best conceptual editor he ever worked with, helped birth Gonzo journalism at *Scanlan's Monthly*. Jann Wenner, whose feeling for the zeitgeist was an essential part of Thompson's success, did more than anyone to promote Thompson and his work. James Silberman, Alan Rinzler, David Rosenthal, and Marysue Ricci developed Thompson's bestselling books at Random House, Straight Arrow Books, Bantam, and Simon & Schuster. In what follows, I pay particular attention to the roles these and other editors played in Thompson's evolution as a writer.

Thompson's key collaborator, however, was Ralph Steadman. Although Gonzo journalism is synonymous with Thompson's output from 1970 on, Steadman's illustrations were an indispensable part of its success. Thompson always understood this point, though it is frequently neglected by critics and commentators. By supplementing Thompson's fantastical prose with powerful visual corollaries, Steadman shaped the reception of Gonzo journalism from the outset. Accordingly, I explore the potent combination of verbal and visual elements in their collaborations, trace the arc of their working relationship, and consider the extent to which Thompson drew on the illustrations for his own inspiration.

A related point is terminological. As a branding tool, "Gonzo journalism" served Thompson and Steadman well, but the label masks one of Thompson's most significant achievements. Whenever necessary, Thompson shrugged off the protocols of journalism, even the relatively elastic ones of New Journalism, to tap the power of fiction. That practice, which also followed the example of his literary heroes, was not lost on his contemporaries. One political strategist remarked that Thompson's description of the 1972 presidential race was the most accurate and least factual account of the campaign. Likewise, novelist William Kennedy observed that Thompson seemed to be writing journalism but was actually developing his fictional *oeuvre*. *The Rum Diary*, the only traditional novel published during his lifetime, wasn't an important work of fiction, but it is a category error to classify *Fear and Loathing in Las Vegas* as journalism or even nonfiction.

Finally, this book's overarching goal—to take Thompson seriously as a writer—does not conflict with Douglas Brinkley's claim that Thompson's most important creation was his persona. It does, however, require us to square that creation with Thompson's evolving model of authorship. There was nothing inevitable about Gonzo journalism, much less Thompson's celebrity. His work responded to shifting conditions, unforeseen events, and fleeting opportunities. Moreover, we know that Thompson understood his literary achievement quite apart from his celebrity. In 1975, for example, he wrote to a Vietnamese colonel that he was "one of the best writers currently using the English language as both a musical instrument and a political weapon." It was a canny assessment of his own standing, and in what follows, I explore the remarkable sequence of events and transformations that led Thompson to his unique niche in American letters.

The inaccessibility of Thompson's archive has made that work more difficult. At the time of this writing, the archive is reportedly housed in a Los Angeles storage facility and contains some eight hundred boxes of material, including a massive trove of letters that Thompson began producing and saving as a youth. Authors often sell or donate their papers to research libraries to enable the scholarly study of their work, but Thompson's archive was purchased in 2008 and has been held privately ever since. Critical neglect is never good for an author's legacy, but it is much likelier when the archival material is sequestered. Until scholars can bring that material to bear on our understanding of Thompson's work, he may be remembered as what his biographer, William McKeen, has called the favorite writer for a lot of people who don't read. In the meantime, we must use the available resources to gauge Thompson's achievement.

Although my primary interest is in Thompson's literary output, many of my precursors have recognized the difficulty of disentangling the work from the person. Thompson was admired and even beloved by his vast network, including women who described him as a perfect southern gentleman. That picture, however, is complicated by the accounts of his closest family members, who recall an angry, domineering narcissist with a record of verbal and physical abuse. Some of Thompson's language and attitudes were problematic even by the standards of his time, and his professional decline was closely linked to his vices. Less than a decade after his arrival on the national stage, he found it difficult to produce a sustained piece of writing without heroic (and largely unacknowledged) assistance from his colleagues. Even with that assistance, much of his writing after 1974 was lackluster. In some cases, he failed to produce any copy at all—or even to attend the event he was sent to cover. San Francisco figured in this later period as well. In the 1980s, Thompson cast himself as the night manager at the O'Farrell Theatre, which he described as the Carnegie Hall of public sex in America. It was a logical extension of his roguish persona, but he produced little writing of note, and his image tilted from louche to sordid. San Francisco, that purest of tornadoes in the 1960s, had turned into a blizzard of cocaine and live sex acts.

Even if we focus on the work instead of the person, the urge to moralize is unavoidable. Indeed, that desire arises from the work itself. Thompson's writing was not produced—or meant to be read—in a moral vacuum. To the contrary, his best work delivered and invited moral judgments at every turn. As early as 1970, novelist James Salter called Thompson a moralist posing as an immoralist, and novelist Hari Kunzru's 1998 review of Thompson's edited correspondence made a similar point. "The true voice of Thompson is revealed to be that of American moralist," Kunzru claimed, "one who often makes himself ugly to expose the ugliness he sees around him." That line is often used as a blurb, but the unabridged version was more specific. Kunzru described Thompson as a "misshapen sort of moralist" who was "largely dismissed by those who require their writers to behave like grownups." That dismissal was a pity, Kunzru added, because Thompson's capacity for mayhem was "a minor side-effect of a personality that functions as a machine for exposing liars and hypocrites." Kunzru's judgment returns us to Streitfeld's point—that Thompson stands in front of his work and often obscures it—but it also calls us to reconsider that work and its durable appeal. Having done so, I would argue that Thompson was not only an accomplished journalist, satirist, and media critic, but also the most distinctive American voice in the second half of the twentieth century.

Rereading Thompson also prompted a wish: that he could have called out the stupidity, cruelty, fraudulence, and corruption that followed his departure from the national stage. As I write these lines, the nation is recoiling from an attack on the US Capitol while Congress was affirming the results of the 2020 election. That spectacle, which left five persons dead, is only the latest in a series of outrages that Donald Trump has inflicted on the nation. Far more lethal was his abject mishandling of a pandemic that so far has claimed 360,000 American lives and ravaged the economy. Equal parts clown show, conspicuous grift, and killing machine, Trump's misrule caught his rivals and the media flatfooted. Even more dispiriting is the fact that, after four years of dividing and demoralizing the nation, Trump racked up 74 million votes in his failed reelection bid.

Thompson would not have been surprised by Donald Trump, his supporters, or the media's reaction to them. His Hell's Angels coverage previewed the politics of resentment, and though his commentary was hyperbolic, it seems prophetic now. He would have argued that Trump was the misbegotten product of the modern conservative movement, and that covering him objectively normalized his depredations. Even misshapen moralists, if they are sufficiently talented, can play an important role in such times. In Thompson's case, it is not his virtue but rather his virtuosity that draws me back, again and again, to his writing and the forces that shaped it. For all of his shortcomings, I now regard his relentless attacks on hypocrisy and mendacity, both in American politics and the media, as a moral force that is too rarely acknowledged and appreciated.

Richmond, California
January 6, 2021

1   Brooding

In the frosty hours before dawn in January 1970, Hunter S. Thompson composed a lengthy letter to his editor at Random House. For more than a decade, the 32-year-old Thompson had used confident, razor-sharp correspondence to build and maintain his literary network. Written over several days from Owl Farm, his home near Aspen, this letter was different. Its tone was anxious, even desperate. He needed help.

Thompson owed James Silberman a book. The contract called for a manuscript by August 1967, and Thompson was almost two and half years late. In his letter, Silberman noted archly that the project was now in its second decade. Thompson claimed to welcome the reminder, which "came as something of a relief. I'd been expecting it for months—like a demand note on a long overdue mortgage."

Thompson's debut effort, published three years earlier, had come together quickly. It began as a magazine assignment while Thompson was living in San Francisco. After spending several weeks with the Hell's Angels, he produced a story about the motorcycle gang for *The Nation* magazine. After it ran in May 1965, he received a dozen contract offers for a book on the same topic. Silberman met him at a bar in North Beach, spiritual home of the Beats, before repairing to Thompson's home near the Haight-Ashbury neighborhood. Ballantine Books was already planning to produce the paperback edition, but Silberman purchased the hardcover rights for Random House and eventually edited the book. After receiving the first part of his advance, Thompson wrote to Charles Kuralt, a friend who would later anchor *CBS News Sunday Morning*. Thompson confided that he would rather receive a fat advance for his novel; nevertheless, this offer was too good to pass up. Instead of repaying a small loan to Kuralt, Thompson reclaimed the guns and camera gear he had hocked.

Thompson spent the next year consorting with the motorcycle gang and finished the manuscript in a four-day rush fueled by bourbon and Dexedrine. Published in 1967, the book was a critical and commercial success. Still short of funds, Thompson accepted an advance from Random House for a novel and two more works of nonfiction. He had already drafted *The Rum Diary*, a novel based on his stint in Puerto Rico. One of the nonfiction works was supposed to be about the death of the American Dream.

That trope had a patchy history. Shortly after the Civil War, Horatio Alger popularized the rags-to-riches stories that showcased America's promise of opportunity. His first success, *Ragged Dick*, appeared two years after Alger resigned from the ministry following sexual abuse charges. It told the story of a poor boy who parlayed his positive attitude and work ethic into middle-class prosperity and respectability. It also became the template for Alger's young adult fiction, which Ernest Hemingway casually lampooned in *The Sun Also Rises*. But it wasn't until 1931 that James Truslow Adams defined the American Dream as such. The idea, Adams wrote, was not "a dream of motor cars and high wages merely." Rather, it was "a dream of social order in which each man and each woman shall be able to attain to the fullest stature of which they are innately capable, and be recognized by others for what they are, regardless of the fortuitous circumstances of birth or position." Hollywood film studios stripped down that bloated formulation, applied some schmaltz, and sold the American Dream to the masses. It was still about opportunity, but the movies added stable families, Main Street virtue, and little guys beating the odds.

Thompson never missed a chance to mention Horatio Alger, but he subscribed to an older version of the American Dream. For him, it was roughly equivalent to what historian Richard Hofstadter called the myth of the happy yeoman. In his seminal 1956 article, Hofstadter argued that early American political rhetoric was "drawn irresistibly to the noncommercial, nonpecuniary, self-sufficient aspect of American farm life." That Jeffersonian ideal, which was broadly accepted in the second half of the eighteenth century, featured independent farmers whose civic rectitude would guide the new nation. The myth's appeal never depended on its descriptive power. "Oddly enough," Hofstadter noted, "the agrarian myth came to be believed more widely and tenaciously as it became more fictional." Even as the United States became more urban, industrial, corporate, and unionized, Americans longed to see themselves as independent agents.

Thompson went to extraordinary lengths to achieve that self-sufficiency. Although he seemed to be a man of the left, especially after the fractious events of 1968, he was no collectivist. From the outset, he cast himself as a rugged individualist tilling the fields of American culture. He chose not to work for others, he said, because Ernest Hemingway had shown that freelancers could make it on their own. In fact, Hemingway's wives offered him significant financial support, especially in his early years, but his perceived independence was what mattered most to Thompson. His own freelance ethic was fortified by a more practical consideration: he lost every regular job he managed to obtain.

If Thompson's American Dream was mostly about self-sufficiency, it also had to do with a patch of land. Like Hofstadter's yeoman, Thompson preferred to live in close communion with beneficent nature. "My only faith in this country is rooted in such places as Colorado and Idaho and maybe Big Sur as it was before the war," he noted in a 1962 letter. "The cities are grease pits and not worth blowing off the map." Editors would bankroll his enthusiastic descents into urban depravity, but most of his homes were set in bucolic landscapes. In 1966, Thompson left San Francisco for Colorado and eventually occupied an abandoned ranch house ten miles outside of Aspen. He immediately wrote to Silberman: "This is my first letter in the new house, new desk, new writing room, etc. . . . painted red, white, and blue by a dope freak that I hired from the trailer court." Almost three years later, Thompson described Owl Farm as his land-fortress; later still, he called it his fortified compound.

Thompson combined his version of the American Dream with a reflexive pessimism. His first-person narrator in *The Rum Diary* articulated that combination precisely.

> Like most others, I was a seeker, a mover, a malcontent, and at times a stupid hell-raiser. I was never idle long enough to do much thinking, but I felt somehow that some of us were making real progress, that we had taken an honest road, and that the best of us would inevitably make it over the top. At the same time, I shared a dark suspicion that the life we were leading was a lost cause, that we were all actors, kidding ourselves along on a senseless odyssey. It was the tension between these two poles—a restless idealism on one hand and a sense of impending doom on the other—that kept me going.

As was frequently the case, Thompson's narrator spoke for him. Despite his sense of impending doom, Thompson clung tenaciously to the American Dream as he understood it.

The income from his writing sustained Thompson's independence, and in his letter to Silberman, his immediate concern was the $5,000 installment he would receive for submitting a partial manuscript for the nonfiction book. Although he had generated hundreds of manuscript pages, he admitted that his draft was "a heap of useless bullshit." He envisioned a narrative that blended fiction with straight journalistic scenes, but he was struggling with that formula and plainly hoped to scotch the project. "I loathe the fucking memory of the day when I told you I'd 'go out and write about The Death of the American Dream,'" he told Silberman. "I had no idea what you meant then, and I still don't." The concept, he said, was too broad and pretentious to address directly. Anything he wrote, he told Silberman, was about the death of the American Dream, but that wasn't the same as writing a book with that working title. Like many dreams, Thompson's subject lay tantalizingly beneath or beyond consciousness. "You might as well have told me to write a book about Truth and Wisdom," he complained to Silberman the previous summer. Now he was even more irate. "Why in the name of stinking Jesus should I be stuck with this kind of book? Maybe later, when my legs go. Fuck the American Dream. It was always a lie & whoever still believes it deserves whatever they get—and they will. Bet on it."

Thompson's frothing might have rattled some editors, but Silberman was a seasoned veteran. After serving in the Second World War, he graduated from Harvard and landed a position in Boston at Little, Brown and Company. By that time, the firm's editor-in-chief was the target of a campaign led by Arthur Schlesinger Jr. Liberal and staunchly anti-communist, the Harvard historian was furious that Angus Cameron had passed on George Orwell's *Animal Farm*, the anti-Soviet fable that Schlesinger called to his attention. In 1947, Schlesinger sought a release from his own contract with Little, Brown. Four years later, Cameron was forced to resign after a right-wing organization called the publishing company a Communist front. That same year, however, *Time* magazine described Cameron as the nation's foremost book editor after he published J. D. Salinger's *The Catcher in the Rye*.

Schlesinger also targeted Cameron's authors. He called one of them, Carey McWilliams, a Typhoid Mary of the left; he and his friends weren't Communists, Schlesinger wrote in the *New York Post*, but they carried the disease. It was an unworthy dig against an accomplished author and editor. In 1929, McWilliams published his first book, a biography of Ambrose Bierce, after H. L. Mencken mentioned the need for a good one. At the time, McWilliams was a 24-year-old Los Angeles lawyer and Mencken acolyte. The Great Depression radicalized McWilliams, and his history of California farm labor, *Factories in the Field* (1939), became a bestseller. He wrote eight more books, including five for Cameron, over the next eleven years. They focused on racial and ethnic discrimination, the Japanese evacuation and internment, and the dangers of rabid anti-communism. Decades later, Schlesinger conceded that McWilliams's books were first-rate, but he maintained that *The Nation* magazine, which McWilliams edited, was insufficiently critical of the Soviet Union. McWilliams deflected the attack and eventually led *The Nation,* founded by abolitionists in 1865, through its most difficult decade. As the magazine celebrated its centennial, McWilliams offered Thompson the Hell's Angels assignment.

By the time Thompson's article appeared, Silberman had moved to New York City, worked his way up to executive editor at Dial Press, and switched to Random House. There he rejoined Cameron, who had been blacklisted before Knopf, a division of Random House, offered him an editorial position. In 1960, Cameron passed on Thompson's novel, *Prince Jellyfish,* but Thompson was grateful that Cameron offered helpful criticism instead of a canned rejection letter. Shortly after signing a contract with Ballantine for the Hell's Angels book, Thompson wrote to Cameron that he wanted to "get this cycle book out of the way" and return to his novel, *The Rum Diary.* He also mentioned his reasons for identifying himself primarily as a novelist. "Fiction is a bridge to the truth that journalism can't reach," he told Cameron. "Facts are lies when they're added up, and the only kind of journalism I can pay much attention to is something like *Down and Out in Paris and London.*" Now classified as fiction, not journalism, Orwell's classic is so auto-biographical that it is frequently considered a memoir. For Orwell as well as Thompson, the lines between participatory journalism, autobiography, and fiction were vanishingly thin.

Midway through his already lengthy letter to Silberman, Thompson paused to review the galleys of a forthcoming article. *Playboy* magazine had rejected his profile of Olympic skier Jean-Claude Killy, but Warren Hinckle quickly agreed to run it in the premiere issue of *Scanlan's Monthly.* Thompson had met Hinckle in San Francisco, where he presided over *Ramparts* magazine. After running blockbuster stories on Vietnam and other topics, *Ramparts's* circulation soared, but the magazine was never solvent, and Hinckle resigned when it filed for bankruptcy in 1969. He quickly cofounded *Scanlan's,* where he hoped to reproduce his editorial success. "God only knows what kind of magazine he has in mind," Thompson told Silberman, "but if he can drum up anything like the old, high-flying *Ramparts,* I know I look forward to reading it." After reviewing the galleys of his article, however, Thompson denounced the *Scanlan's* crew. "The swine have lopped off the whole end of my original ms.—about 25 pages of high white prose that I thought was the best part," Thompson wrote. "Goddamn the tasteless pigs."

For all his venting, Thompson knew he had to produce more than rambling letters. Returning to the problem at hand, he outlined several options to Silberman. One was the *Pump House Gang* approach. Like Tom Wolfe, Thompson could collect his magazine pieces and publish them as a book. Norman Mailer's *Advertisements for Myself,* which Douglas Brinkley described as Thompson's Bible, was a variation on this theme. Thompson admired both authors, but he didn't think his articles would come together as a book. By this time, too, Mailer had also written *The Armies of the Night* (1968). In that book, he used his personal experience as the basis for the novel, whose protagonist was also named Mailer. The plan worked: *The Armies of the Night* won the National Book Award and Pulitzer Prize for fiction. Maybe Thompson could follow Mailer's lead. More than anything, he wanted to be a novelist. But where to start?

Thompson was also pondering Frederick Exley's novel, *A Fan's Notes.* Like Mailer's book, it appeared in 1968 and was profoundly self-referential. Its narrator is named Frederick Exley, and the world reveals its meaning through his warped consciousness. Suffering from alcoholism, madness, and an obsession with professional football, the protagonist presents himself as an intelligent loser coping unsuccessfully with "that long malaise, my life." For Thompson, Exley's narrative technique fell somewhere between Wolfe's and Mailer's. He didn't consider Exley a great writer, nor did he wish to make his acquaintance, but he credited the book's "demented kind of honesty."

Like Mailer and Exley, Thompson planned to create a fictional character to focalize his narrative. That way, he explained to Silberman, he could use the 1968 Democratic National Convention or President Nixon's inauguration "as a framework for the trials and tribulations of my protagonist, Raoul Duke." As he wrote to Silberman in a different letter, his goal was "to let *me* sit back and play reasonable, while *he* freaks out. Or maybe those roles should be reversed . . . ?" The problem lay in the execution. He could not make Duke come to life, and the American Dream motif was a burden. In an aside, he reminded Silberman that F. Scott Fitzgerald wanted to call his book about Jay Gatsby *The Death of the Red White and Blue.* Even while probing his manuscript's most intractable problem, Thompson linked himself to another literary hero. He considered *The Great Gatsby* the most American novel of all and occasionally typed out passages to see how they felt. He also cribbed Fitzgerald's phrase "the high white note" to describe his own style at its best.

With a head full of literary voices, Thompson could not solve the riddle of the second book. He closed his seventeen-page letter by exhorting Silberman to furnish a remedy. "Hell, you're an editor and you're paid to solve this kind of nightmare puzzle," he wrote. "I'll expect a finely reasoned answer very soon." It was a dispiriting conclusion, especially after years of fruitless effort.

Thompson did not know that a solution would appear within months. The inspiration came over dinner with novelist James Salter, who moved to Aspen shortly after Thompson. Salter's third book, *A Sport and a Pastime*, was a stylish erotic novel set in provincial France, where Salter had been stationed during the Berlin crisis. Like much of Thompson's favorite literature, *A Sport and a Pastime* used first-person narration and blurred the lines between fact and fantasy. Published by George Plimpton at the Paris Review Press, it did not sell well, but Salter was flush anyway; he had written screenplays for three films released in 1969, including *Downhill Racer* with Robert Redford.

Dinner parties at Salter's house didn't resemble the high spirits at Owl Farm. The novelist and his wife preferred small gatherings, and on this evening, the Thompsons were the only guests. Having learned that Thompson was from Louisville, Salter asked whether he was planning to cover the Kentucky Derby, which was scheduled for early May. Thompson immediately contacted a receptive Hinckle. He paired Thompson with illustrator Ralph Steadman, who was staying with friends on Long Island. Thompson and Steadman met in Louisville and attended the race, which Dust Commander won by five lengths. But Thompson cared nothing about the outcome, focusing instead on the drunken revelry that accompanied the event. Written mostly in the first person, the piece had an edgy tone that was its dominant feature.

After filing the article, Thompson was concerned. "This whole thing will probably finish me as a writer," he told Steadman. "I have no story." Later, he confided that the piece was "useless, aside from the flashes of style & tone it captures." Even so, he appreciated Steadman's grotesque illustrations, the visual counterpart to his own fantastical prose, and he proposed another collaboration. "I'd like nothing better than to work with you on another one of those savage binges again," he wrote to Steadman, "& to that end I'll tell my agent to bill us as a package—for good or ill."

When it ran in *Scanlan's Monthly*, "The Kentucky Derby Is Decadent and Depraved" was not the disaster that Thompson initially feared. To the contrary, it was celebrated as a *tour de force* and soon labeled Gonzo journalism. No one was more surprised than Thompson, who compared his experience to "falling down an elevator shaft and landing in a pool full of mermaids." Writing to Hinckle in July 1970, Thompson proposed a series of articles in the style of the Kentucky Derby piece. He and Steadman would cover the Super Bowl, Times Square on New Year's Eve, Mardi Gras, the Masters golf tournament, America's Cup, and other spectacles. The idea, he explained to Steadman, would be to "rape them all, quite systematically, and then we could sell it as a book: 'Amerikan Dreams.'" The two men would "travel around the country and shit on *everything.*" Thompson considered the "Rape Series on Amerikan Institutions" a "king-bitch dog-fucker of an idea." They could turn out articles "so weird & frightful as to stagger every mind in journalism."

Scanlan's folded in 1971, but Thompson's idea persisted. The following year, Silberman would have his book. It was narrated by Raoul Duke, the pseudonym Thompson had used to acquire weapons while campaigning for Pitkin County sheriff. (After filing his Kentucky Derby story, Thompson ran on the Freak Party ticket, adopted a mescaline platform, shaved his head, and called the incumbent "my long-haired opponent.") *Fear and Loathing in Las Vegas* was indeed about the death of the American Dream, but it defied categorization. Even Silberman had to ask whether it was fiction or nonfiction. Thompson offered a long, evasive reply, but the correct answer was simple: No.

2 The Storm of Life

The crooked path to Gonzo journalism began in Kentucky, where Hunter Stockton Thompson's paternal ancestors had lived since 1800. Born in 1937, Thompson was the oldest of three boys. His father worked as an insurance adjustor in Louisville, and his mother was a housekeeper. Hunter was an ardent sports fan, and at age 11, he began contributing to a sports newsletter begun by a friend. The following year, he was admitted to a prestigious athletic club, which eventually helped introduce him to Louisville society and parties at the country club. He quickly became known for his pranks, hazing, and theatrics. "Hunter was always where the action was, even if the action wasn't the nicest kind," said one female admirer.

The world of sports usually reflects broader social attitudes and trends, and Louisville in the 1940s was no exception. When Thompson was 9 years old, the Brooklyn Dodgers' farm club arrived to play the Louisville Colonels. The game was delayed, however, when the Colonels walked off the field to protest the visiting team's roster, which included a Black player. It was Jackie Robinson, who would break the color barrier in major league baseball two years later. Firmly in the grip of Jim Crow, Louisville produced its own elite athlete forever associated with racial justice. Born five years after Thompson, boxer Cassius Clay changed his name to Muhammad Ali and became one of the world's most recognizable figures. Thompson would later include Ali, along with Bob Dylan and Fidel Castro, among his heroes. He also mentioned the champ admiringly in his most famous book and later interviewed him for *Rolling Stone* magazine. After his death in 2016, Ali was buried blocks away from Thompson's family home in the Cherokee Triangle neighborhood.

If Thompson admired Ali, he also identified strongly with his regional heritage. "I've always felt like a Southerner," he told one interviewer. "And

I always felt like I was born in defeat. And I maybe have written everything I've written just to win back a victory. My life may be pure revenge." His attachment to the vanquished South was freely chosen. Kentucky was a slave state but not part of the Confederacy, and many more Kentuckians served in the Union army than in the Confederate one. Well after Thompson left Louisville, the city remained a touchstone for him. In 1963, he wrote a story on its entrenched racism for *The Reporter*, a liberal magazine based in New York City. After noting Louisville's civil rights victories and remaining challenges, Thompson concluded that the city was addressing the "Negro problem" better than many northern and midwestern counterparts. (The phrase in scare quotes echoed nineteenth-century works that decried slavery while presuming White supremacy.) Thompson's article was both straight reporting and a form of revenge—not on Louisville, but on the Yankee cities to which he compared it. As for his hometown's customs and traditions, Thompson would lampoon them mercilessly seven years later.

The adult Thompson was by no means a lucid reflector of Jim Crow, but he understood the power of race in America and sometimes used it to animate his work. The racial and ethnic slurs that festooned his communications were also designed to create specific effects, none of them tactful. As one longtime friend said, "Part of it was insulting and part of it was humor and part of it was just provoking you. But there was always this race element buried in his character which popped out every now and then, and it was nasty." Another friend remarked, "Sometimes he would use the word 'nigger' when he was writing, and he was very quick with racial jokes and things like that. But in terms of where his real sentiment was, it was the opposite." By way of support, the friend recalled that he and Thompson planned to run guns from California to Mississippi during the civil rights movement "to level the playing field." Privately, Thompson said he never paid much attention to what he called "the Black/Jew/WASP problem," which he considered a waste of time and energy. It was clear to him by age 10 that most people were bastards, thieves, and pig-fuckers. As a result, he thought his prejudice was "far too broad and sweeping for any racial limitations."

When Thompson was almost 15, his father died. His mother took a job at the Louisville Free Public Library, but the family struggled. Always a hellion, Thompson began acting out more spectacularly than usual—drinking whiskey, vandalizing property, and setting small fires. He stopped participating in sports, and his relationship with his alcoholic mother deteriorated. Yet Thompson was also invited to join the Athenaeum Literary Association, Louisville's most prestigious literary club. His favorite authors were Ernest Hemingway and F. Scott Fitzgerald, and *The Great Gatsby* was especially important to him. In addition to addressing the American Dream, which would become Thompson's signature theme, the novel included a Louisville connection. After spending what she described as her beautiful white girlhood in Louisville, Daisy Buchanan fell in love with Jay Gatsby, an officer stationed at nearby Camp Zachary Taylor, where Fitzgerald served briefly in 1918. A breeding ground for the Spanish flu, which killed 675,000 Americans, it closed two years later.

Athenaeum included boys from the city's leading families, many of whom would attend Ivy League colleges. One of them, Paul Semonin, later described the club. "Athenaeum was tied into the Louisville elite," he said, "and it had this atmosphere of tradition, which I think is important in understanding where Hunter came from." Another friend, Porter Bibb, recalled Thompson's social skills.

> I was always amazed at Hunter's networking ability. He was solidly middle-class, yet he was hanging out with some multi-multi-millionaire families. Paul Semonin's family owned half of Louisville . . . Most of the people that Hunter was close to and who brought him into their circle were very, very wealthy people, and Hunter didn't have a sou. Here he was with a single mom—who had to *work?*

Although one childhood friend described Louisville as "a tight-assed town," Thompson's companions enjoyed extraordinary latitude. As teenagers, they used fake licenses to obtain alcohol effortlessly. "But you really didn't even need them," Bibb said, "because there was so much free alcohol everywhere. Every party at the country clubs, at the hotel ballrooms—it was all open to us. Not to 90 percent of the rest of the city, but it was totally open to us." That privilege manifested itself in other ways as well. When Bibb was old enough to drive, he appeared at the department of motor vehicles, mentioned his name, and collected his license. Some of Thompson's peers thought he longed to join that world, while others maintained that he despised it. "I think Hunter always *hated* what Louisville stood for," said one friend. "What it stood for then and what it will always stand for. It's a boring, provincial, middle-class, family-oriented town that has nothing going for it except the Derby two minutes a year."

As a senior in high school, Thompson had no specific plans for his future, but he outlined his aspirations in the Athenaeum yearbook. In that essay, he associated financial and personal security with complacency, routine, boredom, and emasculation.

> Let us visualize the secure man; and by this term, I mean a man who has settled for financial and personal security for his goal in life. In general, he is a man who has pushed ambition and initiative aside and settled

down, so to speak, in a boring but safe and comfortable rut for the rest of his life. His future is but an extension of his present, and he accepts it as such with a complacent shrug of his shoulders. His ideas and ideals are those of society in general, and he is accepted as a respectable but average and prosaic man. But is he a man? Has he any self-respect or pride in himself? How could he, when he risked nothing and gained nothing?

The teenaged Thompson then posed a rhetorical question: "Who is the happier man, he who has braved the storm of life and lived, or he who has stayed securely on shore and merely existed?"

If that youthful sentiment is commonplace, its expression was not. Nor was the relationship between Thompson's manifesto and the life that followed. Journalist Tim Cahill later remarked on that aspect of Thompson's experience.

> Hunter represents freedom. He has confidence, plus size, plus a certain undeniable fearlessness. We all have a kind of Peter Pan ideal in our lives when we're about twelve. We're going to do this, we're going to do that, and it gets beaten out of us. It gets beaten out of us sometime between puberty and our first job. People often regret things they didn't do. Hunter is the alter ego who got to do *everything*.

Part of that freedom lay in Thompson's refusal to work for others. Over the course of his career, his freelance status entailed endless haggling, but Thompson never oriented his life around financial solvency. Nor would he stay securely on the shore of life; indeed, his improvidence and recklessness were key features of his personal and professional identity.

During his teenage years, Thompson and his friends had many scrapes with the law—so many, in fact, that he later described himself as a juvenile delinquent. "Everybody thought he would end up in prison or dead or something," said one childhood neighbor. "He was fearless. He knew structure and power. He was manipulative. If he wasn't the top banana, the game changed." One friend observed that in his last years of high school, Thompson "was becoming, to a degree, sinister." An early girlfriend speculated about his inner life.

> When Hunter started getting into trouble, part of our minds said, "Wow! This guy has balls!" and the other part was just shocked . . . I have a feeling it had to do with his father's death. And his mother was a pretty good alcoholic. That was probably the big key. Hunter was very private about it. About his whole family. He was full—he was just filled, filled, filled with anger.

After one of his companions relieved a motorist of his wallet, Thompson and another friend were also charged with robbery. Only Thompson, however, served thirty days in jail and missed his graduation ceremony. "Everybody else had money," one classmate noted, "and got out and went to college." When offered a chance to enlist rather than serve more jail time, Thompson joined the Air Force. Before leaving town, however, he decided to settle a score with a teacher who aided his prosecution. On two consecutive nights, Thompson parked in front of his home and threw full beer bottles through the front windows. The retaliation may have satisfied his need for revenge, but Thompson would harbor a deeper grievance that was never resolved.

. . .

After basic training and a course in electronics, Thompson served as a sportswriter at Eglin Air Base in Florida. He chafed under military discipline, but he found the work agreeable and was soon freelancing for a local newspaper as well. During this time, Thompson likely read Furman Bisher, sports columnist for the *Atlanta Journal-Constitution*. Bisher closed his columns with *selah*, the Hebrew word that appears throughout the Book of Psalms and was probably a cue to pause and exalt the Lord. Thompson peppered his communications with the same word. Later in life, he returned to sportswriting in odd ways, including his work on the Kentucky Derby, Muhammad Ali, and the road race that prompted *Fear and Loathing in Las Vegas*. Toward the tail end of his career, he wrote an online column for ESPN and described the huge influence of sportswriting on his work. Sports was a meal ticket for Thompson, but it was also a lifelong interest that never lost its luster.

Discharged from the Air Force in 1957, Thompson worked briefly for daily newspapers in Pennsylvania and upstate New York before catching on as a copy boy at *Time* magazine. With financial assistance from the magazine, Thompson also took courses on literary style and short fiction at Columbia University. During that time, he read Norman Mailer, Jack Kerouac, and Allen Ginsberg. He also worked on his autobiographical novel, *Prince Jellyfish*. Set in New York City, it recounted a pivotal year in the lives of its three major characters. Its first-person narrator, Welburn Kemp, was named after two Louisville residents, Welburn Brown and Penny Kemp. Brown had been killed in an auto accident, and Kemp had been severely injured in another one. But Welburn Kemp mostly resembled his creator. As Thompson biographer William McKeen noted, Kemp is "selfish and arrogant and yet too charming to be firmly repellent."

McKeen also observed that *Prince Jellyfish* bore the influence of J. P. Donleavy's *The Ginger Man*, which its author described as "celebratory, boisterous, and resolutely careless mayhem." Set in postwar Dublin, the comic novel depicts the daily rounds of Sebastian Dangerfield, another self-ish and arrogant charmer who beats his wife and drinks away the family's limited funds. Critics described Dangerfield variously as "impulsive, destructive, wayward, cruel, a monster, a clown, and a psychopath." *The Ginger Man* was first published in 1955 by the Olympia Press, whose cata-log included works by Henry Miller, Vladimir Nabokov, Samuel Beckett, and William Burroughs. Donleavy's novel appeared in the Traveller's Companion series, which was known primarily for its erotica and banned in Ireland and the United States. (Grove Press reissued the novel, which even-tually sold more than 45 million copies worldwide.) Donleavy was furious that the novel was mistaken for smut, but its transgressive status probably heightened the appeal for Thompson. Reading *The Ginger Man*, Thompson said later, "made up my mind that I had to be a writer."

During this time, Thompson met Sandra Conklin at a Greenwich Village bar. A shapely blonde from the affluent town of Dix Hills, Long Island, Sandy was seeing Paul Semonin, but she and Thompson struck up a rela-tionship during her Thanksgiving break from Goucher College in Baltimore. Her father was an executive at a large insurance company, where he even-tually served as CEO and chairman. He also held a PhD in economics and taught finance at New York University. The Conklin family was comforta-ble but unhappy. When Sandy was 12, her mother tried to commit suicide. She began drinking heavily, and Sandy often accompanied her to bars. By the time Sandy was dating Thompson, her father was remarried. He said little about his daughter's new boyfriend, but her mother supported their relationship.

Almost immediately after Thompson connected with Sandy, he landed a job in Puerto Rico. His employer was a new sports weekly in San Juan that quickly went out of business. Nevertheless, Sandy flew down for a roman-tic week and then returned three months later. Semonin also joined Thompson and stayed for the better part of a year. During that time, Thompson produced an article that featured Semonin for the *Louisville Courier-Journal*. Semonin later claimed that Thompson fabricated every quotation attributed to him. Thompson also cast their new home as "voo-doo country" to create what Semonin called "fantastic, eye-grabbing stuff for the reader."

During his time in Puerto Rico, Thompson befriended William Kennedy, managing editor at the *San Juan Star*, a recently established English-language newspaper. Kennedy, who was also writing fiction, recalled Thompson's reading habits.

He was reading voluminously—*Ulysses*, James Agee's *A Death in the Family*, *The Ginger Man* by J.P. Donleavy, Dylan Thomas, Mailer's *Advertisements for Myself*, Dos Passos's *U.S.A.*, *The Plague* by Camus, *Don Quixote*, Proust, *Huck Finn*, D.H. Lawrence, *The Sound and the Fury*, *The Decameron*, *The Inferno*. It was the Western canon. He didn't think there were any serious women writers. He didn't know much about Flannery O'Connor, or if he did he didn't value it. He did like Isak Dinesen's *Gothic Tales*.

Thompson was also keeping up with contemporary fiction. According to Kennedy, he identified strongly with Holden Caulfield in Salinger's *Catcher in the Rye*. He never warmed up to Saul Bellow, who became Kennedy's mentor, but both liked Nelson Algren and James Baldwin. Much later in life, Thompson would rattle off his primary influences: "Conrad, Hemingway, Twain, Faulkner, Fitzgerald—Mailer, Kerouac in the political sense—they were allies. Dos Passos, Henry Miller, Isak Dinesen, Edmund Wilson, Thomas Jefferson."

· · ·

Thompson set his second novel-in-progress, *The Rum Diary*, in San Juan. Its first-person narrator, Paul Kemp, is a newly hired reporter for the *San Juan Daily News*. An Ivy League graduate who had worked in Europe, Kemp shares Semonin's first name and other characteristics. While Semonin was in San Juan, he and Thompson spent a night in jail for failing to pay a restaurant bill, and Thompson included a fictionalized version of that experience in the novel. That episode's prime mover, however, is not Kemp but Yeamon, another *Daily News* reporter. At their pre-dawn arraignment, an American real estate developer named Sanderson threatens to bring in a top Puerto Rican lawyer to represent the defendants. His intervention isn't altruistic; Sanderson has recruited Kemp to write publicity copy for his real estate projects. Although Kemp needs the money, he feels compromised by the arrangement. In particular, he has misgivings about the effect of Sanderson's project on the island's pristine beaches.

Yeamon's beautiful girlfriend, Chenault, catches Kemp's eye on his initial flight to San Juan. Once he discovers she is Yeamon's girlfriend, however, he keeps his feelings in check. When the group travels to St. Thomas for the festival, her wild streak emerges. The festive backdrop resembles Pamplona in *The Sun Also Rises*, but Thompson adds a racial twist when Chenault dances lasciviously in a crowded bar with predominantly Black revelers. (Yeamon has already explained her predilection for dancing by noting that she is "part nigger.") To the crowd's delight, she removes her dress and bra, and her partner—a powerfully built Black man wearing only toreador pants—slips off her panties. Yeamon fights savagely to stop the spectacle, but he and Kemp are physically ejected without Chenault. She is presumably raped, and they cannot find her the next day. She eventually appears at Kemp's door, he comforts her, and they develop a romance. Upon learning of this, Yeamon repudiates both of them. Semonin thought the bar scene had its roots in Louisville. "This never happened in Puerto Rico, but Hunter has this fantasy embedded in his subconscious," Semonin said. "It is a racial nightmare that exists from all the racial stereotyping that went on in his childhood."

The male characters also reflect Thompson's outlook and concerns. Kemp is the reasonable if jaded observer in a remarkable social setting, not unlike Jake Barnes in *The Sun Also Rises* or Nick Carraway in *The Great Gatsby*. Yeamon, who slaps Chenault during one of Kemp's visits, is ornery and unsympathetic, yet Kemp is drawn to his independence, commitment to principle, and fighting spirit. A Kentucky native whose father lost the family farm, Yeamon waxes nostalgic about his childhood home, where a man could "shoot all day and run his dogs and raise all manner of hell, and not a soul in the world would bother him." Yeamon, in short, stands for the American yeoman as described by Hofstadter; his surname is even misspelled Yeoman at one point in the page proofs. Although he loses his job and girlfriend, he never loses his autonomy. After the newspaper folds, the reporters attack its unpopular editor at a party, and he dies of a heart attack. Yeamon is blamed for his death, and Kemp helps him escape the island. As the novel ends, Kemp is planning to return to New York City with Chenault. *The Rum Diary* was not published until 1998, but its major themes revolve around threats to independence, self-sufficiency, and beneficent nature—in short, the key elements of the American Dream as Thompson understood it.

. . .

After Thompson returned to the United States, Semonin invited him to drive a new Ford Fairlane from New York City to Seattle for a car agency. Thompson eagerly accepted. Their trip would be a version of the Beat adventures he had read about in Jack Kerouac's *On the Road* (1957). Kerouac did not drive, but his picaresque novel—which glorified intense experience fueled by alcohol, marijuana, and speed—was a love letter to the American open road. Even the narrator's name, Sal Paradise, signaled its utopian theme. "I was a young writer and I wanted to take off," Paradise says. "Somewhere along the line I knew there'd be girls, visions, everything; somewhere along the line the pearl would be handed to me." By crisscrossing the country, exploring its social margins, and turning those adventures into fiction, Kerouac offered the prospect of ecstatic rapture just over the horizon.

When it appeared, *On the Road* was a breath of fresh air, especially for many younger readers. As Cold War orthodoxy tightened its grip on mainstream America, Kerouac's true subject was freedom. Ironically, the novel's most prominent symbol was linked to President Eisenhower. Citing the need for national defense, he expanded the national highway system and created a new kind of American adventure. (Hopping freight trains, another form of mobility in Kerouac's fiction, was already a fixture in the American folk repertoire.) Kerouac's wingman, Neal Cassady, symbolized the American West to which Kerouac was especially drawn. Thompson wasn't a Kerouac fan as such—in a 1958 letter, he called Kerouac "an ass, a mystic boob with intellectual myopia"—but he admired the way the Beat novelist made his mark. Writing to Silberman in 1971, Thompson called *On the Road* "a long rambling piece of personal journalism" and "the first big breakthrough on this front." Later, he considered Kerouac's effect on him. "I wasn't trying to write like him," Thompson said, "but I could see that I could get published like him and break through the Eastern establishment ice." In particular, he appreciated Kerouac's ability to write about drugs and still reach a large audience. Although Thompson privately mocked the Beat icon and disparaged his style, his most famous work would incorporate elements of Kerouac's picaresque fiction.

As Thompson and Semonin headed west, the 1960 presidential campaign was shifting into high gear, and Thompson attended a John F. Kennedy event in Salt Lake City. Years later, he described the Democratic candidate as little more than an acceptable alternative to the status quo. "The most important thing about Kennedy, to me and millions of others, was that his name wasn't Nixon," he said. "Looking at Kennedy on the stump, it was possible to conceive of a day when a man younger than 70 might enter the White House as a welcome visitor, on his own terms." Yet Thompson was also attracted to the Kennedy style. "With John Kennedy and Bobby Kennedy, Hunter liked that they had such hubris," Douglas Brinkley said. "They could be good politicians but play hard at midnight. That meant a lot. Those were his guys."

After dropping off the car in Seattle, Thompson and Semonin hitchhiked to San Francisco. In a bar outside Salem, Oregon, Thompson watched a televised debate between Kennedy and Nixon. Years later, he identified that night as an important moment in his political education.

That was when I first understood that the world of Ike and Nixon was vulnerable . . . and that Nixon, along with all the rotting bullshit he stood for, might conceivably be beaten. I was 21 then, and it had never occurred to me that politics in America had anything to do with human beings. It was Nixon's game—a world of old hacks and legalized thievery, a never-ending drone of bad speeches and worse instincts.

Thompson followed the presidential campaign, but his central ambition was to flee the country, which he called a "crippled, half-sunk ship." That ambition was closely linked to another one—establishing himself as a novelist. Journalism was a means to that end, not evidence that Thompson was interested in American politics, which he consistently figured as a dead end. Later, the tension between fiction and journalism became the mainspring of his mature work. Moreover, that work focused sharply on American politics—and Richard Nixon.

3   Roughing It

One month before the 1960 election, Thompson made it to San Francisco, which the Second World War had transformed. More than 1 million soldiers and sailors traveled through the Bay Area to and from the Pacific theater, and many chose to settle there after the war. Some used their GI Bill benefits to attend college and buy homes in the rapidly expanding suburbs, but a small fraction formed motorcycle gangs that maintained large chapters in and around San Francisco. Thousands of motorcyclists famously attended a rally in 1947 that overwhelmed the small town of Hollister, just south of San Jose. That spectacle served as the basis for the 1953 film *The Wild One*, Hollywood's version of youthful alienation and rebellion.

The war also changed the region's population and economy. Defense jobs brought the first large influx of Black families to the Bay Area. Migrating from southern states, many settled near shipyards, and a segregated housing market ensured that they stayed there. Meanwhile, Cold War defense spending boosted the regional economy. The electronics sector flourished around Stanford University, and University of California scientists helped design a new arsenal of nuclear weapons. Federal expenditures also funded experiments on LSD and other psychedelic drugs. The CIA thought such drugs could be used to extract state secrets from foreign agents, and the Pentagon hoped to pacify enemy populations by spraying drugs in aerosol form or slipping them into the water supply. That research, much of it conducted at VA hospitals, made up a small fraction of the nation's overall defense spending, but it produced the most unlikely outcome of all. In less than a decade, psychedelic drugs would ignite the San Francisco counterculture.

The local arts scene was changing as well. Ever since the 1860s, when Bret Harte signed his magazine columns as "The Bohemian," San Francisco writers had cast themselves as free spirits rather than custodians of high culture. They also fed the insatiable national appetite for stories set in the West. The most famous writer to emerge from that boisterous scene was Mark Twain, who arrived in San Francisco during the Civil War. With the publication of "The Celebrated Jumping Frog of Calaveras County," a bit of local color set in Gold Rush country, Twain developed a national reputation. Another key writer was Ambrose Bierce, who used his *San Francisco Examiner* column to lampoon public figures. When railroad magnate Collis P. Huntington testified before Congress about a bill to defer the repayment of federal loans, Bierce wrote that he "took his hands out of all pockets long enough to be sworn." Even Bierce's publisher at the *San Francisco Examiner*, William Randolph Hearst, did not escape his scorn. "I don't like the job of chained bulldog to be let loose only to tear the panties off the boys who throw rocks at you," Bierce once told Hearst.

A later generation of Bay Area writers, including Jack London, built on that bohemian legacy. Poet Kenneth Rexroth, who presided over the so-called San Francisco Renaissance after the Second World War, noted that the underground arts scene was the only game in town. Whereas the early bohemians tended to produce journalism and fiction, most of their postwar counterparts were poets. Their coteries reflected a profound need for community—not only among poets, but also in postwar American society generally. "In the spiritual and political loneliness of America in the fifties, you'd hitch a thousand miles to meet a friend," poet Gary Snyder said. "West Coast of those days, San Francisco was the only city; and of San Francisco, North Beach." San Francisco painters, photographers, and filmmakers also banded together at the nearby California School of Fine Arts. When six teachers decided they needed space to show their work, they cofounded the 6 Gallery on Fillmore Street. They used it for parties, openings, and receptions, but poetry readings were also part of the mix.

The Beats began migrating to San Francisco in 1954, and poet Allen Ginsberg read "Howl" at the 6 Gallery the following year. Jack Kerouac fictionalized that event in *The Dharma Bums* (1958), which cast a thinly disguised Gary Snyder, Rexroth's student, as the narrator's spiritual role model. Lawrence Ferlinghetti published Ginsberg's poem at City Lights, the North Beach bookstore he cofounded in 1953. Its explicit references to homosexuality, including anal sex with motorcyclists, led to obscenity charges, but Ferlinghetti was exonerated after a high-profile trial. More obscenity trials would follow in San Francisco, but the Ferlinghetti verdict signaled that the city was a haven for those seeking artistic and sexual freedom.

By the time Thompson landed in San Francisco, key figures in the Beat scene were already missing. Ginsberg left for Morocco and Paris, Kerouac moved to Florida, and Neal Cassady served two years in San Quentin State Prison on marijuana charges. But Ferlinghetti and City Lights kept the Beat legacy alive, and Thompson visited its shrines when not searching for a job. After neither of the city's major newspapers responded to his queries, Thompson composed a short paean to his temporary home and sent it to the *San Francisco Chronicle.* Its title, "Down and Out in San Francisco," echoed Orwell, but the style was pure Beat.

> City of hills and fog and water, bankers and boobs—Republicans all.
> City of no jobs—"sorry, we have no openings here; be glad to talk to
> you, though"—city of no money except what you find at the General
> Delivery window, and somehow it's always enough—city, like all cities,
> of lonely women, lost souls, and people slowly going under.

A later passage reflected Thompson's stubborn desire for independence, no matter the cost.

> Say "no" to San Francisco and be rich—spend your last dollar on
> brandy and swack reality across the cheek. "No, I will not sell out, I will
> not give you the best hours of my day and let you use my blood to
> grease the wheels and cogs of a hundred banking machines, sorry, Jack,
> but I will take your time and your cigarettes and laugh at you quietly
> for the questions you ask and know all the time that your guts have
> dried up and your spine is rubber and you measure me against your
> contempt for the human race and find a disturbing disparity—how so,
> prince jellyfish? will you endorse this check for me? many thanks; now
> I can work against you for another week."

The *Chronicle* never ran the piece, and Thompson's poor prospects only increased his contempt for conformity. Much like Sal Paradise, he was a young writer who wanted to take off, but the Beat movement that excited his hopes was already waning. When a new scene emerged in San Francisco several years later, it would power much of Thompson's most important work, but in 1960, that possibility was inconceivable.

. . .

That fall, Thompson moved 150 miles south to Big Sur, where he was joined by Sandy. It was an odd decision for a journalist but a slightly more sensible one for an aspiring novelist. The rugged coastal outpost was, among other things, a Beat retreat; Ferlinghetti had a cabin in Bixby Canyon, and Kerouac would set *Big Sur* (1962) there. Its earlier history was linked to nearby Monterey, the capital of Alta California during the Spanish and Mexican periods. The Spanish colonists called it *el pais grande del sur,* the big country of the south. They also decimated the native Esselen tribe, who had roamed the coastal mountains fishing, hunting, and soaking in the hot springs. The Anglo presence increased after the Mexican-American War and California statehood. Shortly after the Civil War, a Missouri native named Thomas Benton Slate homesteaded there, hoping that the hot springs would cure his arthritis. But even after the Pacific Coast Highway reached Big Sur in 1935, the area around Slate's Hot Springs remained isolated and sparsely populated.

After the war, Big Sur's beauty and isolation drew Henry Miller, another Thompson idol. Miller's reputation hinged on two novels written in Paris during the 1930s. Both were banned in the United States for their sexual content, but Miller had many advocates, including George Orwell, who described him as "the only imaginative prose writer of the slightest value who has appeared among the English-speaking races for some years past." Returning to the United States in 1939, Miller arranged to drive cross-country with a friend. His plan was to write a book about the trip for a major American publisher, and his companion would provide the illustrations. While producing his manuscript, however, Miller correctly sensed that the publisher would not welcome his disdain for American philistinism and consumerism, especially during wartime. He offered the manuscript to New Directions, which published *The Air-Conditioned Nightmare* in 1945. It was a searing critique of American culture and a precursor to Kerouac's road fiction.

After settling in Big Sur, Miller turned to other projects and maintained his extensive correspondence. Largely through his letters, Miller promoted himself and his books, raised money from friends and supporters, and shared his plans with a select group of peers and advisors. Although he kept a low profile in Big Sur, his presence did not go unnoticed. In 1948, he was featured in Mildred Edie Brady's "The New Cult of Sex and Anarchy," which ran in *Harper's* magazine. A freelance writer from Berkeley, Brady cast Miller as a pillar of Big Sur's bohemian community along with Kenneth Rexroth and Austrian psychoanalyst Wilhelm Reich. Brady's tone was sardonic, but a four-part series in Hearst's *San Francisco Examiner* added a macabre spin, decrying the "hate cult" and "doctrine of doom" that Miller spawned in Big Sur.

A decade later, Miller produced his own portrait of the region. *Big Sur and the Oranges of Hieronymus Bosch* (1957) was a meditation on rustic bohemianism, but it opened on a bleak note.

> The early settlers are dying off. Should their huge tracts of land be broken up into small holdings, Big Sur may rapidly develop into a suburb (of Monterey), with bus service, barbecue stands, gas stations, chain stores, and all the odious claptrap that makes Suburbia horrendous.

Miller also catalogued other threats to reclusive artists. The first was a kind of mental and spiritual torpor. "If an art colony is established here," Miller wrote, "it will go the way of all the others. Artists never thrive in colonies. Ants do." Yet Miller also described Big Sur as a virtual paradise that encouraged personal transformation. Much of it was predicated on rejecting the unexamined life, American style. "Everyone who has come here in search of a new way of life has made a complete change-about in his daily routine," Miller noted. "Nearly every one has come from afar, usually from a big city. It meant abandoning a job and a mode of life which was detestable and insufferable."

The year before Thompson arrived in Big Sur, New Directions published *The Henry Miller Reader*. Edited by Lawrence Durrell, it was a collection of what Norman Mailer called Miller's least obscene writings. The same year, *The World of Sex* was published privately. Its bawdy descriptions, which Miller blended with mysticism and prophecy, made the slight volume unfit for mass consumption. Thompson thought highly of it, but he never endorsed Miller's view that sex was spiritual and self-liberating. Nor did he envision a "world transformed each day through the magic of love, a world free of death." Yet Miller's independence, iconoclasm, sexual frankness, and fearlessness were catnip for Thompson. Miller stood for the freedoms bohemian artists had claimed ever since their appearance in Paris a century earlier. Beholden to no one and working in splendid isolation, Miller produced his singular body of work with little or no compromise. His influence also ran deep. More than any other single figure, one scholar claimed, Miller was the grandfather of the Beat Generation, the counterculture, and the sexual revolution.

Shortly after moving to Big Sur, Thompson sent an unsolicited copy of *The World of Sex* to Norman Mailer. "This little black book of Miller's is something you might like," Thompson wrote. "If not, or if you already have it, by all means send it back. I don't mind giving it away, but I'd hate to see it wasted." Thompson was correct that Mailer admired Miller, to whom he devoted a book in 1976. In his review of that work, Frederick Crews maintained that Hemingway was Mailer's chief influence during the 1950s, but that after his 1961 suicide, Hemingway no longer embodied the "towering authority of masculine style for Mailer or anyone else." That strand of fiction, Crews claimed, "turned away from the clipped and bittersweet Hemingway manner and has become loose, expansive, fantastic— in short, Milleresque." Although Thompson revered Hemingway, his own prose would likewise become looser, more expansive, and more fantastical as the decade wore on.

The rest of Thompson's letter to Mailer was remarkably snotty. He claimed to be dismayed by Mailer's "picayune defensiveness" in response to Thompson's earlier letter, which asked why Mailer hadn't attacked Richard Nixon in print. By that time, Mailer had published three novels, *Advertisements for Myself* (1959), and a slew of articles in high-profile outlets. He also had cofounded the *Village Voice* and covered the 1960 Democratic National Convention for *Esquire* magazine. Yet a cheeky Thompson advised Mailer to "spend more time writing, and less explaining yourself." He concluded with an invitation to join him in Big Sur for a beer. "There ain't much to do here, so I have taken to inviting people down and then flogging them into a coma with my riding crop," he wrote to Mailer. "Between guests, I work on the Great Puerto Rican novel. Watch for it."

Thompson's gesture was richly symbolic. His packet to Mailer conferred several gifts: a copy of Miller's book, condescending advice, the jocular threat of physical violence, and an announcement about his forthcoming novel. The main message was unmistakable: A young and virile writer was on the rise. Here and elsewhere in his correspondence, Thompson was constructing an authorial self that owed much to his heroes. Although Mailer had already fashioned an enviable career by mixing journalism and fiction, Thompson seemed to figure him as a peer or even a rival. Moreover, he openly wished to establish that footing well before he published a novel or even an article for a national magazine. Mailer wasn't the only author with whom Thompson shared his vaulting ambition. William Kennedy was also privy to his aspirations. *The Rum Diary*, Thompson wrote Kennedy in 1961, would do for San Juan what *The Sun Also Rises* did for Paris.

In the meantime, Thompson pursued new pleasures in Big Sur. He befriended sculptor William "Jo" Hudson, who hunted wild boar and deer in the coastal mountains, and developed an interest in weapons and hunting. Those pastimes began to surface in his correspondence as well. In 1962, for example, he shared his view of Kerouac's latest novel with Semonin.

> I have tonight begun reading a stupid, shitty book by Kerouac called *Big Sur*, and I would give a ball to wake up tomorrow on some empty ridge with a herd of beatniks grazing in the clearing about 200 yards below the house. And then to squat with the big boomer and feel it on my shoulder with the smell of grease and powder and, later, a little blood.

If his distaste for Kerouac's novel was clear, so was his budding gun fetish and Hemingway's continuing influence. By the following year, Thompson felt expert enough to pitch an article to the *National Observer* on the difference between hunting with shotguns and rifles. He also reviewed Vance Bourjaily's book on bird hunting, *The Unnatural Enemy*, which the

National Observer ran in December 1963. Bourjaily was another writer whose fiction grew out of his wartime experience, but he was also an avid outdoorsman, legendary host, and instructor at the Iowa Writer's Workshop.

As Thompson and Hudson bonded, the sculptor witnessed his new friend's abusiveness. One day over breakfast, Hudson saw Thompson slap Sandy for failing to retrieve something quickly enough. Tears welling in her eyes, she retreated into the house. "I was shocked by it," Hudson said. "Hunter was wound so tight that little things would set him off." Decades later, Sandy alluded to other examples of similar abuse. She also mentioned a split in Thompson's personality. "He was loving, he was generous," she said. "On the other end of the spectrum, the boy and the man was absolutely vicious." Thompson's second wife, Anita, seemed to concur.

> Hunter had two extremes in him that he lived with constantly: the generous, beautiful Hunter and the scary, mean, cruel Hunter, and he was aware of both. I don't know if he was in control of both all the time, but he was certainly aware of both, and they became present in his life when he was very young, both sides.

That split would take various forms in the years to come, yet Sandy continued to support Thompson and his ambitions.

Looking for cheap rent while he finished *The Rum Diary*, Thompson became the caretaker at Slate's Hot Springs, whose owner was Vinnie "Bunnie" MacDonald Murphy. The family had purchased the property in 1910 to create a spa, but the business was failing by the time Thompson arrived. The Murphys lived in nearby Salinas, an inland farming town where they founded a hospital and maintained close ties to the Steinbeck family. Thompson was well aware of Bunnie's grandson, Dennis Murphy, who had written *The Sergeant* (1958). Set in France after the Second World War, the critically acclaimed novel depicted a US serviceman and a French girl vying for the affection of a handsome young conscript. Thompson thought highly of Murphy and his novel and often mentioned them in letters to his Louisville friends.

While negotiating the film rights to his novel, Dennis Murphy met Kerouac in New York City, and the two became drinking buddies. That same year, Kerouac traveled to California, stayed in Ferlinghetti's cabin, and struggled to write *Big Sur* while in the throes of alcoholism. When the Thompsons lived in "the Big House" at Slate's Hot Springs, Murphy and his wife lived in the property's "small house." Murphy and Thompson formed a friendship, but they never discussed writing. After Sandy declared that Thompson would be a great author, Murphy sneaked into Thompson's room and discovered a thoroughly annotated copy of *The Sergeant* and the beginnings of *The Rum Diary.* "Hunter had studied my book like a Bible, and I didn't even know that he had a copy," Murphy said later. "And as for *Rum Diary,* when I saw some of the vivid scenery from his time in Latin America, I knew that he had the makings of a good writer." Joan Baez also lived on the property, as did Beat poet Lew Welch and Lenore Kandel, who later faced obscenity charges for her poetry. (Kandel would marry poet and Hell's Angel Billy "Sweet William" Fritsch, and Welch's stepson became rock star Huey Lewis.) Dennis Murphy eventually departed for Hollywood, where he worked on the film adaptation of *The Sergeant* with Rod Steiger in the lead role.

Another Big Sur friend and fellow writer was Lionel Olay, whom Thompson would profile in an article called "The Ultimate Free Lancer." In addition to publishing two novels, Olay interviewed stand-up comedian Lenny Bruce for *Cavalier* magazine in 1963. By that time, Bruce had been arrested for obscenity while performing in North Beach. His defenders included Ralph J. Gleason, who covered jazz for the *San Francisco Chronicle.* Bruce was acquitted in the San Francisco case, which many regarded as another landmark free-speech decision. Thompson was no fan of Bruce, but he considered Olay's article exemplary. Olay had no feeling for literary politics, Thompson maintained, and he blew a cushy assignment by describing his subject, a Hollywood producer, as a "pompous toad." That decision only endeared him to Thompson, who admired Olay's independence above all. Thompson's article, which began as a letter to the *Los Angeles Free Press,* was also a eulogy, for the 42-year-old Olay had died after a stroke the month before. Later that year, Thompson's letter appeared in the premiere issue of *The Distant Drummer,* a Philadelphia underground paper. Its editor, John Lombardi, would cross paths with Thompson several years later.

While patrolling the property one morning, Thompson discovered Dennis's brother Michael in Bunnie's bedroom. Thompson woke him and his friend Richard Price with a .22 pistol. The two men were hoping to start a new institute on the property but had not yet received permission from Bunnie. Thompson also kept an eye on the hot springs, where gay men regularly rendezvoused. "We were not trying to pass judgment on anyone," Price said later, "but we couldn't have *that* going on and do what we were planning to do, so we would try and close down the baths at ten in the evening." Thompson described his duties in letters to his Louisville friends. "Yes, there are queers here," he wrote in 1961. "And artists. And farmers. And people who go around naked. I have a bullwhip and a billy club. So far, I have not been bothered." Jo Hudson witnessed Thompson's efforts to intimidate the men who congregated at the hot springs, and Price confirmed that his methods were rough. "Hunter had a lot of aggression and severe homophobia," Price said. "He would go down there and actually try and pick fights. I remember one time they literally tried to throw him off the cliff."

After that episode Thompson described his dilemma to a friend back East.

> I am surrounded by lunatics here, people screeching every time I pull a trigger, yelling about my blood-soaked shirt, packs of queers waiting to do me in, so many creditors that I've lost count, a huge Doberman on the bed, a pistol by the desk, time passing, getting balder, no money, a great thirst for all the world's whiskey, my clothes rotting in the fog, a motorcycle with no light, a landlady who's writing a novel on butcher paper, wild boar in the hills and queers on the road, vats of homemade beer in the closet, shooting cats to ease the pressure, the jabbering of Buddhists in the trees, whores in the canyon, Christ only knows if I can last it out.

Despite these woes, Thompson managed to convert his impressions of Big Sur into an article for *Rogue,* a Chicago-based men's magazine created in *Playboy*'s image. That piece, and a short story that ran in *Rogue* later that year, became his first publications in a national magazine. He called the first article "Big Sur: The Garden of Agony," but *Rogue* changed the subtitle to "The Tropic of Henry Miller." Thompson motivated his photo-essay by debunking earlier descriptions of Big Sur. "If half the stories about Big Sur were true," Thompson wrote, "the vibrations from all the orgies would have collapsed the entire Santa Lucia mountain range, making the destruction of Sodom and Gomorrah look like the work of a piker."

According to Thompson, Miller's home had become a shrine. Miller had moved there to find solitude, but Thompson noted that the onslaught of visitors was unremitting.

> As his fame spread, his volume of visitors mounted steadily. Many of them had not even read his books. They weren't interested in literature, they wanted orgies. And they were shocked to find him a quiet, fastidious, and very moral man, instead of the raving sexual beast they'd heard about.

Thompson did not mention that he, too, had come to Big Sur to investigate the local action; he even staked out Miller's mailbox in a vain attempt to meet his idol. Featuring the region's sex-crazed tourists exemplified a journalistic maneuver that Thompson quickly mastered. He often wrote about sensational topics, subjecting earlier accounts to withering critique even as he kept their lurid nature in sharp focus. In that way, he enhanced his own authority while capitalizing on the very sensationalism he proposed to correct.

In addition to showcasing Thompson's biting humor, the article took notable risks. Perhaps the most obvious is the inclusion of an especially fantastical passage from *The World of Sex*.

> What will happen when this world of neuters who make up the great bulk of the population collapses is this—they will discover sex. In the period of darkness which will ensue they will line up in the dark like snakes and toads and chew each other alive during the endless fornication carnival. They will bury them selves in the earth and go at it hammer and tongs. They will fuck anything within reach, from a keyhole to a mangy corpse. Anything can happen on this continent. From the very beginning it has been the seat of cruel practices, of blood-letting, of horrible tortures, of enslavement, of fratricide, of sacrificial orgies, of stoicism, of witchcraft, of lynching, of pillage and plunder, of greed, of prejudice and bigotry, and so on . . . We have seen everything but the eruption of sexuality. This will be the last outburst, the flood which will carry the robots off.

By including this passage, Thompson stretched the boundaries of local color and prefigured his own savage tone a decade later. More than any other writer, Henry Miller was Gonzo *avant la lettre*.

The *Rogue* article was also notable for Thompson's self-presentation. The title page included a full-page shot of a shirtless Thompson, pipe in mouth, sitting outdoors in front of a typewriter with coastal bluffs in the background. The caption read, "HUNTER S. THOMPSON, AUTHOR AT WORK." Subsequent spreads included photographs of Thompson and Sandy reading the newspaper outdoors, Sandy in a chair overlooking the ocean, and two shots of the gorgeous coastline. It was a direct appeal to the male audience's aspirations: a virile man and his attractive girlfriend sharing a creative lifestyle in a ruggedly beautiful setting. The reality was less glamorous. Sandy, who was working as a maid, had two abortions during their Big Sur stint. Given their situation, she felt she had no other practical option.

> I knew that if I had a baby, Hunter would leave me. There was no question. We weren't married. We had no money. He would have had to have left me, for himself. I mean, as a child he was a narcissist, and later he became a well developed narcissist—a polished narcissist, actually.

To pay for the abortions, Sandy asked an ex-boyfriend and her mother for money. Thompson accompanied her to Tijuana for both procedures, the second of which was especially difficult.

Later that year, *Rogue* ran Thompson's short story "Burial at Sea." It was based on a three-week sea voyage Thompson had taken to Bermuda with Sandy and Semonin. Thompson clashed with the captain and finally avoided him altogether on the fifty-foot boat. In the story, a recently married couple decides to sail back to the mainland after island hopping around Trinidad. Trouble ensues when the captain makes unseemly advances on the wife and berates the husband for his incompetence as a deck hand. One passage encapsulates the internal state of the husband.

> He could never forget the horror of this day. Bruce Laurenson, proud scion of one of Cleveland's best families, insulted and beaten—while his wife watched—by a common sailor, a vicious, ignorant bum. Reduced to hopeless jelly by a cheap sea-thug. And if that wasn't enough, his wife was somehow attracted to the brute, maybe even whoring with him.

As he tries to make sense of his plight, Laurenson begins to form a strategy for preserving his honor.

> He wondered what his friends would say if he came back without her. What about his parents? And hers? What could he say? He thought about it for a while and finally decided he'd simply tell them the truth—that she had suddenly turned into a whore.

A conversation with his wife calms Laurenson, but his worst fears are confirmed when he hears her slip into the captain's berth at night. He leaves the ship in a rowboat, makes his way back to shore, and prepares to return to Cleveland by himself. As in *The Rum Diary*, unregulated female sexuality is a key problem, but this time it is compounded by class, not race, as the brutish sea-thug cuckolds the proud scion. Insofar as he identifies with Laurenson, the reader experiences the traumatic flip side of the masculine aspiration presented in the Big Sur article.

"Burial at Sea" sank into oblivion, but the Big Sur piece queered Thompson's arrangement with Bunnie Murphy. Traveling from her Salinas home in a chauffeur-driven Cadillac, she ordered Thompson to clear out. Before that eviction, Bunnie worried that Michael might sign over the property to "the Hindoos." (He had visited an Indian ashram after his discharge from the army.) After the expulsion, however, Bunnie granted Michael's request to use the property for the Esalen Institute, which quickly became a major node in the human potential movement. In this indirect way, Murphy said, Thompson helped him launch his life's work.

4 Observer

After leaving Big Sur, Thompson returned to New York with Sandy and began to plot his next move. Writing to the *National Observer*, he offered to produce a series of dispatches from South America and was quickly taken up on it. Serving as a foreign correspondent for the *Wall Street Journal's* Sunday edition was a departure for him, but it allowed him to follow in the footsteps of Jake Barnes and Paul Kemp, his own protagonist in *The Rum Diary*. He had not found a publisher for that novel, which William Kennedy thought needed more work. It was "full of digressions and wisdom—his essays on the state of the world, the nation, journalism, Puerto Rico," Kennedy said later.

In May 1962, Thompson landed in Colombia and spent the next eighteen months traveling through eight countries. Brian Kevin, who retraced Thompson's path in South America, claimed that his stories offered glimpses of his emerging style.

> This is sharp, witty, participatory journalism with a keen eye for the
> absurdities of South American life in the 1960s. The pieces are a mix of
> straightforward news reporting and more narrative, feature-style
> articles. The depth of insight into Cold War foreign policy is impressive,
> and the stories contain some memorable prose.

Kevin's overall description is apt, as is his observation that Thompson's time in South America sharpened his view of the United States. "The Thompson who left for the continent was a self-identified seeker and escapist," Kevin maintained. "The one who came back a year later was a narrow-eyed critic of American political culture and social ritual." However, the reportage was not participatory journalism as practiced later by Thompson and others—or even decades earlier by Jack London and George Orwell. Thompson appeared in the stories, but he never reported deeply on the subcultures he encountered. Indeed, his limited grasp of Spanish and Portuguese made that kind of reporting virtually impossible. Years later, however, William Kennedy noted that Thompson's South American tour was a professional breakthrough insofar as he traveled freely, chose his own topics, and established his name modestly.

Reporting from abroad required Thompson to cut through local complexities and offer instant analysis. It also honed his skills as a media critic. His articles often showcased political journalism, both local and American, almost as much as the scenes he observed. Part of the value proposition he offered readers was the unvarnished truth—not only about the subject at hand, but also about the media's distortions and blind spots. His media criticism was on display in a 1963 letter to the *Saturday Review* in which Thompson challenged two of that magazine's articles. He called the first piece, by Barnard Collier, "a nearly perfect case of tunnel vision on the subject of the Latin American press." Collier's chief complaint was the lack of analytical reporting in South America, but Thompson countered that he overlooked Brazil's newspapers, which compared well with American outlets. Thompson dismissed the second article, which called for more research by journalists, by noting a more basic problem: Most American newspapers preferred superficial wire-service reports to more expensive foreign bureaus.

Thompson acknowledged that his letter was much too long to run in the magazine, but he frequently dispatched such missives to raise his profile. During the same period, for example, he struck up a correspondence with *Washington Post* owner Phil Graham. In his introductory letter, Thompson ridiculed a story about Brazil that ran in *Newsweek*, which Graham also owned. "It is a goddamned abomination," Thompson wrote, "a fraud, and a black onus on American journalism that a magazine with *Newsweek*'s money and circulation so slothfully ignores a continent as critical to American interests as this one." He concluded with an even more personal barb. "I'm beginning to think you're a phony, Graham . . . Maybe you should loosen your tie a bit and consider your own hash—because, dollar for dollar, it ain't so tasty, and you're sufficiently old, experienced, and overpaid to have no real excuse at all." Thompson was amazed when Graham replied, asking for "a somewhat less breathless letter, in which you tell me about yourself, and don't make it more than two pages single space—which means a third draft and not a first draft." Thompson never parlayed that correspondence into a job offer, but he maintained it until Graham's suicide in 1963.

Thompson challenged his media colleagues in other ways as well. Writing to the photo editor of *Argosy*, he demanded one hundred dollars for a photograph of Sandy that ran in the December 1963 issue without permission or payment. The photograph shows Sandy in a two-piece bathing suit and walking their Doberman pinscher. *Argosy* also published a letter to the editor purportedly written by Thompson.

> That was like a mildly groovey [*sic*] piece you guys ran on Las Vegas in the October issue. But you didn't tell half the story of what a swinging town it is. You said there were lots of pretty showgirls and lots of pretty visitors, but you didn't say anything about the fact that they walk around town with almost less than the law should allow. It's enough to give a guy a jolt.
>
> How about warning us next time so we can bring more film for our cameras?
>
> Hunter S. Thompson
> Boulder, Colorado

Thompson was having none of it. Failing monetary satisfaction, he wrote to the *Argosy* photo editor, he had "every intention of stomping the shit out of you, either in your office or wherever we happen to meet." Thompson welcomed that prospect. "There's nothing I'd like better—both as a healthy exercise and as good material for my biographers—than to gather some of my ham-fisted friends from McSorley's and clean out your whole damn office." He copied "two other, necessarily unnamed, gentlemen of sporting blood, % McSorley's, East 7th St., New York."

The aggressive tone was partly a matter of honor. Sandy was involved, and the letter attributed to him was fabricated. But the article also contradicted the authorial self he wished to project.

> Too many people in this gutless world have come under the impression that writers are a race of finks, queers, and candy asses to be bilked, cheated, and mocked as a form of commercial sport. It should be noted, therefore, that some writers possess .44 Magnums and can puncture beer cans with 240-grain slugs from that weapon at a distance of 150 yards. Other writers, it is said, tend to enjoy violence for its own sake and feel that a good fight, with the inevitable destruction of all nearby equipment and furniture, is nearly as fine for the nerves as a quart of John Powers Irish [whiskey].

This short passage conveys a great deal about Thompson's model of authorship. First, he demanded proper compensation, a major theme in his correspondence. Second, he rejected the stereotype of the wimpy writer, and he would back up his position with violence if necessary. He also posited, perhaps jocularly, his own biographer several years before the appearance of his first book. Before closing, Thompson assumed the role of southern cavalier who preferred to settle disputes with firearms or fisticuffs—aided by whiskey-swigging "gentlemen of sporting blood."

Thompson's letter was more than a literary exercise. *Argosy* eventually sent him a check for $150.

. . .

At the end of his South American stint, Thompson returned to Louisville. From there, he visited the *National Observer*'s headquarters in Maryland, where he told colleagues that he and Sandy wished to return to California. The couple married in Indiana, then visited Sandy's mother in Florida, where she gave them a 1959 Nash Rambler. Thompson drove west and stopped in Las Vegas, where he was credentialed to cover the heavyweight championship fight between Sonny Liston and Floyd Patterson in July 1963. He watched Liston train at the Thunderbird Hotel and Casino, and when fight night arrived, he sat ringside near former heavyweight champion Rocky Marciano. Even before Thompson finished his first beer, however, Liston knocked out Patterson. Eight years later, Thompson would return to Las Vegas under very different circumstances.

Thompson made his way to Aspen, where Semonin had a cabin. Sandy flew to Colorado, and after a two-month stint with their friend, the couple rented a place in nearby Woody Creek. Soon Sandy learned that she was pregnant. That summer, Thompson wrote to his brother Davison about his impending move. He was wavering between a house in Sonoma County, about fifty miles north of San Francisco, and another house about ten miles outside Aspen. He was leaning toward Sonoma because it was more isolated and lacked the distractions—that is, the nearby bars—of Aspen. The house in Sonoma belonged to Denne Petitclerc, a former correspondent for the *Santa Rosa Press Democrat*. While working for the *Miami Herald*, Petitclerc befriended Hemingway and later converted *Islands in the Stream*, Hemingway's unfinished novel, into a film starring George C. Scott. Much later, that friendship was featured in another Hollywood film, *Papa: Hemingway in Cuba* (2015).

Before Thompson could put his plan into motion, news of President Kennedy's assassination shocked the nation. In a letter to Semonin, who was studying in Ghana by then, Thompson railed against "the death of reason" and those who had killed it. He seemed to include Semonin in his indictment.

> I suppose your boys over there are whooping it up. Another victory for Marxism. Well, they better add up the score again, because they lost as decisively as I did . . . That the bullet should have come from the Far left

is the filthiest irony of all. It was right and proper that the deed was
done in Texas, but a terrible shock to find the "Fair Play for Cuba
Committee" with its name on the slug.

Early reporting on the assassination depicted Lee Harvey Oswald as a lone
Marxist gunman, and in his grief and rage, Thompson railed against
Semonin personally. "All of you cheap bookstore Marxists who had the
answer yesterday had better buy bullets," he wrote. Even Semonin's
sojourn in Aspen, where Thompson would later reside for decades, was a
strike against him. "This is by far the most profound act of the 20th century," he wrote. "But the ski bums in Aspen are still living it up in the Red
Onion. The big laugh. Aspen is a bag of shit. The fact that you like it only
reinforces my opinion of your Marxist leanings."

The same day, Thompson wrote a slightly less bilious letter to William
Kennedy. "There is no human being within five hundred miles to whom I
can communicate anything—much less the fear and loathing that is on me
after today's murder," he wrote. In his grief, Thompson even managed to
slight Kennedy.

> We now enter the era of the shit-rain, President Johnson and the
> hardening of the arteries. Neither your children nor mine will ever
> grasp what Gatsby was after. No more of that. You misunderstand it, of
> course, peeling back only the first and most obvious layer. Take your
> "realism" to the garbage dump. Or the "little magazines." They are like
> a man who goes into a phone booth to pull his pod.

The assassination, Thompson continued, boded ill for the traditional novel.
Fiction was dead, he informed Kennedy, who would win the Pulitzer Prize
for fiction in 1984. "Mailer is an antique curiosity. The stakes are now too
high, and the time is too short. What, O what, does Eudora Welty have to
say? Fuck that crowd." The enormity of the assassination pushed Thompson
toward journalism, though he suspected that his own dreams in the fiction
department could have risen above the chaos. "My concept of the new novel
would have fit this situation," he told Kennedy, "but now I see no hope for
getting it done if, indeed, any publishing houses survive the Nazi scramble
that is sure to come." Two parts of his letter proved durable. "Fear and
loathing" would become his signature phrase, and the idea that the American
Dream died with President Kennedy would underpin his work for years.

In the meantime, Thompson continued his correspondence with
Semonin, who had recommended Frantz Fanon's *The Wretched of the
Earth* (1961). Having read some of the anti-colonial tract and Jean-Paul
Sartre's foreword, Thompson conceded that Fanon was "a dead ringer for
the real thing" but dismissed Sartre as "an eloquent windbag." He also

teased Semonin about the opacity of his recommendation. "If I were Fanon," Thompson wrote, "I wouldn't want you on my side." The next day, he pitched a book review to *The Reporter*, claiming that Sartre's introduction was required reading for those interested in Africa's future. He surmised that Fanon was West Indian and presumably Black, but did not seem to know that Fanon had died two years earlier. Nevertheless, he took the opportunity to tout his sources in Africa.

> For nearly a year, I have maintained a running debt with some contacts at the Institute for African Studies in Ghana (mainly Europeans, but one American) and I have come from a point where I dismissed them all as "bookstore Marxists" to another point, now, where I take their ideas quite seriously. I don't like them, but too much of what they say makes sense when I read the newspapers.

The letter reflected the complexity of Thompson's intellectual friendship with Semonin as well as his own opportunism. When writing to his former classmate, Thompson denigrated him and his worldview. When pitching a book review the next day, however, he lauded Semonin's expertise even as he carefully distinguished his own tough-minded skepticism from his source's bookstore Marxism.

· · ·

In February 1964, with Sandy eight months pregnant, the Thompsons moved to Glen Ellen, a small town in Sonoma County. Upon their arrival, they learned that Petitclerc had rented his home to someone else. All he could offer them was an outbuilding on the same property, which Thompson described as a chicken coop. Their son was born while they were living there. His name, Juan Fitzgerald Thompson, reflected his father's favorite politician, his favorite author, and his stints in Latin America. Their home was primitive, but Sandy made the best of it. "It was actually a shack," Sandy recalled. "Not a bad shack, you know, but a tin shack with a little kitchen and a big room, and then a little room off of that which became Juan's bedroom. It was great. It had electricity and running water."

Glen Ellen was another bucolic town with a literary past. In the early part of the century, Jack London built an enormous home there called Wolf House, which burned down almost as soon as it was completed. Perhaps following London, Thompson dubbed his own modest home Owl House. (That name also echoed the Owl Creek Country Club just outside Louisville as well as a favorite alias, Sebastian Owl.) Thompson had not read London for years, but his precursor's celebrity and professional choices prefigured his own. Known primarily for his adventure stories, London covered the

Russo-Japanese war, the San Francisco earthquake of 1906, and the heavy-weight championship fight between Jack Johnson and Jim Jeffries, the Great White Hope. Moreover, London helped pioneer participatory journalism. *The People of the Abyss* (1903), which was based on London's time in the East End of London, led one writer to cast him as an important precursor to New Journalism. Similarly, *The Road* (1907) recalled London's tramping days and reportedly inspired Hemingway, Steinbeck, and Kerouac.

Like Thompson, London believed that fiction was more truthful than mere fact. "I have been forced to conclude that Fact, to be true, must imitate Fiction," London wrote. "The creative imagination is more veracious than the voice of life." He also rejected the traditional path of the provincial writer. It was never his plan to graduate from local color to fiction, to move to an eastern city, or even to secure steady employment. Rather, he created his own niche in the national media ecology and traveled whenever and wherever it suited him. As a literary celebrity, his biographer Jay Williams observed, London was "always mobile, always independent, answering to no one." After selling his stories to magazines, London republished them in book form; in that way, he resisted changes imposed by magazine editors and ensured that his work would endure. Taken as a whole, London's pro-fessional decisions and practices marked out another kind of adventure—not in the Klondike or South Pacific, but in the world of letters. "IT WAS MY REFUSAL TO TAKE CAUTIOUS ADVICE THAT MADE ME," London once wrote to editor George Brett.

Thompson and London had something else in common—heavy drinking. *John Barleycorn*, London's "alcoholic memoir," occasionally read like a Prohibition tract, but London never swore off alcohol, and his failing kid-neys contributed to his death at age 40. Thompson's drinking was likewise prodigious, but during his time in Glen Ellen, he began to balance it with regular doses of Dexedrine, which helped him maintain his focus while writ-ing. He obtained a prescription from orthopedic surgeon Bob Geiger, whom he befriended in Sonoma. After Thompson and Geiger decided to shoot at gophers on the Glen Ellen property at 4 a.m., the Thompsons were evicted, and the Geigers put them up. Thompson later dedicated *Fear and Loathing in Las Vegas* to Geiger "for reasons that need not be explained here."

A busy lecturer on labor and socialism, London once ran for mayor of Oakland on the Socialist ticket. His key issue was justice, which he defined as "an equal chance for all men." At the same time, much of his writing reflected the so-called scientific racism of his era. During his Glen Ellen sojourn, Thompson told Semonin that he wanted to write about racial poli-tics in San Francisco.

> I am not too worried about being rejected for my whiteness, although I
> do in all truth think the idea of a Negro Nationalist party in the country
> is madness, because there are too many people in this country just
> waiting for an excuse to act like the racists they are. Hell, I even have a
> strain of it myself, and the only thing that has brought me around this
> far is the fact that every time I've seen a black-white confrontation I've
> had to admit the Negroes were Right.

Even that admission was tempered by the potential threat he felt from
Black nationalists. "Once it turns into power politics, the negro loses his
leverage on my conscience," he wrote. "Malcolm X amuses me, and I bear
him no malice at this time, but when he starts carrying a gun and talking
about blowing my head off, there the dialogue ends."

In June 1964, Thompson contacted an editor at *Pageant* magazine about
his interest in "the negro problem." In his query letter, Thompson mentioned his plan, never enacted, to visit Mississippi that summer. That would
have put him at the center of the civil rights movement, but his story idea
for *Pageant* was quite different. With the help of Michael Murphy, he
hoped to arrange an Esalen Institute seminar and parlay that event into a
well-paying article. His dream panel would include comedian and activist
Dick Gregory, Norman Mailer, jazz musician Charles Mingus, and "one or
two of California's black socialists." The key question would be the dilemma
White liberals faced if Black militancy intensified. Specifically, the seminar
would consider "the position of the White Liberal in the event that negro
'militants' gain a dominant voice in the 'civil rights' movement.'" The reason for his quotation marks, Thompson added in his pitch to Murphy, "is
too complex to explain right now."

According to Thompson, the White liberal's dilemma would become
especially acute if Senator Barry Goldwater, who opposed the Civil Rights
Act of 1964, won the GOP presidential nomination later that summer.

> In the event of various "conflicts" predicted by civil rights leaders if
> Goldwater is nominated and the civil rights bill proves toothless in their
> eyes, whose side is the "white liberal" on? Or, as Charley Mingus said
> to Ralph Gleason, "Man, you gotta know where you stand when the
> fighting starts in the streets." Or Louis Lomax when he talks about the
> coming "night of the long knives." Which way do I point my .44
> Magnum if both sides think I'm against them?

Even aside from the handgun reference, Thompson's hypothetical question
was remarkable. The FBI consistently treated the civil rights movement as
a Communist front, and even sympathetic White observers worried that
the movement might be hijacked by radicals. But Thompson's proposal was

not designed to feature that threat—or the more obvious one that White supremacists posed to Black Americans. Rather, he wished to explore the potential threat Black militants posed to White liberals, a group to which he belonged, at least in this formulation.

That imaginary conflict was overtaken by events on the ground. A church bombing the year before had killed four Black girls in Birmingham, Alabama, and civil rights leader Medgar Evers was already dead, shot in his Mississippi driveway. Days before Thompson wrote to *Pageant*, three civil rights workers were slain in Mississippi; their bodies were found almost two months later. In the end, Thompson published relatively little on the civil rights movement as such. *The Reporter* piece on Louisville was a rare exception. A *Pageant* article, which described Los Angeles's dreadful traffic jams, included a lengthy sidebar that featured the plight of Black residents months after the Watts Riots and the desperate conditions that gave rise to them. For the most part, however, Thompson focused on other matters.

As the civil rights movement pressed on, Thompson produced a piece about the Beat generation for the *National Observer* and profiled the Rustic Inn, one of Jack London's watering holes in Glen Ellen. The latter was intended for *The Reporter* but eventually appeared in *Cavalier*, another second-tier men's magazine, well after Thompson left Glen Ellen. The article described the saloon's proprietor as a friend of Jack London who "worked for him and drank with him and was the last man to see London alive."

> Around here that is quite a distinction. London named this valley and built his ill-fated Wolf House—which burned before he could move into it—on a hill overlooking the town. As far as the old-timers are concerned, Jack London is sitting today on the right hand of God, and you begin to suspect after a while that a few of them think it may be other way around.

The Rustic Inn resembled other bars in the valley, Thompson noted, except that its regulars often abused visitors.

> The strange truth is that the Rustic, unlike most "legendary" bars, has not become safe and respectable with fame. London's people still frequent the place, abusing the tourists in all manner of ways, ranging from senseless violence to simple, declarative sentences like: "You're an ass, buddy—I'm takin' your wife home with me." That sort of thing is said to make the Rustic "an interesting place to drink."

If the veracity of these quotations is questionable, the first one chimed well with the cuckold theme in "Burial at Sea."

Thompson's portrait of the saloon resembled his work for the *National Observer*, which remained his bread and butter. When read alongside his first

Big Sur piece, however, it seemed that Thompson was also assembling a literary lineage that included Henry Miller and Jack London. Although he never cited London as an influence, he no doubt recognized his precursor's distinctive model of authorship. Rising out of poverty, London became wealthy on his writing and was no one's subordinate. He managed his public image carefully, always emphasizing his manly adventures, and he lived in bucolic splendor when he wasn't converting those adventures into income and celebrity. Long before Hemingway, London successfully lived out Thompson's teenage dream of forsaking security and embracing vigorous action.

Two months into his Glen Ellen sojourn, the *National Observer* again induced Thompson to travel, this time within the United States. His trip included a stop in Idaho, where Thompson produced an article about Hemingway's final years. "What Lured Hemingway to Ketchum?" was a eulogy for his hero, who had committed suicide three years earlier. It began with the odd claim that Hemingway, who set a novel amid the Spanish Civil War, had no interest in politics. The FBI held a different view; it charted Hemingway's political connections and activities in a file that eventually ran to 122 pages. In Idaho, Thompson maintained, Hemingway "could live among the rugged, non-political people and visit, when he chose to, with a few of his famous friends who still came up to Sun Valley."

According to Thompson, politics was not the only thing Hemingway sought to escape in Idaho; he also wished to avoid modernity itself. Neither he nor Fitzgerald, Thompson claimed, "understood the vibrations of a world that had shaken them off their thrones, but of the two, Fitzgerald showed more resilience." Fitzgerald was writing screenplays in Encino when he died two decades earlier, but in creating *The Last Tycoon*, he was making "a sincere effort to catch up and come to grips with reality, no matter how distasteful it may have seemed to him." Hemingway, in contrast, insisted on living in the past. "The strength of his youth became rigid as he grew older," Thompson wrote, "and his last book was about Paris in the Twenties." Between Fitzgerald's death and the publication of *A Moveable Feast*, Hemingway accompanied the Allied troops at Normandy, faced charges for improperly collaborating with the French resistance, and was awarded a Bronze Star. In 1952, he wrote *The Old Man and the Sea*, for which he received a Pulitzer Prize; two years later, he received the Nobel Prize. Yet he struggled with depression and self-medicated throughout his adult life. As Thompson noted, he was "old, sick, and very troubled" when he moved to Ketchum. "Perhaps he found what he came here for," Thompson concluded, "but the odds are huge that he didn't . . . So finally, and for what he must have thought the best of reasons, he ended it with a shotgun."

While burying Hemingway, Thompson also took aim at novelists who shared his pathology.

> Today we have Mailer, Jones, and Styron, three potentially great writers bogged down in what seems to be a crisis of convictions brought on, like Hemingway's, by the mean nature of a world that will not stand still long enough for them to see it clear and whole.

In this way, Thompson managed to clear the stage of his precursors and rivals. It would take a very different kind of writer, Thompson implied, to thrive in a world where "chaos is multiplying." He never said so explicitly, but Thompson considered himself that new kind of writer. Nevertheless, he also wanted something that would link him to Hemingway. Before leaving Ketchum, he nicked the elk horns that hung over his hero's front door.

· · ·

For Thompson, Glen Ellen was even less satisfactory than Big Sur. He had returned from South America with a fat wallet and promising leads, but the year had been a bust. He was depressed and "bouncing from one midnight to the next in a blaze of stupid drunkenness." Although the *National Observer* provided an office in the *Wall Street Journal*'s San Francisco bureau, it furnished little fellowship. "I would wander in on off-hours and obviously on drugs and ask for my messages," Thompson recalled. "They liked me but I was like the bull in the china shop."

That summer, the Thompsons moved to 318 Parnassus Avenue in San Francisco. Perched on a hill overlooking Golden Gate Park, their new home was walking distance from Kezar Stadium, where Thompson attended the San Francisco 49ers' home games. He also observed the adjacent Haight-Ashbury neighborhood at close range. A fog-shrouded valley of sand dunes and shanties in the nineteenth century, the Haight later became a fashionable neighborhood with direct access to Golden Gate Park. Due to an acute housing shortage after the Second World War, many of its large Victorian homes were divided into flats, and the neighborhood became a plentiful source of low-rent housing, especially for students at nearby San Francisco State College. By the time Thompson moved to the area, some residents were morphing into what the *San Francisco Examiner* would soon call "hippies," or junior-grade hipsters. Three years later, they would make Haight-Ashbury a major news site.

That summer, however, the national media descended on the Cow Palace, the indoor arena that hosted the 1964 Republican National Convention. The raucous event was later described as a bar fight that lasted four days. The GOP's favorite candidate, Barry Goldwater, touted liberty and free markets to counter the spread of communist totalitarianism. But Goldwater's appeal also arose from acute racial tensions. As Dixiecrats abandoned the Democratic Party and swelled the Republican ranks, they subverted the party's tradition of advancing civil rights. At the Cow Palace, White delegates openly taunted their Black counterparts. Reporting for NBC, John Chancellor found an elderly Black delegate leaning against the arena wall, weeping. "The Goldwater delegates had put their cigarettes out all over his suit," Chancellor recalled. Jackie Robinson, the GOP delegate who broke the color barrier in major league baseball sixteen years earlier, said that the convention was "one of the most unforgettable and frightening experiences of my life."

The GOP also targeted the media. On one hotel elevator, television news anchors Chet Huntley and David Brinkley heard partisans grumbling about the coverage. "You know, these nighttime news shows sound to me like they're being broadcast from Moscow," one said to another. The other replied, "Why can't we find Americans to do the television news?" When Dwight Eisenhower's speech scorned "sensation-seeking columnists and commentators," many delegates rose from their seats and waved their fists at the broadcast booths. Black reporters were especially vulnerable to the delegation's wrath. Belva Davis, who became a prominent Bay Area news anchor, recalled the treatment she and her boss, Louis Freeman, received at the convention after Eisenhower's speech: "Suddenly Louis and I heard a voice yell, 'Hey, look at those two up there!' The accuser pointed us out, and several spectators swarmed beneath us. 'Hey niggers!' they yelled. 'What the hell are you niggers doing in here?'" Davis and Freeman packed their equipment and descended the ramps of the Cow Palace. "A self-appointed posse dangled over the railings, taunting," Davis wrote in her memoir. "'Niggers!' 'Get out of here, boy!' 'You too, nigger bitch.' 'Go on, get out!' 'I'm gonna kill your ass.'"

Introduced by Richard Nixon, Senator Goldwater delivered his famous acceptance speech. "Our people have followed false prophets," he claimed. "We must and we shall return to proven ways—not because they are old, but because they are true." The speech climaxed with two reminders separated by forty seconds of wild applause: "I would remind you that extremism in the defense of liberty is no vice! . . . And let me remind you also that moderation in the pursuit of justice is no virtue!" The message was far from unprecedented. As historian Rick Perlstein noted, it echoed President Kennedy's inaugural address, which announced the nation's determination to assure the survival and success of liberty. But context was all. The delegates heard a dog whistle, and most of them howled. Others were repulsed.

Richard Nixon, who restrained his wife from joining the standing ovation, reportedly felt sick to his stomach.

Ironically, Thompson's reaction resembled Nixon's. With the help of a friend, Thompson had obtained a pass and was "genuinely frightened" by the response to Goldwater's speech.

> The Goldwater delegates went completely amok for fifteen or twenty minutes. He hadn't even finished the sentence before they were on their feet, cheering wildly. Then, as the human thunder kept building, they mounted their metal chairs and began howling, shaking their fists at Huntley and Brinkley up in the NBC booth—and finally they began picking up those chairs with both hands and bashing them against chairs other delegates were still standing on.

Witnessing that fervor in the Cow Palace was a key moment in Thompson's political education. Equally formative was Norman Mailer's coverage of it in *Esquire*, which one reviewer described as "brilliant to the point of incandescence, not only in its style and rhetorical energy, but in its witchlike sensitivity to the moods and weathers of the candidates." Douglas Brinkley claimed that Mailer's work, including the convention coverage, influenced Thompson even more than Fitzgerald or Hemingway.

Despite the convention's intensity, Thompson had no reason to believe that the conservative movement was unstoppable. Johnson crushed Goldwater in the general election, and Nixon's political life seemed to have run its course following his loss to California governor Pat Brown. In his remarks to the press after that defeat, Nixon turned out to be something of a media critic himself.

> I leave you gentlemen now, and you will write it. You will interpret. That's your right. But as I leave you, I want you to know, just think how much you're going to be missing. You won't have Nixon to kick around anymore, because gentlemen, this is my last press conference, and it will be the one in which I have welcomed the opportunity to test wits with you.

Nixon added bitterly that the press had a duty even to a candidate they did not like or support. If they decided to "give him the shaft," they should also "put one lonely reporter on the campaign who will report what the candidate says now and then." After Goldwater also went down in defeat, the liberal consensus seemed stronger than ever.

• • •

If Thompson's move to San Francisco was meant to improve his standing at the *National Observer*, his plan failed badly. He still had much to learn about American politics, and his reckless behavior at the convention drew a reprimand from his senior colleagues. Nevertheless, the move allowed him to cover other Bay Area stories of interest. One of them was unfolding across the bay, where University of California students were challenging restrictions on political speech. Put in place during the tumultuous 1930s, those restrictions banned campus events that could "involve the University in political or sectarian religious activities in a partisan way." The rules were meant to restrain student activism and mollify state politicians who controlled the university's budget. As the civil rights movement heated up, however, students began organizing on campus to protest racial discrimination, especially in the Bay Area job market. Business leaders charged that students were using the Berkeley campus as a staging area to attack the community. When UC president Clark Kerr enforced the longstanding speech restrictions, students responded that their speech and assembly rights should be at least as robust on campus as they were anywhere else.

Thompson sensed that the ruckus transcended campus politics. "The Free Speech Movement was virtually nonexistent at the time," he recalled, "but I saw it coming. There was a great rumbling—you could feel it everywhere." Raw demographics powered that revolt. As Baby Boomers came of age, half the nation's population was under 25 years old, and college campuses teemed with students. Nonstudents were subject to the draft, which President Johnson expanded, and that combination prepared the ground for youthful challenges to politics as usual. Cal administrators eventually eased campus speech restrictions, but student activists immediately turned their attention to other causes, especially the conflict in Vietnam. Drawn to Berkeley's culture of dissent, Thompson produced an article about nonstudent activists and was irked when the *National Observer* refused to run it. "It was wild," he said in the same interview, "but Dow Jones was just too far away. I wanted to cover the Free Speech Movement, but they didn't want me to."

Thompson also clashed with his editors over Tom Wolfe's book, *The Kandy-Kolored Tangerine-Flake Streamline Baby* (1965), which Thompson wanted to review for the *National Observer*. In each of the collected articles, Wolfe explored a colorful American subculture. The book drew its title from a 1963 piece on Southern California's hot-rod scene, and another chapter focused on Las Vegas, where the bright lights were "bubbling, spiraling, rocketing, and exploding in sunbursts ten stories high out in the middle of the desert." Although Wolfe mostly wrote for eastern urban elites, he drew heavily on California's lively popular culture. Years later, he reflected on that period.

> When I started writing in what became known as my style, I was trying
> to capture the newness and excitement of the West Coast thing. It's
> where all the exciting youth styles were coming from. They certainly
> weren't coming from New York. Everything I was writing about was
> new to the East Coast.

Wolfe created that style almost by accident. The title essay reportedly
began as a letter to his editor at *Esquire*. It summarized the notes he had
made while struggling with his story, and the magazine simply ran the
letter. The same year, *Esquire* ran "Twirling at Ole Miss," Terry Southern's
first-person investigation of the Dixie National Baton Twirling Institute in
Jackson, Mississippi. It was another step toward what Wolfe would call New
Journalism.

Energized by Wolfe's work, Thompson submitted a book review to his
editors. When they rejected it, Thompson sent it to Wolfe anyway. That letter
began a correspondence and eventually a friendship, yet the two men differed
along many dimensions. Born and raised in Richmond, Virginia, Wolfe was
not a juvenile delinquent but rather student body president, editor of the
school newspaper, and a star athlete at his all-male Episcopal school. Whereas
Thompson took college classes here and there, Wolfe earned a PhD at Yale
University in American Studies, a new discipline powered by the Cold War.
The title of his dissertation—"The League of American Writers: Communist
Organizational Activity Among American Writers, 1929–1942"—reflected
that provenance. After finishing his graduate studies, Wolfe was offered a
teaching job at a midwestern college, but he chose to research his novel-in-
progress by moving furniture for a trucking company. "Jack London of all
people was my model," he said. "Believe me, there is no insight to be gathered
from the life of the working-class milieu." While Wolfe wrote for *Esquire*
and *New York* magazine, Thompson's articles appeared in men's magazines
with centerfold models named Rusty and Misty. If Wolfe represented the
literary equivalent of a southern planter—his father, in fact, edited *The
Southern Planter* magazine—Thompson was the cavalier.

For all of their differences, however, the two men had much in common.
Following Wolfe's example, Thompson carved out a media niche as a student of exotic provincial subcultures, especially on the West Coast. Whereas
Wolfe focused on Southern California's tricked-out automobiles and those
who loved them, Thompson would target the Bay Area's most notorious
motorcycle gang. For Wolfe, the extravagant tastelessness of Las Vegas was
a source of amusement, but Thompson would locate the death of the
American Dream there. Both men imported the techniques of fiction into
their journalism, and each forged a distinctive style. After 1968, they shared

the same agent, and both wrote for *Rolling Stone* magazine. Like Thompson, Wolfe eventually tried his hand at fiction, publishing four novels to diminishing critical acclaim. Before that, however, he edited *The New Journalism* (1973), which described that genre's tenets and collected its key examples, including two pieces by Thompson.

Wolfe didn't rely on participatory reporting, but that approach was strongly linked to New Journalism. There was nothing especially new about it—Jack London and George Orwell were early practitioners—but it was certainly back in fashion. Beginning in 1958, George Plimpton popularized it with a series of *Sports Illustrated* accounts in which he boxed Archie Moore, played quarterback for the Detroit Lions, and tended goal for the Boston Bruins. His patrician background contrasted sharply with Thompson's, but Plimpton recognized their shared interest in participatory journalism. He and Thompson did not meet until 1974, when they flew together from Frankfurt to Zaire to cover the Ali-Foreman championship fight. The two men became friends, and Plimpton later interviewed Thompson for the *Paris Review*, the literary journal he cofounded in 1952.

Despite its popularity, New Journalism had its critics. One was Dwight Macdonald, who argued in the *New York Review of Books* that Wolfe's approach was "a bastard form, having it both ways, exploiting the factual authority of journalism and the atmospheric license of fiction." Worse, perhaps, was the intention behind what Macdonald called para-journalism. "Entertainment rather than information is the aim of its producers," he claimed, "and the hope of its consumers." The criticism would have amused Mark Twain, whose hoaxes enlivened the pages of the *Virginia City Territorial Enterprise* even before he moved to San Francisco. Certainly none of Macdonald's objections dampened Thompson's enthusiasm for Wolfe's project. Publishers were rejecting his novels, and he had little interest in traditional forms of reporting. Wolfe's example showed the way forward.

5   New Journalist

After the *National Observer* thwarted him, Thompson received an appreciative letter from Carey McWilliams, editor of *The Nation*. It was standard procedure for McWilliams, whose lean editorial budget at the venerable leftist weekly turned him into a talent scout. (Calvin Trillin later joked that *The Nation*'s standard fee was "in the high two figures.") Founded by abolitionists, the magazine was celebrating its centennial that year. The anticommunist hysteria of the 1950s had rocked the magazine and its staff, but McWilliams's sure hand kept *The Nation* on course during its most difficult decade. By the time he contacted Thompson, McWilliams was publishing the early work of Howard Zinn, Ralph Nader, Eric Hobsbawm, and other young writers on the rise.

Before taking over at *The Nation*, McWilliams had practiced law in Los Angeles and written prodigiously on California topics. He was later described as the finest nonfiction writer on California and the state's most astute political observer. His works were fact-based, hard-hitting, and consequential. His 1944 book on Japanese-Americans, for example, demolished every argument for their evacuation and internment during the Second World War. One Supreme Court justice cited it four times in his dissenting opinion to *Korematsu v. United States*, the decision that upheld the constitutionality of the internment. In addition to his writing, McWilliams was active in the ACLU and National Lawyers Guild, advocated on behalf of racial and ethnic minorities in and around Los Angeles, and filed an amicus brief for the Hollywood 10, who were cited for contempt of Congress and then blacklisted by the Hollywood studios. Radical writer Mike Davis later called McWilliams "the California left's one-man think tank."

McWilliams's work attracted powerful enemies, including racists and red-baiters in the state legislature. The agribusiness lobby, which resented his critical history of California farm labor, dubbed him "Agricultural Pest Number One, worse than pear blight or boll weevil." Even while McWilliams was serving as California's chief of immigration and housing, FBI director J. Edgar Hoover placed him on the Custodial Detention List, which meant McWilliams could be detained in case of a national emergency. McWilliams never hesitated to work with Communists on specific issues, and he stoutly defended their civil liberties, but after surveilling him for years, the FBI finally decided he wasn't a party member.

Like Thompson, McWilliams loathed Richard Nixon, whose career he had tracked since Nixon's first House race in 1946. Nixon defeated New Dealer Jerry Voorhis and played a key role on the House Committee on Un-American Activities (HUAC). In 1950, he ran for the US Senate against Helen Gahagan Douglas, a House member and former Hollywood actress. That race became known as "one of the most significant, notorious, and lamented election contests in the nation's history." As politicians from both major parties persecuted Reds real and imagined, Nixon declared that his opponent was "pink right down to her underwear." In doing so, he roused the electorate's misogyny as well as its anti-communism. Writing for *The Nation* that year, McWilliams described the 37-year-old Nixon as "a dapper little man with an astonishing capacity for petty malice." It would take the nation two more decades to reach the same conclusion.

Temperamentally, McWilliams and Thompson were opposites. The cerebral editor had a dry wit, enjoyed a drink, and had many brushes with glamour during his years in Los Angeles. But few colleagues felt they knew him well, and younger writers at *The Nation* considered him old-fashioned, even dowdy. He spent long days at the magazine's creaky downtown office, scanning other publications and assembling the weekly issues. Like his hero, H. L. Mencken, McWilliams accepted or rejected ideas quickly and resisted the urge to micromanage stories. Instead, he sent contributors envelopes stuffed with relevant news clippings and rarely fussed over their prose. The magazine's short deadlines reinforced that practice, but his hands-off policy and solid editorial judgment earned him a loyal following.

For Thompson, McWilliams's letter was an opportunity. Placing an article in *The Nation* would connect him to a tradition stretching back to Henry James. In his reply, Thompson mentioned his Berkeley article, and McWilliams published "The Nonstudent Left" that summer. It featured a new state law, sponsored by Oakland assemblyman Don Mulford, to prevent nonstudents from remaining on campus after being ordered to leave. Mulford also figured in a different East Bay saga. When the Black Panther Party for Self Defense formed in 1966, armed party members began shadowing Oakland police officers in Black neighborhoods. Party founder Huey P. Newton justified the armed patrols by citing the relevant passages of the California penal code and the Second Amendment. Mulford quickly sponsored a bill to forbid all residents from carrying loaded firearms in public. To protest the bill, fully armed Black Panthers appeared on the floor of the state legislature and read a strongly worded statement outside the Capitol. They were arrested, but their gesture received widespread media attention and placed the Black Panthers in the vanguard of the Black Power movement. That afternoon, Governor Reagan told reporters that he saw "no reason why on the street today a citizen should be carrying loaded weapons." Claiming that the Mulford Act "would work no hardship on the honest citizen," Reagan signed it into law.

According to Thompson, Mulford's nonstudent bill received a boost from FBI director J. Edgar Hoover's testimony that forty-three Communists were involved in the Free Speech Movement. Thompson seized the opportunity to lampoon both Hoover and a local newspaper that had declined to hire him.

> Where Mr. Hoover got his figure is a matter of speculation, but the guess in Berkeley is that it came from the *San Francisco Examiner,* a Hearst paper calling itself "The Monarch of the Dailies." The *Examiner* is particularly influential among those who fear King George III might still be alive in Argentina.

Thompson's Berkeley article also featured Stephen DeCanio, a graduate student and editor of *Spider* magazine, which Thompson described as "a wild-eyed new magazine with a circulation of about 2,000 on and around the Berkeley campus." The magazine's title, Thompson explained, was an acronym for "sex, politics, international communism, drugs, extremism, and rock 'n' roll." All seven issues of *Spider* appeared between March and October of that year. Its final issue featured a Thompson poem, "Collect Telegram From a Mad Dog," which he tried to include in *Hell's Angels.* By the late 1970s, DeCanio was an economics professor at the University of California, Santa Barbara, where some of us struggled through his statistics course. When contacted about this project, DeCanio indicated that he had little sympathy for the causes and personalities of that period. "I think the 'student movement' was wrong about almost everything and regret my contribution to it," he wrote.

Aside from the Berkeley article, Thompson had few story ideas for McWilliams. Nevertheless, he was desperate for work. "I am long past the point of simple poverty," he wrote McWilliams, "and well into a state of hysterical destitution. The wolves have eaten my door." One of his story ideas concerned "the final collapse of the myth of San Francisco." In

Thompson's view, the city's personality had descended from "neurotic to paranoid to what now looks like the first stages of a catatonic fit." His fall-back story ideas were about Governor Pat Brown's budget proposals and a job Sandy had taken as a telephone solicitor for a dance studio. What would happen, Thompson wondered, if a Black customer accepted the telephone offer? He imagined the dilemma of a hypothetical and hard-pressed solicitor: "Will Sally make the sale and chance the ultimate disaster—a coon showing up at the studio—or will she somehow ascertain the pigment, then do her duty and queer her only sale?"

McWilliams would not have welcomed the racial epithet. Much of his work in the 1940s targeted racial and ethnic discrimination, which was enshrined in law. That work earned him an appearance before the state legislature's Committee on Un-American Activities in California. Committee chair Jack Tenney quizzed McWilliams about his views on interracial marriage, which was still illegal in California. McWilliams said he thought the law should be abolished, and in the committee's published report, Tenney wrote that McWilliams's views were "identical to Communist Party ideology." In 1948, the same year California outlawed racial segregation in public schools, it became the first state to strike down its ban on interracial marriage.

In his reply to Thompson's letter, McWilliams suggested a piece about the Hell's Angels motorcycle gang, and Thompson eagerly accepted. The state's attorney general, Thomas C. Lynch, had recently issued a report targeting motorcycle gangs. That report was prepared at the request of State Senator Fred S. Farr, whose district included the city of Monterey, the site of a 1964 Labor Day rally by members of the Hell's Angels motorcycle gang. In its background section, the Lynch Report summarized the events of that weekend.

> Early on the morning of September 6, complaint was made by the erstwhile companions of two girls, aged 14, and 15, that they had been taken away from the boyfriends by some Hell's Angels at the site of the camp. Shortly, deputies found one completely nude and another with only a small amount of clothing on her. Both alleged that they had been raped by five to ten men just prior to the arrival of the officers. They professed to be unable to identify any responsibles at that time. Some hours later, four men were arrested after being identified by the girls. Two of the men identified themselves as presidents of the North Sacramento and Richmond Hell's Angels groups, respectively.

Farr asked Lynch to investigate, and Lynch sent a circular letter to all district attorneys, sheriffs, and police chiefs asking for information about the motorcycle gang and for suggestions about "methods to control them." The Lynch Report, which distilled that information, appeared in March 1965.

There was nothing flashy about Thomas Lynch, who had risen through the ranks on Pat Brown's coattails. But Lynch had his own ambitions, and many thought his report was designed to attract publicity. If so, the plan worked beautifully. The *New York Times* quoted the report in two stories that ran five days apart in March 1965. The first story opened with the following paragraph:

> A hinterland tavern is invaded by a group of motorcycle hoodlums.
> They seize a female patron and rape her. Departing, they brandish
> weapons and threaten bystanders with dire reprisals if they tell what
> they saw. Authorities have trouble finding communicative witnesses, let
> along arresting and prosecuting the offenders.

Only in the second paragraph do readers learn that the first wasn't a report of a specific incident, but rather a model scene posited by the Lynch Report.

> This, the California Attorney General's office reported today, has been
> the pattern of innumerable crimes committed throughout the state in
> the last few years by organized gangs of cycle-mounted outlaws whose
> aggregate membership numbers nearly 1,000.

The Lynch Report urged "increased firmness" in prosecuting offenders, protecting witnesses from retaliation, and alerting law enforcement officials to "the threat that members of the group pose to the peace of the state." The following month, Lynch circulated another report on paramilitary organizations in California, which included sections on the American Nazi Party, Minutemen, and Black Muslims. Both reports suggested a crackdown not only on crime, but also on unpopular groups.

The Lynch Report gave Thompson a starting point, but he also wanted to meet the motorcycle gang members. For that he turned to Birney Jarvis, a police reporter for the *San Francisco Chronicle*. A charter member of the motorcycle gang, Jarvis was "the only guy who could talk to the Hell's Angels on anything like human & realistic terms." Jarvis appeared in Thompson's work under his own name as well as a pseudonym, Preetam Bobo. After recounting Jarvis's violent past in *Hell's Angels*, Thompson described his career in journalism: "It was only then, after exhausting all other means of demoralizing the public, that he turned seriously to writing." Several years later, Denne Petitclerc used Jarvis as the model for his protagonist in *Then Came Bronson*, a 1969 television show whose protagonist was a former newspaperman who hit the road on a Harley-Davidson motorcycle.

Jarvis put Thompson in touch with the gang's San Francisco chapter, and he crashed their meeting in Hunters Point, a rough neighborhood near the shipyard and naval base. After a tense introduction, Thompson emphasized his desire to "do the ultimate favor of telling the American people the truth" about the motorcycle gang. Later, he invited five Hell's Angels back to his home, where Sandy and Juan retreated to a back room. Thompson wrote to friends that he established a balance of terror by showing the gang members his shotgun. Evidently, the gambit worked. Thompson spent the next month with the motorcycle gang before filing his story. His piece ran next to an analysis of Vietnam rather than the usual stories about sex, celebrities, and diets.

Thompson was clearly proud to be a *Nation* contributor. It was an honor to write for Carey McWilliams, he told a friend in 1966. Although the magazine did not pay well, "When your article appears in *The Nation*, you feel clean." He wrote to McWilliams almost weekly for years, usually searching for story ideas but also commenting on California, which McWilliams left behind to edit *The Nation*. Not surprisingly, Thompson saw the death of the American Dream at every turn. In 1966, he told McWilliams that California was "a nightmare of failed possibilities." McWilliams did not share Thompson's tragic view. He had once hated Los Angeles but came to respect its volcanic energies and foresaw its growing importance. Borrowing a trope from H. L. Mencken, McWilliams wrote that he cherished his "ringside seat at the circus." Two decades later, Thompson took his own seat in the front row.

Thompson's byline for the Hell's Angels article noted that he was living in San Francisco and completing a novel. At the time, *The Rum Diary* seemed to be the best candidate for his first book-length work. Soon after the article appeared, however, he received multiple offers to write a book about the Hell's Angels. Only one offer, from Ballantine Books, required no proposal and mentioned a specific advance against royalties—$6,000, with $1,500 payable upon signing. Writing to a friend, Thompson noted an irony: Although he received only one hundred dollars for the *Nation* article, no other outlet could have generated that advance.

Before signing the contract, Thompson received a personal visit from Ian Ballantine. Having launched Penguin USA in and Bantam Books, Ballantine was a pioneer in paperback publishing even before he founded the house that bore his name. When he entered the house at 318 Parnassus, Ballantine sensed that Thompson and Sandy had been quarreling. After a brief exchange about the book's prospects and the advance, Thompson retreated to the bedroom. To Ballantine's horror, Thompson began beating Sandy. When he returned, he tried to negotiate a larger advance, but Ballantine stood firm. They shook hands on the deal and parted amicably, but Ballantine left with grave reservations about this new author. "I didn't know if he was a Hell's Angels or was just writing a book about them," he recalled. "All in all, he was remarkably bad behaved."

· · ·

Thompson had one year to research and write the book. During that time, Ballantine sold the hardcover rights to Random House, and editorial responsibility for the project fell to senior editor James Silberman and assistant editor Margaret Harrell. "He didn't need any help writing the book," Silberman recalled, "but he needed help organizing the narrative. He hadn't yet discovered his full voice, but he was already beyond standard journalism."

Harrell became the publisher's primary contact person with Thompson. Although many authors were eventually invited to work face-to-face with their editors in New York City, Silberman decided that Thompson's presence in the office was unlikely to be productive. When Random House's lawyers vetted the manuscript and wanted Thompson to verify his facts, Harrell delivered that news. Thompson sourced his work as he went along but did not realize he would need further documentation to support his reporting. As Harrell recalled, "They didn't tell me things until it was time to tell him." As a result, Thompson was busily gathering and mailing documents to Random House well after submitting the manuscript.

Diplomacy was part of Harrell's job, and she always made sure she demonstrated her interest in, and understanding of, the author's work. Handholding wasn't a problem with Thompson, however, whom she called the most stimulating author she had been assigned to keep happy. There was just enough explosiveness, she thought, to keep things interesting, and she felt rejuvenated by her exchanges with him. Moreover, the diplomacy worked both ways. Harrell noted that Thompson was good at picking up vibrations and turned that skill to advantage. In part because he rarely contacted Silberman directly, Thompson often recruited her to achieve his ends, especially when it came to money. He was resourceful in other ways as well. When the legal department directed him to alter his manuscript— for example, by concealing Neal Cassady's identity in a key passage—he complied but managed to put across his meaning. Harrell was also struck by Thompson's attention to detail. As a former sports editor, he kept a close eye on the layout and made sure the final pages reflected his preferences. Because he was relatively unknown, he also wanted reassurance that Random House understood his intended audience. He asked Harrell to remind the publicity department not to target "the Argosy-Popular

Mechanix market." When he saw the original cover concept, he objected to it immediately and offered to send along a suitable cover photograph. Surprisingly, Random House accepted his substitute.

As the publication date approached, Thompson fretted over the dedication page. He wanted to thank unnamed friends for their support, but he also considered mentioning McWilliams, sculptor Ron Boise, and musician Sandy Bull. Boise, who had recently died, was famous for his 1964 obscenity trial in San Francisco. Thompson was under the impression that Bull, too, had died, even asking Harrell to confirm his death with his record label. But Bull was very much alive. The son of an East Coast magazine editor and a banking heiress, he developed a serious drug problem and carried on a lengthy affair with the wife of Jann Wenner, even living with the couple for a time in San Francisco. Thompson would later include Bull's *Inventions* (1965) on a list of favorite albums from that decade and mention his "Saigon mirror-shades" in *Fear and Loathing in Las Vegas*. In the end, Thompson thanked only his unnamed friends on the dedication page of the cloth edition. In January 1967, however, he told Harrell that McWilliams continued to amaze him. "I should have dedicated the book to him on general principles." The Ballantine paperback noted that McWilliams furnished the idea for the book and influenced its framework and perspective.

Harrell and Thompson collaborated from afar, but one of his Bay Area friends met her in New York City. David Pierce was a defense attorney who became mayor of Richmond at age 32. Only five miles north of Berkeley, the city was mostly notable for its shipyards and Standard Oil refinery, but it also had a large Black community and a prominent Hell's Angels chapter. Pierce tried to bring his left-wing politics to bear on the blue-collar city. While running for office, he visited the refinery's manager, who wondered why he wanted to build parks for Black people. Folk singer Rosalie Sorrels, a Thompson favorite, lived in Pierce's guest house and was another reason for Thompson's East Bay visits. Thompson was disappointed that Pierce resigned from public office—by postcard from Paris—instead of running for governor. Instead, Pierce followed Swami Muktananda to India and finally settled in Thailand.

After Pierce met Harrell, Thompson arranged a visit to New York City. Before he arrived, he sent Harrell a packet that included two tablets of Dexedrine. He described them as "sort of a temporary zapp. 4–5 hours duration. Not at all dangerous. One at a time—at least until I get there." Young, single, and attractive, Harrell was eager to meet Thompson in person. When he finally visited the Random House office in 1966, the two began a romance. "That night we started the tradition of snatched moments," she wrote in her memoir.

. . .

As Thompson worked on his book, his life changed significantly. In July 1965, he met Ken Kesey, who joined him on a public radio program to discuss the Free Speech Movement. Raised in rural Oregon, Kesey had moved to the Bay Area to study creative writing at Stanford University. His first published novel, *One Flew Over the Cuckoo's Nest*, appeared in 1962 and was an immediate success. Set in a mental hospital and narrated from the perspective of a schizophrenic Indian, it depicted a symbolic rebellion against a suffocating, authoritarian system embodied by the Big Nurse. It also reflected Jack Kerouac's influence. "Everybody I knew had read *On the Road*," Kesey recalled, "and it opened up the doors to us just the same way drugs did." It was no coincidence that Neal Cassady, the model for Dean Moriarty in *On the Road*, joined Kesey's cohort after serving time in state prison for selling marijuana. Nor was it mere chance that *Cuckoo's Nest* inverted the model scene of Kerouac's fiction. Like Moriarty, Kesey's protagonist was a boisterous rambler. But whereas Kerouac's characters enjoyed ecstatic rapture, the open road, and male camaraderie, Randle P. McMurphy challenged the mental hospital's joyless, static, and isolating regime. To put down McMurphy's rebellion, the hospital lobotomized him, but his sacrifice sparked the narrator to free himself from the institution's sinister grip.

At first, Thompson claimed to be unimpressed by Kesey's bestseller. Writing to Lionel Olay, he grudgingly conceded that the novel was good but compared it to drinking water when you wanted whiskey. By the time Thompson met him, Kesey had published a second novel, *Sometimes a Great Notion* (1964). He was also strongly associated with LSD. While at Stanford, he had volunteered to take psychedelic drugs for VA hospital experiments. A few weeks later, he became a night attendant in its psychiatric ward. Soon after that, LSD was flowing freely among Kesey's friends. With his royalties from *Cuckoo's Nest*, Kesey bought a woody retreat in the nearby coastal mountains. There he began to assemble the Merry Pranksters, who were playfully preparing for what they called the great freak forward. The drug experimentation began in earnest, this time without VA supervision.

In 1964, Kesey and the Merry Pranksters launched a cross-country trip in a brightly decorated school bus. The official destination was the World's

Fair in New York City. With Cassady at the wheel, the trip reenacted Kerouac's adventures, but the journey did not feed Kesey's fiction; instead, he planned to produce a film from the footage shot on the trip. Upon their arrival in New York City, Kesey met Ginsberg and Kerouac and described the encounter in frontier terms. "We had been accepted by the old gunfighters," Kesey said. Unlike Thompson, who cast himself as a defeated southerner in search of revenge, Kesey was an optimistic westerner. Even as Thompson was exploring the death of the American Dream, Kesey insisted that his work was a continuation of the frontier experience. "I thought this was as American as you could get," he said about his project, "because we were exploring a new territory—just the same way we went to the moon or sent the Lewis and Clark expedition here to Oregon."

After their radio appearance, Thompson and Kesey repaired to a bar. When Thompson left to meet some Hell's Angels, Kesey tagged along and hit it off with the gang members. "I could see that it was a love affair from the start," Thompson observed. Kesey invited the gang members to a party in La Honda the next weekend, and Thompson attended with Sandy and Juan. He recoiled in horror, however, when the Hell's Angels pulled up and were offered LSD. The Thompsons left for a picnic on the beach. When they returned, they passed the police, who were stationed outside the property and observing it carefully. Much to Thompson's surprise, he found the guests peacefully watching the film footage from the Merry Pranksters' cross-country trip. Allen Ginsberg, Neal Cassady, and Richard Alpert had arrived, and the party seemed far less dangerous than Thompson expected. By that time, Thompson had come to know Ginsberg well. "I met Allen in San Francisco when I went to see a marijuana dealer," Thompson later told the *Paris Review*.

> I ended up going there pretty often, and Ginsberg—this was in Haight Ashbury—was always there looking for weed, too. I went over and introduced myself and we ended up talking a lot. I told him about the book I was writing and asked if he would help with it. He helped me with it for several months; that's how he got to know the Hell's Angels.

The party turned out to be something of a literary event. Ginsberg's poem, "First Party at Ken Kesey's with Hell's Angels," later appeared in a City Lights chapbook called *Planet News* (1968).

The Thompsons decided to spend the night at Kesey's place. Sandy and Juan turned in, and Thompson continued to circulate. Before midnight, he noticed some activity in a nearby cabin. When he walked over to investigate, he could see the silhouettes of several figures behind a curtain. One man was lowering himself onto a woman while others held her legs. According to Thompson, the woman was "lying on the floor with her dress, kind of a shift, pulled up to around her ribcage, and one of them sticking his dick in her mouth, and another one was screwing her, and just a mad, mad scene." Thompson was horrified. The gang's sexual practices were no longer a media hook but a disturbing reality.

Thompson was unaware of the incident's backstory. Frequently identified as Cassady's ex-wife, the woman seems to have been his girlfriend, Anne Murphy. She, Cassady, and two other women had been living together in the weeks leading up to the party. Sex with Cassady, Murphy said, often sprang from his jealous fantasies about imagined infidelities. Later, some of the fantasies became real when the women acted out his accusations. That night, some of the Hell's Angels retrieved Cassady, who had been taunting police officers while drunk, high, and naked. He, too, had sex with Murphy. In a Merry Prankster publication called *Spit in the Ocean*, Murphy recalled the night that she was "joyously 'gang-banged' by the Hell's Angels" in front of Cassady.

After midnight, an agitated Thompson decided to take LSD, reasoning that nothing much worse could happen to him that night. Years earlier, Michael Murphy had advised him against taking the drug because of his violent tendencies, but he was glad he ignored that warning. Although the party at Kesey's continued for two more days, the Thompsons left before dawn and drove back through the coastal fog to San Francisco. Only then did Thompson mention what he had seen to Sandy. "When we left," Sandy recalled, "Hunter said, 'Do you know what was happening in there?' And I said, 'What do you mean?' And he said, 'Well, there was a gang bang going on.'" Back home, Thompson pulled out his tape recorder and recounted the incident.

At the time, Tom Wolfe was researching his story on Kesey and the Merry Pranksters. After Kesey was arrested on a marijuana charge, Wolfe interviewed him in jail, spent several weeks in the Bay Area, and wrote a three-part story for *New York* magazine. Wolfe did not take LSD or even "get down to shirtsleeves" with Kesey and his cohort. His approach, which he described as "saturation reporting," involved living with Kesey and the Pranksters for long stretches and describing their experiences. Later, Thompson would contrast his work with Wolfe's. "Wolfe's problem is that he's too crusty to *participate* in his stories," he wrote later. "The people he feels comfortable with are dull as stale dog shit, and the people who seem to fascinate him as a writer are so weird that they make him nervous." Yet Thompson gave Wolfe full credit for his ability to capture a story: "The only thing new and unusual about Wolfe's journalism is that he's an abnormally good reporter."

Although Wolfe didn't trip with the Pranksters, he famously altered his style to reflect the psychedelic scene he observed. His author's note explained that he "tried not only to tell what the Pranksters did but to recreate the mental atmosphere or subjective reality of it." His use of the historical present tense, which created a sense of vividness and immediacy, suggested eyewitness accounts, but he furnished little or no source information for particular passages. Instead, he noted that "the events, details and dialogue I have recorded are either what I saw and heard myself or were told to me by people who were there themselves or were recorded on tape or film or in writing." Thompson was one of those people. Although Wolfe missed the party in La Honda, Thompson forwarded his tape-recorded notes to him. When *The Electric Kool-Aid Acid Test* appeared in 1968, it described the gang bang and acknowledged Thompson as the source.

· · ·

Four days after Kesey's infamous party, Los Angeles exploded. The Watts Riots left thirty-four residents dead, more than one thousand injured, and the neighborhood's business district in flames. The uprising came as no surprise to many observers. The predominantly Black neighborhood was home to eighty thousand of the city's poorest residents, and its unemployment rate stood at 30 percent. Nevertheless, Mayor Sam Yorty had declined the Johnson administration's offer to expedite anti-poverty funding and to facilitate communications between city officials, civil rights groups, and the federal government. Governor Brown, who was vacationing in Greece when the riots erupted, was unable to calm the city. "Nobody told me there was an explosive situation in Los Angeles," he remarked to the press, adding absurdly that California was "a state where there is no racial discrimination." A commission appointed by Brown later confirmed that unemployment and a lack of opportunity contributed to the ghetto's spiral of failure.

The Watts Rebellion expressed the Black community's frustrations, but it also rattled White residents. LA police chief William Parker praised those who purchased guns to protect their communities. He also claimed that the trouble started "when one person threw a rock, and like monkeys in a zoo, others started throwing rocks." Regarding his department's success in suppressing violence, Parker said, "We've got them dancing like monkeys on strings." Responding to complaints from the Black community, Parker said, "We didn't ask these people to come here, and they've taken over a whole section" of the city. It was true that Black residents had not received formal invitations from the Los Angeles Police Department; most migrated to the city during the Second World War, when wartime mobilization required thousands of new workers to build ships and aircraft.

Thompson did not try to cover the Watts story. Instead, he wrote another article about Big Sur for *Pageant*. "It Ain't Hardly That Way No More" emphasized the paradise-lost angle of "the last bastion of Bohemia where a cheeseburger cost $3.50 and is listed on a bill of fare as 'cheddar steak.'" Several scenes of *The Sandpiper* with Elizabeth Taylor and Richard Burton had been shot in Big Sur, effectively putting the tiny hamlet on the Hollywood star map. "There was a time, and not very long ago, when Hedda Hopper didn't know Big Sur from Big Daddy Lipscomb," Thompson quipped, name-checking the Hollywood gossip columnist and NFL lineman, "but now that wrong has been righted." In the meantime, the region's "reputation as a hideaway for artists, writers, and other creative types" was in peril. "Big Sur is no longer a peaceful haven for serious talent, but a neurotic and dollar-conscious resort area," he concluded.

That piece ran the same month that the Berkeley article appeared. When added to the Hell's Angels piece, the trio suggested that Thompson was less interested in covering the major issues of the day than in cataloging West Coast exotica. In the Hell's Angels book, however, Thompson branched out. He compared the media frenzy over the motorcycle gang with the paucity of reporting on racial tensions in Los Angeles, which erupted "without an inch of pre-riot press coverage." He opened one chapter by quoting Chief Parker, and though he didn't say so explicitly in the book, he implied that the riots were a response to the city's systemic racism. Thompson could not address the Watts Riots more directly without disfiguring his story, but he left the clear impression that California's criminal justice priorities were out of whack.

The gubernatorial campaign also occurred in the interval between the Hell's Angel article and book. As Governor Brown sought a third term, former actor and GOP candidate Ronald Reagan vowed to clean up the mess in Berkeley and send the welfare bums back to work. Reagan's campaign drew much of its power from the Goldwater surge that Thompson had observed firsthand at the Cow Palace. From his perch at *The Nation*, Carey McWilliams linked Reagan's strategy to the state's rising racial tensions. The Watts Riots were only one symptom; another was discriminatory housing. Although the state's fair housing law was enacted in 1963, a statewide ballot initiative to reverse it passed by a two-to-one margin the following year. The courts struck down the initiative, but Reagan understood its popularity. He decried racism but claimed that property rights were "inseparable from the right of freedom itself." Delivered to an audience of real estate brokers, Reagan's dog whistle received a standing ovation. "There will be more of this kind of demagogy as the campaign comes to a climax," McWilliams predicted, "with Reagan using code words and phrases to let the electorate know his right-wing stand on racial issues without his having to voice outright racist sentiments." In November, Reagan defeated Brown decisively. Among statewide officeholders, Thomas Lynch was the only Democrat to survive the conservative backlash.

. . .

Yet another incipient story grew in Thompson's proverbial backyard. Hippies in Haight-Ashbury were pioneering a new lifestyle that grew out of the Beat experience but was now distinguishable from it. One of its tastemakers was George Hunter, a student at San Francisco State College who formed a band called the Charlatans. In the summer of 1965, the Charlatans landed a long-term gig in Virginia City, Nevada, the silver-mining town where Mark Twain wrote for the newspaper a century earlier. A small group of hippies decided to refurbish a decrepit gambling hall that they dubbed the Red Dog Saloon. "We completely decorated the place," Hunter said. "We brought rugs and Victorian tapestries from the city. We were re-creating the Wild West, pretending it had never gone away." Having laid in a significant supply of LSD, they spent the summer tripping in vintage drag, making music, and dancing on the arid eastern slope of the Sierra Nevada mountain range. To promote the Charlatans, Alton Kelley created the first psychedelic poster. Toward the end of that stint, Kesey and the Merry Pranksters wheeled the bus to Virginia City to investigate.

The Family Dog, a San Francisco commune that included some of the Virginia City crew, began hosting weekend house parties that fall. When those parties outgrew their home, promoter Chet Helms booked union halls. In October, the Family Dog hosted their first rock dance at Longshoremen's Hall. "A Tribute to Dr. Strange" featured the Charlatans, Jefferson Airplane, and the Great Society, which included Grace Slick, the debutante and model who chose San Francisco hippies over high society. "About 400 or 500 people showed up—it was such a revelation," Alton Kelley recalled. "Everybody was walking around with their mouths open, going, 'Where did all these freaks come from? I thought my friends were the only guys around!'" Covering the event for the *San Francisco Chronicle*, Ralph J. Gleason noted that the apparel ranged from "velvet Lotta Crabtree to Mining Camp Desperado, Jean Lafitte leotards, I. Magnin Beatnik, Riverboat Gambler, India Imports Exotic to Modified Motorcycle Rider Black Leather-and-Zippers."

As the folk revival and Beat scene gave way to something more spectacular, Thompson became an avid participant. He attended shows at The Matrix, a small club in the Cow Hollow neighborhood that featured Jefferson Airplane. In September 1965, he shared his enthusiasm for that group with his brother Jim. Jefferson Airplane, he said, would "lift the top or your head off" and "make those silly goddamn Beatles look like choirboys." He reportedly telephoned Gleason to alert him to the band, though their press agent also reached out to Gleason. His column appeared on September 13 under the headline, "Jefferson Airplane—Sound and Style." One line in particular motivated the music industry's A&R men: "I don't know who they will record for, but they will obviously record for someone." Singer Marty Balin said the band was fielding offers immediately after its publication, and bassist Bob Harvey corroborated that account. "After Ralph Gleason did that column, there was pandemonium," Harvey said. "I never believed that a newspaper column could have that kind of effect until I actually saw it happen." Jefferson Airplane became the first San Francisco rock band to sign with a major record label, and Gleason wrote the liner notes for their 1966 debut album. The band went on to record "White Rabbit" and "Somebody to Love," both of which cracked *Billboard*'s top-ten singles list.

When another San Francisco resident surveyed the fledgling scene, he saw a business opportunity. Bill Graham was born in Berlin, but his family sent him to New York City to escape Nazism, and many of his relatives were killed in the Holocaust. In the early 1960s, he joined his sister in San Francisco and became the business manager for the San Francisco Mime Troupe, which staged free shows in the city's public parks. After the troupe's leader was arrested for obscenity, Graham organized a benefit concert that featured Jefferson Airplane. He later described it as "the most significant evening of my life in theater." Journalist and anti-war activist Robert Scheer recalled his time with Graham that night, when the two men went out to dinner on Graham's motor scooter. "We went to get this chopped liver sandwich," Scheer said, "and I remember talking at dinner because we were worried that *no* one would show up." After dinner, they returned to Graham's loft on Howard Street.

> Anyway, we pull around there, and the fucking line is going around the building. It wasn't just hot. It was *incredible*. It wasn't like five or six people. It was this fucking *line* . . . Then Bill turned around on the motor scooter and said to me, "*This* is the business of the future." I'll never forget that.

The following month, Graham organized another wildly successful benefit that included the Grateful Dead.

When Kesey and others hosted the Trips Festival, the largest of the Acid Tests, Graham helped with its planning and promotion. A three-night public entertainment at Longshoreman's Hall, the Trips Festival featured virtually every significant avant-garde group in the Bay Area. According to one scholar, it was "a watershed event in the history of the underground arts scene in San Francisco." Light shows, an art form pioneered in the Bay Area, blazed behind the bands while they performed. Grateful Dead guitarist Jerry Garcia described the event as "thousands of people, man, all helplessly stoned . . . It was magic, far-out beautiful magic." It was a brief intersection between the avant-garde art scene and the emerging counterculture, but the crowd clearly preferred ecstatic dancing to artistic experimentation. "When the dull projections took over, it was nowhere," Gleason noted in his *Chronicle* review. "When the good rock music wailed, it was great."

Within weeks, Graham was renting the Fillmore Auditorium and promoting shows that featured "the sights and sounds of the Trips Festival." To design promotional posters, both he and Chet Helms turned to artists inspired by the opulence of Art Nouveau posters. The poster artists experimented with intense colors, revolving patterns, and wild typography. Although they worked on short schedules, the artists appreciated the quick display and wide dissemination of their work. In short order, psychedelic posters became an indispensable part of the music's reception. Sensing their popularity, political activists also began using posters to promote their events and causes. Even as hippies were refashioning the rock concert, San Francisco poster artists were converting a medium traditionally used for government purposes into a vehicle for dissent.

· · ·

By the end of that summer, Thompson was wrapping up his book manuscript. He claimed he spent six months writing the first half of his book and four days writing the second half.

> I got terrified about the deadline; I actually thought they were going to cancel the contract if I didn't finish the book exactly on time. I was in despair over the thing, so I took the electric typewriter and about four quarts of Wild Turkey and just drove north on 101 until I found a motel that looked peaceful, checked in, and stayed there for four days. Didn't sleep, ate a lot of speed, went out every morning and got a hamburger at McDonald's and just wrote straight through for four days—and that turned out to be the best part of the book.

Once again, Thompson took aim at the Lynch Report and focused on the national media's shortcomings. Indeed, he sometimes seemed more interested in critiquing the press than in describing the motorcycle gang. He opened the second chapter with a quotation from nineteenth-century Danish philosopher Søren Kierkegaard on the pernicious effects of newspapers.

> The daily press is the evil principle of the modern world, and time will only serve to disclose this fact with greater and greater clearness. The capacity of the newspaper for degeneration is sophistically without limit, since it can always sink lower in its choice of readers. At last it will stir up all those dregs of humanity which no state or government can control.

Thompson's reporting validated Kierkegaard's prophecy about the degenerate media. After describing various profiles of the Hell's Angels in high-circulation outlets, he claimed that the national coverage turned them into celebrities by focusing excessively on rape charges.

> Weird as it seems, as this gang of costumed hoodlums converged on Monterey that morning they were on the verge of "making it big," as the showbiz people say, and they would owe most of their success to a curious rape mania that rides on the shoulder of American journalism like some jeering, masturbating raven. Nothing grabs an editor's eye like a good rape.

In this short passage, Thompson offered two unnerving ideas. First, he implied that American journalism was reflexively sensationalistic. Second, his notion of "a good rape" set off alarms. The likeliest reading is that certain kinds of rape stories drew large readerships, but the sentence seemed designed to disturb.

Thompson concluded that the national media coverage, in concert with questionable reports from law enforcement agencies, effectively invented the story it purported to cover. "If the 'Hell's Angels Saga' proved any one thing," Thompson claimed, "it was the awesome power of the New York press establishment. The Hell's Angels as they exist today were virtually created by *Time*, *Newsweek*, and the *New York Times*." He was especially critical of the *Times*, which he described as "the heavyweight champion of American journalism." He called one of its stories "a piece of slothful, emotionally biased journalism, a bad hack job that wouldn't have raised an eyebrow or stirred a ripple had it appeared in most American newspapers." Nevertheless, Thompson added, the *Times* was "a heavyweight even when it's wrong, and the effect of this article was to put the seal of respectability on a story that was, in fact, a hysterical, politically motivated accident."

Thompson's media criticism served two purposes, both of them carried over from his *Nation* article. The first was to clear the stage of other credible sources. That purpose required Thompson to challenge earlier accounts of the motorcycle gang, especially from trusted news outlets. A related goal had to do with the story's provenance. Thompson's implicit claim was that the Hell's Angels story could not be covered from midtown Manhattan—or even from a desk in downtown San Francisco. Rather, it required the kind of participatory journalism that he alone was willing and able to provide.

Although Thompson dismissed earlier accounts of the Hell's Angels, his book managed to exploit much of the sensationalism he derided in other coverage. Even as he excoriated mainstream outlets and law enforcement agencies for their hysteria, he kept rape and brutal violence, both real and imagined, in sharp focus. He did not deny the substance of the Lynch Report: namely, that the motorcycle gang posed a threat to public order. Moreover, he situated the Hell's Angels squarely within the American myth of the western outlaw. In this sense, Thompson ate his cake and had it, too, but his audacity reflected the most potent source of his authority—the physical courage he displayed in reporting the story. Writing to his editor at the *National Observer*, Thompson articulated his comparative advantage: "I dare say I'm the only reporter in the history of the world who ever got wound up in a story to the point of going to a Hell's Angels meeting and then taking five of them home for a drinking bout." As Thompson acknowledged to McWilliams, even Birney Jarvis warned him against taking such risks. The *New York Times Book Review* echoed Thompson's remark, calling the book "a close view of a world most of us would never dare encounter." As a result of his participatory reporting, Thompson came to enjoy a reputation for bravery that was usually reserved for war correspondents.

The middle section of *Hell's Angels* ventured beyond the *Nation* article. It described the club's Labor Day run to Bass Lake, a small resort near Yosemite National Park, and it was perceptive and frequently funny. It showcased Thompson's participatory reporting, but it also featured the cool leadership of Ralph "Sonny" Barger and the adroit crisis management of Madera County sheriff Tiny Baxter. The weekend lacked the violent mayhem that Thompson described in other parts of the book, but he never loosened his grip on the prospect of violence, even if that required frequent departures from the facts on the ground. Consider, for example, the following passage about Barger's relatively uneventful encounter with vigilantes near Bass Lake (italics added).

> If Barger *had been stomped* by a mob of locals, nothing short of a
> company of armed militia *could have kept* the main body of outlaws
> from swarming into town for vengeance. An attack on the Prez *would
> have been* bad enough, but under those circumstances—a police-
> planned beer run—it *would have been* evidence of the foulest treachery,

a double cross, and the Angels *would have done* exactly what they all
came to Bass Lake expecting to do. Most *would have finished* the
weekend in jail or the hospital, but they were expecting that, too. It
would have been a good riot, but looking back, I no longer think the
initial clash *would have been* evenly matched. Many of the vigilantes
would have lost their taste for the fight the moment they realized
that their opponents mean to inflict serious injury on anybody they
could reach.

The absence of declarative sentences turned this passage into a long exercise in counter-factuality.

Thompson's article argued that sensational attention to sexual assault
drove the motorcycle gang's media coverage, and the book spent even more
time discussing rape and rape culture. Thompson showed how the gang's
ideas about sex, which were bound up with notions of revenge and punish-
ment, too rarely proceeded from consent. He also suggested that the criminal justice system was unable to distinguish between rape and the gang
bangs that the Hell's Angels favored. As a result, many rape charges were
filed against the Hell's Angels but eventually dropped. Finally, Thompson
suggested that many of the women who consorted with the Angels were
guilty of either very poor judgment or of inviting sexual assault. Although
he cast the Angels' behavior as despicable, his own treatment traded vigorously in ugly ideas and images.

Hell's Angels also bristled with racist language, usually but not always
attributed directly to gang members. Much of that language appeared in
Thompson's account of the most violent episode he witnessed—not on the
Bass Lake run, but at the El Adobe, the Oakland bar favored by the Hell's
Angels. A fight in the bar's parking lot ended with gang members swarming
over an imposing Black man who appeared at the bar. After an altercation
with photographer Don Mohr, the man was beaten senseless by gang members. Miraculously, he was able to walk off under his own power when the
police arrived. The police warned Barger that the victim might press
charges, but the Angels were more concerned about massive retaliation.
"The case never came to court," Thompson noted, "but it whipped the
Angels into a very agitated state of mind. There was no doubt in their heads
that the niggers would try to get even." After describing this imaginary
retaliation, Thompson described their preparations. "Every time I talked to
the Angels in the weeks after the Big Nigger incident, they warned me that
the cork was ready to blow." He doubted the retaliation would come at all,
but he could not be sure. "Several months earlier, I would have laughed the
whole thing off as some kind of twisted adolescent delusion . . . but after

spending most of that summer in the drunk-bloody, whore-walloping taverns of East Oakland, I had changed my ideas about reality and the human animal."

Thompson suggested but never asserted that the Hell's Angels were racist. Indeed, he furnished limited evidence to the contrary, including their friendly if guarded relations with the East Bay Dragons, an all-Black motorcycle gang. But he was crystal clear about their reactionary world view. After describing the motorcycle gang's assault on anti-war demonstrators in 1965, Thompson summarized that view as follows: "The attack was an awful shock to those who had seen the Hell's Angels as pioneers of the human spirit, but to anyone who knew them it was entirely logical. The Angels's collective viewpoint has always been fascistic." His point was echoed a half century later by Susan McWilliams, Carey's granddaughter and a professor of politics at Pomona College. "What's truly shocking about reading the book today," she wrote in *The Nation*, "is how well Thompson foresaw the retaliatory, right-wing politics that now goes by the name of Trumpism." Her observation supported Thompson's repeated prediction that the gang's political outlook was likely to spread, even if its membership remained limited.

Thompson also addressed drug use within the Hell's Angels. Although the gang members consorted with the Pranksters, Grateful Dead, and other psychedelic enthusiasts, they had no interest in expanded consciousness as such. Nor was their systematic derangement of the senses an aesthetic strategy. Rather, it was a debased version of the Beat and hippie ethic, which celebrated ecstasy, mobility, and community. As Thompson made clear, the gang members also liked to party, loved the open road, and prized their fraternity even more than their motorcycles. The Hell's Angels and hippies were strange bedfellows, but their projects were not entirely distinct.

. . .

Thompson's book included a lengthy section, completely absent from the article, about the gang's "genes and real history." For Thompson, that genealogy involved the influx of Okies, Arkies, and hillbillies to California before and during the Second World War. "The old way of life was scattered back along Route 66," he observed, "and their children grew up in a new world. The Linkhorns had finally found a home." Thompson used that fictional family, which Nelson Algren created in *A Walk on the Wild Side*, to illuminate the freebooting brawlers who later joined the ranks of the motorcycle gang. Its protagonist, Dove Linkhorn, leaves Texas to seek his fortune in New Orleans. "Ten years later," Thompson maintained, "he would have gone to Los Angeles." According to Thompson, Algren's novel opened with "the best historical descriptions of American white trash ever written." In effect, Thompson used *A Walk on the Wild Side* to write the "real history" of the Hell's Angels. By doing so, he paid a compliment to both Algren and the power of fiction.

The genealogy section, however, feels general and abstract compared to the carefully observed passages elsewhere in the book. It also deviated from what Thompson originally intended. Well before his book appeared, Thompson wrote to Algren, whose work he wished to quote extensively in *Hell's Angels*. Algren's most famous novels were already a decade old, but even years later, Thompson could recite the opening paragraph of *The Man with the Golden Arm* from memory at 3 a.m. By that time, Algren's career had been buffeted by the forces of reaction. A former member of the Communist Party, he was surveilled by the FBI and repeatedly denied a passport. When Thompson contacted him, he was a freelance journalist writing for *Playboy, Rogue, Cavalier, The Nation,* and other magazines on Thompson's radar. An outspoken critic of the Vietnam War, Algren would also write for *Ramparts* magazine, the fledgling San Francisco muckraker edited by Warren Hinckle.

Unlike Algren, Thompson never met Hemingway or had a long affair with Simone de Beauvoir. In other ways, however, Thompson's life and work resembled Algren's. *A Walk on the Wild* Side was lauded for its ironical parody of the American Dream, Thompson's abiding theme. Moreover, Algren arranged to cover the 1958 Kentucky Derby for *Sports Illustrated.* Although the magazine never ran the piece, his biographer described it as a precursor to New Journalism. "Much of what happens in the story is either fictitious or greatly exaggerated, and the subject—the Derby—is less important than the narrator's character and impressions." Finally, Algren subscribed to *Police Chief* magazine so he could "keep an eye on the opposition." Several years later, Thompson would write a review of the same magazine.

In his letter to Algren, Thompson noted that he had reviewed two books by or about him: *Conversations with Nelson Algren* (1964) and *Notes from a Sea Diary: Hemingway All the Way* (1965). Although the *National Observer* rejected the latter review, Thompson's homage to Algren was clear enough. As with his earlier missives to Norman Mailer, however, Thompson could not resist the urge to dispense advice. "You have got to get over the idea that you have a sense of humor," he added. "No, that's not it. It's this gag-line stuff. You're not a comedy writer." Six days later, Algren replied to the main point of Thompson's letter, stating that "using 500 words of *anything*, without permission, would lay you open to the legal department of the copyright owners of that book, i.e.: Farrar, Straus & Giroux." He added that he didn't see what good "stuffing somebody else's material" into a book would do. "It's always a good idea for a writer to do the best he can with what he has," Algren concluded before offering his best wishes.

Thompson's letter could have been clearer. Why would a nonfiction book about a California motorcycle gang need extensive quotations from a novel set halfway across the country and decades earlier? Moreover, Algren was increasingly attuned to the value of his intellectual property. He had benefited significantly from shrewd repackaging and rights sales of his earlier work, but he also had been ripped off by the usual Hollywood villains, including a producer who purchased and resold the film rights for *The Man with the Golden Arm* without paying the author his share of the windfall. Algren was by no means averse to helping younger writers; in fact, he was teaching at the Iowa Writers' Workshop, and he informally mentored Don DeLillo and Russell Banks early in their careers. But his letter to Thompson wasn't encouraging.

Thompson quickly cracked off a longer and more pointed reply. "Regardless of what you think," he wrote, "I know damn well that no law prevents me from quoting you. If you want to call it 'stealing,' that's cool, but don't exclude yourself. I'm also using that [quote] that you stole from [medieval French poet Francois] Villon. So I guess I'll see you both in court." After documenting exactly what he wished to quote and why, Thompson mocked Algren even as he praised his work.

> I'm sorry if my letter of February 10 led you to believe I was going to steal a portion of your book. Maybe the letter wasn't very clear. But I should think this letter is about as clear as it has to be, and although it's not necessary that you reply, I wanted to get it down in writing to make sure you don't sue me for the wrong reasons. If you are addled enough to think you can't be quoted or even mentioned in the public prints, it makes me feel kind of sad, and the best advice I can offer is that you change your lawyers . . . In any case, I don't want you roaming up and down Muscatine Street, brooding and bitching about some punk on the Coast who's stealing your stuff. I happen to think you've written some very good stuff, and not even the most swinish letter from you will change opinion or my tastes.

A month later, Thompson wrote Algren a shorter letter which noted that Candida Donadio, Algren's agent, had contacted him. (Three years earlier, Donadio had declined to take on Thompson as a client.) Thompson also assured Algren that *Hell's Angels* would not be worse off for losing six paragraphs of Linkhorn material. Even without it, however, the *New York Times* review of his book, "On the Wild Side," recognized the Algren connection.

True to his word, Thompson continued to hold Algren's fiction in high regard. "I admired Algren and still do," he said in a later interview. "I thought at the time [1956] that no living American had written any two books better than *The Man with the Golden Arm* and *A Walk on the Wild Side.*" Algren would eventually return the compliment, writing a brief but insightful review of *The Great Shark Hunt* for the *Chicago Tribune* in 1979.

. . .

The final section of *Hell's Angels* traced Thompson's disillusionment with the gang members. Again, the media played a major role in that development. "It was about this time that my longstanding rapport with the Angels began to deteriorate," Thompson noted. "All the humor went out of the act when they began to believe their own press clippings, and it was no longer much fun to drink with them." That deterioration culminated in a beating, delivered by several Hell's Angels, during the 1966 Labor Day weekend run to Squaw Rock (now Frog Woman Rock) on the Russian River in Mendocino County. The book's postscript recounted the entire event, and though the assault left Thompson battered and bruised, he counted himself lucky that one gang member intervened before more damage could be done. His editor also looked on the bright side. "He needed that ending," Silberman recalled, "because he was really struggling with an ending for the book." As a final flourish, Thompson swiped and juxtaposed two passages from Conrad's *Heart of Darkness:* "The horror! The horror! . . . Exterminate all the brutes!"

In a letter to Barger later that month, Thompson mentioned the assault in Mendocino. He also acknowledged that the Hell's Angels had expected consideration for their cooperation with him.

> Anyway, I'm off on another book now, and if you people want to sue me for any money regarding the Hell's Angels book, I think you should get as much as you can. I can't go into detail—especially in a letter—but if we had sat down and talked, I think we could have worked something out. I'm still willing to talk, but it will have to be on my turf next time. I don't ever intend to be that much outnumbered again.

Several months after that, Thompson wrote a more conciliatory letter to Barger, whose girlfriend had been killed in a motorcycle accident. It indicated that he retained a high opinion of the motorcycle gang's leader. That feeling wasn't mutual. In a *Washington Post* online interview that appeared in 2000, Barger was asked about Thompson.

> Hunter found out I was upset with him because he never paid us the keg of beer he was supposed to pay us at the finish of the book. He sent word back via my ex that he was willing to pay it now; I said the beer was due in the 60s, not the 90s. The book is great reading, and he's a great writer, but I don't think much of him as a person. He reneged on our deal.

Barger also disparaged Thompson in his memoir. He wrote that he liked the *Nation* article even though it was exaggerated, but he didn't meet Thompson face-to-face until after its appearance. "Hunter turned out to be real weenie and a stone fucking coward," Barger recalled. "He's all show and no go. When he tried to act tough with us, no matter what happened, Hunter Thompson got scared. I ended up not liking him at all, a tall, skinny, typical hillbilly from Kentucky. He was a total fake."

Part of Barger's disdain for Thompson arose from the effect his book had on law enforcement.

> I read the book, *Hell's Angels: A Strange and Terrible Saga,* when it came out in 1967. It was junk. The worst part was that it became a law enforcement guide on the club. There was a lot of writer's exaggeration along with a writer's dream-and-drug-induced commentary, like when he talks about members pissing on their patches or members having to wear pants dipped in oil and piss . . . The cops claimed that for years after. That kind of stupid mythology came right out of Hunter's book.

Barger's contempt did not extend to Kesey, Cassady, or Jerry Garcia. He generally liked hippies, who wanted to "get loaded, fuck, and party." The Berkeley radicals, however, were idealistic students whose politics he did not share. "Some were violent," he wrote in his memoir, "but not in a stand-in-the-middle-of-street-and-fight kind of way. They preferred sneaking around and blowing up buildings and creating chaos."

If Thompson's book cramped the motorcycle gang's style, it also changed his own life dramatically. His improvidence meant he would continue to struggle financially, but he would never again be anonymous. Moreover, *Hell's Angels* demonstrated that the Bay Area was an important focus of his work. "That book made him realize that there was a market in the freak circus of the sixties," Douglas Brinkley later observed. "And it became this thing that was going on out in the Bay Area, and Hunter was deeply involved in it."

For Thompson, the Hell's Angels book also served another purpose, which he described in *Songs of the Doomed* (1990). Until he took on that project, he had "always been writing in the same mold as the newspaper hacks, and I thought that was the way to do it." That story, however, opened up new literary horizons for him.

> But this subject was so strange that for the first time in any kind of journalism, I could have the kind of fun with writing that I had had in the past with fiction. I could bring the same kind of intensity and have the same kind of involvement with what I was writing about, because there were characters so weird that I couldn't even make them up. I had never seen people this strange. In a way, it was like having a novel handed to you with the characters already developed.

In retrospect, the Hell's Angels project was an important step toward the complex blend of journalism and fiction that would become his signature.

Hell's Angels also changed his public image. As William Kennedy observed, Thompson's persona not only became increasingly spectacular, but also the focus of his work.

> I noted the transformation of Hunter into a public personality for the first time when he was doing publicity for *Hell's Angels* in 1968. He was in New York and he turned up with a cowboy hat and very bizarre sunglasses, bright red or green, glow in the dark. It was a costume for Halloween, and that persona was what he was after, that look. I asked him, "What are you made up for? What are you trying to prove?" He had always shown up at my house wearing sweaters, slacks—clothes, not costumes. But now the image was foremost. I believe Hunter was captured by that persona, and that his writing was transformed. More and more it was about that persona, not about what it used to be about. And it seemed he was reveling in it.

In the years to come, Thompson would also sport wigs, lipstick, and women's purses. In doing so, he seemed to take a page out of the Hell's Angels publicity playbook, which included gang members French kissing each other when photographers were on hand.

Thompson's interest in gender-bending was reflected in his other work as well. In August 1967, *Pageant* ran "Why Boys Will Be Girls: A Special Report on How More & More Hes Behave Like Shes." It featured hippie indifference to social expectations and quoted literary critic Leslie Fiedler on the changing nature of masculinity. He did not offer his own views, and friends later maintained that he was not judgmental about sexual preferences. His Big Sur experience indicated otherwise, however, and he never accepted his younger brother's homosexuality. In 1969, Jim Thompson sent him a carefully composed letter on that topic. "He never responded," Jim noted later. "Nor has he *ever* responded. I never heard any comment. It has never been discussed. *Never* been discussed."

The *Pageant* article also offered Thompson another chance to shape his public image. In an inset called: "Cool Facts About a Cool Cat," he again plumped his novel-in-progress.

> Says Hunter Thompson about Hunter Thompson: "Hunter Thompson is a freelance writer and ex-foreign correspondent, also the author of a fantastic best seller entitled *Hell's Angels,* a strange and terrible saga (*sic*). His next bestseller will be a savage and defamatory novel called *The Rum Diary,* which he is currently polishing at his villa in Woody Creek, Colorado. Random House will publish this book when the time is ripe. Mr. Thompson is given to excess in all things and currently is in very poor health. He is 29 years old and is responsible for a blonde wife, Sandy, and a 3-year-old son, Juan. Mr. Thompson's essays, articles, and screeds have appeared in the *Nation, Esquire,* the *Reporter,* the *New York Times Magazine,* and *Spider.*"

Thompson was beginning to live into the public image he had constructed for himself. With a bestselling book under his belt, articles in important national magazines, and a novel on the way, he finally could be mentioned in the same breath as some of his heroes.

6   Hashbury

As Thompson's career blossomed, he continued to correspond with Carey McWilliams, but he never again published in *The Nation*. Instead, a very different editor boosted the next phase of his career.

Thompson met Warren Hinckle in the San Francisco office of *Ramparts* magazine. Founded in 1962 as a Catholic literary quarterly near Palo Alto, *Ramparts* initially ran articles by Thomas Merton, John Howard Griffin, and other Catholic intellectuals. A product of San Francisco's parochial schools and Jesuit university, Hinckle hired on as the magazine's publicist. When he became editor in 1964, he converted *Ramparts* into a monthly, shifted its focus to politics, and moved the office to San Francisco. He also recruited a new cohort of staff writers, including many from Berkeley. Chief among them was Robert Scheer, a former graduate student whose publications included *Cuba: An American Tragedy* (1963) and *How the United States Got Involved in Vietnam* (1965).

After Hinckle and Scheer joined forces with art director Dugald Stermer, *Ramparts* achieved liftoff. The upstart magazine, which Hinckle described as a "radical slick," combined hard-hitting content, high production values, and playful humor. With its hoaxes and sly media criticism, *Ramparts* tapped the tradition of frank and cheerful irreverence that stretched back to the days of Mark Twain, Bret Harte, and Ambrose Bierce.

Hinckle's showmanship was an important part of the magazine's success. He frequently echoed playwright George M. Cohan's motto: "Whatever you do, kid, always serve it with a little dressing." He had a knack for identifying and promoting stories that larger news outlets found irresistible. *Ramparts* staff writer Adam Hochschild, who later cofounded *Mother Jones* magazine, described Hinckle's recipe for success: "Find an exposé that major newspapers are afraid to touch, publish it with a big enough splash so they can't afford to ignore it, and then publicize it in a way that plays the press off against each other." By using larger outlets to amplify his stories, Hinckle expanded the magazine's media niche and impact, influenced major figures, and inspired a new generation of political journalists. One example of the magazine's influence involved "The Children of Vietnam," a photo-essay that showed the effects of US bombing on that country's youth. Immediately after reading it, and despite advice to the contrary, Dr. Martin Luther King announced his intention to speak out against the war for the first time. As his advisors predicted, King was criticized in the mainstream media for taking that position, but he never regretted it.

Ramparts also figured modestly in California's electoral politics. In 1966, three of the magazine's principals ran for Congress as peace candidates. Publisher Edward Keating and financial backer Stanley Sheinbaum lost in the San Mateo and Santa Barbara Democratic primaries, respectively, but both surprised experts by receiving more than 40 percent of the vote. Robert Scheer's campaign was the most remarkable of all. He challenged Democratic incumbent Jeffery Cohelan in California's District 7, which included Oakland and Berkeley. In the end, Scheer drew 45 percent of the primary vote and showed that Cohelan was vulnerable. Four years later, Ron Dellums unseated him and became an outspoken critic of US militarism.

Thompson later described his respect for the San Francisco muckraker and its editor.

> I met [Hinckle] through his magazine, *Ramparts*. I met him before
> *Rolling Stone* ever existed. *Ramparts* was a crossroads of my world in
> San Francisco, a slicker version of *The Nation*—with glossy covers and
> such. Warren had a genius for getting stories that could be placed on the
> front page of *The New York Times*. He had a beautiful eye for what
> story had a high, weird look to it. You know, busting the Defense
> Department—*Ramparts* was real left, radical. I paid a lot of attention to
> them and ended up being a columnist.

Thompson agreed to write a series of columns for $1,500 per month, and his name appeared on the masthead, but he never published anything in *Ramparts*.

Hinckle also matched Thompson in the drinking department. Boozing with Hinckle, one colleague said, "was like going to Vietnam." To maxi-mize efficiency, Hinckle worked out of Cookie Picetti's, a North Beach cop bar that also catered to the drinking press. The decor was primitive. "Cookie's was a narrow dim room, like a railroad car in a tunnel with the lights turned off," Hinckle later wrote. "The weathered wooden bar was marked like smallpox scars with the sweating of a million cocktails." Some of Hinckle's left-wing colleagues disliked drinking with police officers, but Hinckle silenced their protests by challenging them to name a decent left-wing bar.

Thompson's first visit to the *Ramparts* office, where Hinckle kept a capuchin monkey named Henry Luce, quickly became legend. The two men left for drinks and returned to find Thompson's backpack open, pills of various colors strewn across the floor, and the deranged monkey racing around the office. Henry Luce was rushed to the veterinarian's office to have his stomach pumped. "That fucking monkey should be killed—or at least arrested—on general principles," an unsympathetic Thompson later wrote to Hinckle. He closed his letter with general encouragement and specific suggestions.

> Again . . . it was a good show over there, and my advice to you is to give up all forms of booze and bookkeepers for the duration of the crisis. Moderation in all things. When you turn up a freak on the staff, don't just fire him/her—pursue him into the very bowels of the economy and queer his act for all time. And get that nigger off the premises. You've got to get a grip on yourself. Otherwise . . . they'll cut your throat.

"That nigger" presumably referred to Eldridge Cleaver. In 1966, *Ramparts* helped obtain Cleaver's release from state prison by offering him a staff position. The following year, he covered the Black Panthers protest against Don Mulford's gun control bill at the state Capitol. Cleaver also witnessed a dramatic showdown between Black Panthers and San Francisco police officers outside the *Ramparts* office. He decided to join the Black Panther Party and soon became its Minister of Information. The success of *Soul on Ice* (1968), which included his pieces for *Ramparts*, made him a key figure in the Black Power movement.

Ramparts had many enemies, including Henry Luce's *Time* magazine. One of its articles, "A Bomb in Every Issue," described the muckraker's explosive impact while criticizing its sensationalism. Noting that *Ramparts* had moved to "one of those topless streets in San Francisco's New Left bohemia," the article spelled out the moral for readers in the last paragraph.

> *Ramparts* is slick enough to lure the unwary and bedazzled reader into accepting flimflam as fact. After boasting that the January issue would "document" that a million Vietnamese children had been killed or wounded in the war, it produced a mere juggling of highly dubious statistics and a collection of very touching pictures, some of which could have been taken in any distressed country.

Nothing to see here, *Time* told its readers, effectively urging them to ignore *Ramparts* magazine as well as the US bombing of Vietnamese children.

The CIA was also a dedicated adversary. After *Ramparts* published a whistleblower story about the agency's activities in Vietnam, CIA director William Raborn ordered a high-priority rundown on the magazine. The order seemed to violate the National Security Act of 1947, which prohibited the agency from spying on US residents. By linking *Ramparts* to foreign funding, however, the CIA could justify its surveillance. Officers spent two months researching the magazine's investors and staff. They identified two Communist Party members on the payroll, but the magazine's most outspoken CIA critic was former Special Forces sergeant Donald Duncan, an anti-communist Catholic whose first-person account of his Vietnam experience became the February 1966 cover story. The cover photograph of Duncan in uniform combined with the caption ("The Whole Thing Was a Lie!") became a *Ramparts* icon.

The following year, *Ramparts* exposed another covert operation. In January 1967, Hinckle met 24-year-old Michael Wood in New York City. A former fundraiser for the National Student Association (NSA), Wood had learned that the CIA was funding his organization. The intelligence agency's goals were to counter similar groups under Soviet control abroad and to recruit foreign students. Wood, who was one of the few NSA officers who hadn't signed a secrecy oath, decided to contact Hinckle. His story checked out, and when the CIA learned of Hinckle's plans to publish it, the agency planned to stage a press conference at which NSA leaders would admit to their CIA relationship and insist it was over. That admission would make the *Ramparts* story look like old news when it appeared. Hinckle, however, discovered the CIA's plan before the press conference could be held. He bought full-page advertisements in the *New York Times* and *Washington Post*, effectively scooping himself. Immediately after the advertisements appeared, eight congressmen signed a letter of protest to President Johnson.

Admitting that the NSA story was factually accurate, *Time* took aim at the messenger. *Ramparts* was "the sensation-seeking New Left-leaning monthly" whose article was predictably "larded with pejorative clichés." Those who were concerned about the story were captive to "the emotionalism of young Americans who worship honesty." *Time* also suggested that the *Ramparts* story wasn't news in the first place. "The use of front foundations to handle CIA money is an old technique," the story maintained. The only problem in this case was that "red-bearded New Leftist Michael Wood" had learned about the CIA connection. After plumping the agency and its new director, Richard Helms, the *Time* article closed by clarifying the moral of the story.

In an open society like the U.S., there will always be a degree of conflict between the policymaking and the secret, empirical processes by which decisions must be made and implemented. What is usually overlooked, when the CIA is the subject of controversy, is that it is only an arm—and a well-regulated one—of the U.S. Government. It does not, and cannot, manipulate American policies. It can only serve them.

In fact, oversight of the CIA was lax, and as the agency attracted more scrutiny in the 1970s, its ability to influence public opinion through its media network was also exposed. One CIA director privately referred to this influence as the Mighty Wurlitzer, the organ that accompanied silent films and signaled how audiences should feel at any given moment. The attacks on *Ramparts* showed that the Mighty Wurlitzer was pitch perfect, but the NSA story was yet another milestone in the magazine's development. Circulation spiked to 229,000, more than half of it newsstand sales. The same month that the NSA story appeared, *Ramparts* received the George Polk Award for excellence in magazine reporting. Ironically, it shared that award with *Time*, its sharpest critic.

Oddly, the NSA bombshell wasn't a *Ramparts* cover story. That honor went to "The Social History of the Hippies," Hinckle's piece about the San Francisco counterculture. Its cast of characters included the Hell's Angels, who attended rock concerts and otherwise attached themselves to hippie culture. It also mentioned the Human Be-In, which drew more than twenty thousand young people to Golden Gate Park and touched off an avalanche of national media coverage. By the end of that summer, almost every major American news outlet had run at least one story about San Francisco hippies. Most of them featured the so-called Summer of Love, which attracted some hundred thousand young people to the city and created an even more spectacular scene. The media coverage tilted toward drugs and general weirdness, but it also converted the Haight into what Todd Gitlin later called "the center of the nation's fantasy life."

Hinckle took a dim view of the counterculture. "The hippies grew up in my backyard," he noted in his memoir. "I did not find them good neighbors." In his *Ramparts* article, he also critiqued their politics. He argued that the counterculture's Beat precursors personified two dissonant political strains: fascism (as embodied by Jack Kerouac) and resistance (as embodied by Allen Ginsberg). Yet too many hippies were willing to renounce politics altogether.

The danger in the hippie movement is more than overcrowded streets and possible hunger riots this summer. If more and more youngsters begin to share the hippie posture of unrelenting quietism, the future of activist, serious politics is bound to be affected. The hippies have shown that it can be pleasant to drop out of the arduous task of attempting to steer a difficult, unrewarding society. But when that is done, you leave the driving to the Hell's Angels.

Hinckle was correct that many hippies ignored electoral politics. They turned their attention to creating new ways of life for themselves and their friends. Nevertheless, few observers connected the Beats to fascism, and fewer still thought the Hell's Angels would fill any political vacuums left by the hippies.

Ramparts had other blind spots as well. It tended to overestimate the strength of the liberal consensus that it questioned and frequently mocked, and to underestimate the power of the right-wing backlash that was already under way. Growing out of Barry Goldwater's 1964 campaign, the modern conservative movement was busily targeting liberal values and institutions. Ronald Reagan, who challenged incumbent governor Pat Brown in 1966, also derided campus activists, decried welfare benefits, defended discriminatory housing, and denigrated hippies. Yet Hinckle's radical slick did not portray the challenger as a threat to the state's future. Instead, it argued in its October 1966 issue that "the triumph of the right is inevitable because liberalism—not just unfortunate, well-meaning Pat Brown—had failed California."

Reagan vanquished Brown and made good on his promises. Two months after his victory, his finance director proposed a 10 percent budget cut for the university and new student fees. With the help of FBI Director J. Edgar Hoover, the university's Board of Regents also dismissed UC president Clark Kerr. Kerr was a celebrated educator, but conservative regents thought he had appeased left-wing faculty during the McCarthy Era and failed to thwart campus activists in the 1960s. As the Free Speech Movement played out, Hoover also sabotaged President Johnson's efforts to appoint Kerr to a cabinet position. Kerr later remarked that he left the UC presidency the same way he entered it—fired with enthusiasm.

· · ·

Like Hinckle, Thompson seized the opportunity to write about the San Francisco scene—not for *Ramparts,* but for the *New York Times Magazine.* Two months after Hinckle's article appeared, "The 'Hashbury' Is the Capital of the Hippies" connected the San Francisco counterculture to Berkeley campus activism.

Now, in 1967, there is not much doubt that Berkeley has gone through a revolution of some kind, but the end result is not exactly what the original leaders had in mind. Many one-time activists have forsaken politics entirely and turned to drugs. Others have even forsaken Berkeley. During 1966, the hot center of revolutionary action on the Coast began moving across the bay to San Francisco's Haight-Ashbury district, a rundown Victorian neighborhood of about 40 square blocks between the Negro/Fillmore district and Golden Gate Park.

As a result of this shift, Thompson maintained, the Haight was becoming a new kind of vice district.

The "Hashbury" is the new capital of what is rapidly becoming a drug culture. Its denizens are not called radicals or beatniks, but "hippies"—and perhaps as many as half are refugees from Berkeley and the old North Beach scene, the cradle and the casket of the so-called Beat Generation.

Thompson also described the San Francisco hippies as far less worldly than their Beat precursors.

The North Beach types of the late 1950s were not nearly as provincial as the Haight-Ashbury types are today. The majority of beatniks who flocked into San Francisco 10 years ago were transients from the East and Midwest. The literary-artistic nucleus—Kerouac, Ginsberg, et al.—was a package deal from New York. San Francisco was only a stop on the big circuit: Tangier, Paris, Greenwich Village, Tokyo, and India. The senior beats had a pretty good idea what was going on in the world; they read newspapers, traveled constantly, and had friends all over the globe.

By comparison, the hippies were long on idealism and short on experience—except with psychedelic drugs.

Like Hinckle, Thompson featured the Diggers in his piece. As the street actors turned activists tried to house, feed, and clothe hippies for free, they were becoming the "invisible government" of the Hashbury. Yet Thompson's analysis of hippie politics differed from Hinckle's. In his view, the counterculture was responding to the conservative electoral sweep the year before. That victory, Thompson maintained, demonstrated the futility of fighting the establishment on its own terms. It was no coincidence that the scene "developed very suddenly in the winter of 1966–1967 from the quiet, neo-Bohemian enclave that it had been for four or five years to the crowded, defiant dope fortress that it is today." The hippies realized that a new approach was needed.

There had to be a whole new scene, they said, and the only way to do it was to make the big move—either figuratively or literally—from Berkeley to the Haight-Ashbury, from pragmatism to mysticism, from politics to dope, from the hangups of protest to the peaceful disengagement of love, nature, and spontaneity.

Where Hinckle saw political quietism in the San Francisco counterculture, Thompson saw a rejection of traditional politics and protest in favor of creating new alternatives to the status quo.

Thompson later described his own piece as second-rate, but it had several virtues. Linking the hippies to the Beats and then contrasting the two groups was instructive. Also, many hippies had Berkeley roots or connections, and drugs were a key part of the burgeoning counterculture. Nevertheless, the omissions were notable. Thompson gave ample space to drugs and politics, but he declined to explore the Haight's fledgling music and art scene. One would never know from his piece that a relatively small group of hippies was reinventing the modern rock concert not far from his home. Certainly much had changed since August 1966, when the Beatles ran out to a Candlestick Park stage in matching suits. As teenyboppers shrieked, the Fab Four sang eleven songs in thirty minutes. After dashing off to an armored car, the Beatles decided to stop touring for good. Across town, however, a new combination of long jams, light shows, modern sound systems, freestyle dancing, and psycho-activity was already making the previous rock conventions look quaint. The following year, George Harrison returned to San Francisco to witness the Summer of Love, and two years after that, John Lennon and Yoko Ono visited the city to investigate the scene. During that brief interval, San Francisco became a global rock capital.

·   ·   ·

Another New Journalist, Joan Didion, also arrived in San Francisco to survey the Haight-Ashbury scene that summer. A Sacramento native who attended Cal in the 1950s, Didion distinguished herself sharply from the Beats and their project. In 1956, she moved to New York City to work for *Vogue* magazine, and four years later, she profiled her alma mater for *Mademoiselle*. "Call it the weather," she wrote, "call it the closing of the frontier, call it the failure of Eden; the fact remains that Californians are cultivating the lushest growth of passive nihilism right along with their bougainvillea." It was a curious claim. After years of bipartisan investments in infrastructure, education, and other public goods, the state's economy was booming. That year, California passed its Master Plan for Higher Education, which was hailed as a blend of bold vision and shrewd practicality. It landed Clark Kerr on the cover of *Time* magazine, but much of the credit also went to Governor Brown. President Kennedy would soon tap Cal alumni for top advisory roles, including secretary of state, secretary of defense, CIA director, and chairman of the Atomic Energy Commission. None of this suggested passive nihilism, but Didion's standards were her own.

Like Thompson, Didion relied heavily on her distinctive style, sensibility, and self-presentation. Her author photographs, many of them made by her friend Ted Streshinsky, resembled glamour shots. In other ways, however, she had little in common with Thompson. In Sacramento, she had absorbed her family's Republican outlook. Anthony Kennedy, whom Ronald Reagan would appoint to the US Supreme Court, was a family friend. Nina "Honey Bear" Warren, daughter of Governor Earl Warren, was a sorority sister at Cal. In 1960, Didion began contributing to the conservative *National Review;* four years later, she voted for Barry Goldwater. Her manner also contrasted sharply with Thompson's. Whereas he projected brawny masculinity, Didion was precise, fragile, even neurasthenic. After moving to Los Angeles in the mid-1960s, however, she quickly became known as a gifted hostess on the Hollywood party circuit. "She seemed to be the only sensible person in the world in those days," said album designer and novelist Eve Babitz. "She could make dinner for 40 people with one hand tied behind her back while everybody else was passed out on the floor." Although Thompson frequently held court at Owl Farm, he was rarely described as the only sensible person in any social setting.

Venturing north from Los Angeles, Didion began researching her story for the *Saturday Evening Post.* Paul Hawken, whom Didion met through Streshinsky, was deeply involved with the counterculture and became one of her guides to it. Later, he built a successful gardening tools business and wrote bestselling books about commerce and the environment. Despite his familiarity with the scene, however, Didion didn't share his view of the counterculture. In fact, her description bore a strong resemblance to a *Time* magazine article that figured hippies as "dangerously deluded dropouts, candidates for a very sound spanking and a cram course in civics—if only they would return home to receive either." Although the *Time* story made little effort to understand the hippies on their own terms, it finally conceded that they "have not so much dropped out of American society as given it something to think about." For Didion, even that concession was too generous.

"Slouching Towards Bethlehem" drew its title and thesis from Yeats's "The Second Coming." The center was not holding, Didion claimed, and San Francisco "was where the social hemorrhaging was showing up." In the course of making that point, she identified several important players in the counterculture. She watched the Grateful Dead rehearse and quoted lead guitarist Jerry Garcia in passing. Only 21 years old that summer, Garcia and his friends were at the center of a vibrant music scene, yet Didion seemed more interested in the vacuous girls who were dancing to their music. Didion also talked to Chet Helms, the music promoter who observed that America's youth constituted a new and important market. She spoke to Arthur Lisch, a member of the Diggers, but she reported that he "just keeps talking about cybernated societies and the guaranteed annual wage." Didion declined to credit any of this, but the Grateful Dead would thrive for decades, the youth market was real, and the digital revolution would eventually transform work, commerce, media, and politics at the global level. Even the guaranteed annual wage, which struck Didion as fantastical, would become a national issue.

Although many hippies regarded their community as an important source of identity and significance, Didion saw it as the epitome of social disintegration.

> At some point between 1945 and 1967, we had somehow neglected to tell these children the rules of the game we happened to be playing. Maybe we had stopped believing in the rules ourselves, maybe we were having a failure of nerve about the game. Or maybe there were just too few people around to do the telling. These were children who grew up cut loose from the web of cousins and great-aunts and family doctors and lifelong neighbors who had traditionally suggested and enforced the society's values.

Didion also quoted a San Francisco psychiatrist's dire political predictions.

> Anybody who thinks this is all about drugs has his head in a bag. It's a social movement, quintessentially romantic, the kind that recurs in times of real social crisis. The themes are always the same. A return to innocence. The invocation of an earlier authority and control. The mysteries of the blood. An itch for the transcendental, for purification. Right there you've got the ways that romanticism ends up in trouble, lends itself to authoritarianism.

To be sure, the counterculture was not all about drugs, and it was indeed a Romantic social movement. But the psychiatrist's political forecast was oddly abstracted from its immediate context. The counterculture had many faults, but aiding authoritarianism was not one of them. Soon after the Summer of Love, in fact, Thompson would credit hippies for their commitment to individual freedom.

According to Didion's biographer, her portrait of the Haight could not be separated from worries about her young daughter, who would struggle with alcoholism and depression until her death at age 39. Later, Didion also admitted that she was ill while working on the piece.

> I was in fact as sick as I have ever been when I was writing "Slouching
> Towards Bethlehem"; the pain kept me awake at night and so for
> twenty and twenty-one hours a day I drank gin-and-hot-water to blunt
> the pain and took Dexedrine to blunt the gin and wrote the piece.

Didion's intake resembled Thompson's, but in national media stories about
the Haight's drug culture, alcohol and prescription speed were not drugs in
the relevant sense.

"Slouching Towards Bethlehem" was not Didion's final comment on the
counterculture. She followed up with "The White Album," which recalled
her encounters with Black Panthers, The Doors, and student activists at San
Francisco State College, whose revolutionary activities amounted to "indus-
trious self-delusion." That article also referred to the Manson Family,
whose ghoulish murders haunt the essay. "The White Album" continued
many themes from "Slouching Towards Bethlehem" but was more self-
reflexive. Didion opened that essay by claiming that narrative itself, her
stock in trade as a journalist, was meant to order raw experience and give it
meaning. Yet many of her encounters in those years, she noted, "were
devoid of any logic save that of the dreamwork."

A related and equally self-reflexive motif was her own psychological
disintegration. She offered a detailed description of that decline, even
including a long passage from a psychiatric report. On the surface, Didion
said, she appeared to be a "competent enough member of one community
or another," and her life "was an adequate performance, as improvisations
go," but she dreaded the social disorder she saw around her.

> The only problem was that my entire education, everything I had ever
> been told or had told myself, insisted that the production was never
> meant to be improvised: I was supposed to have a script, and had mislaid
> it. I was supposed to hear cues and no longer did. I was meant to know
> the plot, but all I knew is what I saw: flash pictures in variable sequence,
> images with no "meaning" beyond their temporary arrangement, not a
> movie but a cutting-room experience.

In short, the social breakdowns she documented in her work mirrored the
psychological ones she was experiencing personally. Her hope lay in narration, which provided structure and a modicum of predictability. The valorization of order—in her life, work, and society—distinguished Didion from
figures like Ken Kesey, Jerry Garcia, and Jim Morrison, who courted spontaneity and improvisation. Didion implied that their project led to a nightmare devoid of meaning, but by embracing it three years later, Thompson
would invent a new genre.

"Slouching Towards Bethlehem" and "The White Album" became Didion's signature works. Well before they appeared, however, the hippie story was fixed. Its weirdness worried mainstream Americans, especially parents, even as it attracted a horde of young people to San Francisco for the Summer of Love. Some hippies welcomed that influx on the theory that more turned-on people would change the world for the better. For the local arts and music community, however, the Summer of Love was overwhelming. Most of the new arrivals brought little talent or creativity to the mix, and Jerry Garcia later described the result as an ecological disaster. As summer turned to fall, many hippies accused the media of creating the scene it purported to describe. Even Didion noted the self-reflexive nature of the coverage. "There were so many observers on Haight Street from *Life* and *Look* and CBS that they were largely observing one another," she wrote. When the Diggers performed the "Death of Hippie" event the month after Didion's essay appeared, the funeral notice described the deceased as "Hippie, beloved son of Mass Media."

The Diggers were not alone in that view. Shortly after the mock funeral, San Francisco police officers arrested members of the Grateful Dead for marijuana possession at their Haight-Ashbury home. In a press statement the next day, band manager Danny Rifkin claimed that the mass media had created the so-called hippie scene, which depended on "the long-haired dropout who performs his exotic rites for the convenience of visiting cameramen." That ritual, in turn, encouraged police officers to arrest young people who fit the description. Because police routinely ignored drug use in the city's more respectable neighborhoods, Rifkin concluded that the drug law was a lie, and that "the hippie, as created by the media, is a lie as well."

Thompson's Hashbury article seemed to reinforce that lie, but in other outlets, he echoed the hippie critique. In August, for example, the *Aspen News* solicited various views on the influx of hippies to that area, and Thompson's response diverged sharply from the others.

> There is no such thing as a hippy. The word is a desperate, cynical misnomer croaked by late-night, half-souled headline writers at the *San Francisco Chronicle* and then picked up with all the hooks showing by frightened word-hustlers who need a word like *hippy* to define the shadow of what they might have been—or might still be—but maybe not, because it's getting late and a lot of things that used to be fun just don't make it anymore. So hippies are crippled remains of other people's fantasies. Gatsby had a green light and a good biographer; the other losers have hippies and *Time* magazine.

Thompson was playing the media critic, not to mention the Fitzgerald afi-
cionado, but the hippie migration was already changing Aspen significantly.
Indeed, Thompson himself would soon convert the city's freak power into
a local political force.

. . .

As the national media skewered San Francisco hippies, two local observers
were more sympathetic. In a three-part article for *The Nation*, history professor Theodore Roszak famously coined the term *counter culture*. Much
like Thompson's earlier article for the same magazine, Roszak's work
bloomed into an important book. *The Making of a Counter Culture:
Reflections on the Technocratic Society and Its Youthful Opposition* (1969)
described the budding interest in radical politics, psychedelic experience,
ecology, sexual freedom, mysticism, and Eastern religions. Roszak's analysis was by no means an uncritical celebration. He punctured the counterculture's rhetorical excesses, wondered about its "frantic search for the
pharmacological panacea," and faulted its histrionic resistance to traditional
values. Yet he also credited its idealism and concerns about technocracy and
managerial liberalism. Where Thompson and Didion saw drug fortresses
and social disintegration, Roszak saw youthful resistance to unchecked
materialism, spiritual poverty, Cold War militarism, and environmental
despoliation. In the decades to come, the mainstream culture would absorb
the hippie critique even as it turned its creators into stereotypes.

Ralph J. Gleason, the *San Francisco Chronicle* columnist, was especially
receptive to the counterculture and its music. A New York native and
Columbia graduate, he immersed himself in the Manhattan jazz scene
before moving to the Bay Area in 1950. In addition to his work at the
Chronicle, he produced a syndicated column on jazz and hosted radio pro-
grams and a public television series. Well before the Summer of Love, he
cofounded the Monterey Jazz Festival, wrote liner notes for Lenny Bruce's
comedy albums, and testified for the defense at Bruce's obscenity trial in
San Francisco. If Gleason had done nothing else, his career would have been
remarkable. But in the mid-1960s, he also began championing San
Francisco's emerging rock groups. RCA Victor signed Jefferson Airplane the
same month Gleason sang their praises. Writing to a friend, he described
the city's music scene as almost unprecedented. "There has been no point
in American history that I know of, except the street bands of New Orleans,
where music has had such a direct role in the culture of any area as it has in
San Francisco at this point in our history." Music industry insiders took
notice. Ahmet Ertegun, president of Atlantic Records, told Gleason that no

other city could match the San Francisco music scene's commercial appeal during this period. "Something like 15 out of the first 19 albums recorded by San Francisco bands made the best-seller charts," Ertegun said. "There's something different about the San Francisco bands, some mystique."

In 1967, Gleason also supported the Monterey Pop Festival, which was conceived by John Phillips and his label's president, Lou Adler. Working out of Los Angeles, Phillips and Adler realized they needed the San Francisco bands for the festival to succeed, but those bands had misgivings about the Los Angeles labels and their slick commercialism. With Gleason on board, however, those bands agreed to participate. When former Beatles publicist Derek Taylor added his talents, the festival became the key musical event of the summer. Its success, along with the film that documented it, boosted the careers of Jimi Hendrix, Janis Joplin, The Who, and Otis Redding. Both the outdoor festival format and the film's success cleared the way for Woodstock two years later.

Compared to Hinckle and Thompson, Gleason was less focused on politics, yet he was far from neutral politically. Americans would later learn that he was the only music journalist on President Nixon's Enemies List, which Gleason considered the highest honor his country could bestow on him. His network included radical labor union leader Harry Bridges, political journalist I. F. Stone, and Marxist historian Eric Hobsbawm, who wrote jazz criticism under a pen name. Gleason was also a contributing editor at *Ramparts* magazine, but he confessed that "the square, myopic, UNHIP left" antagonized him "like the bandilleras in the bull." He was convinced that politics followed culture, not vice versa, and that young people were far ahead of leftist intellectuals and activists in changing American culture. "You make the social revolution first and politicize it, don't you?" he asked one friend rhetorically. Trying to politicize hippies, he noted privately, was "discussing them in the wrong framework."

Gleason hosted an informal salon at his Berkeley home that included Jann Wenner, a Cal student and avid reader of Gleason's *Chronicle* column. "It was the only place I knew to find a certain social, cultural, and political mix that was coming to define my world," Wenner wrote later. Wenner's music column for the Cal newspaper was an homage to his mentor. An English major and political science minor, Wenner was also an editor for SLATE, the student group that helped launch the Free Speech Movement. In his spare time, he worked at the NBC radio affiliate, where he covered the Berkeley campus. He was reporting from the Greek Theatre in December 1964 when police famously hauled off Mario Savio, the Free Speech Movement leader. An AP photograph showed Wenner in a trench coat, microphone in hand, only yards behind the apprehended Savio. Gleason, who was in the audience, wrote about the event in a *Chronicle* column he called "Tragedy at the Greek Theatre."

After Wenner dropped out of Cal, Gleason arranged a job for him at the *Sunday Ramparts,* the magazine's spinoff newspaper. Wenner worked on the entertainment section and tried to interest Hinckle in the burgeoning counterculture. "They were oblivious to the cultural changes in San Francisco," Wenner recalled. "Warren ridiculed it, and Scheer had no use for it." But Wenner's time at *Ramparts* was well spent. He met his future wife, learned the value of showmanship from Hinckle, and admired Dugald Stermer's layouts. When *Hell's Angels* appeared, Wenner lifted the galleys from the *Ramparts* office and mentioned the book in his *Daily Cal* column.

Meanwhile, Gleason was planning to orchestrate the Summer of Love coverage at *Ramparts.* When Hinckle ran his own cover story without consulting him, Gleason flew into a rage. He resigned from *Ramparts* magazine, which he later described as "the white hope of the square left." Hinckle also shut down the *Sunday Ramparts,* leaving Wenner out of work. Within months, Gleason and Wenner conceived a new magazine. Gleason suggested *Rolling Stone* as the title, and Wenner began assembling the first issue in a spare room at the *Ramparts* office. He consulted Stermer about layout ideas, lifted design elements from *Ramparts,* and later moved the operation to a loft over Garrett Press, which printed both *Ramparts* and *Rolling Stone.*

The premiere issue of *Rolling Stone* appeared in November 1967. Its design outclassed other early rock magazines, and its countercultural emphasis distinguished it from trade and teenybopper publications. Gleason's stature also gave *Rolling Stone* an edge, especially with the record labels that became the magazine's chief advertisers. But *Rolling Stone* was always more than a music magazine. Above all a creature of the San Francisco counterculture, the magazine also absorbed the influence of *Ramparts* and the Free Speech Movement. Many of *Rolling Stone*'s early editors and contributors studied at Cal, and their political outlook figured heavily in magazine's unique editorial formula. "The Free Speech Movement had an enormous effect on everyone and in many ways," *Rolling Stone* editor and Cal alumnus Greil Marcus recalled. "We measured ourselves against it and its values. *Rolling Stone* wouldn't have happened without the Free Speech Movement. Everything that I had learned at Berkeley, that I had learned to care about, there was room for that at *Rolling Stone.*"

In many ways, Marcus's arrival at *Rolling Stone* reflected the magazine's early operations. Like Wenner, Marcus was a regular visitor at Gleason's home, but he joined *Rolling Stone* only after complaining to associate editor Charles Perry about the magazine's album reviews. Days later, Marcus received an offer to edit that section for $35 a week. Perry's arrival was no less typical. Another Cal graduate, he had once shared a home in North Berkeley with Owsley Stanley, the LSD chemist who became the Grateful Dead's patron and sound engineer. After graduation, Perry attended dance parties in San Francisco, sampled psychedelic drugs, and tended animals in the psychology department's facility in the Berkeley hills. After connecting with *Rolling Stone* through another Cal roommate and friend of Gleason, Perry worked his way up to associate editor.

Rolling Stone quickly found a large audience, which Wenner later traced to the Bay Area's distinctive culture.

> The San Francisco Bay Area was a hotbed of a lot of rock and roll stuff, drug culture, psychedelics, Kesey, politics, campus activism. It was more on the edge culturally than any other place in the country. There was more freedom. *Rolling Stone* began and merged all those elements. We just felt it was time for a new kind of politics, and it would emerge out of the rock-and-roll consciousness and that rock-and-roll ethos.

Despite that early success, Warren Hinckle was unimpressed. In his 1974 memoir, he specifically disavowed Wenner and *Rolling Stone.*

> What I found objectionable about the hippies—or rather about some hippie promoters—was the attempt to make a serious political stance out of goofing off . . . One of the leading merchandisers of this counterculture bullshit was *Rolling Stone,* the rock culture tabloid that was started by two disgruntled *Ramparts* types. One of them was Jann Wenner, then a fat and pudgy kid hanging around the office . . . The truth of the matter is that I hardly knew the kid; and the only thing that *Ramparts* gave him to help start his paper was a bottle of rubber cement to paste up the first issue, and I screamed about *that.*

Hinckle was slightly more deferential to Gleason. He apologized for dumping on Gleason's flower children "without giving him a chance to defend the little fascists." By the time Hinckle's memoir appeared, however, *Rolling Stone* was winning awards, expanding its readership, and running Thompson's work.

Despite Hinckle's characterization of *Rolling Stone* and its publisher, Wenner did not see his magazine as a typical product of hippie culture.

> We didn't want to be part of that hippie way of life. We didn't want to be communal. We didn't want to have a hippie design. Our values were more traditional reporting. We wanted to be recognized by the establishment. Part of it was our own mission; part of it was what we were looking for, music. We wanted the music to be taken seriously.

Certainly the magazine's album reviews took the music seriously, and its clean design underscored its professionalism. Wenner also hired Alan Rinzler, a young editor at a major New York City publisher, to launch *Rolling Stone*'s book division. Even as he professionalized the operation, however, Wenner stole his company's name, Straight Arrow Press, from Chet Helms, the hippie impresario who planned to start a magazine with that title. Wenner also commissioned psychedelic poster artist Rick Griffin to produce *Rolling Stone*'s lush title logo. From the beginning, Wenner threaded the needle between mainstream recognition and countercultural appeal.

· · ·

When the first issue of *Rolling Stone* hit the newsstands, Thompson had been living in Colorado for a full year. He certainly wasn't the only person to leave San Francisco for the hinterlands. Many hippies abandoned the Haight after it devolved into what Thompson called "a cop magnet and bad sideshow." After the drug arrest at 710 Ashbury, members of the Grateful Dead drifted north to bucolic Marin County along with Janis Joplin, Bill Graham, and other fixtures in the San Francisco music scene. Ken Kesey returned to the family farm in Oregon and mixed light literary production with occasional public appearances. Other hippies migrated to California's northernmost counties, where they started communes, grew cannabis, and eventually created one of California's largest cash crops.

Thompson was well aware of the back-to-the-land movement. In his Hashbury piece, he noted that Gary Synder was urging young people to "move out of the cities, form tribes, purchase land, and live communally in remote areas." Snyder's experience encapsulated much of the counterculture's origin story. A Beat poet from the Pacific Northwest, he studied with Kenneth Rexroth, immersed himself in Zen Buddhism and Asian literature, and served as the model for Kerouac's hero in *The Dharma Bums*. He also lived out his back-to-the-land prescription. In 1969, *Look* magazine featured his family on their backcountry acreage in the Sierra Nevada foothills. The profile noted that Snyder was looking forward to "a new Neolithic age that will combine the love of nature, sex, and life based on mythical truths."

The back-to-the-land movement also had a soundtrack. The acoustic guitars, sweet harmonies, and folksy iconography of Crosby, Stills & Nash made their debut album a commercial and critical success in 1969. The cover photograph showed them wearing blue jeans, plaid shirts, and boots, not the spectacular costumes associated with the Haight. That summer, the new supergroup performed Joni Mitchell's new song, "Woodstock," at Max

Yasgur's farm in upstate New York. With its exhortation to "get ourselves back to the garden," Mitchell's lyric channeled the movement's spirit. The following year, the Grateful Dead released *Workingman's Dead,* which signaled a return to the band's folk roots. In the voice of his alter ego, Raoul Duke, Thompson included that album—along with *Buffalo Springfield,* Sandy Bull's *Inventions,* and Bob Dylan's *Highway 61* and *Bringing It All Back Home*—on his list of the top ten recordings of the decade. Although Thompson had no desire to live communally, his musical tastes suggested that he, too, was ready for the country.

Thompson called Woody Creek home for the rest of his life, but San Francisco remained an important touchstone. His initial reaction to the city had been negative, but he eventually came to identify with its freewheeling spirit. "His utopia, which he had experienced before I met him, was San Francisco in the early sixties," said Timothy Crouse, who worked closely with Thompson at *Rolling Stone* in the early 1970s. Almost a decade after his San Francisco stint, Thompson reflected on the hippies and their significance.

> The hippies threatened the establishment by dis-interring some of the most basic and original "American values," and trying to apply them to life in a sprawling, high-pressure technocracy that has come a long way, in nearly 200 years, from the simple agrarian values that prevailed at the time of the Boston Tea Party.

Among the American values Thompson had in mind was liberty, which he prized above all. Any thinking hippie, he wrote, took note of the fear-oriented warfare state that could no longer tolerate "even the minor aberrations that go along with 'individual freedom.'" In effect, Thompson cast hippies as fellow libertarians who shared his Jeffersonian outlook.

If Thompson's move to Woody Creek reflected the back-to-the-land movement, it also recreated the bucolic bohemianism of Big Sur. Unlike Henry Miller, however, Thompson was no recluse. He was a fixture in the taverns and quickly became involved in local affairs. Aspen also attracted many hippies during that period, which eased the transition to what was otherwise a high-end ski resort with old-fashioned views about land use and law enforcement. Finally, Thompson's move gave full expression to his inner hillbilly, a term he frequently applied to himself. In particular, he enjoyed the freedom to behave as outrageously as he pleased on his own property with no complaints from neighbors.

At the same time, Woody Creek presented few professional advantages to a freelance journalist. Even compared to San Francisco, Aspen was a literary backwater. Reflecting on his arrangement and its costs, Thompson noted he had "put a lot of work into living out here where I do and still making a living." Much like Miller in Big Sur, he used his unflagging correspondence to grow and maintain his literary network. Thompson also resembled Miller, who by that time was holding court in Pacific Palisades, by converting Owl Farm into a clubhouse for friends and visiting celebrities. In Woody Creek, Thompson could be the writer he imagined in the 1950s: a bright white golf ball in a fairway of windblown daisies. If politics was the art of controlling your environment, as Thompson famously maintained, his political prospects were much brighter in Pitkin County than in San Francisco.

As Thompson settled into Owl Farm, he wrote very little. The lull was due in part to problems with his agent, Scott Meredith, who also represented Norman Mailer and other luminaries. In May 1967, Thompson told Silberman he didn't trust Meredith and asked him to tell literary agent Lynn Nesbit, who had worked for Sterling Lord, that he was still alive. In 1961, Lord had declined to represent Thompson, who did not take the news well. In a letter to Lord, Thompson called his decision a "pompous and moronic rejection of my work" and threatened to cave in his face and scatter his teeth over Fifth Avenue. Now Thompson began courting Nesbit and directing his wrath at Meredith. In a long letter to Paul Krassner, he called his agent "a fascist soul-fucker" and detailed his plans for revenge, which included "cracking his teeth with a knotty stick and rupturing every other bone and organ I can make contact with."

Thompson returned to full production only after his deal with Meredith expired later that year, at which point Nesbit took over. Having left Sterling Lord's shop in 1965, she ran the literary department for what later became International Creative Management. She knew about Thompson from his success with *Hell's Angels*, but she quickly learned that he was no ordinary client.

> He'd come blundering into our offices, and there were always some
> secretaries who were quite smitten with him. Some people were
> terrified of him. He'd be talking at the top of his voice with some
> strange baseball cap on and a bag full of funny things. Even when it was
> quite cold out, he'd be in shorts.

According to Nesbit, Thompson was obsessed with receiving enough money for his work. He also had a propensity to squander whatever he made. "The arguments we had about money went on and on," she recalled.

. . .

That summer, Thompson met Oscar Acosta in Aspen. The introduction came through local resident Michael Solheim, who owned a bar that both men had patronized while visiting Hemingway's home in Idaho. Over the next several years, Acosta's frenetic lifestyle and gargantuan appetites would stimulate Thompson and figure heavily in his work.

Born in El Paso, Acosta was raised in Riverbank, California, a farming town in the San Joaquin Valley. After serving in the Air Force and as a Baptist missionary in Panama, he studied creative writing at San Francisco State College. One of his mentors was Mark Harris, whose 1956 novel, *Bang the Drum Slowly*, was later turned into a film with Robert DeNiro. A productive journalist as well as a novelist, Harris wrote a long article for the *Atlantic Monthly* on the Summer of Love in which he navigated the space between Thompson and Roszak. Like Didion, he noted the media's role in creating, rather than merely reporting on, the San Francisco countercul-ture. Hippies, he wrote, were "in part a hoax of American journalism, known even to themselves only as they saw themselves in the media." Although he focused on the hippie community's immaturity and privilege, he also credited their nonviolence while the city's establishment pushed the police to crack down on them. As for Acosta and his future, Harris's advice was simple: If he wanted a literary career, he should drop everything else and pursue it ardently. Acosta resisted that advice but never gave up on his literary dreams.

During his time in San Francisco, Acosta lived in the Polk District, worked as a copyboy at the *San Francisco Examiner*, and attended law school at night. He also hurled himself into San Francisco's bohemian scene, an experience he recorded in *The Autobiography of a Brown Buffalo* (1972). After a string of nervous breakdowns, the protagonist feels he must leave the city to find himself. "Five years of madness in this hideout," he says. "No wonder I'm cracking up." Eventually, he treks across the southwest to his birthplace, El Paso, in his 1965 Plymouth. Acosta's book, scholar Hector Calderon has argued, is best understood as a sixties-style drug adventure whose origins lay in Kerouac's fiction. Acosta read both Kerouac and Henry Miller voraciously, and critics noted a kinship between his work and theirs. "In terms of style," another critic observed, "his was free flow-ing, chaotic in structure and content, responding only to the goddess of spontaneity." Calderon also listed many resemblances between Acosta and Thompson. Born four years apart, both men "responded intellectually to forties and fifties American culture by buying into the Beat Generation's myth of the road, drifting and breaking away, searching and writing." Likewise, both men served in the Air Force, lived in Latin America, found their way to San Francisco during the 1960s, and wanted to write novels based on their outsized experiences. That both men had visited Hemingway's final home was the proximate cause of their introduction.

Having deserted San Francisco, Acosta landed in Aspen, where he washed dishes, worked construction jobs, and tore through the local bars. Although his beefy frame was racked by ulcers, he drank heavily and favored LSD sprees that he called "walking with the king." Writing to his parents that July, he acknowledged that he was conflicted.

> As you well know, I have been at war with myself and the universe,
> with mankind and God, with the whole of society and all it has to offer.
> I have been in this conflict for so many years I can't even remember
> when was the last time I felt at peace.

Acosta left Aspen for El Paso but was jailed for insulting a police officer in Juarez. In January 1968, he recounted the experience in his first letter to Thompson, and for the next several years, they maintained a vigorous and occasionally pointed correspondence. In much of it, Thompson dispensed writing and publishing advice to Acosta, but the exchange was mutually beneficial. Eventually, Acosta would lead Thompson to an important story and figure prominently in his most famous book.

FIGURE 1. Thompson served in the Air Force as a sportswriter. That experience shaped his style, and much of his notable later work was related to sports.

BIG
SUR:
THE
TROPIC OF
HENRY
MILLER

article By HUNTER S. THOMPSON

FIGURE 2. Henry Miller was the hook for Thompson's first article in a national magazine. Miller's work and model of authorship influenced Thompson profoundly. (Courtesy of the Hunter S. Thompson Estate)

FIGURE 3. Carey McWilliams urged Thompson to write about motorcycle gangs for *The Nation*. Despite his admiration for McWilliams, Thompson never wrote for the magazine again. (Courtesy of the Bancroft Library, University of California, Berkeley)

FIGURE 4. Tapping the demand for New Journalism, Thompson parlayed the Hell's Angels article into a bestselling book.

FIGURE 5. James Silberman edited most of Thompson's books, first at Random House and then at Simon & Schuster. He was known for his meticulousness, intuition, and patience. (Courtesy of the Silberman family)

FIGURE 6. Thompson met Warren Hinckle, editor of *Ramparts* magazine, in San Francisco. By pairing Thompson and Ralph Steadman at *Scanlan's Monthly*, Hinckle helped create Gonzo journalism. (Courtesy of the Hunter S. Thompson Estate)

FIGURE 7. Thompson wrote to Jann Wenner after reading *Rolling Stone*'s coverage of Altamont. Wenner enlisted Thompson even before *Scanlan's* folded. (Mark Seliger/Courtesy of Jann S. Wenner)

FIGURE 8. Oscar Acosta persuaded Thompson to cover the Chicano movement in Los Angeles. While Thompson was researching "Strange Rumblings in Aztlan," the two men drove to Las Vegas, and Thompson returned with the beginnings of his Gonzo masterpiece.

FIGURE 9. Ralph Steadman did not make the trip to Las Vegas, but his illustrations created Gonzo's distinctive iconography. (Courtesy of Jann S. Wenner)

FIGURE 10. While covering the 1972 presidential campaign, Thompson overcame many obstacles to create what one McGovern insider called the least factual and most accurate account of the campaign. (Annie Leibovitz)

FIGURE 11. In a San Francisco hotel room, Alan Rinzler helped Thompson lash together *Fear and Loathing: On the Campaign Trail '72*. (Courtesy of Alan Rinzler)

FIGURE 12. Whereas Theodore White famously converted campaign seasons into polished narratives, Thompson declined to smooth out his jagged dispatches for the book.

The Murder of California's Last Wild Bears • L.A.'s Mean Streets at 150 mph • A Sober Chat With Dennis Hopper

$2.00 MARCH 1987

California

Willie Hearst and His Boys:
PUTTING SOME GUTS BACK INTO THE WEST COAST PRESS

FIGURE 13. Will Hearst hired Thompson to write for the *San Francisco Examiner*. They are seen here with Warren Hinckle and editor Larry Kramer.

7 Totally Gonzo

At the end of 1967, Thompson met with his editors in New York City and agreed to complete three books. Two were on short schedules. The first manuscript, on LBJ's reelection campaign, was due that April, and *The Rum Diary* was due only three months later. A manuscript on the death of the American Dream was scheduled for July of the following year.

If Thompson's publishing arrangements were settled, the nation was not. On March 31, 1968, President Johnson announced he would not seek reelection. That decision killed one of Thompson's book projects, but it gave Robert F. Kennedy an opening to run for president. Thompson offered his speech-writing services to Kennedy family advisor Ted Sorensen. "All I really want to do," he wrote, "is get that evil pig-fucker out of the White House and not let Nixon in . . . and the only real hope I see right now is your friend Robert." But two events quickly altered the political landscape. In April, Dr. King was shot in Memphis, prompting riots in eleven cities, including Louisville. Two months later, Kennedy met the same fate in Los Angeles after winning the Democratic primary in California.

In the meantime, Richard Nixon's campaign was gaining momentum, and Thompson traveled to New Hampshire to cover his adversary for *Pageant*. Writing to Charles Kuralt, he described it as a fluff assignment that would help him with his Johnson campaign book. While following Nixon in New Hampshire, he was surprised when two aides, Ray Price and Pat Buchanan, offered him a chance to ride in Nixon's car, provided he spoke only about football. Thompson promised to comply and was impressed by Nixon's expertise. "It was a very weird trip," Thompson wrote later, "probably one of the weirdest things I've ever done, and especially weird because both Nixon and I enjoyed it."

That colloquy did not blunt Thompson's contempt for the Republican candidate. In July, *Pageant* ran "Presenting: The Richard Nixon Doll." An illustration portrayed Nixon as a smiling windup doll, and the article listed the various personae Nixon had acquired over the years before attempting "to find the man behind all these masks, or maybe to find that there was no mask at all." It was possible, Thompson conceded, that Nixon "was neither more nor less than what he appeared to be—a plastic man in a plastic bag, surrounded by wizards so cautious as to seem almost plastic themselves." Thompson made no pretense of objectivity. Admitting that Nixon had "never been one of my favorite people, anyway," he denounced the candidate's character.

> For years I've regarded his very existence as a monument to all the rancid genes and broken chromosomes that corrupt the possibilities of the American Dream; he was a foul caricature of himself, a man with no soul, no inner convictions, with the integrity of a hyena and the style of a poison toad.

By making himself a character in the story, Thompson remained well within the bounds of New Journalism, but his personal attack on a presidential candidate distinguished his work from Wolfe's and Didion's. The caustic portrait was also out of step with *Pageant*'s other articles, which included "How to Avoid Bedroom Boredom," "Warn Your Kids About Homosexuals," and "Finally—A Safe Diet Pill That Works."

The following month, Thompson attended the 1968 Democratic National Convention in Chicago. He asked Semonin to join him there. Semonin declined but noted that the Chicago convention aroused Thompson's political consciousness. His own candidate, Thompson wrote later, had been murdered in Los Angeles two months earlier. That terse formulation belied his deep attachment to Robert Kennedy, whose assassination "probably drove a stake into his heart," Semonin said. Thompson had no assignment or plan to write anything in particular about Chicago. "I just wanted to *be there* and get the feel of things," he recalled. Nevertheless, he asked Random House to arrange press credentials for him. He told Silberman that Peter Collier, managing editor at *Ramparts*, assured him that "all manner of hell is going to break loose."

Collier was correct. Thousands of demonstrators flooded Chicago's streets and public parks. As television cameras rolled, police officers flayed provocateurs, peaceful protestors, and observers alike. The clashes, which continued for three days and nights, provided a dramatic backdrop for the political maneuvers inside the convention. The key debate concerned the party's peace plank. Congressman Phil Burton of San Francisco urged withdrawal from Vietnam, while Senator Edmund Muskie maintained that the anti-war contingent wanted peace at any price. Other speakers followed in the same vein, and the peace plank was defeated. Reporting for *Harper's* magazine, Norman Mailer observed that the debate echoed the measured rhetoric of Secretary of State Dean Rusk, who was "always a model of sanity on every detail but one: he had a delusion that the war was not bottomless in its lunacy."

For Thompson, however, the real story was in the streets, where he recoiled from the police violence he witnessed. Scampering from agitated cops on Michigan Avenue, he encountered two officers blocking his retreat to his hotel. As he later recalled, "I finally just ran between the truncheons, screaming, 'I live here, goddamnit! I'm paying fifty dollars a day!'" When he submitted his expenses to Silberman, Thompson wrote that the protestors' militancy made "all the Berkeley protests look like pastoral gambols from another era." The protestors "stood and fought, and took incredible beatings," Thompson reported. "I witnessed at least ten beatings in Chicago that were worse than anything I ever saw the Hell's Angels do."

The GOP convention in San Francisco had been a political lesson for Thompson, but the meltdown in Chicago was a turning point. The police riot he witnessed shocked him into a deeper personal, civic, and professional reckoning.

> That week at the Convention changed everything I'd ever taken for granted about this country and my place in it. I went from a state of Cold Shock on Monday, to Fear on Tuesday, then Rage, and finally Hysteria—which lasted for nearly a month. Every time I tried to tell somebody what happened in Chicago, I began crying, and it took me years to understand why.

Although he published very little about Chicago, it changed him as a writer. Before the convention, he focused on exotic provincial subcultures—artists in Big Sur, radical activists in Berkeley, and motorcycle gangs in San Francisco and Oakland. That strategy, which he modeled on Tom Wolfe's example, had served him reasonably well. His new book projects addressed broader topics, and his *Pageant* piece on Nixon targeted a presidential candidate, but especially after Chicago, Thompson began to take direct aim at the political class.

While Thompson coped with the mayhem in Chicago, Hinckle was developing a novel way to cover it. The concept originated in San Francisco, where his assistant managing editor asked for a week off. During that time, Fred Gardner wanted to produce a daily leaflet for demonstrators in Chicago.

Hinckle liked the idea but suggested a wall poster. One side of a full-folio sheet would be news from the street, the other side would cover the convention. "The idea sprang fully formed from his head," Gardner said. "It was the most brilliant thing I ever saw a publisher do." The *Ramparts Wall Poster*, which recalled the publications of Mao Zedong's Red Guard during the Cultural Revolution, left a deep impression on Thompson. The Chicago convention, however, was Hinckle's last hurrah at *Ramparts*. Despite its impressive circulation, the magazine never developed a reliable advertising base. Hinckle's mentor, advertising executive Howard Gossage, called the magazine's finances "a twenty-four hour crap game." Having burned through two private fortunes, *Ramparts* filed for bankruptcy and reorganized in 1969.

Hinckle resigned and launched a new magazine, *Scanlan's Monthly*. His partner in that venture was Sidney Zion, a former federal prosecutor and legal reporter for the *New York Times*. A fixture at New York's celebrity watering holes, Zion was a cigar-smoking raconteur whose friends included mobsters, actors, and politicians. He was by no means a leftist. In 1971, Zion revealed Daniel Ellsberg as the source of the Pentagon Papers, the classified documents that exposed the US government's history of deceit in Vietnam. Later, Zion completed and published the autobiography of his friend, Roy Cohn, who acted as chief counsel to Senator Joseph McCarthy, served as Donald Trump's personal lawyer, and was later disbarred for cheating his clients.

Hinckle lost no time in publishing Thompson, whose piece on skier Jean-Claude Killy appeared in the first issue of *Scanlan's*. *Playboy* had commissioned the article about the Olympic champion but declined to run it. By that time, Hugh Hefner's magazine was reaching millions of readers with its blend of interviews, fiction, cartoons, and nude photo-spreads. Hefner also launched a chain of nightclubs, hosted a television show, and was touting the "Playboy philosophy" at every turn. When Thompson landed the Killy assignment, Hefner's empire was worth more than $70 million. Thompson's work for *Rogue* and other men's magazines seemed to qualify him for inclusion in *Playboy*, but in other ways he was a poor fit. A beatnik detractor, Hefner preferred to tout "the UpBeat generation." But there was nothing chipper about the Killy piece, which lampooned the routines and rituals of American marketing. Killy's three gold medals at the 1968 Winter Olympics had made him the world's dominant skier, but after his retirement from amateur sports, his handlers converted him into a well-paid pitchman for Chevrolet. American automakers bought a lot of magazine advertising, and Thompson heard from the editor who assigned his piece that Hefner had been wooing Chevrolet for five years. In an internal discussion, another *Playboy* editor said that Thompson's article would be good for *Esquire;* yet another regarded it as an attack on the *Playboy* ethos: "Thompson's ugly, stupid arrogance is an insult to everything we stand for."

Thompson was grateful that Hinckle accepted the piece, which had been difficult to write. Killy's flat personality was a challenge, as were his handlers, who restricted Thompson's access to Killy. Thompson responded by folding both obstacles into the story. When Killy skirted Thompson's questions, or when Killy's handlers thwarted him, Thompson wrote about that. He also made his traveling companion, *Boston Globe* writer Bill Cardoso, a character in the story. Both moves would become staples in Thompson's later work. Although Cardoso counted Thompson as a friend, he later admitted that Thompson frightened him.

> Hunter's such an amazingly brutish physical specimen. I couldn't believe his stamina. I remember he tore apart his hotel room in New Hampshire when he was covering Jean-Claude Killy. It was a fucking mess. He tore it apart, physically, tore it apart. I mean just demolished it . . . You know, his violence always scared me. I was fat when I was a kid, and I was shot. That was the end of my gangster period. So Hunter's violence always scared me.

Cardoso's description resonated with others. One of Thompson's editors, Alan Rinzler, described Thompson as "a big, scary, athletic, rednecked guy." After David Pierce disparaged a country song that Thompson liked, Thompson produced a .44 Magnum, aimed it at Pierce's chest, and pulled the trigger. The cartridge was a blank, but the force knocked Pierce across the room. "So Hunter could be really sweet and everything," Pierce remarked. "But he could also be extraordinarily painful and stressful to be around."

Even family members found Thompson menacing. "I was afraid of the guy," his brother Jim admitted. "And I still am. Always unnerved by his presence." That feeling surfaced when Jim visited his older brother after dropping out of college. Virginia Thompson suggested the visit in hopes that Jim's suicidal thoughts would abate under his brother's care. But Jim was thoroughly cowed, and the mood was tense. "I used to dread Hunter getting up in the afternoon—three or four o'clock in the afternoon, and immediately he would be very grouchy, very sleepy, and very domineering from then on." Anything could set him off, Jim recalled. If the breakfast Sandy had prepared displeased him, Thompson might throw it off the deck, and she would prepare another. When Thompson dropped off his brother at the airport, he finally asked about "this suicide business." Embarrassed, Jim downplayed it. "I didn't want to look bad in his eyes. Because he indicated that that was a pretty pathetic thing to do."

. . .

"The Temptations of Jean-Claude Killy" presented a practical man with little charisma or curiosity. "Killy reacts," Thompson observed. "Thinking is not his gig." Killy was converting his celebrity into cash with the same determination he displayed as a downhill racer. "There was a hint of decency—perhaps even humor—about him," Thompson wrote, "but the high-powered realities of the world he lives in now make it hard to deal with him on any terms except those of pure commerce." Thompson noted that Killy's financial instincts were clear even during his amateur years. When Avery Brundage, the elderly president of the International Olympic Committee, called on Killy and others to return their medals because they had accepted money from "commercial interests," Killy replied that Brundage should come and fetch the medals himself.

Thompson was sympathetic but noted that Killy's new role meant avoiding such outbursts.

> Chevrolet doesn't pay him to say what he thinks, but to sell
> Chevrolets—and you don't do that by telling self-righteous old men to
> fuck off . . . You smile like Horatio Alger and give all the credit to Mom
> and Dad, who never lost faith in you and even mortgaged their ingots
> when things got tough.

The Horatio Alger reference returned the piece to familiar ground. For Thompson, Killy's temptations revealed the emptiness of the American Dream. That emptiness hit Thompson hardest when he found himself bound for The Stockyards Amphitheatre, which hosted the 1968 Democratic Party convention. He and his companions were "heading for that rotten slaughterhouse where Mayor Daley had buried the Democratic party," and the ride evoked unpleasant memories. "I had been there before, and I remembered it well. Chicago—this vicious, stinking zoo, this mean-grinning, Mace-smelling boneyard of a city; an elegant rockpile monument to everything cruel and stupid and corrupt in the human spirit." In this way, Thompson yoked Killy's experience to the nation's crisis. If American marketing was a charade, American politics was an abomination. Along the way, Thompson also compared Killy to Jimmy Gatz, the Fitzgerald character who reinvented himself as Jay Gatsby. In doing so, Thompson linked Killy's robotic sales pitches to another longstanding preoccupation. Finally,

Thompson managed to slam Chicago, where *Playboy* magazine was head-quartered.

The Killy piece included two secondary characters, John DeLorean and O.J. Simpson, both of whom would endure high-profile criminal trials. After defending himself against cocaine trafficking charges in 1982, DeLorean eventually declared bankruptcy; Donald Trump bought his estate in Bedminster, New Jersey, and turned it into a golf club. Simpson, the USC football star who had yet to play a professional game, was already preparing himself for a career in television. After watching Killy and Simpson tout Chevrolets at the Chicago Auto Show, Thompson compared their styles.

> Killy's public pitch is very low-key, a vivid contrast to O.J. Simpson, whose sales technique has all the subtlety of a power-slant on third and one . . . O.J. *likes* this scene. His booming self-confidence suggests Alfred E. Neuman in blackface or Rap Brown selling watermelons at the Mississippi State Fair. O.J.'s mind is not complicated; he has had God on his side for so long that it never occurs to him that selling Chevrolets is any less holy than making touchdowns.

Thompson regarded Simpson's appeal to Black Americans as his main asset.

> O.J. is a Black Capitalist in the most basic sense of that term; his business sense is so powerful that he is able to view his blackness as a mere sales factor—a natural intro to the Black Marketplace, where a honky showboat like Killy is doomed from the start.

But the arc of Simpson's career revealed a different aspiration, a form of celebrity that transcended race. Sportswriter Robert Lipsyte caught a glimpse of that ambition while dining with Simpson. After overhearing another diner say, "Look at those niggers sitting with O.J.," Lipsyte expressed sympathy. But Simpson claimed that Lipsyte was missing the point. "Don't you understand?" he said. "She knew I wasn't black. She saw me as O.J." Later, Simpson was found not guilty on two counts of murder after a racially charged trial in Los Angeles.

As usual, Thompson was a significant character in his own story. In one passage, several teenage boys approached him while he was smoking a pipe at the Chicago Auto Show. Mistaking him for Killy, they asked what he was doing. "Well," he replied, "I'm just sitting here smoking marijuana." He held up his pipe and added, "This is what makes me ski so fast." Later, he parried with the marketing director of Head Skis, one of Killy's sponsors. "Look," the executive told Thompson, "I'll give you all the help you need on this thing, and I think I'm in a position to give you the kind of help you need. Naturally, I'd expect some play for Head Skis in your photo coverage and of course that's my job." Thompson replied, "Fuck the skis. I couldn't give a hoot in hell if he skis on metal bowls; all I want to do is talk to the man, in a decent human manner, and find out what he thinks about things." By foregrounding such negotiations, which were often part of a profile's backstory, Thompson challenged the norms of both modern marketing and celebrity journalism. When he discovered that his approach offended *Playboy*'s editors, he made that part of the story as well.

When the article appeared in *Scanlan's*, Thompson was unhappy with the layout. "Graphically, it was a fucking horror show," he wrote to Hinckle. "It looks like it was put together by a compositor's apprentice with a head full of Seconal." He especially disliked the illustrations: "On lesser fronts, I want to impose a condition on anything I may or may not sell you in the future—to wit: That any 'cartoon/illustration' by Jim Nutt will not be allowed within 15 pages on either side of my byline." Despite his misgivings about the art, Thompson again found himself in smart company. The March issue of *Scanlan's* included Murray Kempton on Dean Acheson, Maxwell Geismar on Mark Twain, screenwriter Ben Hecht on mobster Mickey Cohen, Peter Collier's review of *The French Lieutenant's Woman*, and former *Ramparts* editor Sol Stern on the disaster that was Altamont. It was several steps up from the articles about *Hell's Angels* that ran in *Stag Annual* and *For Men Only*, which also featured advertisements for books called *The Three Loves of a Backwater Nympho*, *The Girls Who Star in Stag Movies*, and *Blonde Bait for a Sex-Thrill Kidnapper*.

• • •

Thompson and Hinckle would collaborate again within months. After novelist James Salter suggested a story on the upcoming Kentucky Derby, Thompson pitched the idea to Hinckle. He also asked that Pat Oliphant, political cartoonist for the *Denver Post*, produce the illustrations. Oliphant passed, and Hinckle instead chose Ralph Steadman, who would later describe the opportunity as his big break. Steadman had placed his first cartoon, on the Suez Canal controversy, in the *Manchester Evening Chronicle*. In 1960, one of his illustrations appeared in *Punch*, where he eventually advanced to cover designs. He also illustrated children's books and contributed to *New Musical Express* and other publications. It was his work for *Private Eye*, however, that caught Hinckle's attention. Founded in 1961, the satirical news magazine modeled some of what Hinckle would create at *Ramparts* and *Scanlan's*. In the first issue of *Scanlan's*, Hinckle included a Steadman cartoon that the *New York Times* had rejected.

Although Steadman was mild-mannered, he used his drawings as a weapon. One of his heroes was George Grosz, who was arrested for insulting the German army and prosecuted for anticlerical drawings during the Weimar era. Grosz's audience, which included Hannah Arendt, was profoundly dissatisfied with German politics. "We young students did not read the newspapers in those years," Arendt recalled. "George Grosz's cartoons seemed to us not satire but realistic reportage: We knew those types; they were all around us." Steadman likewise hit the mark by overshooting it. His most famous illustrations would appear in *Rolling Stone*, but they bore little resemblance to psychedelic posters or other hippie art. Drawing on the Art Nouveau, Dada, and Pop traditions, those posters were more likely to evoke a sense of "cosmic initiation." Steadman, however, had no interest in psychedelic drugs or the occult as such. Authority was the mask of violence, and satire was a way to retaliate and change things for the better. "The only thing of value is the thing you cannot say," he said in a 2013 interview. "But you can draw it."

In 1969, Steadman visited New York City and drew the people he encountered on skid row, which he described as "a museum of misery and desperation." What he saw did not endear him to America. "I don't think he even liked the idea of this country, much less the reality" Thompson said later. While staying with friends in the Hamptons, Steadman received a call from Donald Goddard, an Englishman and former *New York Times* editor who was serving as *Scanlan's* managing editor. Steadman accepted the Kentucky Derby assignment and stopped at Goddard's apartment on the way to the airport. Having left his ink and colors in the taxi cab, Steadman borrowed lipstick and make-up materials from Goddard's wife, who worked for Revlon. "They were the ultimate in assimilated flesh color and, bizarrely, those Revlon samples were the birth of Gonzo art," Steadman wrote later. After meeting Thompson in Louisville, Steadman sketched steadily. In his memoir, he recalled Thompson chastising him for the grotesque quality of his illustrations. "You scumbag!" Thomson said over breakfast on their last day in Louisville. "This is Kentucky, not Skid Row. I love these people. They are my friends, and you treated them like scum." Yet Thompson made his companion part of his article, even including a scene in which he reprimands Steadman for his filthy habit of drawing.

If Thompson rebuked Steadman in Louisville, he consistently maintained that the illustrations were far better than the story he filed. Over the years, he also offered significant insight into Steadman's work and process. "He catches things," Thompson noted. "Using a sort of venomous, satirical approach, he exaggerates the two or three things that horrify him in a scene or situation." That form of attention stimulated Thompson. "He gives me a perspective that I wouldn't normally have because he's shocked at things I tend to take for granted." For that reason, Thompson began to seek out or create conditions that would alarm Steadman. "His best drawings come out of situations where he's been most anguished," Thompson said. "So I deliberately put him into shocking situations when I work with him." Many of Thompson's remarks about Steadman applied equally well to himself. "His view of reality is not entirely normal," Thompson said. "Ralph sees through the glass very darkly. He doesn't merely render a scene, he interprets it, from his own point of view." That effort, Thompson also noted, was difficult to sustain. One couldn't expect "a mind like Ralph's to stay up on the wire *all the time;* it's too fucking painful, even when you do it in short doses." Especially over time, Thompson would have even more difficulty performing on the high wire. Steadman also recognized a kinship between his work and Thompson's. "I think what he saw in our connection was somebody that somehow saw the thing in pictures that he saw in his work." That chemistry, Steadman believed, made Gonzo possible.

After the race, Thompson repaired to New York City. By that time, he told Lynn Nesbit, he hadn't slept for six days. He also could not stop thinking about the events at Kent State University, which had boiled over that week. Students were protesting the US invasion of Cambodia, which President Nixon had announced before the weekend. Black students were pushing for increased admissions, others were trying to shut down the ROTC program, and Jerry Rubin had given a speech on campus earlier that month urging students to kill their parents. "And I mean that quite literally," Rubin said, "because until you're ready to kill your parents, you're not ready to change this country. Our parents are our first oppressors."

Kent State was one of many campuses experiencing such protests, and tensions elsewhere were running even higher. The previous year, police used deadly force to disperse an unruly crowd in Berkeley. Governor Reagan maintained that permissive college administrators, not the police, killed bystander James Rector. As he ran for reelection, Reagan did not shy away from more violence. "If it's to be a bloodbath, let it be now," he said four days before Kent State exploded. "No more appeasement." As the temperature was rising at Kent State, Attorney General John Mitchell ordered the Pentagon to station four thousand National Guard troops in New Haven, where Yale students had mobilized to support Black Panthers about to go on trial. Meanwhile, President Nixon disparaged campus protestors. "You know, you see these bums, you know, blowing up the campuses," he told the press. "Listen, the boys that are on college campuses today are the luckiest people in the world, going to great universities, and here they are, burning up the books." After Kent State, Nixon's top aide noted privately that he "obviously realizes but won't admit, his 'bums' remark very harmful." Yet the president's insult also validated the anger and resentment many Americans felt for campus activists.

The day before the Kentucky Derby, Kent State protestors surrounded the ROTC building and eventually set it on fire. When firefighters arrived, some protestors interfered with their efforts. The next morning, the governor arrived by helicopter and told the press he would "eradicate the problem." Monday classes were interrupted by bomb threats and outdoor demonstrations, which the governor had forbidden. Students threw rocks at guardsmen, who responded by marching up a slope and returning fire with tear gas canisters. They were approaching a fence, however, and had to reverse course as students continued to throw rocks and shout at them. Several guardsmen suddenly turned around, dropped to one knee, and shot at a cluster of students in a parking lot on the other side of the fence. Within thirteen seconds, thirteen students were down, most of them bystanders. One was paralyzed, and four were dead. A Gallup poll found that 58 percent of Americans blamed the victims, while only 11 percent thought the National Guard was at fault.

In his room at the Royalton Hotel near Times Square, Thompson brooded over the bloodshed. But the clock was ticking. Hinckle had already laid out the other stories, Steadman's illustrations were finished, and the deadline was Sunday. "I would lie in the bathtub at this weird hotel," Thompson recalled. "I had a suite with everything I wanted—except I couldn't leave." Three days later, he began to tear pages out of his notebook and feed them into the telecopier. Back in San Francisco, Hinckle received Thompson's fragments in Howard Gossage's restored firehouse on Pacific Avenue. From there, Hinckle walked over to Columbus Avenue and pulled into Tosca Cafe, the North Beach bar across the street from City Lights. Sitting alone in a large red booth, he assembled and reassembled the text. He later compared his editorial task to finishing a jigsaw puzzle without access to the picture on the box cover. Thompson made his deadline, but only in what he considered "the foulest and cheapest way, like Oakland's unclean touchdown against Miami." Hinckle was elated, but Thompson felt only grief and shame.

Hinckle knew that Thompson's basic approach was hardly new. Many writers had blended fact with fiction, placed themselves at the center of their stories, and presented them as truthful accounts. Nevertheless, Hinckle maintained, "*Scanlan's* version of the genre, powered by Hunter's pills, activated a dormant volcano in the geography of contemporary journalism."

> What distinguished the Kentucky Derby piece from the earlier 50s and 60s first-person New Journalism pioneered by Terry Southern and perfected by Tom Wolfe was Hunter's hallucinatory stimulant-fueled novelistic attention, on a sporting assignment, given not to the horses but to the outdoor loony bin of boozed-up burgher spectators.

Hinckle was correct that Thompson made Southern and Wolfe seem tame by comparison, but the Kentucky Derby piece had one other asset— Steadman's illustrations. When those arrived the next morning, Hinckle knew he had a "game-changer."

.   .   .

"The Kentucky Derby Is Decadent and Depraved" begins with Thompson's arrival in his hometown airport. In the lounge, he meets a garrulous visitor from Houston named Jimbo, who chides him for ordering a margarita.

> "Look." The man tapped me on the arm to make sure I was listening. "I know this Derby crowd, I come here every year, and let me tell you one thing I've learned—this is no town to be giving people the impression you're some kind of faggot. Not in public, anyway. Shit, they'll roll you in a minute, knock you in the head and take every goddamn cent you have."

Jimbo's insult plays out at two levels. The obvious affront is to Thompson's manliness, but his local knowledge also exceeds Jimbo's, making the visitor's presumption an additional offense. Thompson affably changes his drink order and begins to exact his revenge. When Jimbo asks about his work, Thompson replies that he is a *Playboy* photographer whose assignment is to document the Black Panther riot that will disrupt the Derby. It was not the last time Thompson would deploy that trope, which he used to arouse White fear. He adds alarming (and imaginary) detail after detail, leading Jimbo finally to cry out, "Oh . . . Jesus! What in the name of God is happening in this country!" Later, Thompson reflects on his performance. "I felt a little guilty about jangling that poor bugger's brains with that evil fantasy. But what the hell? Anybody who wanders around the world saying 'Hell yes, I'm from Texas,' deserves whatever happens to him." Teasing the rubes would become another Gonzo staple.

Thompson picks up the local newspaper and scans the headlines: "Nixon Sends GIs into Cambodia to Hit Reds" and "4,000 U.S. Troops Deployed Near Yale as Tension Grows Over Panther Protests." He also mentions another story notable for its absence. "There was no mention of any trouble brewing at a university in Ohio called Kent State," he notes tersely. The brevity of these references belies their significance. Connected to the Derby by coincidence, the stories provide an important backdrop for the Louisville scene and point to an even more important truth: Whatever Thompson experiences at Churchill Downs pales in comparison to more lethal forms of American mayhem.

Thompson acquires a rental car, which he dubs the Pontiac Ballbuster. (Careful attention to cars would also characterize Gonzo journalism.) He then turns his attention to securing a room, acquiring his press credentials, and locating Steadman. He finds his partner at the racetrack, their credentials in hand, then walks the grounds and plots his strategy. Unlike most of the press, he and Steadman "didn't give a hoot in hell what was happening on the track. We had come there to watch the *real* beasts perform." Thompson scans the infield and describes the debauchery to come.

> Now, looking down from the press box, I pointed to the huge grassy meadow enclosed by the track. "That whole thing," I said, "will be jammed with people: fifty thousand or so, and most of them staggering drunk. It's a fantastic scene—thousands of people fainting, crying, copulating, trampling each other, and fighting with broken whiskey bottles."

In narrative terms, Thompson's prediction works better than his musings in *Hell's Angels*. When describing what could have happened at Bass Lake, for example, his fanciful deviations from the facts on the ground were necessarily limited. At Churchill Downs, however, Thompson can offer a description of what he has witnessed, an embellished version of that description, or even a hellish prophecy. Moreover, his prediction works as explication. By educating Steadman, Thompson also sets the stage for his readers. Having frightened Steadman with his prediction, however, Thompson assures him that he is kidding. Besides, he adds, he is prepared to pump Mace into the crowd at the first sign of trouble. In effect, Thompson plans to solve the problem of mayhem with more potent mayhem.

Thompson then describes the search for a certain face, one he associates with the Derby. Steadman had already made several good sketches, but they needed something specific for their lead drawing.

> It was a face I'd seen a thousand times at every Derby I'd ever been to. I saw it, in my head, as the mask of the whiskey gentry—a pretentious mix of booze, failed dreams, and a terminal identity crisis: the inevitable result of too much inbreeding in a closed and ignorant culture.

That mask, he adds, is a symbol of "the whole doomed atavistic culture that makes the Derby what it is." On their way to dinner that night, Thompson continues to play the prodigal by briefing Steadman on the dangers of the local culture. "You should keep in mind," he says, "that almost everybody you talk to from now on will be drunk. People who seem very pleasant at first might suddenly swing at you for no reason." Once again, Thompson's warning also prepares readers for the big day.

That night marks the beginning of "a vicious, drunken nightmare." The next morning, Thompson rebukes Steadman for sketching his brother over dinner. When Steadman maintains that his caricatures offend no one in England, Thompson cuts him off. "Fuck England. This is Middle America. These people regard what you're doing to them as a brutal, bilious insult." Thompson blames the sketches for the social awkwardness at dinner the previous night, but Steadman suggests that spraying the headwaiter with Mace might have been the real problem. Thompson concedes the point and tries to call a truce. "Yeah . . . well, okay . . . Let's just figure we fucked up about equally on that one. But from now on, let's try to be careful when we're around people I know. You won't sketch them, and I won't Mace them. We'll just try to relax and get drunk." "Right," Steadman agrees. "We'll go native."

When race day arrives, Thompson presents a series of jagged impressions from the scene at Churchill Downs. These are almost certainly the raw notes that Thompson thought would doom the article, and they resemble what Joan Didion decried as "flash pictures in variable sequence." For Didion, such disconnected images fell well short of finished narrative, which she regarded as an important survival strategy, but Thompson's fragments effectively put across what his booze-soaked narrator was registering at the track. As the race begins, the narrative focus returns. Thompson quickly summarizes the race results and returns to the press box for more drinking. "The rest of that day blurs into madness," he says. "And all the next day and night. Such horrible things occurred that I can't even bring myself to put them down in print."

When a haggard Steadman wakes him the next morning at the motel, Thompson watches him stumble toward the beer bucket and open a can of malt liquor.

> My eyes had finally opened enough for me to focus on the mirror
> across the room, and I was stunned at the shock of recognition. For a
> confused instant I thought that Ralph had brought somebody with
> him—a model for that one special face we'd been looking for. There he

was, by God—a puffy, drink-ravaged, disease-ridden caricature . . . like an awful cartoon version of an old snapshot in some once-proud mother's photo album. It was the face we'd been looking for—and it was, of course, my own.

The reflection dissociates the narrator from himself, which makes the shock of recognition even more powerful. The epiphany also alters the piece's narrative mode. When the two men depart for the airport in the Pontiac Ballbuster, the story switches to the present tense and third-person narration; now the characters are called "the journalist" and "his passenger." A radio bulletin reports that the National Guard is massacring students at Kent State and that Nixon is still bombing Cambodia. The passenger has removed most of his clothing, which he holds out the window to rid it of Mace. "His eyes are bright red," the narrator notes, "and his face and chest are soaked with the beer he's been using to rinse the awful chemical off his flesh. The front of his woolen trousers are soaked with vomit; his body is racked with fits of coughing and choking sobs." The transformation is complete; a long weekend in Middle America has debauched the innocent English visitor.

At the airport, the journalist shoves the passenger out of the car and showers him with epithets—worthless faggot, twisted pig-fucker, scum-sucking foreign geek. "We can do without your kind in Kentucky," he finally snarls. The journalist is no longer the worldly scribe who slyly jangles Jimbo's brain. Rather, he is the drink-ravaged man in the motel-room mirror, a synecdoche for the Ugly America that decimates Southeast Asia, murders students who protest that crime, and then blames the slain students for their own deaths. The man in the mirror might even vote for Richard Nixon. In the meantime, Thompson sees decadence and depravity, and they are him.

. . .

Well after submitting the piece, Thompson confessed to Donald Goddard that he could not "look back on that effort with anything but shame and horror." He thanked Goddard and hoped that Steadman's drawings would redeem the piece "because the writing is lame bullshit." When Thompson saw the June issue of *Scanlan's*, he offered a similar assessment to Steadman.

The article is useless, except for the flashes of style & tone it captures—but I suspect you & I are the only ones who can really appreciate it. The drawings were fine, although I think they fucked up the layout—as usual—quite badly. They also cut about one-third of the article, in

> addition to the 4,000 or so words that Don & I cut in NY. In all, a bad
> show, & I'm sorry it wasn't better. Maybe next time. I'd like nothing
> better than to work with you on one of those strange binges again, & to
> that end I'll tell my agent to bill us as a package—for good or ill.

But Thompson misjudged the article's reception. As soon as it appeared, he
began to receive letters and calls. "People were calling it a tremendous
breakthrough in journalism, a stroke of genius. And I thought, *What in the
shit?*" One of the letters was from Bill Cardoso, who described the piece
as "totally Gonzo." Thompson also heard Cardoso use that term while covering the 1968 New Hampshire primary. Its origins have been debated ever
since, but whatever its provenance, Thompson began to apply that label to
his own work.

William Kennedy later described the Kentucky Derby piece as an effective way for Thompson to wed fiction with journalism. It was a wonderful
story and departure piece, he thought, the first one that used "all his fictional talent to describe and anatomize those characters and just make it all
up. I'm sure some of it was real." Well after winning the Pulitzer Prize for
Ironweed (1983), Kennedy also traced the arc of Thompson's Gonzo journalism. "In time he found a way to turn himself into this singular first-
person itinerant journalist who was interesting no matter what he wrote
about," Kennedy noted. "He put himself into the picture, and he became
the story."

If the Kentucky Derby piece was a milestone in Thompson's career, it
also marked a decline in his stamina and craftsmanship. "This was no longer
the Hunter who would sit down and rewrite a piece three times," Sandy
said. "He could get out a page, maybe, or a paragraph, a really neat, wild
paragraph—and then some gibberish. He couldn't come out with a full
piece." That challenge, however, was part of a larger and more complex
pattern. Thompson's life, work, and persona were recombining in a way
that was simultaneously degenerate and generative. William Kennedy
recalled that Thompson's early goal was to create new forms.

> And that's what he did. Not only forms of writing, but forms of
> living—and the two fed each other. The more he behaved in a radical
> way, the more radical his writing could be, and the more he had to write
> about. Nobody could imitate Hunter, because nobody had his
> personality or stamina. It was a spectacular roundelay.

After years of experimentation, Thompson had created not only a remarkable piece of journalism, but also a new model of authorship. Like Jack
London, he would soon come to believe that his biggest asset was the char-

acter he had built up. In London's case, the constructed nature of that character did not mean it was subject to revision. If he misunderstood what his readers valued in his work, London told his editor, he would quit writing before abandoning that character. So, too, with Thompson. His persona, which was fixed to the new genre he was creating, became his most valuable asset. Indeed, it would eventually eclipse his literary output and outlast his most productive period.

8   Rolling Stone

By the time Thompson hit the high white note in *Scanlan's,* he had been corresponding with Jann Wenner for months. He sent his first dispatch after reading *Rolling Stone's* coverage of the Altamont disaster, which ended the Rolling Stones' 1969 tour. The Stones had missed Woodstock that summer and had not toured the United States since 1966. During that time, almost everything about rock concerts had changed, largely under the influence of the San Francisco counterculture. The Monterey Pop Festival in 1967 had paved the way for even larger outdoor rock performances, including Woodstock. Moreover, both Monterey Pop and Woodstock were accompanied by successful documentary films. Hoping to reestablish their primacy, the Rolling Stones commissioned a film to document their tour. They also promised to finish that tour with a free concert in San Francisco. The concert was originally conceived as a modest event in Golden Gate Park, but when it was billed as "Woodstock West," San Francisco officials scratched the park as a venue.

Days before the scheduled concert, the Stones were still searching for a site when a major news story emerged from Southern California: Charles Manson and his followers were arrested for murder. The police broke the case when a member of the Straight Satans, a Southern California motor-cycle gang, said that Manson had mentioned the homicides to him. To many, the Manson Family story read like a ghoulish inversion of Haight-Ashbury flower power. Psychedelic drugs, communal living, crackpot spir-ituality, and rock music weren't producing a peaceful world but instead a chaotic and murderous one.

As the nation absorbed the Manson Family horror, the Rolling Stones looked to the windswept hills of the East Bay hinterland as a site for their free concert. A businessman had recently built the Altamont Raceway there, and he hoped that the event would help his new enterprise. The show's lineup was certainly impressive. It included Santana, Jefferson Airplane, Crosby, Stills, Nash & Young, and the Grateful Dead, all of whom had performed at Woodstock. After the Dead played their set, the Rolling Stones would close the show. But the last-minute relocation made it impossible to provide adequate facilities for what turned out to be three hundred thousand spectators. Security was also a question mark, but the Rolling Stones' road manager, Sam Cutler, offered the Hell's Angels $500 worth of beer to sit near the stage and help out as needed. That stage, which was only one meter high, had been built for a different site. When the music started, the crowd surged toward it, and the Hell's Angels retaliated with pool cues, bottles, and fists. Cutler watched the bloody skirmishes with mounting horror. "Before me was the ugly truth of what we had collectively wrought, manifested in greed, blood, drug overdoses, spilled guts, and hatred," he recalled. "The peace and love generation was smashing itself to bits."

After witnessing the violence, some of which was directed at the musicians and their crew members, the Grateful Dead decided not to play. The Rolling Stones were not ready to go on, and tension mounted during the lengthy pause. When the music resumed at nightfall, the violence intensified. A young Black man from Berkeley named Meredith Hunter brandished a handgun and was swarmed by Hell's Angels; one stabbed him, several others stomped him, and he died before he was evacuated from the concert. Police used the documentary film footage to identify the killer, a Hell's Angel from San Jose who was eventually acquitted on grounds of self-defense.

In his 1973 memoir, Warren Hinckle claimed that the Altamont violence confirmed his analysis of hippie politics. Ralph Gleason, who had once praised the counterculture's Dionysian spirit, ruminated on the disaster in his *San Francisco Chronicle* column. "Is this the new community? Is this what Woodstock promised?" he asked rhetorically. "Gathered together AS a tribe, what happened? Brutality, murder, despoliation, you name it." Gleason did not see Altamont as the dark side of hippie utopianism but rather as its death knell. The following year, he wrote a related article for *Esquire*. "If the name 'Woodstock' has come to denote the flowering of one phase of the youth culture," he concluded, "'Altamont' has come the mean the end of it." Gleason also quoted Sonny Barger on the violence that day. Much of it, Barger explained, flowed from the crowd's shabby treatment of their choppers. Even Thompson was taken aback by that violence. In a letter to Silberman one month after the debacle, he remarked, "I trust you noticed the unspeakably savage public rebirth of the Hell's Angels. Did you read the coverage in *Rolling Stone?* That scene at the Altamont rock festival shames my worst fantasies; the sharks finally came home to roost."

For *Rolling Stone,* Altamont was also an opportunity. Mainstream outlets missed the story, and by investigating the concert's feckless planning and lethal violence, *Rolling Stone* landed its first National Magazine Award. (It won a second award that year for an article on the Manson Family.) Behind the scenes, much of the credit went to Gleason, who insisted that *Rolling Stone* "either go out of business right now or else cover Altamont like it was World War II." For various personal and business reasons, Wenner had been reluctant to antagonize Jagger, but the "Let It Bleed" issue was unstinting in its judgment. It described Altamont as "the product of diabolical egotism, hype, ineptitude, money, manipulation, and, at base, a fundamental lack of concern for humanity." The National Magazine Awards signaled the magazine's arrival to the world of credible journalism. They also showed that *Rolling Stone* could cover stories the mainstream press could not or would not address. As Wenner biographer Joe Hagan noted, it was an inflection point for the magazine. Wenner realized that *Rolling Stone* could become something far grander than a rock publication, something more like *Ramparts* or *New York* than *CREEM* or *Crawdaddy.*

The achievement wasn't lost on Thompson, whose letter to Wenner opened with high praise. "Your Altamont coverage comes close to being the best journalism I can remember reading, by anybody," he wrote. After comparing the magazine favorably to two precursors, Art Kunkin's *Los Angeles Free Press* and Paul Krassner's *The Realist,* he shifted quickly to earthy advice: "Kunkin and Krassner never came close to what you're doing . . . so don't fuck it up with pompous bullshit; the demise of *R.S.* would leave a nasty hole." The tone of the letter reflected Thompson's sense of himself as an established writer and savvy media veteran. Wenner affirmed that status in his reply. "Having once read your *Angels* book in galley proof forms (stole them when I worked at *Ramparts*) and having really dug it in its precut form, I've been a fan of yours," he wrote. "Glad you are now a fan of ours." He invited Thompson to contribute something to *Rolling Stone,* and Thompson replied that he wanted to write about Aspen politics. Wenner encouraged the idea, sparking a more sustained correspondence.

That spring, *Rolling Stone* staffer John Lombardi invited Thompson to the magazine's San Francisco office. The two men had not met, but three years earlier, Lombardi published Thompson's elegy for Lionel Olay in *The Distant Drummer.* Hoping to upgrade the quality of *Rolling Stone's* writing, Lombardi and Wenner met Thompson in the office on a Saturday. When he finally arrived, Lombardi described him as "a bizarre sight."

He was wearing his famous "gook" Hawaiian shirt and carrying a six-pack of beer, which he didn't offer to anyone. He had a little case under his arm, a straw bag or something with all kinds of things coming out of it: papers, string, very strange-looking. And he wore a Dynell wig; a cheap gray lady's wig that he kept taking off, straightening, putting back on. And his sunglasses, which he did not remove. And, of course, the cigarette holder.

Thompson held forth for the entire meeting, pausing only to relieve himself. During one of those breaks, Wenner said to Lombardi, "I know I am supposed to be the youth representative in this culture . . . but what the fuck is that?"

Neither Wenner nor Thompson could have predicted the significance of their new relationship, but each had something the other needed. *Rolling Stone* was growing but not yet solvent, and Wenner was facing an internal revolt. His staff writers wanted more editorial independence, and some suspected Wenner of tweaking the album reviews to appease the record labels. For his part, Wenner thought his writers were dragging *Rolling Stone* toward radical politics. "Our core mission was the purpose of the music," he said later. "I didn't like their particular politics, and I wanted to do what I wanted to do, which was about music." There was another wrinkle as well. As Wenner's staff decried the deaths at Kent State, he was collecting money from the major labels to keep the magazine alive. The implicit understanding was that *Rolling Stone* would continue to focus on music, not radical politics. Some of the money came from Xerox executive Max Palevsky, which led some activists to charge that Wenner had betrayed the revolution. By the end of 1970, many staff members left or were fired. One described the situation as "a ship jumping off a sinking rat."

Thompson was by no means a typical *Rolling Stone* contributor. Especially in the magazine's early years, Wenner recruited many fellow students at the University of California, Berkeley. Although Thompson acquired a mail-order Doctor of Divinity certificate from the Universal Life Church, he never earned a college degree. He was also older than most of the other writers and an Air Force veteran. Nevertheless, Lombardi and Wenner thought Thompson's iconoclasm and humor might click with *Rolling Stone*'s audience. Thompson wanted to write about politics, but he would never be mistaken for a revolutionary; like Wenner, he was drawn to Kennedy-style Democrats and would eventually support George McGovern and Jimmy Carter. More important, he added a touch of New Journalism to *Rolling Stone* and pushed it toward the general interest category.

If Thompson was an outlier at *Rolling Stone*, the magazine also differed from his normal outlets. Its connection to *Ramparts* was a positive, but

Gleason was not a fan of his work, and it was not yet clear that *Rolling Stone* was a suitable home for Thompson. As the Altamont coverage showed, the magazine's unique editorial formula included a serious side, but even after Thompson became its star contributor, he told Wenner that *Rolling Stone* had yet to reach a large potential readership that "doesn't give a flying fuck what the Jackson Five eats for breakfast." Yet each man was happy to use the other, especially in the start-up culture that characterized *Rolling Stone*.

. . .

As the courtship with Wenner played out, Thompson assembled his story on Aspen politics. The previous year, he had persuaded 29-year-old attorney Joe Edwards to run for mayor. Edwards made his name in Aspen by filing a lawsuit on behalf of hippies arrested for vagrancy; his clients prevailed after the police magistrate railed against hippies in open court. For Thompson, the Edwards campaign promised to replicate David Pierce's experience in Richmond, where the young attorney challenged the powers that be and became mayor. It also reflected the lesson of other bohemian enclaves. "What happened in the Haight echoed earlier scenes in North Beach and the Village," Thompson wrote, "and it proved, once again, the basic futility of seizing turf you can't control." Pitkin County he hoped, would be different. Edwards lost the election by six votes, but Thompson was encouraged.

In 1970, Thompson decided to run for Pitkin County sheriff on what he called the Freak Party ticket. Thompson later said the events he witnessed in Chicago prompted the decision to run.

> I'm still not sure what launched me. Probably it was Chicago—that brain-raping week in August of '68. I went to the Democratic convention as a journalist and returned a raving beast. For me, that week in Chicago was far worse than the worst bad acid trip I'd even heard rumors about. It permanently altered my brain chemistry, and my first new idea—when I finally calmed down—was an absolute conviction there was no possibility for any personal truce, for me, in a nation that could hatch and be proud of a malignant monster like Chicago.

His key issue was drug enforcement, but he was also running against Aspen's rapid growth and Nixon. In one radio advertisement, James Salter put across the basic message.

> Hunter Thompson is a moralist posing as an immoralist. Nixon is an immoralist disguised as a moralist. There will be thieves and auto

wrecks in Aspect whoever gets elected. But Hunter represents
something wholly alien towards the other candidates. Ideas. And a
sympathy towards the young, generous, grass-oriented society, which is
making the only serious effort to face the technological nightmare
we've created. The only thing against him is he's a visionary. He wants
too pure a world.

Convinced that many voters shared his contempt for conventional
candidates, Thompson framed the election as a local race with national
significance.

Thompson's campaign was deeply irreverent but not a prank. His so-
called mescaline platform called for Aspen's streets to be ripped up and
replaced with sod. He also proposed that Aspen be renamed "Fat City" in an
effort to thwart "greed heads, land-rapers, and other human jackals from
capitalizing on the name 'Aspen.'" As for the sort of drug enforcement he
favored, Thompson declared that it would be "the general philosophy of the
Sheriff's office that no drug worth taking should be sold for money." In a
post-election letter to Carey McWilliams, he noted this his drug tastes were
discussed openly, and that he had refused to say he would stop taking mescaline if elected. Despite his outlandish campaign rhetoric, however,
Thompson remained cool and on point during the campaign's only public
debate. A third candidate refused to participate, calling it a sideshow, but
Thompson easily upstaged the incumbent.

To support his campaign, Thompson approached graphic artist Tom
Benton and suggested that they collaborate on a wall poster. It was mostly
a campaign tool, but they also hoped to fill the gap left by the *Aspen
Illustrated News*, the liberal weekly that folded in February 1970.
Thompson, Benton, and Edwards formed the Meat Possum Press, whose
board of directors included Oscar Acosta, lawyer John Clancy, William
Kennedy, and journalist Loren Jenkins. As their first official act, they purchased a fifty-millimeter flare gun, which they fired in town at night. "It
was wonderful," Benton said. "I still have the gun." In March, they began
distributing wall posters on the street. The first number targeted Robert
Delaney, the attorney for Pitkin County, whose business ventures included
an ore mine, slag heap, trailer court, and sewage plant. After fourteen years
of service, Delaney resigned amid conflict-of-interest charges, including the
manipulation of county zoning laws to benefit himself.

Thompson touted the *Aspen Wallposter* to his entire network. He gave
copies to Wenner, McWilliams, and *San Francisco Chronicle* columnist
Herb Caen. He attempted to recruit *Washington Post* columnist Nicholas
Von Hoffman and ran a Steadman illustration of Richard Nixon. He also

promised to send Hinckle a copy of his latest work. "And if the Wallposter name rings a bell," he told Hinckle, "well, I'll never deny it." In the meantime, Hinckle published Thompson's review of *Police Chief* magazine in *Scanlan's*. Thompson, who began reading *Police Chief* to stay current on new weapons, used Raoul Duke as a pseudonym. He later explained that he employed it regularly as "a vehicle for quotations for things no one else would say." In the final issue of *Scanlan's*, Thompson plugged the *Aspen Wallposter*, which he said was "conceived more as a political tool than either a newspaper or a poster—but it has evolved, very quickly, into a combination of all three. And on that basis we intend to run the bugger full bore for as long as there's room to run."

Less than three weeks before the election, Aspen police captain Glen Ricks received an anonymous handwritten letter about Thompson. Ricks, who was also the GOP candidate for sheriff, forwarded the letter to the FBI office in Denver. It was ostensibly written in Louisville, but the envelope had an Aspen postmark.

Dear Mr. Ricks:

   I think but do not know that Hunter Thompson has a police record in Louisville. He was *the* bad boy of our neighborhood when he was high school and college-age—it would probably be around 1954-, 1955-6 or 7. At that time, he lived on Ransdell Ave.
   I would sign my name but am afraid I might be sued. I am interested in good government.

The letter landed in Thompson's file, which the bureau opened in 1967. At that time, Thompson subscribed to *People's World*, the weekly Communist newspaper published in San Francisco. When interviewed by the FBI, his postal carrier said Thompson received "a lot of quality magazines" in addition to *People's World*. The bureau then tracked his subscription to Woody Creek and interviewed a local shopkeeper there. She furnished information about his housing arrangements, his work in South America, and his appearances to promote *Hell's Angels*. She also saw some "very obscene publications" come through the mail for him from an unknown publishing company in New York. Although an FBI memo noted that the letter from Kentucky contained "information concerning THOMPSON which may be of value in the future," it appears to be the final entry in his file, which also included *Aspen Wallposters* and articles about his campaign.

In the end, Thompson won a majority of votes in Aspen, but he lost the county as a whole by some twenty percentage points. In his concession speech, delivered with a wig perched precariously on his shaved head,

Thompson channeled Richard Nixon: "This is my last press conference. You won't have Hunter Thompson to kick around anymore, you motherfuckers." In his *Rolling Stone* article, he noted that similar campaigns were likewise unsuccessful. Oscar Acosta pulled almost 108,000 votes but lost the sheriff's race in Los Angeles County. Thompson's candidate for Pitkin County coroner, Bill Noonan, was defeated, as was Ned Ware, who ran unsuccessfully for county supervisor but retained his Aspen city council seat. Back in the Bay Area, Yippie Stew Albert lost his bid for Alameda County sheriff while collecting sixty-five thousand votes.

Another Yippie, George Kimball, ran for sheriff in Douglas County, Kansas. He and Thompson had a bit of history. The son of an army colonel, Kimball entered the University of Kansas on an officer-training scholarship but was expelled for picketing the local draft board. He then moved to New York City and worked for the Scott Meredith Literary Agency, where Thompson met him. When Olympia Press published *Only Skin Deep*, Kimball's erotic novel, publisher Maurice Girodias offered Thompson $500 for a ten-word blurb. Thompson refused to endorse what he called "that heap of deranged offal that Kimball has coughed up in the shameful guise of art." He also said he was planning to visit New York City "to beat the living shit out of Kimball. *Only Skin Deep* is a vicious and intolerable mockery of the whole filth industry." Girodias promptly used the second sentence as a blurb. After a stint at the Iowa Writers' Workshop, Kimball returned to Kansas to run against the sheriff who arrested him in 1965. He won the uncontested Democratic primary but was beaten decisively in the general election. After that, Thompson recommended him to Wenner, but Kimball landed at the *Boston Phoenix*, where he eventually became a renowned sportswriter.

Despite Thompson's defeat at the polls, his campaign furnished a new and exciting platform. He communicated some of that excitement in a letter to Silberman.

> On election night, our Jerome Hotel headquarters was a scene out of some other world. Every freak in Christendom was there, it seemed, including those from *Life, Harper's, LOOK*, and a film crew from London—along with the camera crew from Woodstock and a bona fide Swami from India.

Thompson wondered whether the campaign could serve as the linchpin for the nonfiction book he still owed Random House.

> Maybe "The Battle of Aspen" might be a working title for a book that would actually delve into politics far beyond Aspen . . . all the way back to New Hampshire in early '68, Chicago, election day in L.A. and all the

other things. Because all that really led to the scene that just happened here. Without Chicago, I would never have run for Sheriff—or even launched the Joe Edwards campaign.

Thompson hadn't quite convinced himself, much less Silberman, that his book idea was sound. Once again, he put the onus on his editor.

> If you want to go with "The Battle of Aspen," that decision will amount to far more than just a working title. It will amount to that definitive framework that we've lacked ever since you shackled me with that nebulous "American Dream" bullshit. Which has hamstrung me ever since.

That plan was never enacted, but Thompson's campaign marked a new and more direct form of political engagement as well as a significant shift in his public persona. Before settling in Colorado only three years earlier, he had never entertained the idea of running for public office. Several peers, however, had entered the ring. Thompson later distinguished his bid from Norman Mailer's quixotic mayoral campaign in New York City. Instead, he likened it to Robert Scheer's 1966 Congressional race in the East Bay, where the *Ramparts* editor almost unseated the incumbent in the Democratic Party primary. Four years after Scheer's loss, left-wing challenger Ron Dellums beat the incumbent and became a key voice in the Congressional Black Caucus. Six years after Thompson's loss, Aspen elected his friend, Dick Kienast, to serve as sheriff. A former college instructor with a graduate degree in theology, Kienast and his staff became known as "Dick Dove and the Deputies of Love." He was succeeded in 1987 by Bob Braudis, another Thompson friend, who served for twenty-four years. Pitkin County was a microcosm at best, but Thompson's intervention there was significant.

· · ·

The same year Thompson campaigned for sheriff, Kate Millett's *Sexual Politics* was published. Based on her Columbia University dissertation, it coolly surveyed the objectification of women in the fiction of D.H. Lawrence, Henry Miller, and Norman Mailer. Although Millett credited those authors for their overall achievements, she selected and analyzed sex scenes that, when presented sequentially, seemed more ridiculous than erotic. She failed to attribute some quotations to characters rather than their creators, and she made little effort to contextualize the passages in the broader sweep of each author's work. Yet the book's main argument—that fictional representations of sex had a political dimension—

came across forcefully. The book received a strong endorsement from *New York Times* critic Christopher Lehmann-Haupt, who devoted two consecutive columns to it.

Mailer responded to Millett's book with a sprawling *Harper's* magazine article called "The Prisoner of Sex." His third-person narrator, whom he called "the prizewinner," realized he was "apparently being chewed half to death by a squadron of enraged Amazons, an honor guard of revolutionary (if we could only see them) vaginas." Reading a few lines of Millett's article in the *New American Review,* the prizewinner claimed, "was enough to think she wrote like a gossip columnist." Later, Mailer described "the land of Millett" as "a barren and mediocre terrain, its flora reminiscent of a Ph.D. tract, its roads a narrow argument, and its horizon low." He then developed the trope with gusto.

> So her land was a foul and dreary place to cross, a stingy country whose treacherous inhabitants (were they the very verbs and phrases of her book?) jeered at difficulties which were often the heart of the matter, the food served at every inn was a can of ideological lard, a grit and granite of thesis-factories turned out aggregates of concept-jargon on every ridge, stacks of such clauses fed the sky with smoke, and musical instruments full of the spirit of intellectual flatulence ran in the river, and bloody ground steamed with the corpse of every amputated quote. Everywhere were signs that men were guilty and women must win.

Mailer's rebuttal pitted men against women, but it also rehearsed the ancient feud between poets and philosophers. It did not refute Millett's argument so much as overwhelm it with a cascade of images, associations, and flourishes linked to his favorite themes. His performance, which Pete Hamill later compared to a bebop jazz solo, ran 47 double-columned pages that appeared the following year as a 240-page book. But the portents of Millett's study were clear enough. Feminist critics would henceforth scrutinize fiction for evidence of misogyny and patriarchy.

The literary lineage Thompson had constructed for himself was now a high-profile target. Miller was figured as a tool of the patriarchy, not a liberationist, and Mailer was routinely described as a sexist. Warren Hinckle did not escape unscathed; two years earlier, one magazine named him "Male Chauvinist of the Month." Under his leadership, both *Ramparts* and *Scanlan's* exuded men's house culture, but the bellwether for men's magazines was still *Playboy,* which interviewed Thompson in 1974. Its circulation peaked at 5.6 million readers the next year and then fell steadily for decades. *Rolling Stone* was another holdout. "It was a guy's magazine," said editorial assistant Christine Doudna. "It was a very *male sensibility,* always." Even after Marianne Partridge became the magazine's first female editor, that sensibility was literally on display in the office. "There was a sign over Jann's secretary's desk in huge letters: 'Boys' Club,'" said Barbara Downey (later Barbara Landau). "I'll never forget that."

Although Thompson rarely visited the San Francisco office, he was an important influence on its mood and temper. Staff member Sarah Lazin described headquarters as "a rollicking male culture, spearheaded by Hunter and Hunter wannabes." When Thompson did appear in the office, his mischief both amused and exasperated the staff. In a memo written after she found a smashed telephone, scattered papers, and several albums missing, Lazin implored Wenner to intervene with Thompson. "There are those who see Hunter's destructive tendencies as cute, and then there are those who have to clean up," she wrote. "If you could head him off toward some other pass, we'd appreciate it."

If the rise of feminist criticism boded ill for Thompson, his professional future was uncertain for other reasons as well. His dream of becoming a novelist seemed more remote than ever. It was unclear how long New Journalism would remain in favor, and his book project was foundering. His primary outlets were *Scanlan's*, which was faltering, and a fledgling rock magazine in San Francisco. True to his youthful manifesto, Thompson had forsaken security and complacency, but his professional success, or even survival, was by no means assured.

· · ·

By the time Thompson's second piece appeared in *Rolling Stone*, he was listed as a contributing editor. Instead of following up on the Freak Power story, which he still considered the framework for his forthcoming book, he turned his attention to Los Angeles. The article he produced was a rare detour into relatively straight journalism on an important issue.

The idea grew directly out of his contact with Oscar Acosta, whose post-Aspen wanderings led him to Los Angeles. His sister reportedly encouraged him to use his legal acumen to assist the emergent Chicano movement there. She also called his attention to *La Raza*, the underground Chicano newspaper that Raul Ruiz later turned into a monthly magazine. Born in El Paso, Ruiz moved to Los Angeles with his family and studied history at California State University, Los Angeles. A radical professor introduced him to Carey McWilliams's *North From Mexico* (1949), a history of Latinos in the southwest, which transformed Ruiz's understanding of historical agency. Ruiz committed himself to *el movimiento* as a journalist, activist, and instructor at San Fernando Valley State College. In a similar way, *La Raza* transformed

Acosta. He contacted the movement's leaders, who initially suspected he was a police plant. Compared to his peers, he was more educated and comfortable with the White world, and his relationship with Thompson was grounds for concern. Nevertheless, Acosta began to associate himself with the movement and the street activists who were drawn to it.

Throughout this period, Thompson and Acosta maintained an active correspondence. Thompson said he was too busy to read Acosta's novel-in-progress, but he recommended cutting it to fifty thousand words and writing another book about the Chicano movement in Los Angeles. That project, Thompson maintained, would help Acosta place the novel. Thompson, who had pursued the same strategy, also urged Acosta to be less didactic. He could sell the movement book only if he removed "that goddamn missionary instinct" from his writing. When Acosta furnished an outline for a book about Brown Power the following month, Thompson sent it to his editor at Ballantine but predicted that "damn few publishers are going to want a flat-out piece of bugle-blast propaganda." In another letter, Thompson suggested that Acosta write a three-thousand-word article and send it to Carey McWilliams. If McWilliams ran the piece in *The Nation*, Thompson reasoned, Acosta would be in better position to place the book. That plan was also plucked out of Thompson's playbook.

Acosta was busy on other fronts as well. Shortly after the assassination of Dr. King in April 1968, he described his mission to Thompson.

> Hunter, I came here to blow minds, as usual, and as a secondary thing to stir the Mexican-American Liberation. It has happened all too fast. The slogans have become reality. And now with the King thing fucking our heads, it is not inconceivable that this largest of cities could be on fire before this letter reaches you. I'm scared shitless because the anger within me looks forward to seeing the fear in their faces . . . and the burning.

Convinced that the frenzy Acosta described was consuming him, Thompson urged Acosta to buy a ranch on the western coast of Mexico. "Get hold of a good green hillside looking down on the sea and build something on it," he said. "Make a decent human place where people can come and really feel peace—if only for a few hours, before rushing out again to that stinking TV world." It was a Mexican version of Thompson's American Dream, but Acosta had no desire for peace and quiet.

Meanwhile, Chicano activists were organizing a student strike to protest unequal conditions in the Los Angeles Unified School District. Scholars would later recognize that effort as the beginning of the urban Chicano movement in Los Angeles and California. Some fifteen thousand students in seven high schools participated in the so-called blowouts of March 1968. Because school funding was based on attendance, the walkouts hit the school district in the pocketbook. Later that month, a committee representing the students submitted a list of demands to the school board. The board denied them, and the committee members walked out of the meeting. Three days later, police arrested thirteen movement organizers on felony conspiracy charges to disrupt public education.

For Acosta, the arrests furnished an opportunity to contribute his services. He offered to represent the defendants and soon became counsel for the so-called Eastside 13. "Oscar popped up out of nowhere offering to help," one defendant recalled decades later. According to this account, Acosta had been waiting tables at an Aspen restaurant when he saw news footage of Los Angeles police officers chasing and beating students. "Oscar said he took off his apron, threw it down on a table and announced, 'Those people need a lawyer!' Then he drove to L.A.'" But defendant Moctesuma Esparza recalled that Acosta had been getting high with the *vatos locos* and *pachucos* for months before the arrests. When Acosta contacted the defendants, he urged them to make their trial a political one. "He was the only one who was offering to pursue our defense as a political defense," Esparza said, "to turn our trial into a further chapter in the Chicano struggle. That was unique." Acosta was one of many attorneys on the defense team, but as the only Chicano, he became an important figurehead and media spokesman.

The defense argued that the protestors were legally exercising their First Amendment rights. After an appeals court struck down those indictments, Acosta shifted his attention to another case. Six Chicano activists had been accused of setting fires inside the Biltmore Hotel in downtown Los Angeles while Governor Reagan was speaking there. Acosta and his colleagues argued that the indictment should be quashed because the grand jury was illegally constituted. At the time, Superior Court judges recommended grand jury candidates; by questioning some of those judges in court, the defense showed that they knew few Latinos personally. They also presented lists that showed that only 1.7 percent of grand jurors over the past eleven years had Spanish surnames, even though that group represented about 13 percent of the county's population. The absence of Latinos on grand juries, the defense argued, violated the due process and equal protection clause. During the trial, Acosta was jailed for contempt of court, but the jury deadlocked, and the judge declared a mistrial.

Acosta also defended members of a group called Catolicos por La Raza, who were arrested for demonstrating against the Los Angeles diocese and its leadership. That protest took place inside a church, and the charge was conspiracy to disrupt a religious assembly. Acosta's clients included Raul Ruiz, who understood that Acosta was no ordinary attorney. "Oscar didn't want to be a lawyer," Ruiz recalled. "He wanted to be a writer." Acosta was also insane, Ruiz added, but he mounted a brilliant defense and "showed no deference to the judge or to the judicial procedure. In fact, he displayed nothing but contempt." Acosta's defiance worried his clients, but some of them, including Ruiz, were found not guilty.

Acosta afflicted judges in other ways as well. Thompson recalled driving to Santa Monica one night with Acosta, who poured ten gallons of gasoline on a judge's front lawn and lit it on fire. According to Thompson, Acosta had decided that this was the only meaningful way to communicate with the judge. Instead of fleeing, Acosta "stood in the street and howled through the flames at a face peering out from a shattered upstairs window." His impromptu sermon on social justice was taken from the New Testament. Acosta was sure that the judge recognized him but would never admit it. Thompson drew his own conclusion about the gesture and its significance: "The Lawn of Fire was Oscar's answer to the Ku Klux Klan's burning cross, and he derived the same demonic satisfaction from doing it."

In the middle of these legal cases, Acosta ran unsuccessfully for sheriff. His campaign statement, issued in February 1970, announced a full-scale attack on the system.

> The history of Los Angeles County is one of violence, vice, and corruption in high places . . . Because the forces of oppression and suppression—the law enforcement agencies—continue to harass, brutalize, illegally confine, and psychologically damage the Chicano, the black, the poor, and the unrepresented, I hereby declare my candidacy for the office of Sheriff of Los Angeles County.

Acosta's platform shared the Thompson campaign's iconoclasm but none of its sly humor. His seven-point program called for the ultimate dissolution of the Sheriff's Department, its immediate withdrawal from barrios and ghettos, investigations of its conduct, and the establishment of community review boards.

Despite his defeat at the polls, Acosta harbored dreams of becoming an even more important figure in the Chicano community. He changed his middle name to Zeta and often signed his documents with a Z. The name change, scholar Hector Calderon observed, indicated that Acosta was reinventing himself.

> This marks the transformation from Oscar Thomas Acosta to Oscar Zeta Acosta, Chicano lawyer, from English to Spanish language, from

Legal Aid lawyer to outlaw hero. Militancy, ethnicity, drugs, and
literature were all coming together for Acosta, as he fashioned a persona
that would be the subject of his work.

Acosta would be remembered for that persona, which Thompson both
refracted and immortalized in his most famous book.

· · ·

With Acosta's encouragement, Thompson pitched a story about the Chicano
movement to *Scanlan's*. Hinckle accepted, and Thompson claimed to write
half of the story by hand on a red-eye flight from San Francisco to New
York City in September 1970. By that time, the story had taken a dramatic
turn. In August, journalist Ruben Salazar was killed during an anti-war
demonstration in East Los Angeles. Salazar was a respected figure not only
in the Latino community, but also in the mainstream media. After reporting for the *Los Angeles Times* from Vietnam and Mexico City, he was called
back to Los Angeles to cover the Chicano movement. In January 1970, he
accepted a position as news director at KMEX, a Spanish-language television station, but continued to contribute columns to the *Los Angeles Times*.
Many of them criticized the city's White power structure, especially the Los
Angeles Police Department. When asked why he was leaving objective
journalism and venturing into advocacy, Salazar replied, "Objectivity is
impossible. And I don't think there's a newsman alive who really thinks
that objectivity is the name of the game in the news media."

In August 1970, Salazar was covering the National Chicano Moratorium
March in Laguna Park when it devolved into what some participants called
a police riot. Salazar and his colleagues sought relief in the Silver Dollar
Cafe on Whittier Boulevard, some ten blocks away from the main action,
but a sheriff's deputy standing outside the cafe shot a tear gas canister
through the front door and killed the 42-year-old Salazar. The sheriff's
department denied any responsibility, but Raul Ruiz had taken a photograph of the deputy pointing the tear gas launcher at the cafe's front door,
and other eyewitnesses refuted the department's official statements. The
district attorney filed no charges against the deputy, but the county eventually paid the Salazar family $700,000 to settle a wrongful death lawsuit.
Weeks after the incident, Laguna Park was renamed Ruben F. Salazar Park.

Even before the inquest, however, Sidney Zion spiked Thompson's story
at *Scanlan's*. By that time, the magazine was struggling to survive. President
Nixon directed US Attorney General John Mitchell to begin an FBI investigation of *Scanlan's*, and the Royal Canadian Mounted Police impounded
the December 1970 issue at a Montreal printing press. Nixon also ordered

newly hired White House counsel John Dean to probe *Scanlan's* finances. "I'm still trying to find the water fountains in this place," Dean complained to one Nixon advisor. "The President wants me to turn the IRS loose on a shit-ass magazine called *Scanlan's Monthly.*" After eight issues, *Scanlan's* went down in flames.

Thompson returned to East Los Angeles to update his story, this time for *Rolling Stone.* Running more than nineteen thousand words, "Strange Rumblings in Aztlan" appeared in April. The title alluded to the mythical homeland of the Aztecs, which Chicano activists said they wished to restore. But Thompson was less interested in the movement than in his suspicion that the sheriff's department targeted a troublesome journalist for execution. Sifting through the evidence, Thompson saw no indication of premeditation, but he labeled Salazar's death "a second-degree job" insofar as it was committed unlawfully and with malice aforethought. "The malignant reality of Ruben Salazar's death," he maintained, "is that he was murdered by angry cops for no reason at all—and that the L. A. sheriff's department was and still is prepared to defend that murder on the grounds that it was entirely justified." Thompson also left no doubt that officials were untruthful about Salazar's death. Recounting the collapse of each public statement, he dismissed them as "garbled swill" and documented the official mendacity that had long been a favorite target.

As usual, Thompson paid careful attention to other media outlets, including *La Raza* and other movement publications. He singled out the *Los Angeles Herald-Examiner* for special criticism, noting that one of its editorials supported LAPD Chief Ed Davis's claim that the violence was attributable to a "hard core group of subversives who infiltrated the antiwar rally and turned it into a mob." In the same speech, Chief Davis added that the Communist Party in California had said it was "giving up on the blacks to concentrate on the Mexican-Americans." Thompson dismissed the *Herald-Examiner* as "a genuinely rotten newspaper" whose perverted purpose was a monument to "everything cheap, corrupt, and vicious in the realm of journalistic possibility." He wondered how "the shriveled Hearst management can still find enough gimps, bigots, and deranged Papists to staff a rotten paper like the *Herald.*" Its very existence, he concluded, "explains a lot about the mentality of Los Angeles—and also, perhaps, about the murder of Ruben Salazar."

"Strange Rumblings in Aztlan" was unique in Thompson's body of work. Written after the Kentucky Derby piece but before *Fear and Loathing in Las Vegas*, it lacked most of the pyrotechnics of the Gonzo *oeuvre*. Thompson enlivened what he later called a murder mystery with his keen wit, but the piece was never meant to be comical or satirical. He was a figure in the story, but the reporting wasn't especially participatory, and the world didn't reveal its meaning through his warped consciousness. He flouted the norms of journalistic objectivity with his frank personal asides, but he also laid out a detailed fact pattern and reviewed it discerningly. By the time he delivered his conclusions, they were persuasive and damning. The article was also a deviation for *Rolling Stone*. Running almost half as long as Thompson's next book, it did not revolve around the counterculture as Wenner and his readers understood it. Nevertheless, "Strange Rumblings in Aztlan" was a clear sign that Thompson had the green light at *Rolling Stone*.

9   Las Vegas

Although the Salazar piece was a high point in Thompson's journalistic output, it was quickly overshadowed by another work hatched in the middle of that project.

After an especially tense week in East Los Angeles, Thompson accepted an assignment from *Sports Illustrated* to cover the Mint 400 Off-Road Rally. Sponsored by Del Webb's Mint Hotel & Casino, the event featured a motorcycle and dune buggy race in the desert outside Las Vegas. Claiming he needed a break from the Salazar story, Thompson invited Oscar Acosta to join him. Part of his plan was to separate Acosta from his militant colleagues, who openly wondered about his friendship with a White journalist. As Thompson would note later, "We were always in the midst of a crowd of heavy street-fighters who didn't mind letting me know that they wouldn't need much of an excuse to chop me into hamburger." A road trip would allow the two men to speak openly and at length. Thompson rented a convertible, which he later dubbed the Great Red Shark, and the two men drove to Las Vegas on March 20, 1971.

Their destination resembled no other city in the United States, but it was the most American of places. Founded in 1905 as a railroad town, Las Vegas bloomed in the 1930s, when the federal government commissioned the Hoover Dam. Nevada had legalized gambling, and the city's cowboy casinos and bordellos made it a destination for thousands of laborers. That traffic waned after the dam's completion, but when Los Angeles cracked down on the rackets in the late 1930s, local mobsters saw an opportunity in the desert 270 miles away. They established a race wire in Las Vegas, took offtrack bets, and poisoned their main competitor. Two new defense installations boosted their business during the Second World War, and the Flamingo Hotel's 1946 premiere kicked off a postwar casino boom. Eastern and midwestern mob figures began to invest heavily in Las Vegas, and its swanky new gambling palaces looked like they might have been airdropped from Miami Beach or Havana.

Thompson's favorite literary figure used his underworld connections to reinvent himself as a Long Island socialite, but Las Vegas operators plied their trade openly and become pillars of the community. "When these guys came here, it was like a morality or ethical car wash," said mob expert Nicholas Pileggi. "You came here, you were cleansed of your sins, you were now legitimate and legal. I didn't care what you did, you got a wash." A prime example was Morris "Moe" Dalitz, a bootlegger from the Mayfield Road Gang in Cleveland. With the repeal of Prohibition in 1933, Dalitz operated illegal casinos in Ohio and Kentucky, but in 1949, he came to Las Vegas to finance the Desert Inn hotel and casino. Over time, Dalitz became an important local builder who regarded the Las Vegas Convention Center as his greatest achievement. "He was a success of Southern Nevada's gaming economy as any one person could be," said a former Nevada governor after Dalitz's death. "His conduct has always been exemplary, and in my opinion, he was a good citizen in every way." Dalitz sold the Desert Inn to business magnate Howard Hughes, who took up residence there in 1966 and did not leave the bedroom of his penthouse suite for four years.

When the US Senate investigated organized crime in the 1950s, the Las Vegas tycoons were undaunted. However, the hearings pressured gambling operations elsewhere, and more racketeers streamed to the desert. Their fortunes rose as the city became a major tourist destination. The appeal was simple: In Las Vegas, Americans could pursue desires that were illegal or frowned upon elsewhere. One observer noted the city's niche in the national psyche.

> I think this notion that Vegas is a place where the underside of the American psyche could express itself a little more, could come out from under the rock as it were, has been there for a long time. Las Vegas was created as this place in which sort of good people could be bad and yet not lose any points for doing so.

The Strip, which was placed outside city limits to minimize taxes, hosted much of the gambling. As its built landscape became increasingly spectacular, one writer described its growth as "completely inorganic" and noted that nothing about its placement made intrinsic sense. "It's the middle of the desert," he noted. "And this anomalous and overriding sense of dislocation and fantasy plays out in the city's architectural eclecticism." Disneyland, which also emerged as a major tourist destination in the 1950s, was subtle by comparison.

The casino moguls didn't finance their expansion with bank loans. Instead, they turned to the International Brotherhood of Teamsters, which Jimmy Hoffa led after the AFL-CIO expelled the union for corruption in 1957. The union's pension fund financed at least eight casinos, including the Desert Inn. Thompson certainly knew about Hoffa and the mob. In the late 1950s, he was riveted by the televised Senate hearings on labor racketeering. According to one of his Air Force colleagues, Thompson was especially drawn to Robert Kennedy, the Senate committee's chief counsel.

> Hunter was absolutely obsessed with the Senate hearings and Robert Kennedy. It was the only damn thing he would write about in that period. He was fascinated with all that shit. He really liked the job Bobby Kennedy was doing, and he stopped writing about sports altogether.

As attorney general, Robert Kennedy continued to target Hoffa. By the time Thompson and Acosta made their way to Las Vegas, the Teamster leader was serving a thirteen-year term for jury-tampering and pension fund fraud. Kennedy's zeal pushed Hoffa into the arms of the GOP, and shortly after Thompson's Las Vegas article ran, President Nixon granted Hoffa a "conditional commutation" that prevented him from returning to his leadership role in the Teamsters. In exchange, the union supported Nixon's reelection bid in 1972.

Gambling made Las Vegas a tourist destination, but entertainment turned it into an adult theme park. In 1951, Frank Sinatra made his first appearance at the Desert Inn. Two years later, he began playing the Copa Room at the Sands Hotel and Casino and eventually became its co-owner. "He was the spark that changed Vegas from a dusty Western town into something glamorous," said one former lieutenant governor. Sinatra and his friends pursued their pleasures openly and were glorified for it. Most of the Las Vegas talent was represented by MCA, whose field general was Lew Wasserman. A Cleveland native, Wasserman knew Moe Dalitz, represented Ronald Reagan, and later became president of MCA/Universal. By the time Thompson made his fateful trip to Las Vegas, Wasserman was said to be the most powerful man in Hollywood. His best friend of five decades was Sidney Korshak, whose clients included the Chicago mob, Dalitz, and Hoffa. When Korshak arrived in Las Vegas during a Teamsters' meeting in 1961, his hotel dislodged Hoffa from the largest suite to accommodate him.

The Strip put its founders' aspirations and aesthetic on display. Many Americans considered Las Vegas garish, but to the counterculture it was grotesque. Certainly no place was less spiritual, organic, or communal. Its popularity made Las Vegas Exhibit A in the case that square America, and not the counterculture, was truly weird. The antipathy worked both ways, of course. In *Fear and Loathing in Las Vegas*, Thompson included a long passage about the barbarous treatment his longhaired Aspen neighbor received from the criminal justice system in Las Vegas.

. . .

When Thompson and Acosta arrived in Las Vegas, they checked into the Mint Hotel and drove to the Desert Inn for a drink. Debbie Reynolds was performing there with Harry James. She was only five years older than Thompson, but James's career had peaked during the swing era, when he hired an unknown baritone named Frank Sinatra. In every conceivable way, Thompson was a long way from The Matrix. As his narrator notes in *Fear and Loathing in Las Vegas*, "The Fillmore style never quite caught on here. People like Sinatra and Dean Martin are still considered 'far out' in Vegas." Thompson also met Aspen musician Bruce Innes at Circus Circus casino for a drink. Innes had already written "One Tin Soldier," a cover version of which was the theme song for *Billy Jack*, a popular countercultural film released in 1971. After their visit with Innes, Thompson and Acosta repaired to the Mint Hotel bar and then to their room, where they stayed up all night.

Early the next morning, Thompson drove out to Floyd Lamb State Park to cover the race. That task was more difficult than he expected, largely because the motorcyclists were shrouded in the dust clouds they generated. Thompson completed his notes on the race, returned to the hotel, picked up Acosta, and dropped him off at the airport. He soon realized, however, that Acosta had left his attache case in the car. Back at the hotel, Thompson opened it to find a Colt .357 Magnum, a box of bullets, and a large bag of marijuana. Exhausted by his Dexedrine-fueled weekend, he panicked. Nevada had some of the toughest marijuana laws in the country. Moreover, Thompson had little cash, an unreliable credit card, and no confirmation that *Sports Illustrated* would pay his hotel bill. As he considered his predicament, he watched the early morning gamblers, many of them elderly, filling the slot machines with change. The scene filled him with despair.

Thompson decided to return to Southern California without paying his hotel bill. He drove to Arcadia, checked into a Ramada Inn, and fleshed out his notes for the *Sports Illustrated* piece. At 2,500 words, his draft far exceeded the 250-word slot the editors had set aside. They declined to run it, and he was predictably irate. Once again, a setback prompted a major work. Thompson decided to recast his Las Vegas story and offer it to *Rolling Stone*. "The rejection by *Sports Illustrated* infuriated him," Douglas

Brinkley said. "And it was only at that point that he started realizing, like, 'Eureka!' Chicago may not be where the death of the American Dream is. It's Las Vegas."

He drafted an even longer version of his Las Vegas adventure with Raoul Duke and his attorney, Dr. Gonzo, as the protagonists. Sensing the beginnings of a book-length work, he showed an early version to *Rolling Stone* editor David Felton, who lived in nearby Pasadena. Felton had grown up in the area before attending San Francisco State College to study creative writing under Mark Harris. He returned to work for the *Los Angeles Times,* but as the Haight-Ashbury scene developed, Felton began to write about it. He had already worked for John Burks, who ran the student newspaper at San Francisco State College before guiding *Rolling Stone*'s coverage of Altamont and Kent State. (Burks fell out with Wenner that year and later taught journalism at his alma mater.) For one year, Felton was also *Rolling Stone*'s Los Angeles editor; during that time, he teamed up with David Dalton to write the award-winning Manson Family story.

Felton, who was also Thompson's editor on the Ruben Salazar piece, encouraged him to pursue the Las Vegas project. Shortly after that, Thompson circulated its first chapter at the magazine's San Francisco office. Editor Paul Scanlon described the circumstances.

> One day Hunter came in, and I'm standing there with Charlie Perry and another editor, Grover Lewis, and he pulls out a sheaf of manuscript, legal sized and all neatly stapled together, and he handed one section to me and one to Charlie and one to Grover, and then stomped out . . . I went to my office to read it, and I started howling when the bats started coming out of the sky, and by the time I finished reading it, I was pounding on my desk and couldn't stop laughing. I wandered into Grover's office, and he was hunched over his desk wheezing. And he turned around, and there were tears in his eyes, and he couldn't stop laughing.

"Everybody was knocked out," Scanlon recalled. "I know Jann was. Nobody expected it."

The Mint 400 expedition sufficed for a long *Rolling Stone* article, but Felton alerted Thompson to another event in Las Vegas. Later that month, the Third National Institute on Narcotics and Dangerous Drugs would convene there. Sponsored by the National District Attorneys Association, the four-day conference was held at the Dunes Hotel, which also had a checkered history. For that trip, Thompson and Acosta flew to Las Vegas and rented a white Cadillac convertible. Thompson brought a tape recorder and collected more than one hundred minutes of commentary and conversations. The two men stayed at the Flamingo Hotel & Casino, which had served as a location for *Ocean's 11* with Frank Sinatra and *Viva Las Vegas* with Elvis Presley. Presley was strongly associated with Las Vegas for other reasons as well. Three years before Thompson and Acosta checked in, Presley played a four-week engagement at the Flamingo that propelled his comeback. He eventually performed more than six hundred concerts there, many of them in his signature jumpsuits and capes. Especially as his weight ballooned in the 1970s, Presley embodied the deeply unhip reputation that Las Vegas earned in the freak community.

Presley also played a minor role in the drug crackdown to which the Las Vegas conference was dedicated. Only months before Thompson's first trip to Las Vegas, Presley requested an impromptu meeting with President Nixon in the White House. His goal was to become a "Federal Agent at Large" in the federal narcotics bureau. He explained his motives in a handwritten letter to Nixon. "The drug culture, the hippie elements, the SDS, Black Panthers, etc. do *not* consider me their enemy, or as they call it, The Establishment," Presley wrote. "I have done an in-depth study of drug abuse and Communist brainwashing techniques, and I am right in the middle of the whole thing, where I can and will do the most good." The meeting itself was surreal. When Presley arrived at the White House, aides accepted his gift to President Nixon—a nickel-plated handgun and ammunition—and ushered him into the Oval Office. Nixon quickly approved Presley's request for a federal badge. When the drug-addled Presley died in 1977, he was still a credentialed Special Assistant in the Bureau of Narcotics and Dangerous Drugs.

By the time Thompson made the second trip to Las Vegas, he was relishing the audacity of his project. His narrator, Raoul Duke, notes that he and Dr. Gonzo were mere observers during their first visit.

> But this time our very presence would be an outrage. We would be dealing, from the start, with a crowd that was convened for the stated purpose of putting people like us in jail . . . If the Pigs were gathering in Vegas for a top-level Drug Conference, we felt the drug culture should be represented.

Thompson and Acosta attended several conference sessions, which made Acosta uncomfortable. "They're all a bunch of lily-colored liverworts," he said on tape. "Dodging all the significant issues of the day. They're spending millions and billions of dollars on rehabilitating persons that they'd obviously like to kill." To compound the irony, the prosecutors never seemed to notice or care that the city hosting their convention was built by bootleggers.

. . .

Thompson returned to Woody Creek that summer to develop his manuscript. As late as mid-June, however, he was unsure how it would appear in
book form or even who would publish it. He assured Silberman that
Random House would have first crack at it, but there was a snag. Although
Lynn Nesbit and Silberman thought the Las Vegas material could be
included in the American Dream book, Thompson disagreed. In his mind,
that material would undermine the seriousness of the American Dream
project, which he still pinned to the Battle of Aspen. He intended to satisfy
his contractual obligations, he assured Silberman, but he was "a bit leery of
making a Public Fool of myself, just to get a book out." The last thing he
wanted was to "confuse payment of a legitimate debt with the permanent
destruction of my credibility." One year after filing the Kentucky Derby
piece, Thompson still did not realize that his Gonzo persona, which the Las
Vegas project would crystallize, was his most valuable asset.

Village Voice staff writer Lucian K. Truscott IV visited Thompson in
Woody Creek that summer and realized that a serious project was under
way.

> In the days before the Freak Power spirit, Thompson's ranch served as a
> war room and R&R camp for the Aspen political insurgents. Needless to
> say there was rarely a dull moment. When I arrived last summer, however,
> things had changed. Thompson was in the midst of writing a magnum
> opus, and it was being cranked out at an unnerving rate. I was barely
> across the threshold when I was informed that he worked (worked?)
> Monday through Friday and saved the weekends for messing around. As
> usual, he worked from around midnight until 7 or 8 in the morning and
> slept all day. There was an edge to his voice that said he meant business.

Truscott also quoted one of their exchanges about the manuscript.

> "I'm sending it off to Random House in 20,000-word bursts," he said,
> drawing slowly on his ever-present cigarette holder. "I don't have any
> idea what they think of it. Hell, I don't have any idea what it is."
> "What's it about?" I asked.
> "Searching for The American Dream in Las Vegas," replied
> Thompson coolly.

. . .

As Thompson labored over his manuscript in Woody Creek, President
Nixon was positioning himself for reelection. In June, he gave a major policy speech. "America's public enemy number one in the United States is

drug abuse," Nixon said. "In order to fight and defeat this enemy, it is necessary to wage a new, all-out offensive." He presented the drug war as a bipartisan measure, promised to fund it adequately, and appointed a drug czar who reported directly to him. Later, he reshuffled the bureaucracy to create the Drug Enforcement Agency (DEA). None of this improved Nixon's standing in Thompson's eyes; indeed, he detested the president more than ever.

Nixon's plan included significant resources for drug treatment, which pleased liberals, but the underlying political calculation was partisan. The drug crackdown targeted what White House aides privately called "*their* people"—young, poor, and Black Americans who were unlikely to vote for Nixon anyway. The president's top domestic advisor, John Ehrlichman, later acknowledged that the drug war was political from the outset.

> The Nixon campaign in 1968, and the Nixon White House after that, had two enemies: the antiwar left and black people. You understand what I'm saying? We knew we couldn't make it illegal to be either against the war or black, but by getting the public to associate the hippies with marijuana and blacks with heroin, and then criminalizing both heavily, we could disrupt those communities. We could arrest their leaders, raid their homes, break up their meetings, and vilify them night after night on the evening news. Did we know we were lying about the drugs? Of course we did.

Nixon's key metaphor was also a stroke of genius. By framing the crackdown as a war, the president distinguished it from other social services, which conservatives tended to oppose. That framework also set the stage for heavy federal spending. Between 1969 and 1974, the federal drug enforcement budget rose from $65 million to $719 million. The DEA also took over the task of classifying drugs from public health experts. Marijuana became a Schedule One drug, which meant it was highly dangerous, had high potential for abuse, and lacked any medical value. Nixon's war on drugs, which President Reagan later militarized, had far-reaching consequences. Between 1925 and 1975, the male incarceration rate in the United States was relatively stable. Between 1975 and 2008, however, that rate increased fivefold.

Although Pitkin County never embraced Thompson's outlandish views on drug enforcement, its sheriffs were not drug warriors in the classic sense. Early in his career, Sheriff Dick Kienast relished drug raids. "We were really going to clean up this town," he recalled. "I enjoyed it." But several mishaps led Kienast to rethink his position. In one, an Aspen police officer almost shot a suspected drug dealer on a residential street; the perp turned out to be an undercover federal agent. Angry that such agents were working in Aspen without his knowledge, Kienast directed them to stay out. That controversial decision received widespread media coverage, including an appearance by Kienast on *60 Minutes*.

Nixon's drug speech was a milestone, but it was quickly swamped by other news. A week after his address, the *New York Times* began publishing excerpts from the so-called Pentagon Papers. That classified report, commissioned by Secretary of Defense Robert McNamara in 1967, showed that the Johnson administration misled Congress and the American people about the conflict in Vietnam. Daniel Ellsberg, a military analyst at the RAND Corporation, released the top-secret report to the *Times* and other outlets. The following month, and in response to the leak, Nixon aides began to assemble a group called the White House Plumbers. In September, Ehrlichman ordered that group to raid the office of Ellsberg's psychiatrist in search of discrediting information. Ellsberg was eventually tried under the Espionage Act, but his case was dismissed. The White House Plumbers, and those who directed them, would not be so lucky.

. . .

When "Fear and Loathing in Las Vegas" appeared in November 1971, Thompson suspected that *Rolling Stone* was the only American magazine that would publish it. Porter Bibb, his boyhood friend and *Rolling Stone*'s publisher, agreed with that assessment.

> Who else would have given Hunter the encouragement? The space? The complete freedom? Who else would have let him go on and on for ten thousand, fourteen thousand words? Not Harold Hayes [at *Esquire*]. *Playboy* was rejecting his stuff. Only Jann Wenner. Without Jann, Hunter would not have become Hunter.

Bibb had a point. With the collapse of *Scanlan's*, *Rolling Stone* became Thompson's key outlet, and Wenner his most important ally. The 25-year-old publisher was keenly aware of the drug culture and its appeal, and though *Rolling Stone* had never published such scorching satire, he understood its value immediately. Thompson's voice further distinguished *Rolling Stone* from its direct competitors, and Raoul Duke's view of the San Francisco counterculture captured the magazine's sense of itself. As Duke notes in *Fear and Loathing in Las Vegas*, it seemed entirely reasonable to think that "every now and then, the energy of a whole generation comes to a head in a long fine flash, for reasons that nobody really understands at the time." More than any other publisher, Wenner was channeling that long fine flash for a large and growing audience.

Unlike most of the copy Thompson submitted to *Rolling Stone*, "Fear and Loathing in Las Vegas" came in clean, yet editors grappled with it, checking facts and constructing timelines. As they did so, Thompson told Wenner that it required a different editorial approach. The problem was that Wenner was "working overtime to treat this thing as Straight or at least Responsible journalism." He would be better off, Thompson said, fact-checking a Bob Dylan song, *The Ginger Man*, or *Naked Lunch*. The generic confusion was understandable. The Las Vegas story was neither New Journalism nor traditional fiction, though it overlapped with each. Thompson's advice was on point, but he also wanted to prevent *Rolling Stone*'s editors from tampering with his manuscript.

At the same time, Thompson could not resist the opportunity to complain about his unpaid expenses. When he learned that *Rolling Stone* would not reimburse him for his outlays—which included a rented Cadillac, a hunting knife, and a flute—he wrote directly to David Felton.

> You scurvy pig-fucker. I was about to send you some mescaline when I talked to Jann & found out that all my daily expenses on the Salazar/ Vegas stories were disallowed—for reasons of gross excess and irresponsible outlay. That $500 you sent me wasn't for my expenses at all; it was my fucking *June retainer*, which means I was spending my own money all that time.

Now that the story, which began as a *Sports Illustrated* project, was going into print at *Rolling Stone*, Thompson reminded Wenner about the money.

> Let's keep in mind that this was never a commissioned piece of journalism; it was a strange neo-fictional outburst that was deemed so rotten and wasteful, journalistically, that neither [*Rolling Stone*] nor [*Sports Illustrated*] would even reimburse me for my expenses. So I'm not in much of a mood, right now, to act grateful for any editorial direction.

Such haggling was nothing new, but this time Thompson's angle was to exploit his work's generic ambiguity. When it came to editing, he presented his work as fiction. For his expenses, however, he expected the norms of journalism to prevail.

The relationship between fiction and journalism was top of mind for Thompson. Neither one, Thompson declared in the so-called jacket copy for the book, was necessarily truer than its counterpart. Both were arbitrary categories and different means to the same end. In this case, Thompson claimed, the work began as a piece of journalism.

> My idea was to buy a fat notebook and record the whole thing, *as it happened*, then send in the notebook for publication—without editing.

That way, I felt, the eye & mind of the journalist would be functioning as a camera. The writing would be selective & necessarily interpretive—but once the image was written, the words would be final; in the same way that a Cartier-Bresson photograph is always (he says) the full-frame negative. No alterations in the darkroom, no cutting or cropping, no spotting . . . no editing.

That plan, Thompson conceded, was too difficult to execute. In the end, he found himself "imposing an essentially fictional framework on what began as a piece of straight/crazy journalism." For that reason, he maintained, the book was a failed experiment in Gonzo journalism, but its failure was complex enough to make it interesting. He later called the Las Vegas book a "nonfiction novel," which only deepened the generic ambiguity.

Thompson's taste in fiction also informed the book's title. Thompson probably drew the first part from Thomas Wolfe's *The Web and the Rock* (1939). He had used "fear and loathing" in his correspondence for years—including after John F. Kennedy's assassination—and he would reuse it many more times at *Rolling Stone*. But the subtitle—"A Savage Journey to the Heart of the American Dream"—evoked Conrad as well as Thompson's favorite theme. *Hell's Angels* closed with lines from *Heart of Darkness*, and Thompson admired *The Nigger of the Narcissus*, which Conrad hoped would access the truth in a particular way.

> My task which I am trying to achieve is, by the power of the written word, to make you hear, to make you feel—it is, before all, to make you see. That—and no more, and it is everything. If I succeed, you shall find there according to your deserts: encouragement, consolation, fear, charm—all you demand; and, perhaps, also that glimpse of truth for which you have forgotten to ask.

Thompson's book likewise offered a glimpse of truth for which many Americans had forgotten to ask. That it was set in a major tourist destination, not the Congo, only sharpened the satire.

Unlike Conrad, Thompson had another way to make readers see. Ralph Steadman did not make the journey to Las Vegas, but he was asked to illustrate the article and book. His drawings—a dozen in all—combined with Thompson's fevered prose to raise Gonzo journalism to a new and more demented level. The book's cover illustration depicted Dr. Gonzo as an amphibious creature and Raoul Duke in a full-throated howl as they tore across the desert in their convertible. More than any other illustration, it laid the foundation for Gonzo's distinctive iconography.

· · ·

The story of Raoul Duke and Dr. Gonzo begins on the road, with the two men wheeling their way to Las Vegas. Many reviewers have noted that the scene evokes Kerouac and other poets of the open road. Thompson certainly had that tradition in mind; if Nixon were reelected in 1972, he predicted in the jacket copy, the myth of the road would be dead. But Duke also differed from the road warriors who preceded him. Whereas Sal Paradise trekked across America and explored its social margins, Duke was hallucinating wildly while racing across the desert at top speed.

> We were somewhere around Barstow on the edge of the desert when
> the drugs began to take hold. I remember saying something like "I feel
> a bit lightheaded; maybe you should drive." . . . And suddenly there was
> a terrible roar all around us and the sky was full of what looked like
> huge bats, all swooping and screeching and diving around the car, which
> was going about 100 miles an hour with the top down to Las Vegas.
> And a voice was screaming: "Holy Jesus! What are these goddamn
> animals?"

From the outset, the reader suspects that Duke's ordeal will be more extreme, and also more comical, than the typical Beat adventure. Much of the humor is produced by juxtaposing the rhetoric of sanity with madcap psycho-activity. In the opening scene, for example, Duke quite reasonably wishes to turn over the wheel, but even before that suggestion can be acted upon, he hears the sound of his own dissociated voice crying out.

Although Duke's experience is intense, it is by no means mystical. His hallucinations portend no epiphany or self-realization; they are chemical, not transcendental. That aspect of Thompson's work was not lost on *Rolling Stone* editor Charles Perry, who identified it as a turning point in the American discourse about drugs.

> At that point, there was still kind of that Timothy Leary approach to
> psychedelics going around, where it was this very pious thing where
> you sat on a Persian rug and listened to Indian music. There had been
> very little in the way of actually dealing with the fact that when you're
> stoned on psychedelics, you're often just way out of control. You don't
> know how you're going to handle things, and Hunter made that his real
> topic.

Thompson would affirm his outlook in the 1974 *Playboy* interview. "I've never believed in that guru trip," he said. "I like to just gobble the stuff right out in the street and see what happens, take my chances, just stomp on my own accelerator."

That theme of survival also had a political dimension. Many commentators pointed to Altamont and the Manson murders as the figurative end of the 1960s. Although Duke frequently refers to counterculture's failed utopian project, he casts the 1971 heavyweight championship fight between Muhammad Ali and Joe Frazier as an even more fitting denouement.

> A very painful experience in every way, a proper end to the sixties:
> Tim Leary a prisoner of Eldridge Cleaver in Algeria, Bob Dylan clipping
> coupons in Greenwich Village, both Kennedys murdered by mutants,
> Owsley folding napkins on Terminal Island, and finally Cassius/Ali
> belted incredibly off his pedestal by a human hamburger, a man on
> the verge of death. Joe Frazier, like Nixon, had finally prevailed for
> reasons that people like me refused to understand—at least not out
> loud.

The question was no longer how to stop the war or achieve a more perfect union; rather, it was how that generation would survive the loss of its cultural heroes.

As the book opens, a more immediate form of survival is at issue. Duke has to fend off the imaginary bats without crashing the Great Red Shark. Pulling over to the side of the highway, he decides to open the trunk, which resembles "a mobile police narcotics lab."

> We had two bags of grass, seventy-five pellets of mescaline, five sheets
> of high-powered blotter acid, a salt shaker half full of cocaine, and a
> whole galaxy of multi-colored uppers, downers, screamers, laughers . . .
> and also a quart of tequila, a quart of rum, a case of Budweiser, a pint of
> raw ether and two dozen amyls.

The car Thompson actually drove to Las Vegas contained only marijuana, Dexedrine, and Benzedrine, but the narcotics cache is an essential part of the work. It depressed Thompson to learn that Silberman did not believe the characters were on drugs, and he urged his editor to keep that interpretation to himself. His editors at *Rolling Stone,* he said, were absolutely convinced that he had spent his expense money on contraband. "Probably we should leave it that way," he concluded.

Although the stash was mostly fictional, the drug cornucopia prefigured other excesses. Thompson had long ago mastered hyperbole, the work's foundational trope, but it was more timely than ever. By the end of 1971, a measured assessment of America's shortcomings seemed pointless. The counterculture was flaming out, a victim of its own misdirected energies. After years of official mendacity and slaughter in Vietnam, public officials who promoted and defended the war had exhausted their credibility, especially among young people. Violence had taken the lives of a charismatic president and the most visible symbols of the civil rights movement. Little more could be said dispassionately about Richard Nixon, his policies in

Southeast Asia, or his drug war. At these moments, Richard Klein points out in a very different context, another rhetorical strategy is required.

> In these circumstances, hyperbole is called for, for it raises its objects up, excessively, way above their actual merit: it is not to deceive by exaggeration that one overshoots the mark, but to allow the true value, the truth of what is insufficiently valued, to appear. The validity of hyperbole, the truth that exaggeration may often convey, depends on a principle well recognized by marksmen: there are times when aiming to overshoot the mark is the condition of hitting it.

That form of marksmanship was Thompson's specialty. By exaggerating an already gaudy scene, Thompson dramatized the gap between Nixon's America and the ideal republic his characters are seeking.

As they approach Las Vegas, Duke considers the significance of their trip. His impressions reflect death and decay, not the ecstatic raptures of Kerouac's road trips. "Old elephants limp off to the hills to die," he notes, while "old Americans go out to the highway and drive themselves to death with huge cars." Yet Duke ironically insists that their prospects are bright.

> But our trip was different. It was a classic affirmation of everything that was right and true and decent in the national character. It was a gross, physical salute to the fantastic *possibilities* of life in this country—but only for those with true grit. And we were chock full of that.

Those fantastic possibilities, readers soon learn, are even more fantastical than usual. The contents of the trunk generate most of them, and they are less decent than Duke suggests. "Hallucinations are bad enough," he remarks at one point. "But after a while you learn to cope with things like seeing your dead grandmother crawling up your leg with a knife in her teeth."

The next day, Duke sets out to cover the motorcycle race. That night, when he and Gonzo see Debbie Reynolds and Harry James, Gonzo exclaims that they have wandered into a time capsule. Ejected by security, they drive to Circus Circus. After huffing the ether, they stagger toward the entrance. The narration switches to the second person as Duke describes his cognitive collapse.

> What's happening here? What's going on? Then you hear yourself mumbling: "Dogs fucked the Pope, no fault of mine. Watch out! . . . Why money? My name is Brinks; I was born . . . born? Get sheep over side . . . women and children to armored car . . . orders from Captain Zeep."

Mistaken for a drunk at the door, Duke enters the casino and describes the scene before him as "what the whole hep world would be doing on Saturday night if the Nazis had won the war."

Back at the suite, Dr. Gonzo trips in the bathtub while Duke reflects on his early experiences with psychedelics. He recalls the nights he left the Fillmore Auditorium and sped his motorcycle across the Bay Bridge toward Oakland, Berkeley, and Richmond. "There was madness in any direction, at any hour. If not across the Bay, then up the Golden Gate or down 101 to Los Altos or La Honda." He and his friends "were riding the crest of a high and beautiful wave." But less than five years later, he adds plangently, you could climb a steep hill in Las Vegas, look west, and "almost see the high-water mark—that place where the wave finally broke and rolled back." Thompson later called his book an epitaph for the 1960s, but Duke's elegy is situated geographically as well as historically. His Bay Area experience, we gather, is the psychedelic part that stood for the utopian whole.

The next day, Dr. Gonzo flies back to Los Angeles, and Duke begins to panic. He has an expensive rental car, no cash, no story, and a gigantic room-service tab. He also has his attorney's .357 Magnum, which he finds on the passenger seat of the Great Red Shark. Duke realizes he must flee without paying the hotel bill. As he plans his escape, he scans the morning edition of the *Las Vegas Sun*. The scene recalls a similar one in the Kentucky Derby piece; this time the headlines concern heroin-related deaths, the US military's use of torture in Vietnam, a random shooting that leaves five wounded, and the arrest of a Las Vegas pharmacist after one hundred thousand pills go missing. Weirdly, the stories give Duke hope; compared to these horrors, his own crimes are trivial. His hope ebbs, however, when he reaches the sports page and realizes that Muhammad Ali, who received a five-year sentence for refusing to serve in the military, has not yet won his appeal.

After fleeing the city, Duke pulls off the highway to call Dr. Gonzo, who recommends an upcoming drug conference in Las Vegas. Duke returns to Las Vegas and ditches the Great Red Shark. When the agency offers a Mercedes, he responds angrily, "Do I look like a goddamn Nazi? I'll have a natural *American* car, or nothing at all!" He selects a white Cadillac Coupe de Ville, which he dubs the White Whale. The name extends the Great Red Shark trope, but it also echoes Melville's classic novel and sets the stage for more madness. Duke quickly discovers that the White Whale signals his support for the local economy, the community's sole concern. "If Charlie Manson checked into the Sahara tomorrow morning," he observes, "nobody would hassle him as long as he tipped big."

The men book a room at the Flamingo, which Duke describes as "a sort of huge under-financed Playboy Club in the middle of the desert." When he arrives at the room, he discovers a young woman named Lucy with a stark naked Dr. Gonzo. Both are under the influence of LSD. The room is festooned with her Barbra Streisand portraits, but Duke sees only trouble.

> It was bad enough if she were only what she appeared to be—a strange young girl in the throes of a bad psychotic episode—but what worried me far more than that was the likelihood that she would probably be just sane enough, in a few hours, to work herself up into a towering Jesus-based rage at the hazy recollection of being picked up and seduced in the Los Angeles International Airport by some kind of cruel Samoan who fed her liquor and LSD, then dragged her to a Vegas hotel room and savagely penetrated every orifice in her body with his throbbing, uncircumcised member.

Once again the specter of rape propels the plot. To extricate Acosta from a delicate situation, Duke doubles down on the indelicacy. He suggests that they turn Lucy out to raise money. His strategy hinges on hyperbole; by exaggerating her sexual exploitation, he shocks Dr. Gonzo into apprehending the danger to him—a Mann Act felony, kidnapping, rape, prison time, and disbarment.

Their only chance, Duke reasons, is to ditch Lucy without provoking a disastrous backlash, but Dr. Gonzo is still turning over the situation in his acid-addled head.

> "It just occurred to me," he said, "that she has *no witnesses*. Anything she says about us is completely worthless."
> "Us?" I said.
> He stared at me. I could see that his head was clearing. The acid was almost gone. This meant that Lucy was probably coming down, too. It was time to cut the cord.

Although they finally shake Lucy, Duke imagines their ineffective defense at their imaginary trial. Another drug binge ensues, this time with adrenochrome, before the pair visits a diner, where they watch "four boozed-up cowboy types kick a faggot half to death between the pinball machines." After some eighty hours without sleep, Duke returns to the hotel and prepares for the drug conference.

The keynote speech does not bode well. "These poor bastards didn't know mescaline from macaroni," Duke concludes. Dr. Gonzo heads for the casino bar, where Duke finds him bullshitting a district attorney from Georgia about the depravity of California's dope fiends. The scenarios are even more fantastical than their Kentucky Derby precursor, and the prosecutor predictably bemoans the nation's moral direction. After more misadventures, Duke and Dr. Gonzo land in a coffee shop at three in the morning. Dr. Gonzo propositions the middle-aged server, who responds forcefully.

"You sonofabitch! I take a lot of shit in this place, but I sure as hell don't have to take it off a *spic pimp!*" Dr. Gonzo responds by pulling his large hunting knife, slicing the receiver from the pay telephone's cord, returning to his seat, and asking how much the lemon meringue pie costs. When she tells him the price for a slice, he laughs, fetches the entire pie from the display case, and leaves five dollars. "The waitress was clearly in shock," Duke reports. "The glazed look in her eyes said her throat had been cut. She was still in the grip of paralysis when we left." It is not the first time Dr. Gonzo has pulled his knife, but the encounter dramatizes his menace.

Where to go after this unsavory scene? The next chapter opens with an editor's note explaining that Duke has broken down. All that remains is a transcript of the two men's banter while searching North Las Vegas for the American Dream. Structurally, the passage resembles the raw notes Thompson inserted into the Kentucky Derby piece—a texture break that resets the story after peak lunacy. Sarah Lazin, who prepared a transcript from Thompson's tape recordings, later noted that its passages appeared verbatim in the magazine and book, except that the speakers are Duke and Gonzo. When they ask a short-order cook where they might find the American Dream, he suggests the old Psychiatrist's Club on Paradise Road, adding that only drug dealers hang out there now. When Duke and Gonzo arrive at that location, they learn that the building burned down three years earlier. So much for the American Dream.

After a high-speed airport run to catch Dr. Gonzo's flight, Duke returns to the Flamingo to ponder their crimes. That reflection gives way to a broader rumination on sanity, the doom-struck era of Nixon, and "the *survival* trip." Leary, Barger, Ginsberg, Kesey, Altamont, and Manson all surface as "grim memories and bad flashbacks." By this time, Duke's suite resembles the site of "disastrous zoological experiment involving whiskey and gorillas." He recalls that the last time the maid tried to clean it, he awoke to find a naked Dr. Gonzo throttling her. Leaping out of bed, Duke flashed a press badge and placed her under arrest. "Here we were," Duke says, "both naked, staring down at a terrified old woman—a hotel *employee*—stretched out on the floor of our suite in a paroxysm of fear and hysteria. She would have to be dealt with." They accuse her of spying on them for a dope ring; she denies it, and they finally offer to put her on the payroll if she remains silent about them. Once again, the duo triumphs over a woman they have terrified—in this case, to conceal the gratuitous destruction of their suite.

The mirth is wearing thin, and the behavior seems more puerile than ever. If *Fear and Loathing in Las Vegas* is about the breakdown of values in

the twentieth century, it does not exempt its heroes from that disintegration. It is not a comical version of *Heart of Darkness,* where Marlow bears
witness to various forms of savagery, or *Under the Volcano,* where the dip-
somaniacal Consul copes with an extreme situation within his own extremity. Instead, the story presents Duke and Dr. Gonzo solving problems of
their own creation in increasingly objectionable ways. Thompson seems to
have expected the criticism. He prefaces the entire tale with Samuel
Johnson's famous adage: "He who makes a beast of himself gets rid of the
pain of being a man." The beastliness is obvious, but what counts as manliness remains opaque.

Duke describes the conference as "a waste of time, a lame fuckaround
that was only—in clear retrospect—a cheap excuse for a thousand cops to
spend a few days in Las Vegas and lay the bill on the taxpayers." The pro-
jection is striking. Duke's plan, like Thompson's, was precisely to spend a
few days in Las Vegas and charge it to someone else. Duke concludes that
the prosecutors are "about ten years behind the grim truth and harsh
kinetic realities of what they have only recently learned to call 'The Drug
Culture' in this foul year of Our Lord, 1971." On this point, Duke is prophetic. Those harsh realities, and the federal government's determination to
understand them in military terms, would disfigure the American criminal
justice system for decades.

Toward the end of his journey, Duke reunites with Bruce, his musician
friend from Aspen. He also recounts an event that occurs months later.
Having listened to Bruce's set in an Aspen club, former astronaut Wally
Schirra—who is named in the *Rolling Stone* article but not in the book—
takes issue with the socially conscious lyrics: "What kind of nerve does a
goddamn *Canadian* have to come down here and *insult this country?*" Duke
responds that he is an American and agrees with every fucking word Bruce
says. The following night, Duke continues, The Astronaut is dining with a
large party when a 14-year-old boy requests his autograph. When The
Astronaut complies, the boy looks at the autograph, tears it into pieces, and
drops the pile into The Astronaut's lap. "Not everybody loves you, man,"
the boys says before returning to his nearby table. Duke clearly approves,
and the story points to a larger cultural schism, especially within the White
middle class. Partly generational, partly regional, and deeply political, that
fracture would shape American politics for the rest of Thompson's life.

The Astronaut, Duke supposes, would never experience that awkwardness in Las Vegas. Its perfect mayor would be Richard Nixon, with John
Mitchell as sheriff and Spiro Agnew as Master of Sewers. Duke's observation completes the identification between Las Vegas and Nixon's America.

Those who visit and populate the city, vote for Nixon, and fight his drug war are even more warped than Raoul Duke and Dr. Gonzo. Once again, Thompson's narrator has come to see the real beasts perform, but the Las Vegas caper differs significantly from the scene at Churchill Downs. Whereas Thompson explained Louisville to Steadman as only a prodigal son could, the Strip is foreign territory, no more Duke's than the Congo is Marlow's. As Duke searches in vain for the American Dream, he feels no kinship with the locals and sees nothing of himself in that weird landscape. The adventure is more outlandish than the Louisville one, the drugs stronger, the place more fantastical, and the wingman more volatile. The pair's alienation from their surroundings generates comic energy, but the story lacks anything as powerful as Thompson's shock of recognition in the Louisville motel room. Duke is guilty of much, but he is not complicit. In lieu of an epiphany, his experience suggests that the culture war has begun, and that Las Vegas is its most spectacular scrimmage line.

• • •

And what of the good doctor? Acosta's response to the book was a tale in itself. Duke describes Dr. Gonzo as a three-hundred-pound Samoan attorney; Acosta, of course, was famously and militantly Chicano. We do not know how or why Thompson chose that character's ethnicity, but Samoa figured prominently in his fantasy life. In 1964, he wrote a letter to President Johnson offering his services as governor of American Samoa. He received a short, noncommittal reply from White House aide Larry O'Brien. In a burst of optimism, Thompson bought six white sharkskin suits. Three years later, he followed up with O'Brien, who by then was serving as US Postmaster General. His letter described his shock and despair after learning that a Congressman's son—Owen Aspinall of Grand Junction, Colorado—had been appointed governor or American Samoa. "A few years ago," Thompson told O'Brien, "you seemed like a man with his balls intact and with maybe even a small sense of humor. But I guess it was just a reflection." He closed by noting that he would keep his eyes open along Interstate 70, which connects Denver and Grand Junction, for the Larry O'Brien Memorial Drinking Fountain. Thompson continued to send disparaging letters to O'Brien, who chaired the Democratic National Committee in 1968 and later became commissioner of the National Basketball Association. In the meantime, Thompson's preoccupation with American Samoa persisted. After the Las Vegas book appeared, Thompson informed Nixon aide Pat Buchanan that he was still interested in the governorship.

Random House's lawyers fretted over Dr. Gonzo. His Samoan origins did not disguise his resemblance to Acosta, and because he commits a string of serious felonies over the course of the book, the lawyers insisted on a release from Acosta before going to press. They were correct that Acosta was irate, but not over Dr. Gonzo's crimes. Rather, he was angry that Thompson fictionalized him in the first place. He chastised Thompson for depicting him as a three-hundred-pound Samoan and pushed to have his name and photograph appear on the cover. By that time, Acosta had parlayed his connection to Thompson into a contract with Straight Arrow Books, but he remained dissatisfied with the way Thompson handled the Las Vegas book. In his view, he and Thompson had formed a partnership on the Salazar story and, by extension, the Las Vegas adventure. "Like, did you even so much as ask me if I minded your writing & printing the Vegas piece?" Acosta asked. "Not even the fucking courtesy to show me the motherfucker." (In fact, Acosta had seen the first half of the piece while they were staying at the Flamingo.) He was also dismayed by Thompson's condescension. "All I want," Acosta explained in a long letter to Thompson, "is for you to quit playing the role that I'm some fucking native, a noble savage you discovered in the woods."

For documentary filmmaker Phillip Rodriguez, Acosta had a valid point. Produced by Benicio Del Toro, *The Rise and Fall of the Brown Buffalo* (2018) maintained that Acosta was much more than Thompson's ethnic mascot. Whereas Thompson glorified Freak Power among Pitkin County's six thousand mostly Anglo souls, Acosta took on the entire criminal justice establishment of Los Angeles County, with its diverse population of 7 million and long history of violent, racist law enforcement. Of the two men, Thompson was the more accomplished writer, but Acosta captured the chaos, confusion, fury, and appetite that was airbrushed from the lives of civil rights leaders once their public images were shaped and polished. For these and other reasons, Rodriguez claimed that Acosta was the more committed, more revolutionary, and more interesting figure. In one interview, Rodriguez compared the two men to a 45 record where the B side was the heavier tune.

Thompson certainly did not regard Acosta as a mascot. Commenting on the 1998 film made from his book, he noted that Acosta was decidedly more complex than Benicio Del Toro's version of Dr. Gonzo.

> Oscar was suave in a weird way. You know, he's portrayed here as kind of a dumb brute. But Oscar could shift personality in the blink of an eye and become suave, almost like an actor, you know. And he could be also very menacing. I mean, he was a scary-looking guy, and he carried himself as a scary guy. He was a handful.

To emphasize Acosta's complexity and substance, Thompson also referred to the important criminal cases he handled. The book makes no mention of those cases, however, and the film barely acknowledges the nature of Dr. Gonzo's work.

Whatever the merits of Acosta's complaints, they were not well received. Instead, Thompson fired off a ferocious reply.

> You don't know how fucking lucky you are that I didn't run into you cold, as a stranger, on something like the Salazar piece—because, with an act like yours, I'd have crucified you on general principles. Shit, you're *lucky* that the LA press is a bunch of lame hacks; anybody good would screw you to the fucking floor.

As for the book, Thompson refused to let Acosta touch a word of it. He noted that Random House would probably use a photograph of them taken at Caesar's Palace, but it would appear on the back of the jacket and without identification. "Let me know if you plan to object," Thompson wrote. He also offered some advice. "You'd better write that fucking book," he warned, predicting that Acosta would have a difficult time conning another publisher if he blew the opportunity. Finally, he advised Acosta to cut back on the psychedelics.

> In the meantime, for fuck's sake get off the acid. There's too much paranoia in it—especially for you, because you seem to enjoy cultivating it, and that's suicide. There's too much good in your head— and all the rest of you, for that matter—to bog it all down in sick gibberish like that last letter to me.

Though pointed, Thompson's conclusion was gentle compared to the tone of the opening paragraphs.

When Acosta threatened a libel action, Thompson lost all patience. "Dear Oscar," he wrote in April 1972. "You stupid fuck; send me a mailing address so I can explain what's happening because of what you've done." Acosta's legal threat served neither of them, Thompson maintained, and he sarcastically called Acosta a credit to his race. "I assume you had some excellent, long-stewing reason for doing this cheap, acid-crippled, paranoid fuckaround," he added. As for Acosta's book, Thompson concluded darkly, "You'll get all the help you deserve when the time comes." The discord continued even after Acosta signed the release. The next year, Acosta told Lynn Nesbit he was planning to sue Thompson for gross fraud over the sale of the film rights. Later, he wrote directly to Thompson.

> I've been silent on the subject for almost two years because of the blackmail threats from both you and Jann that ultimately my book

would be stopped. Well, old pal, the book is out now, and I'm coming after you. You cocksuckers have been ripping me off for a long time.

Acosta urged Thompson to make him an offer. "It would be better for all if we settled it and forgot it. Besides, you can afford it now." Acosta was not deluded. In a letter to his mother, Thompson confided that Acosta had "an apparently valid claim" against him for $25,000. He did not specify the grounds for that claim, but it may have been related to a section of the book that transcribes the tape recordings he made with Acosta.

Toward the end of that year, Acosta's tone took a dramatic turn. Arrested by undercover deputies for illegal possession of Benzedrine, he was acquitted in 1972. Even so, prospective clients gave him a wide berth. In a letter to Thompson, he explained that he had been blackballed in San Francisco and Los Angeles, and that he was living on food stamps and petty theft. "I am still looking to you as my only serious white connection for the big contract . . . the way it looks from here, I'd even settle for a small one." He asked that Thompson send immediate "seed money" to explore a political alliance between Thompson's freaks and his *cucarachas*. Finally, he asked that Thompson forward Acosta's share of the film rights for the Las Vegas book, deduct his outstanding loans, and wish him well, as he did Thompson. "Money-wise, I am desperate," he closed. "Send help to the above address, quick . . . thanx."

Thompson replied immediately. "What in the fuck would cause you to ask me for *money*—after all the insane bullshit you've put me through for the past two years?" The film rights for the Las Vegas story had not been purchased, Thompson claimed, and Acosta's legal threats might have scotched that sale for good. "Anyway, good luck with your grudge. No doubt it will make you as many good friends in the future as it has in the past." He closed with a salvo.

> As for me, my attorney advises me that I can at least deduct something around $10,000 for losses you have caused me in '73. In the meantime, why don't you write a nice movie? Or a book? You shouldn't have any trouble selling the fucker, considering all the people you've fucked over & burned.
>
> Good luck,
> Whitey

By that time, Straight Arrow Books had published Acosta's second work, *The Revolt of the Cockroach People*, but his personal life was a mess. In a 1980 interview, Thompson said he last saw Acosta at the Seal Rock Inn in San Francisco. Acosta had drifted away from the legal profession, and

Straight Arrow Books had folded. "So he decided to get another business, and he needed money," Thompson told David Felton. Thompson declined the request. "Yeah, it sounds good," Thompson said he told Acosta, "it makes perfect sense, but I wouldn't touch it at all, man. I'm sorry; I know it's doomed. And the next thing I heard is that he was killed doing it." Acosta was last heard from in May 1974, when he called his son from Mazatlán. He was, he said, "about to board a boat of white snow." A private investigator concluded that Acosta's disappearance was either a political assassination or murder at the hands of drug dealers.

Two years before Acosta's death became official, Thompson wrote an elegy for *Rolling Stone*. "The Banshee Screams for Buffalo Meat" was a long piece, even by Thompson's standards. It was also relatively straightforward, tough-minded, and moving. "Oscar was one of God's own prototypes—a high-powered mutant of some kind who was never even considered for mass production," Thompson wrote. "He was too weird to live, and too rare to die." The article's length and detail reflected an important fact: Acosta contributed directly to one of Thompson's most significant works of journalism as well as his most famous nonfiction novel. In doing so, he joined a small cohort of figures who helped Thompson become himself.

. . .

Fear and Loathing in Las Vegas was not an immediate bestseller, but the critical reception was overwhelmingly positive. In the *New York Times*, Christopher Lehmann-Haupt called it "a kind of mad, corrosive prose poetry that picks up where Norman Mailer's *An American Dream* left off and explores what Tom Wolfe left out." The comparison to *An American Dream* was remarkable. Mailer's first-person narrator murders his estranged wife and has sex with her maid. That opening sequence led Kate Millett to claim that Mailer had once again framed male heroism as a conjunction of sex and violence against women. Lehmann-Haupt's endorsement of Thompson's book was notable for another reason as well. His brother Sandy had joined the Merry Pranksters, installed a new sound system at Kesey's home in La Honda, and was a principal source for Tom Wolfe's *The Electric Kool-Aid Acid Test*. Yet Sandy's experience with the Pranksters wasted him. He never fully recovered and later regretted the way Kesey and his followers glorified drugs. Given Thompson's connection to Kesey, his brother's book review might have railed against a book about the counterculture, even one that eulogized it. Instead, the review recognized the book's energetic style and placed it in favorable (if savage) literary company.

Another reviewer for the *New York Times*, Crawford Woods, described *Fear and Loathing in Las Vegas* as "by far the best book yet written on the decade of dope gone by" and "the funniest piece of American prose since *Naked Lunch*." Like Lehmann-Haupt, Woods compared Thompson to Mailer, describing each man's version of the American Dream as "a fanfare of baroque fantasy." But Woods added that Thompson's book was more vicious than *The Armies of the Night*, so much so that readers might miss his moral purpose. "He is moving in a country where only a few cranky survivors—Jonathan Swift for one—have gone before," Woods wrote. "And he moves with the cool integrity of an artist indifferent to his reception."

In the *Village Voice*, Lucian K. Truscott IV was even more taken by Thompson's achievement.

> He has permanently altered the landscape of The American Dream, that's what he's done. In one fell swoop, he's created a modern cross between Kerouac's *On the Road* and *The Dharma Bums*. This book is the final word, a brilliant vision, a terrible magnificently funny telling of what happened to this country in the 1960s.

The *New Republic* was less impressed: "The book is in the zonked, road-writing tradition of Jack Kerouac, but it lacks Kerouac's bleeding feelings. Despite some hip ironies and several funny episodes, Thompson's world is loveless". It is a curious comparison. One does not expect love or even tenderness from satire, which was no part of Kerouac's project; indeed, his characters are earnest to a fault. Moreover, Thompson's anti-heroes never experience, or even strive for, the ecstatic raptures that propelled Kerouac's crew. But the review indicated that the book's sharp edges made it difficult for some readers to embrace.

Fear and Loathing in Las Vegas made Thompson a cultural icon, but it also helped *Rolling Stone* become what music journalist Joel Selvin called "the voice of its generation." Although Gonzo was born at *Scanlan's*, Wenner lashed it firmly to his masthead. He even converted his office into the Raoul Duke Room, which he used for editorial conferences. At the same time, Thompson's success at *Rolling Stone* was a blow to Hinckle. "He inherited Hunter," Hinckle said of Wenner, "and fell into it very luckily, because the *Stone* was a piece of shit. It was just there to sell records." Wenner put it differently. "I think part of what led to Hinckle's bitterness toward me was that Hunter became mine," he said. "I got all the glory."

Thompson's arrival was also a turning point in the magazine's history. "The reinvention of *Rolling Stone* around Hunter Thompson," Wenner biographer Joe Hagan claimed, "would be nearly as important as the invention of the newspaper itself." Wenner made it clear that Thompson's work was setting the bar. More and more, he expected his contributors to challenge the norms of conventional journalism and "kick away the barriers." Other contributors began to dramatize their own eccentricities and appetites. Joe Eszterhas, for example, developed a reputation for excess that challenged Thompson's. "The leader of the pack in the office came to be Joe Eszterhas," Wenner remarked, "but the star was always Hunter. It created a bit of rivalry. Joe was jealous, but Hunter never seemed to feel that at all." Even Wenner seemed to be under his influence. During this time, he altered his name on the masthead. He was no longer Jann Wenner, but Jann S. Wenner.

During this period, *Rolling Stone* earned a reputation as a writer's magazine. Some began to see the magazine as literary, maybe even important. It ran very long pieces, and editors routinely deferred to contributors. David Felton had come from the *Los Angeles Times,* where editors were in charge, but he credited Thompson with teaching him that nothing was gained from imposing a rigid style on unorthodox writers. Thompson was "so belligerent and stubborn—I mean he just *insisted* on more freedom for individual styles," Felton said. That sense of authorship pervaded the magazine's culture. When an art director deleted a comma from a pull quote, Eszterhas protested, "I *wrote* that comma!"

Thompson was still basking in his Las Vegas glory when Wenner convened an editorial meeting at the Esalen Institute in December 1971. "The Gonzo journalist was the star of the conference," Robert Draper noted in his history of *Rolling Stone,* "and he did not disappoint." Thompson arrived with a red police light on top of his Mustang, wore surgeon's scrubs, pretended to inject rum into his stomach, threw a fit when he failed to gain Wenner's immediate attention, and narrowly escaped arrest for drunk driving and drug possession. "Everybody was poking the elephant with a stick," recalled staff writer Robert Greenfield. "They were all standing around waiting for Hunter to do something." The hot baths, staff writer Robin Green noted, staged Thompson's athletic physique to advantage. Many in attendance also recalled that he pulled his car up to his cabin door one night to prevent entry. Green added that chief photographer Annie Leibovitz, the only woman invited to the first part of the meeting, was also in his room at the time.

The chief idea to emerge from the raucous meeting was already months in the planning. *Rolling Stone* investor Max Palevsky had offered to support the magazine's coverage of the 1972 presidential campaign. Palevsky thought *Rolling Stone* could channel the youth vote after the voting age was lowered to 18 in 1970. Political strategist Frank Mankiewicz, who would eventually work for the McGovern campaign, was Palevsky's friend and an important contact. At Esalen, Wenner announced that Thompson would move to Washington and cover the campaign. Newcomer Timothy Crouse volunteered to assist him. Crouse did not enjoy Wenner's favor, but he could see that Thompson did. Indeed, he thought it was fair to say that Wenner was in love with Thompson. "That's what I saw," Crouse said. "Jann really worshipped Hunter." Together, Thompson and Crouse would take the magazine into new territory.

10 Campaign Trail

For the 34-year-old Thompson, the National Affairs Desk was a plum. Less than a decade earlier, he had considered politics a dead end, but as Richard Nixon consolidated his power, Thompson was spoiling for opportunities to write about current affairs. The new assignment brought other benefits as well. He had more freedom than ever, the pay was steady, he no longer had to pitch stories, and his work was disseminated quickly and broadly. At the end of the campaign season, he could produce a book, perhaps even another bestseller.

Yet the campaign assignment was also daunting. Thompson attended party conventions in 1964 and 1968, but his immaturity in San Francisco was noticeable, and the turmoil in Chicago traumatized him. Moreover, he published almost nothing about those events. The Nixon profile for *Pageant* showcased his powers of observation and flair for invective, but that was a relatively brief foray. Full-time reporting from the campaign trail was arduous, and not only for those who rose at the crack of noon. Thompson would be surrounded by seasoned reporters from the major news organizations. He knew few insiders and lacked savvy colleagues who could serve as a sounding board. The candidates often groused about the major news outlets, but they cared deeply about how they were covered there. A fledgling rock magazine was another matter. In short, Thompson lacked the experience, access, guidance, resources, and leverage that his colleagues enjoyed. He and Crouse would occupy the lowest rung of an established hierarchy.

Although Crouse's mission was to support his senior colleague, Thompson treated him as part of the team. Each evening, they ordered room service and reviewed the day's events. Thompson, who felt disrespected by the other reporters, suggested that Crouse observe them carefully. Soon Crouse had a project of his own. *The Boys on the Bus* (1973), which began as a *Rolling Stone* article, offered a detailed description of the campaign and White House press corps. Crouse studied their motives and challenges, their competition and camaraderie, and their complex dealings with campaigns. He outlined the group's internal hierarchy—national political reporters at the top, then campaign reporters, wire-service men, network correspondents, and reporters from the smaller papers. He noted that the five female reporters, who were excluded from the clubby world of their male counterparts, wrote some of the toughest pieces on the Nixon campaign. Ranging back decades, he observed that reporters rarely wrote about candidates' personal foibles yet eagerly shared that information with one another. He also explained the press's risk-averse approach to reporting, much of which could be traced to the dry style and vast audience of the wire-service accounts. Reporters at other outlets dreaded "call-backs" from their editors, which required them to justify any variations from the cautious wire-service stories. "There is an inverse proportion between the number of persons a reporter reaches and the amount he can say," Crouse claimed. "The larger the audience, the more inoffensive and inconclusive the article must be."

As part of his study, Crouse itemized the instruments press secretaries used to discipline reporters. He also described how Ron Ziegler, Nixon's press secretary, wielded those tools and weapons to manage the White House press corps. Crouse dramatized the miseries of that insular world.

> Here was this awful little POW camp, with an officious pouter pigeon of a junior officer—the camp commander's favorite—who bullied the prisoners, studied their flaws, rewarded their failures, beat them for their successes, and encouraged them to turn each other in. And yet, under the mind-bending strain of four years' captivity, nearly all the prisoners had convinced themselves that the little bully was really not that bad a guy. They were grateful for the times when he kidded around with them.

It was no wonder, Crouse concluded, that Ziegler disdained the press. The White House preferred the example set by one reporter, who was "an absolutely thorough and 'objective' stenographer, recording every official happening, never tainting his copy with the smallest speck of insight." The press corps could have acted collectively to curb Ziegler's power, but Crouse claimed that reporters tended to work as a herd when independent action was called for, and to insist on their individuality when closing ranks was more effective. The Watergate story, which did not take hold until after the election, revealed another asymmetry between the White House and the press. Carl Bernstein, whose reporting for the *Washington Post* helped bring the Watergate scandal to light, told Crouse that he and his colleagues "realized one crucial fact about the White House: *they know our business, and we don't know their business.*"

Finally, Crouse showed how the rules of objective journalism led to misleading coverage. By way of example, he mentioned the case of one *New York Times* reporter who hoped to impress the Nixon campaign with his "fresh eye." In one piece, he described the New Nixon as a walking monument to reason, civility, and frankness. When that reporter's enthusiasm for Nixon waned, however, he found it difficult to express his doubts within what Crouse called "the narrow, hard-news form of reporting preferred by the *Times.*" After the election, the reporter admitted that the press needed a new way to deal with the White House's skillful manipulation of the news. In effect, he realized what Thompson had told Angus Cameron almost a decade earlier—that facts were lies when added up.

The most forceful criticism of objective journalism came from Brit Hume, who worked for syndicated columnist Jack Anderson, *Ramparts* magazine, and ABC News before his long career at Fox News. "These guys on the plane," Hume said, "claim that they're trying to be objective."

> They shouldn't try to be objective. They should try to be honest. And they're *not* being honest. Their so-called objectivity is just a guise for superficiality. They report what one candidate said, then they go and report what the other candidate said with equal credibility. They never get around to finding out if the guy is telling the truth. They just pass the speeches along without trying to confirm the substance of what the candidates are saying. What they pass off as objectivity is just a mindless kind of neutrality.

If a candidate or even the president spouted demonstrable lies every day— at that time, this scenario was still hypothetical—the rules made it impossible for reporters to say so directly.

Some of the sharper reporters felt stymied by those conventions, but few writers were allowed to ignore them. Magazines dispatched Norman Mailer, Germaine Greer, and Kurt Vonnegut to cover the 1972 conventions without requiring them to genuflect before the dark god of objectivity. Bob Greene, only 25 years old at the time, offered the youth perspective at the *Chicago Sun-Times,* and Ron Rosenbaum wrote colorful pieces for the *Village Voice.* According to Crouse, however, only one "non-objective journalist" covered the campaign full-time from January through November. It was his colleague, Hunter S. Thompson, who created the greatest sensation of all.

. . .

Crouse was the first to examine the press corps in such detail, but presidential campaigns had already produced a short shelf of acclaimed books. Joe McGinniss's bestseller, *The Selling of the President 1968*, exposed the political theater behind that year's election, but its title was a nod to an even more influential book. When it appeared in 1961, Theodore White's *The Making of the President 1960* offered a new and decidedly literary approach to American politics. Its own backstory also encapsulated a key theme in twentieth-century American journalism and threw Thompson's efforts into sharp focus.

Born to a poor Jewish family in Boston, White attended Harvard University on a scholarship awarded to newsboys. During the Second World War, he covered China for *Time* magazine. Its founder, Henry Luce, believed that by writing what ought to be instead of what was, *Time* was performing journalism's noblest function. In that spirit, White glossed over Chiang Kai-shek's corruption and ineptitude in an effort to serve American interests. Even so, his copy was rewritten by editors, including anti-communist Whittaker Chambers, to further obscure what was actually happening in China. A frustrated White quit *Time* and later became a European correspondent. Most of his work fell neatly into the category of consensus journalism, but his two books about China persuaded the FBI to open a file on him. Years later, President Johnson pointed to a manila folder on his desk and told White House aide Richard Goodwin, who would later write for *Rolling Stone*, "It's Teddy White's FBI file. He's a communist sympathizer."

White also published two novels, both of which were converted into Hollywood films. Even before the second one appeared, he decided to tap that fictional genre to write about the 1960 presidential campaign. It was an important innovation. Campaign coverage before White focused on the public aspects of the campaign, including announcements, speeches, conventions, and elections. In effect, it created a historical record rather than a way for readers to understand the personalities and motives of the candidates. White's plan was to present the entire campaign as a polished narrative.

> It would be written as a novel is written, with anticipated surprises as, one by one, early candidates vanish in the primaries until only two final jousters struggle for the prize. Moreover, it should be written as a story of a man in trouble, of the leader under the pressure of circumstances.

White's formula omitted material that did not support the work's main theme. "A book, to be a great book," he once told a friend, "must have a unity, a dramatic unfolding from a single central theme so that the reader comes away from the book as if he had participated himself in the development of a wonder." His stylized approach had at least two consequences. It created a grandiose image of the president and reinforced a particular conception of American power at the height of the Cold War. In that contest, the United States was also struggling with another jouster for the prize— not the presidency, but global dominance.

As it turned out, the popular vote in 1960 was especially close. Only 113,000 votes, or 0.2 percent of the overall tally, separated the candidates. Election fraud in Illinois and Texas—reportedly engineered by Mayor Daley, the Chicago mob, and Lyndon Johnson's allies—contributed to Kennedy's victory. Such fraud was not unprecedented. Biographer Robert Caro claimed that Lyndon Johnson had benefited from similar measures to win his Senate primary in 1948. "I don't disagree with the accuracy of anything Bob has in there," one of Johnson's former aides said about Caro's book, but he also added, "There was a lot of stealing in that election." Another Johnson biographer, Doris Kearns Goodwin, found evidence that a rigged recount probably sank Johnson's first Senate bid in 1941. In the 1960 presidential race, Nixon decided not to challenge the results publicly, but his allies and aides aggressively pursued that option. Twelve years later, he directed his own election machinations.

None of this muck soiled White's account of the 1960 campaign, a national bestseller that won the Pulitzer Prize for general nonfiction. Sensing a franchise, White followed up with books about the 1964, 1968, and 1972 campaigns. Very little in that *oeuvre* suggested that anything in American politics was amiss. Feeling that he had slighted Nixon in his 1960 coverage, he atoned for that lapse in his 1968 campaign book, which he sent to Nixon with his apologies. Reporters laughed out loud, Crouse said, when they read White's description of that contest. "In 1968," White wrote, "Nixon conspicuously, conscientiously, calculatedly denied himself all racist votes, yielding them to [George] Wallace." In fact, Nixon skillfully deployed the so-called Southern strategy, which harnessed the racism of white voters, to win the presidential election that year.

White also touted Nixon in his 1972 book, whose publication was postponed by the Watergate revelations. Nixon's perfidy caught White by surprise, and his next book was *Breach of Faith: The Fall of Richard Nixon*, which appeared in 1975. Political journalist Richard Rovere, who had criticized Senator Joseph McCarthy and Nixon in the 1950s, said that White's respect and love for America's political culture "led him to celebrate some rather shabby characters." Another colleague, Marvin Kalb, noted that White "had all the correct instincts, but he lived by very few of them." When asked about his critics, White replied, "Look, the only leaders I really

hated were Hitler and Stalin. I've tried to see the different sides of people.
I've been called anti-Nixon and pro-Nixon. Just say I'm soft on the human
race."

Both novelistic and heroic, White's books offered an appealing alternative to traditional campaign reporting. According to media scholar Joyce
Hoffmann, they also reflected a particular style of American journalism
that prevailed during and after the Second World War. By writing as patri-
ots first and journalists second, reporters and columnists produced a form
of consensus journalism that supported American power. In White's case,
that pattern included a tendency to glorify American leaders. A prime
example appeared in the aftermath of President Kennedy's assassination.
Jacqueline Kennedy invited White to Hyannis Port and asked him to write
about the Kennedy White House for *Life* magazine. She especially wanted
him to compare it to Camelot. (At the time, *Camelot* was enjoying a successful run on Broadway.) White consented but later described his piece for
Life, which ran in December 1963, as "a misreading of history" and a gesture to a distraught widow. For historian Rick Perlstein, however, White's
article was "a nadir in the history of court journalism."

· · ·

Thompson, who had no plans to flatter anyone, was well aware of the challenges he faced. At the beginning of his 1973 book, he mentioned the steps
he took to overcome them. One was to ignore the regular press's norms. As
far as he was concerned, there was no such thing as "off the record." In fact,
he knew few sources whose unattributed information would be newswor-
thy, but Thompson also realized that his strategy could turn his marginal
status to advantage. His colleagues cultivated inside sources and considered
their interests, but Thompson saw no need to play the long game. He wrote
for *Rolling Stone*, not a major news outlet, and he had no plans to return to
the campaign trail. That freed him to tell the truth as he understood it, and
he mentioned that liberty early in his book.

> Unlike most other correspondents, I could afford to burn all my bridges
> behind me—because I was only there for a year, and the last thing I
> cared about was establishing long-term connections on Capitol Hill. I
> went for two reasons: (1) to learn as much as possible about the
> mechanics and realities of a presidential campaign, and (2) to write
> about it the same way I'd write about anything else—as close to the
> bone as I could get, and to hell with the consequences.

That approach came naturally to Thompson, but now it combined with
Rolling Stone's liminal status to create a unique opportunity.

Despite his willingness to forswear long-term connections, Thompson developed a strong rapport with the McGovern campaign. Mostly that connection reflected his preference for McGovern, but it also grew out of his desire to learn as much as possible. Pollster Pat Caddell noticed Thompson's determination to master the inner workings of the campaigns.

> Hunter worked his ass off to understand what was going on. He saw things that nobody else was seeing . . . He didn't know about politics, so he insisted that you explain every detail, and he would pick it up like that. That's why he was so much better informed than most of the political reporters traveling on the campaign, because they were covering it by the book—and Hunter didn't have the book. He was making one up.

Once again, Thompson turned a liability into an asset. Precisely because he was unfamiliar with campaigns, he worked harder to master their mechanics and realities. That labor, in turn, positioned him to explain the campaigns in terms that lay audiences could understand.

If Thompson ignored certain journalistic norms, he also spurned—or perhaps superseded—Theodore White's literary innovations. In particular, he had no intention of presenting the campaign as unified story with a single theme. Instead, his "jangled campaign diary" would attempt to record the volatile campaign in real time. That goal resembled his original conception of the Las Vegas project, and as with the Hell's Angels story, his participatory reporting became a source of authority. In this case, however, the campaign dispatches did not need to form a shapely arc. Even while assembling the book, he renounced what he called "the luxury of hindsight" and resisted the urge to fashion a polished narrative.

Thompson also drew on the force of his personality. One veteran reporter noted that several stiff-necked colleagues resented his presence, but many were drawn to him and his freewheeling style. He did not claim any special political expertise, but he relished the chance to mark his beliefs to market. His coverage often referred to the bets he was placing, and usually winning, with other reporters. The horserace aspect of his coverage brought the campaign closer to the ground he knew well, and he used those wagers to strengthen his connections with colleagues. Drinking was another activity that united the press corps, and he yielded to no one in that department. Over time, one reporter noted, Thompson created a niche for himself in the press corps.

> He was viewed with a combination of love and fear by the reporters. I think they were all mystified by him at first—he was such a different animal than you usually see in the press corps—but most of them

quickly came to appreciate the fact that he was a pretty good writer. Even the big mainstream writers from the *New York Times* and *The Washington Post*—R.W. Apple and that crowd—grudgingly learned to appreciate and respect him. The younger reporters, of course, loved him.

Especially after the race, campaign veterans of all stripes greeted him warmly, expressed their affection, and shared their Thompson anecdotes with others.

Thompson's experience as a media critic was another asset. As usual, his coverage included reporting by other outlets as well as the main story as such. Crouse's book was an even deeper dive into the press corps and its habits, but Thompson's self-reflexive dispatches had the advantage of time-liness during the campaign season. His media criticism did not follow the well-worn path of singling out individual reporters or outlets for bias or other shortcomings. Rather, he believed that traditional journalism in general was failing to meet the moment. To capture Nixon's monstrosity, he argued, journalists needed an alternative approach and lexicon. Years later, he made the same point more forcefully.

> Some people will say that words like *scum* and *rotten* are wrong for Objective Journalism—which is true, but they miss the point. It was the built-in blind spots of the Objective rules and dogma that allowed Nixon to slither into the White House in the first place . . . You had to get Subjective to see Nixon clearly, and the shock of recognition was often painful.

Unlike Crouse, Thompson did not subject the press's blind spots, rules, or dogma to detailed analysis. But even his brief critique implied that objective journalism's conventions, when followed slavishly, could normalize the deeds of bad actors. That normalization proceeded in part from journalism's predictability. No matter how disturbing the daily news was, any alarm it aroused was contained in advance by the promise that a fresh batch of generically identical stories would arrive the next day. In addition to calling out those conventions, Thompson was making an important point: As campaign journalism ossified into empty ritual, it became an intellectual narcotic whose most effective antidote was the truth of powerful writing. If professional norms prevented reporters from capturing Nixon's depravity, a more subjective approach was a necessary improvement. Far from soothing readers, it offered what Kafka called an axe for the frozen sea within them.

In his own un-theoretical way, Thompson was referring to what historian Hayden White later called the content of the form. Narrative conventions in historiography, White observed, did not furnish a clear window through which we could perceive reality. Rather, those conventions created meaning above and beyond the particulars of any story. "What wish is enacted," Hayden asked, "what desire is gratified, by the fantasy that real events are properly represented when they can be shown to display the formal coherency of a story?" Reviewing the historical record, White linked that desire to the maintenance of legitimate authority. So, too, with narrative conventions in journalism. In "The White Album," Joan Didion equated narration with survival. "We tell ourselves stories in order to live," that essay began. She was not referring to "the survival trip" that Thompson had in mind during the Age of Nixon, but rather to the way writers ordered and made sense of raw experience. Thompson did not share Didion's fear of disorder—indeed, he liked to create it. If his experiences were chaotic and fragmented, so was his reporting. His critique of objective journalism revealed its limitations, but his jagged style also challenged the social and political arrangements such journalism reinforced as a matter of course.

Finally, Thompson brought his formidable powers of invective and satire to his coverage. From the outset, he targeted the leading candidates in both parties. In the early primaries, he drew a bead on Senator Edmund Muskie, the Democratic frontrunner. Working for Big Ed, he wrote, "was something like being locked in rolling box car with a vicious 200-pound water rat." Thompson never adopted the party line that Muskie was the only Democrat who could beat Nixon. "This was bullshit, of course," he wrote. "Sending Muskie against Nixon would have been like sending a three-toed sloth out to seize turf from a wolverine." Nixon's thugs, he continued, would have Muskie "screeching on his knees by sundown on Labor Day." If he were running a campaign against Muskie, he continued, he would air national television ads with an anonymous creep announcing that "twenty-two years ago, he and Ed spent a summer working as male whores at a Peg House somewhere in the North Woods." Nothing else would be necessary, Thompson added.

Muskie was also the target of Thompson's most outrageous satire. After the Wisconsin primary, Thompson reported a leak to the effect that Muskie was addicted to ibogaine. A psychoactive substance drawn from the iboga tree, ibogaine was used for spiritual purposes in Central Africa but was completely unknown to most Americans. Sandwiched between relatively straight reports, Thompson's scoop included an outlandish but professionally packaged lede.

> Not much has been written about The Ibogaine Effect as a serious factor in the Presidential Campaign, but toward the end of the Wisconsin

primary race—about a week before the vote—word leaked out that some of Muskie's top advisors had called on a Brazilian doctor who was said to be treating the candidate with "some kind of strange drug" that nobody in the press corps had heard of.

That leak, Thompson continued, helped account for Muskie's erratic behavior on the campaign trail. In fact, Muskie had lashed out on several occasions and famously wept during his remarks to the press in New Hampshire. But The Ibogaine Effect, Thompson wrote, explained why Muskie fell apart during a speech in Miami. "It is entirely conceivable—given the known effects of Ibogaine—that Muskie's brain was almost paralyzed by hallucinations at the time."

The satire clicked for several reasons. First, it was the sort of leak that reporters might decline to share even if true. Although the entire White House press corps knew about Franklin Roosevelt's disability, for example, no one wrote about it. Likewise, John F. Kennedy's extensive philandering went unreported. That custom would change in the 1980s, when reports of Gary Hart's extramarital affairs dashed his bid for the Democratic nomination for president. In 1972, however, such matters were still largely out of bounds. Second, Thompson's satire was tailored for the drug culture, which made up a substantial portion of *Rolling Stone*'s readership. The idea that the humorless Muskie might scan his audience and see a collection of Gila monsters had comic potential. Finally, the satire reinforced the hippie conviction that official America was capable of weirdness that far outstripped their own. It delighted them to imagine Muskie in the grip of a drug that not even they had heard of.

When Muskie's campaign collapsed, Thompson trained his sights on Hubert Humphrey, the former vice president who lost to Nixon in 1968. Humphrey's resume cut no ice with Thompson, who called him "a treacherous, gutless old ward-heeler who should be put in a goddamn bottle and sent out with the Japanese current." His insult, Thompson noted with satisfaction, appeared in consecutive issues of *Newsweek*. Before the California primary, Thompson said he wanted to "follow Hubert for a while, track him around the state like a golem, and record his last act for posterity." He then addressed Humphrey directly.

Remember me, Hubert? I'm the one who got smacked in the stomach by a billy club at the corner of Michigan and Balboa on that evil Wednesday night four years ago in Chicago . . . while you looked down from your suite on the 25th floor of the Hilton, and wept with a snout full of tear gas drifting up from Grant Park.

Thompson also combined his takedown of Humphrey with his critique of standard journalism.

> There is no way to grasp what a shallow, contemptible, and hopelessly dishonest old hack Hubert Humphrey really is until you've followed him around for a while on the campaign trail. The double-standard realities of campaign journalism, however, make it difficult for even the best of the "straight/objective" reporters to write what they actually think and feel about a candidate.

Thompson claimed that journalists ridiculed Humphrey, especially in the midnight conversations conducted in hotel bars, but he offered no specifics.

As Thompson flayed the last candidate standing between McGovern and the Democratic nomination, he reviewed his own handiwork.

> I have never been one to hold a grudge any longer than absolutely necessary, Hubert, and I get the feeling that we're about to write this one off. Big Ed was first . . . then you . . . and after that—The Other One.
>
> Nothing personal. But it's time to balance the books. The Raven is calling your name, Hubert; he says you still owe some dues—payable, in full, on June 6th. In the coin of the realm; no credit this time, no extensions.

The Other One, of course, was Nixon, for whom Thompson would save his most savage invective. Grounding his preference for McGovern in the language of vendetta, he left the cool analysis to others, including Carey McWilliams, who used his editorial perch at *The Nation* to hammer away at the president and his policies.

· · ·

Thompson's "merciless, ball-busting approach" had several advantages, but it also generated its own problems. The least serious one concerned his reception in Washington, DC. In both his comportment and his writing, Thompson announced that the usual forms of press discipline did not apply to him. As a result, however, the few friends he had there began treating him "like a walking bomb." Some were reluctant even to share a drink with him "for fear that their tongues might get loose and utter words that would almost certainly turn up on the newsstands two weeks later." Locals knew that Washington journalists routinely used dinner-party chatter, lubricated with stiff martinis, to inform their own columns.

A more complex problem arose from Thompson's clear preference for McGovern, who pledged to end the war in Vietnam. Thompson wrote freely (and humorously) about McGovern's weaknesses as a candidate, but he worked easily with his staff during the early primaries. "He had better access to our campaign than any other reporter," strategist Frank Mankiewicz noted. "He was around, and he was friendly. It was partly a case of no one else treating us seriously at the beginning. But in addition to that, I thought he was the smartest." When McGovern emerged as the top Democratic candidate, however, Thompson was perceived as a liability and sidelined. He responded by lamenting McGovern's decision to court centrist voters even as he hoped for—and bet on—a McGovern victory. As the campaign wore on, he also focused on the striking contrasts between the candidates. Only "a blind geek or a waterhead" could miss the difference between McGovern and Nixon.

> Granted, they are both white men; and both are politicians—but the similarity ends right there, and at that point the difference is so vast that anybody who can't see it deserves whatever happens to them if Nixon gets re-elected due to apathy, stupidity, and laziness on the part of potential McGovern voters.

He also contrasted their campaign styles. The McGovern campaign resembled a Grateful Dead tour, he said, whereas covering Nixon was like traveling with the Pope. More often than not, the press corps was not allowed to see, much less question, the president.

Thompson was still touting McGovern when that campaign made a catastrophic error. Having named Senator Thomas Eagleton of Missouri as his running mate, a move that Thompson questioned, McGovern learned that Eagleton had received electroshock treatments for depression. McGovern initially declared his continued support for Eagleton but then distanced himself, hoping that Eagleton would take the hint and step down. The story dragged on, and McGovern never recovered. Despite committing what Thompson called "a series of almost unbelievable blunders," the Democratic candidate was still his man. "McGovern made some stupid mistakes," he wrote, "but in context they seem almost frivolous compared to the things Richard Nixon does every day of his life, on purpose, as a matter of policy and a perfect expression of everything he stands for."

No one expected impartiality from Thompson, but for all his advocacy, he was not partisan in the classic sense. To the contrary, he still bore a major grudge against the Democratic Party. While McGovern was surging in the primaries, Thompson shared his mixed feelings.

> I am suddenly facing the very distinct possibility that I might have to drag myself into a voting booth this November and actually pull the

lever for the presidential candidate of the Democratic Party. O'Brien's party. That same gang of corrupt and genocidal bastards who not only burned me for six white sharkskin suits eight years ago in South Dakota and chased me through the streets of Chicago with clubs & tear gas in August of '68, but also forced me to choose for five years between going to prison or chipping in 20 percent of my income to pay for napalm bombs to be dropped on people who never threatened me with anything; and who put my friends in jail for refusing to fight an undeclared war in Asia that even Mayor Daley is now opposed to.

That grudge deepened after the party's toppled leadership refused to support McGovern fully in the general election. In one poll, Thompson noted, 48 percent of respondents who said they would vote for Humphrey in the California primary pulled the lever for Nixon in the general election. Even if that figure was closer to 30 percent, as Democratic pollster Pat Caddell claimed, Thompson called it "a hell of a defection."

Thompson did not try to conceal his disappointment. Crouse noted that for professional reasons, many reporters wanted the campaigns they covered to succeed, but Thompson's commitment to McGovern did not reflect his personal ambition. As McGovern's political fortunes sagged, so did Thompson's spirits. Some considered Thompson naive even as others called him a cynic. The latter label, Matt Taibbi later maintained, missed the mark completely.

> People who describe Thompson's dark and profane jokes as "cynical humor" don't get it. Hunter Thompson was always the polar opposite of a cynic. A cynic, in the landscape of Campaign Trail '72, for instance, is someone like Nixon or Ed Muskie, someone who cheerfully accepts the fundamental dishonesty of the American political process and is able to calmly deal with it on those terms, without horror.

Thompson's disappointment was compounded by fatigue and his hatred for Nixon. As his stamina waned and McGovern's chances slipped away, Thompson's coverage became more fantastical. In the final days of the campaign, his dispatches merged real-time observations from the so-called Zoo Plane, which transported the rowdier reporters and crew members covering the campaign, with flashbacks from his Hell's Angels and Kentucky Derby experiences. He imagined looking up from his notes at Churchill Downs to see Frank Mankiewicz and Sonny Barger in Hell's Angels colors with heavy chain-whips. Steadman was also there, sketching as usual, along with Tiny, Frenchy, Terry the Tramp, and several McGovern advisors. Following that passage, an Editor's Note explains that Thompson suffered a seizure, and the rest of the book is made up largely of transcribed conversations and unedited monologues.

. . .

When it arrived, McGovern's loss did not resemble Goldwater's. The GOP defeat in 1964 realigned American politics and prepared the party for future success, but McGovern's defeat left the Democrats stunned. To prevent similar losses in the future, the party responded by creating superdelegates—party regulars who could guide, temper, or even offset the popular vote in Democratic primaries. That change, which favored insiders over grassroots campaigns, only compounded what Thompson saw as McGovern's chief mistake.

> My own theory, which sounds like madness, is that McGovern would have been better off running against Nixon with the same kind of neo-"radical" campaign that he ran in the primaries. Not radical in the left/right sense, but radical in the sense that he was coming on with . . . a new . . . a different type of politician . . . a person who would grab the system by the ears and shake it.

Ironically, McGovern would blame his defeat on the media, which covered his relatively transparent campaign extensively while neglecting Nixon's opaque one. Yet Thompson claimed that nothing, not even the early stages of the Watergate story, could have derailed a Nixon victory at that point. To judge by his reaction, the election was a calamity comparable only to Kennedy's assassination nine years earlier.

After Nixon's reelection, *Rolling Stone* ran Thompson's reflections on the campaign. He began by rehearsing his claim that the choice for president was clearly defined. The contrast between McGovern and Nixon went far beyond political differences; it also extended to personalities, temperaments, and principles. After staging that contrast carefully, Thompson launched an unprecedented screed against a sitting president who only days before had won a landslide victory.

> It is Nixon himself who represents that dark, venal and incurably violent side of the American character that almost every country in the world has learned to fear and despise. Our Barbie-doll president, with his Barbie-doll wife and his boxful of Barbie-doll children is also America's answer to the monstrous Mr. Hyde. He speaks for the Werewolf in us; the bully, the predatory shyster who turns into something unspeakable, full of claws and bleeding string-warts on nights when the moon comes too close . . .

As Thompson continued, his hyperbole reached new heights.

> At the stroke of midnight in Washington, a drooling red-eyed beast with the legs of a man and a head of a giant hyena crawls out of its

bedroom window in the South Wing of the White House and leaps fifty feet down to the lawn . . . pauses briefly to strangle a Chow watchdog, then races off into the darkness . . . towards the Watergate, snarling with lust, loping through the alleys behind Pennsylvania Avenue, and trying desperately to remember which one of those four hundred identical balconies is the one outside Martha Mitchell's apartment . . .

Thompson characterized his reverie as a bad dream and a joke. "Ah . . . nightmares, nightmares. But I was only kidding," he quickly added. "The President of the United States would never act that weird. At least not during football season." Despite that hedge, the election's outcome pushed Thompson's diction into a new and darker register.

Returning to the realm of political commentary, Thompson wondered how voters regarded a *New York Times* editorial that appeared less than one month before the election. It made the astounding charge that Nixon was presiding over "a complex, far-reaching, and sinister operation on the part of White House aides and the Nixon campaign organization . . . involving sabotage, forgery, theft of confidential files, surveillance of Democratic candidates and their families, and persistent efforts to lay the basis for possible blackmail and intimidation." Especially by that time, Thompson considered the Nixon administration's corruption an open secret.

> "Ominous" is not quite the right word for a situation where one of the most consistently unpopular politicians in American history suddenly skyrockets to Folk Hero status while his closest advisors are being caught almost daily in nazi-style gigs that would have embarrassed Martin Bormann.

Thompson wondered what, if anything, could make Nixon's turpitude plainer.

Nixon was not the only problem, of course. His victory meant that Americans approved of, or at least could live with, everything that Thompson detested. In his view, McGovern's defeat reflected poorly on American voters, not the candidate.

> This may be the year when we finally come face to face with ourselves; finally just lay back and say it—that we are really just a nation of 220 million used car salesmen with all the money we need to buy guns, and no qualms at all about killing anybody else in the world who tries to make us uncomfortable.

Thompson's analysis shared several features with Carey McWilliams's. Toward the end of his long career as a Nixon watcher, McWilliams wondered how Nixon had become his generation's dominant politician. "Again and again," he wrote in his memoir, "I asked myself why it was that so many Americans either found it difficult to take Nixon's measure or were prepared to give him the benefit of the doubt." Although Nixon was unpredictable, he was not that hard to read. Despite the view that he himself once advanced— that Nixon played on the emotions of a gullible electorate—McWilliams later acknowledged that many Americans had not been fooled. To the contrary, they understood Nixon perfectly. "A section of the public," he concluded, "apparently felt that the times called for a bastard and that Nixon fit the specifications." That conclusion was even more sobering than the notion that Nixon was a demagogue. If voters knowingly placed a soulless opportunist in the White House, they were at least partly responsible for the results.

However the blame was assigned, Thompson's contempt for Nixon remained untempered. In a 1978 interview, he detailed his aversion to the besmirched president.

> Richard Nixon represents the dark side of the American Dream. Richard Nixon stands for me for everything that I would not want to happen to myself, or be, or be around. He stands for everything that I not only have contempt for but dislike and think should be stomped out. Greed, treachery, stupidity, cupidity, positive power of lying, total contempt for any sort of human, constructive political instinct . . . Nixon represents everything that's wrong with this country. Down the line.

He later claimed to miss Nixon as an adversary, but his view of the former president never improved. By the time he wrote Nixon's obituary in 1994, that view had crossed into demonology. "Richard Nixon was an evil man— evil in a way that only those who believe in the physical reality of the Devil can understand it," he maintained. Thompson's biographer, William McKeen, later described Nixon as Thompson's muse.

• • •

After the election, Thompson turned his attention to his book project. Most of the manuscript consisted of the dispatches he produced from the campaign trail. The publisher, Straight Arrow Books, already had Steadman's illustrations from the *Rolling Stone* articles. But there was still work to do on the manuscript's connective tissue, and editor Alan Rinzler was nervous about the schedule. After exchanging hostile letters with Thompson, he realized that the complete manuscript would not arrive on time or perhaps not at all. After his arrival in San Francisco, Thompson failed to appear in *Rolling Stone*'s office, where space had been cleared for him to finish the work. Eventually he checked into the Seal Rock Inn on Geary Boulevard near the beach.

Rinzler faced a formidable task. Editors usually read complete drafts before weighing in with comments. In some cases, especially on short deadlines, they read chapters in batches. Rinzler realized, however, that he would have to sit with Thompson and wring the final sections out of him. Having faced that fact, he arrived at the Seal Rock Inn along with forty pounds of supplies, which Thompson itemized in his Author's Note: two cases of Mexican beer, four quarts of gin, a dozen grapefruits, and "enough speed to alter the outcome of six Super Bowls." The other supplies included a Selectric typewriter, two reams of paper, plenty of firewood, and three tape recorders. Thompson's list echoed the drug inventory in the opening pages of *Fear and Loathing in Las Vegas*, but this time the adventure would be finishing the manuscript, not a road trip through the desert. As was his custom, Thompson noted the weather (foggy) and added another detail— the frenzied reaction of Rinzler's poodle to the barking seals off the coast. Nothing about this scenario fit the script for efficient literary production.

The work sessions were brutal. Thompson described them as "55 hours of sleepless, foodless, high-speed editing." Rinzler confirmed the basic story.

> Food was brought in constantly, but he didn't eat much because he was taking so much speed and cocaine. It was a nonstop, you know, 72 hours at a stretch, collapse, 72 more at a stretch, collapse, kind of experience. And we had tape machines in those days. People would come pick up the tapes, rush away to the office and work all night transcribing the tapes, or all day, and bring back the pages. And that was the kind of way you had to work to get it done with Hunter.

His ordeal at the Seal Rock Inn, Thompson noted in the book, resembled the one he used to produce the campaign dispatches in the first place. Almost every paragraph of that coverage was produced "in a last-minute, teeth-grinding frenzy." As the two men rushed to complete the manuscript, Rinzler noted the centrality of drugs to Thompson's literary production. "He tried to tune up his mind through drugs and alcohol to the point where he was having grandiose visions and flights of tremendous creative imagination," he said. "But then there would be too much of it, and he would turn to jelly, and he couldn't think straight at all." The editorial process was hands-on, exhausting, and adversarial. Later, Rinzler would see himself as battle-tested. If he could edit Thompson, he could edit anyone. Eventually the manuscript was turned into page proofs that included scratched-out words. Nevertheless, they were sent to the printer in Reno, Nevada, and reviewers received their galleys less than six months after Nixon's reelection.

When the book appeared, it did not read like a novel. Rather, it blended Thompson's first-person reports with blistering invective, wicked satire, fantastical digressions, and chronic complaints about life in the campaign bubble. In some ways, it had less in common with *The Making of the President 1960* than with pitcher Jim Bouton's *Ball Four* (1970), the inside account of a single season of major league baseball. After that book was denounced by players, sportswriters, and baseball commissioner Bowie Kuhn, it became the bestselling sports book of all time. Sportswriters in particular were upset about its revelations that ballplayers took pep pills, got drunk, stayed out late, talked dirty, had groupies, and were rude to fans. But as Bouton pointed out, if sportswriters had been reporting what actually went on in the major leagues, there would have been no sensation around his book in the first place. That irony was not lost on Pulitzer Prize winner David Halberstam. In an article for *Harper's* magazine, he maintained that sportswriters were not judging the accuracy of Bouton's revelations, but rather his right to share them. "A reporter covers an institution, becomes associated with it, protective of it, and, most important, the arbiter of what is right to tell," Halberstam explained. "He knows what's good for you to hear, what should remain at the press-club bar." Halberstam concluded that Bouton's book was "deep in the American vein," and that the reaction was also deeply American. Like *Ball Four*, Thompson's book was characterized by its irreverent tone, episodic narration, and references to alcohol and drug abuse—not on the road with the Seattle Pilots, but on the Zoo Plane with the political carnival.

Once again, the critical reception was excellent. *New York Times* critic Christopher Lehmann-Haupt praised the campaign while comparing Thompson to his earlier incarnation.

> But behold—we find here a Hunter Thompson rather different from the savage who gave us *Fear and Loathing in Las Vegas*. Gaze in awe— for this is almost a sane man. True, he is not yet exactly Theodore S. White soberly reflecting from the suites of power. He bitches endlessly about the pressure of his deadlines, keeps wandering off on obscure, if amusing, tangents, has nervous breakdowns before our eyes, and generally deports himself like a man who would rather be doing any thing else than reporting politics.

Lehmann-Haupt facetiously worried that Thompson might go overboard with his newfound sanity.

> That would be a shame, for while he doesn't exactly see America as Grandma Moses depicted it, or the way they painted it for us in civics class, he does in his own mad way betray a profound democratic concern for the polity. And in its own mad way, it's damned refreshing.

Two months later, another *New York Times* review called Thompson's book "the best account yet published of what it feels like to be out there in the middle of the American political process." The sales figures supported that claim. By 1992, some 1.5 million copies of *Fear and Loathing: On the Campaign Trail '72* had been sold in cloth and paperback editions.

· · ·

By the time the campaign book landed on the shelves, the Watergate scandal was consuming the Nixon administration. Before the election, the White House dismissed the *Washington Post*'s coverage as a vendetta launched by the liberal establishment. In March 1973, however, convictions in the Watergate burglary case revealed evidence of obstruction. As a grand jury investigated that charge, President Nixon announced that he would begin his own "intensive new inquiries" into Watergate. When asked about the myriad contradictions between the president's statement and earlier ones, Ron Ziegler replied that all other statements were "inoperative." Even *Time* magazine did not buy the White House spin, concluding that the scandal was "rapidly emerging as probably the most pervasive instance of top-level misconduct in history." The Senate launched its own investigation, which eventually aired on television. During his testimony before the Senate committee that summer, White House counsel John Dean revealed that the president's public statements about Watergate were lies.

As fall arrived, Nixon was still holding on, and Thompson considered the president's predicament in the pages of *Rolling Stone*.

> The vultures are coming home to roost—like he always feared they
> would, in the end—and it hurts me in a way nobody would publish
> if I properly described it, to know that I can't be with him on the sweaty
> ramparts today, stomping those dirty buzzards like Davy Crockett
> bashing spics off the wall of the Alamo.

Thompson also mentioned the president's Enemies List, which by that time had become public. Drawn up in the summer of 1971, it predated much of Thompson's most pointed attacks on Nixon. Thompson was disappointed by his exclusion from the list and complained about Ron Ziegler's refusal to read *Rolling Stone*. "This is a matter of journalistic ethics—or perhaps even 'sportsmanship'—and I take a certain pride in knowing that I kicked Nixon before he went down," he wrote. "Not afterwards—though I plan to do *that*, too, as soon as possible."

Thompson reviewed the national press's performance as well. Noting that he was underwhelmed by his colleagues on the campaign trail, he acknowledged that "the bastards had this Watergate story nailed up and bleeding from every extremity." There was little room for Gonzo journalism while the Washington press corps "was working very close to the peak of its awesome but normally dormant potential." His own coverage blended fact, fiction, genres, and personae. Much of it remained tangential to the underlying story—a complex drama that dominated all three branches of the federal government—but as Thompson noted, his colleagues already had documented that story thoroughly.

In 1974, Nixon lost a legal battle over his tape-recorded White House conversations. The transcripts revealed his direct role in the burglaries and cover-up and dramatized the gap between Nixon's stiff public self and brutal political style. Although he was losing ground on every front, the president resisted calls to resign. When Senator Goldwater informed him that he would not survive an impeachment trial in the Senate, Nixon finally relinquished the White House. His replacement, Gerald Ford, quickly granted him a full, free, and absolute presidential pardon.

In a long article for *Rolling Stone*, Thompson described the somber aftermath of Nixon's resignation. "Within hours after Nixon's departure, every bar in downtown Washington normally frequented by reporters was a sinkhole of gloom." Thompson found Democratic speechwriter Richard Goodwin nursing a drink near the White House. "I feel totally drained," Goodwin said. "It's like the circus just left town." Thompson admitted that he, too, felt deflated. "My interest in national politics withered drastically within hours after Nixon resigned." He was appalled by President Ford's pardon, but the war of attrition had taken its toll.

> After more than ten years of civil war with the White House and all the swine who either lived or worked there, I was ready to give the benefit of the doubt to almost any president who acted half human and had enough sense not to walk around in public wearing a swastika armband.

Thompson had always needed an adversary to produce his best work. With Nixon's evacuation from the national scene, he lost the worthiest one of all.

11   After Nixon

If Thompson's literary formation was largely a San Francisco story, his peak output coincided with Nixon's presidency. When his chief adversary resigned in August 1974, Thompson's literary practices, public profile, and media niche were largely established. After years of freelance itinerancy, he would call Woody Creek home for the final three decades of his life. Although he would write for other outlets during that time, Wenner remained the editor most closely associated with him and his work. He would devise new ways to capitalize on his image, but his basic model of authorship changed little, and most of his finest writing was behind him.

As Thompson's professional arrangements stabilized, his main outlet continued to evolve. With his help, *Rolling Stone*'s profile rose steadily during its first decade. "Being the premier rock magazine wasn't a coveted title in 1967," one staff writer recalled, "but it was a big deal ten years later." By that time, the magazine occupied a unique niche in the national media ecology. Neither an underground publication nor a traditional outlet, it overlapped with teen and trade magazines. Politics and current affairs were part of the editorial mix, but its coverage was not radical; in fact, Abbie Hoffman described Wenner as the Benedict Arnold of the revolution. Music was *Rolling Stone*'s strong suit, but especially as the magazine matured, it did not discover new talent so much as ratify it. More than any other outlet however, *Rolling Stone* balanced countercultural cachet and professional respectability. "We were hipper than anyone better," staff writer Abe Peck recalled, "and better than anyone hipper."

Even before Nixon's resignation, Wenner was eager to expand *Rolling Stone*'s political coverage. At Thompson's suggestion, he sponsored a retreat with seven veterans of Democratic campaigns in February 1974. To minimize distractions, the participants met in Elko, Nevada, where they exchanged views on a wide range of issues. The goal was to fashion an editorial platform for the 1976 election, but Wenner also hoped to produce a book based on their colloquy. Little was accomplished, and Thompson later dismissed the transcript as "gibberish" and "liberal elitism at its worst." Nevertheless, Wenner recruited one of the participants, former Kennedy speechwriter Richard Goodwin, to establish a Washington bureau and contribute six columns to *Rolling Stone*. Wenner even considered launching a new magazine called *Politics* under Goodwin's guidance. Larry Durocher, *Rolling Stone*'s publisher in the early 1970s, took a dim view of the arrangement. What their readers wanted, he said, "was cultural politics, the kind of stuff Hunter Thompson and Timmy Crouse wrote." Durocher also criticized the impetus behind Goodwin's appointment. "But along came Dick Goodwin, and Jann once again got star-fucked. He walked into a room and said in a sense, 'What does it cost me to kiss your ass?'" Wenner was thrilled when Goodwin introduced him to Jackie Kennedy Onassis, but the two men split acrimoniously after that.

Wenner remained on the lookout for big stories, and in 1975, *Rolling Stone* published an important investigative piece. The Patricia Hearst saga had received heavy coverage from the moment the Symbionese Liberation Army kidnapped the 19-year-old media heiress from her Berkeley apartment. The frenzy escalated when Hearst announced that she had joined the rag-tag outfit, and it peaked when some of her comrades and former captors perished during a shootout with the police in Los Angeles. After watching the confrontation on live television, Hearst disappeared. Even after the FBI arrested her in September 1975, little was known about the sixteen months she spent underground. That changed when Howard Kohn and David Weir detailed her movements in their two-part *Rolling Stone* article. Their sources included sports activist and former *Ramparts* contributor Jack Scott, who drove Hearst cross-country twice while FBI agents were working furiously to determine her whereabouts. Another source was Patricia Hearst's cousin, Will Hearst, whom Wenner met as the story took shape.

Published after Hearst's capture but before her trial, the story once again showed that *Rolling Stone* was more than a music magazine. Less obvious but equally important, perhaps, was the fact that *Rolling Stone* never depended on such stories to stay in business. Although several political magazines had survived for decades, they failed to attract advertisers even when they enjoyed healthy circulations. *Ramparts*, where Wenner began his magazine career, was a parade example of that failure, but right-wing magazines also struggled with the same problem. Many outlets solved it by bundling their political coverage with more popular fare. Newspapers had been doing that for decades, and by the mid-1970s, the largest ones were also exploiting regional monopolies to book fat profits. Weekly magazines such as *Time* and *Newsweek* likewise flourished by blending political content with lighter news. In 1968, the news division at CBS found the sweet spot when it launched *60 Minutes*, which tempered hard-hitting investigative journalism with softer feature stories. Presenting the program as "a kind of a magazine for television," the network created that medium's most successful and durable franchise.

When it came to advertising, *Rolling Stone* had a secret weapon—the music labels. Politics and current affairs were a key part of the editorial mix, but the magazine's appeal to rock fans underwrote its finances. Wenner insisted that *Rolling Stone* had a mission, not a business model, yet its musical focus, and the advertising that came with it, provided a sturdy platform for its political coverage and commentary. That arrangement distinguished the magazine from its direct competitors, which were not designed to break big stories. In some cases, it also afforded *Rolling Stone* an advantage over larger news organizations, whose beat reporters could not afford to alienate newsmakers and sources. As Thompson's campaign coverage demonstrated, *Rolling Stone* was well positioned to report that the emperor had no clothes.

During this period, Thompson was a central figure at the magazine. Although he did not write about music, he was its most popular contributor, and Abe Peck observed his primacy at close range. After editing an underground newspaper in Chicago, Peck worked for *Rolling Stone* in the mid-1970s and later taught journalism at Northwestern University. In his estimation, *Rolling Stone* was one of the most important American magazines of its era, and Thompson defined its nonmusical voice during the 1970s. In particular, Thompson linked readers to their youthful iconoclasm even as their tastes changed. "He kept the sparks flying when the readership was starting to settle down," Peck said. As he did so, Thompson turned his growing renown to advantage. He began to lecture on college campuses, and though the work was easy and lucrative, he never enjoyed it. Rather than delivering speeches, Thompson limited himself to answering questions, which were often submitted in advance. Sensing that audiences were drawn to his alter ego, Raoul Duke, he played that role onstage. That approach, one of his friends noted, had the added benefit of masking Thompson's shyness in public.

Even as Thompson flaunted his penchant for drugs and alcohol, those appetites were beginning to hamper his literary production. The Dexedrine he relied on to maintain his literary output was no longer producing the desired effect, and he began using cocaine after the campaign book appeared.

Before that time, editor David Felton said, Thompson considered cocaine "a bullshit drug." In short order, however, it became part of his writing process. It sometimes turned his brain into cement, Felton said, and he began to struggle with flow and continuity. No one described Thompson as a drunk—indeed, he was famous for holding his liquor—but he had been drinking all day, every day, for decades. Despite his amazing constitution, his habits were finally taking their toll—not only on him, but also on the colleagues who worked with him. "When Hunter had problems," Felton said, "they became your problems. And they could be quite excruciating."

Thompson's lifestyle affected his professional decisions as well his writing process. At one party, Goodwin deputy Joe Klein suggested that Thompson write a novel. Gesturing to the drugs, Thompson replied, "Well, if I did that, I'd have to give *those* up." Other colleagues also tried to offer advice. During one of Thompson's slumps, *Rolling Stone* editor Paul Scanlon suggested he put Raoul Duke behind him and start producing again. By way of reply, Thompson pulled a tab of LSD out of his wallet, tore it in half, put one half back in his wallet, and washed the other half down with his beer. The gesture signaled an unwillingness both to check his drug use and to refashion his public image. Although he felt constrained by that image, much as Fitzgerald felt trapped by his Jazz Age persona in the 1930s, it was now his most valuable asset. Rather than abandon it, he would seek new ways to monetize it, especially as writing became more problematic.

The editorial support Thompson received at *Rolling Stone* reflected his stature as well as his diminishing attention to literary craft. He later admitted he had not produced a second draft of anything after *Fear and Loathing in Las Vegas*. Every subsequent assignment, Wenner noted, became "a full-out siege." Wenner had to be available to read copy and talk to Thompson for hours before the story came together.

> Generally the lede was easy, describing the invariably dramatic weather wherever he was writing from. Then a flurry of headlines and chapter headings and the transitions he had to produce on demand to create the flow and logic, and always, sooner or later, the conclusion which we always called "the Wisdom."

"Editing Hunter required stamina," Wenner added, "but I was young, and this was once in a lifetime, and we were clear on that."

The magazine supported Thompson in other ways as well. Office staff lined up hotel reservations, airline tickets, and rental cars. They found locations for Thompson to finish his stories, preferably somewhere isolated and with a good bar. In addition to hiring researchers, handlers, and assistants, the magazine flew in IBM Selectric typewriters with the correct typeface.

Back at the office, Thompson's copy arrived in eight-to-ten page bursts over the Xerox telecopier, which he called the Mojo Wire. Each page took seven minutes to print. When the transmissions were complete, editors spread out the fragments and assembled them into a cohesive piece. In some cases, Sandy retrieved discarded drafts from the waste basket, ironed them, and fed them into the telecopier. Thompson was usually grateful for the editorial help, but one *Rolling Stone* staff member recalled waiting for his copy to burble slowly out of the telecopier, only to discover the transmission's full content: "Fuck you."

The most detailed description of Thompson's *modus operandi* was produced by Robert Love for the *Columbia Journalism Review* in 2005. Love, who edited Thompson for three magazines over more than two decades, noted that Thompson's process "was utterly idiosyncratic and unique."

> Other writers more or less turned in manuscripts that were more or less finished, or needed some editorial tweaking. If further revisions were required, we sent them back for rewriting. With Hunter, these deadline sessions were part Mardi Gras, part falaqua. And that's not even mentioning that there were just as many feints and false starts during these twenty-three years as there were pieces that worked out.

The Mardi Gras aspect was signaled by "little multimedia creations that he controlled entirely, like an auteur." Those transmissions arrived on customized letterhead, including some that Thompson had acquired from Congress. Thompson added handwritten heralds at the top: URGENT, BEWARE, BONUS: 4 PAGES TO FOLLOW, HOT DAMN, STAND BACK BUBBA, INSERTS XXX TO FOLLOW. He also decorated them with heart-shaped valentines or other drawings. These productions, Love wrote, "were like the legendary live performances of a band that were never to be captured in a recording."

Thompson's process was seldom smooth or efficient—indeed, it was almost always protracted and theatrical—and editors paid the physical and emotional price. "I don't think there's an editor that's worked with Hunter that hasn't at some point in the process of a story, broken down in tears," Felton said. Some of that despair was due to exhaustion. Editors had to work on Thompson's schedule, which Felton thought was partly determined by his cocaine use.

> He would mojo stuff in—a page or half page—and you'd have to spend that time working on it as it was coming in. And he would be up for three solid days. You'd be up three solid days, getting the stuff and trying to work on it. But then he would crash, but you'd have to stay awake in order to try to assemble the pages into a piece, and edit and

sketch questions that you'd have to ask next time you talked. So he'd be
sleeping, and then he'd be up again, so you would go a full week
without any sleep and be pretty brittle by the end of it.

Thompson taxed his editors in other ways as well. If he was unhappy with
the art direction, he might threaten to pull the piece. Love learned that such
threats were "just a necessary step in the process." Although that process
demanded time, energy, and patience, it was not always productive. "People
have worked on stories with him and failed to get them," Felton said. "Even
if it was a cover story, it might not come in. So if you could get a piece in, it
was a victory, no matter how much you might have cried over it."

Rolling Stone editor Terry McDonell recalled that Thompson made little
effort to hide the transactional nature of his professional relationships. "He
had a riff about it," McDonell recalled, "how he used to suck editors into his
pieces as conspirators, all of us wanting to prove ourselves good enough—
hip enough—to edit him." But if Thompson was difficult to work with, he
also made his colleagues feel special. "When Hunter paid attention to you,"
McDonell noted, "it could feel like a gift, or currency that could be spent
telling stories about him." Moreover, Thompson "could put anyone at ease
when he felt like it."

> This happened more often than his reputation suggests, and it always
> struck me as kind. Although his friendships could be situational, or
> transactional even, he was sentimental about them. One Christmas
> he send me an expensive pocket knife with "The Long Hunt" engraved
> on it.

Timothy Ferris also recalled Thompson's "unwavering generosity" after
he was laid off at *Rolling Stone* during a downturn. Ferris called Owl Farm
and spoke to Sandy, who said Thompson was in his room at the Watergate
in Washington. When Ferris asked about her, she said they were worried
about money. They had only $400 in the bank and nothing on the way.
After Ferris rang off, he called Thompson and reported that Wenner had
fired him. "Do you need any money?" Thompson asked. "I can lend you
four hundred dollars." Along with the editorial support Thompson received,
such gestures strengthened his in-house reputation as *Rolling Stone*'s top
writer.

• • •

As Love and Felton noted, Thompson often failed to produce at all, and two
botched assignments during this period were especially important. Shortly
after Nixon's resignation, Thompson traveled to Kinshasa, Zaire, to cover

the heavyweight championship fight between Muhammad Ali and George Foreman. By that time, Ali was a global media superstar and one of Thompson's personal heroes. The bout appeared to be Ali's last chance to regain the title he lost for resisting the draft, but after crushing Joe Frazier in Jamaica to win the title, Foreman was the heavy favorite. Having cast the first Ali-Frazier fight as the end of the 1960s, Thompson certainly understood the significance of the moment, and his sportswriting experience prepared him well for it. Norman Mailer and George Plimpton were also in Kinshasa to cover the fight, and Ralph Steadman was on hand to produce the illustrations. When Foreman was cut during his training, however, the promoters were forced to delay the bout by one month. Thompson and Bill Cardoso reportedly used that time to make mischief in and around Kinshasa.

When the main event finally came off, Thompson was not ringside. Instead, he chose to float in the hotel swimming pool, into which he had dumped more than a pound of local marijuana. It was an absurd defeat for the Gonzo franchise, which hinged on Thompson's reaction to the event at hand—or, more precisely, the spectacle that surrounded it. Privately, Mailer expressed misgivings about Thompson's approach, which he compared to playing tennis without a net. In Zaire, however, the problem was not Thompson's method so much as his indolence, or perhaps the literary paralysis that it signaled. Even if his Gonzo articles were finally about himself, he could not ignore the occasion for the story. That was especially true of this event, which attracted a massive global audience. Nearly one billion viewers, the largest television audience ever at that time, tuned in to watch the fight. Worse for Thompson, they witnessed what was later described as the greatest sporting event of the twentieth century. To frustrate Foreman, Ali deployed his "rope-a-dope" strategy, which he concealed even from his trainer before the fight. Foreman wore himself out with ineffective punches, Ali scored a knockout at the end of the eighth round, and Thompson returned home without the story. According to Sandy, he slept for a day and a half and had trouble writing after that.

Thompson's excursion to Vietnam the following year was another major setback. He and Wenner had discussed that assignment even before he covered the 1972 campaign, but the window of opportunity in Vietnam was closing quickly. As the American phase of the conflict came to a close, Saigon's fall was imminent. Thompson flew to Southeast Asia via Hawaii, where one local friend noticed that Thompson sounded nervous on the telephone. "But there he was," the friend recalled, "zipping through Honolulu on his way to Vietnam, hoping to get there in time to be thrown out." After his arrival in Saigon, Thompson checked into the Continental

Hotel, the setting for much of Graham Greene's *The Quiet American* (1955). There he joined Loren Jenkins, an Aspen neighbor who was covering the war for *Newsweek*. Veteran correspondent Philip Caputo recognized Thompson and wondered what he was doing there. His colleague, Nick Proffitt, replied, "Well, if he wants fear and loathing, he sure as hell has come to the right place."

Jenkins introduced Thompson to Caputo and Proffitt, both of whom had misgivings about the new arrival. Caputo thought Thompson was "almost like a celebrity or a movie actor who was so identified with the role he played that he couldn't get out of it." He and Proffitt allowed Thompson to join them on a reporting expedition, which typically involved driving out of Saigon until they met gunfire, then returning to file a report. But Proffitt issued a stern warning to Thompson. "You are not in Las Vegas now," he said. "This is a war zone. We leave at 6 a.m., and if you're not there, we are gone. Come along with us, but I don't want any of your shit. *No Gonzo bullshit!*" Despite that warning, Proffitt and Caputo rebuked Thompson for his carelessness during the expedition.

Back at the hotel, Thompson joined the press corps in the interior courtyard, where correspondents ate, drank, and speculated about the imminent invasion. After two days, Thompson flew to Hong Kong and returned with electronic communications equipment he had purchased on *Rolling Stone*'s credit. He thought the gear might help the press corps cope with the city's fall. "I don't think anyone took him seriously," Jenkins said. In another odd move, Thompson decamped for Laos. "Laos was the middle of nowhere," Jenkins said, "clearly out of the picture on anything." Jacques Leslie, who was covering the war for the *Los Angeles Times*, crossed paths with Thompson there and described him as a nervous wreck, even though the situation was relatively calm.

After a month in Vietnam, Thompson returned with little to show for his efforts. It was another disappointment, but he quickly changed the subject to Wenner's treachery. Before he departed for Saigon, Thompson wrote a scathing letter to Wenner about his decision to close Straight Arrow Books. In particular, Thompson claimed he was owed $75,000 for an advance on his next book. In a 1990 interview, he recalled that exchange and its aftermath.

> While in Saigon, I found I'd been fired when Wenner flew into a rage upon receiving the letter. Getting fired didn't mean that much to me. I was in Saigon, I was writing—except that I had no health insurance. Here I was in a war zone, and no health insurance. So, essentially, I refused to write anything once I found out.

Wenner also had taken out a life insurance policy on Thompson, later claiming that it paid out to his family. Upon his return, an enraged Thompson could focus on little else. As Lynn Nesbit recalled, "One day, a forty-foot fax unrolled across my office floor—all about Jann and the expenses and 'Where is my life insurance?' and 'He's canceled it.'" Thompson criticized Wenner publicly and insisted that his name, and Raoul Duke's, be removed from *Rolling Stone*'s masthead.

The insurance flap marked a low point in Thompson's complex relationship with Wenner. Early on, both men had shared an interest in building the brand, and though Wenner had similar relationships with other writers, Thompson was his biggest asset. "Jann was always good at picking a horse," Peck said. Wenner also realized that Thompson needed an adversary, and he often cast Wenner in that role if no one else was handy. For his part, Thompson knew that few publishers would pay well for his work and furnish the editorial resources required to produce it. Many writers and staff members also clashed with Wenner, but managing editor Terry McDonell credited him for pushing Thompson to produce quality work. Thompson had an unerring sense of weakness in others, including his editors. "If you rolled over with Hunter," McDonell said, "you were fucked." Thompson was said to hate Wenner, but he also claimed that arguing with him about money was better than sex.

In the end, Wenner absorbed the abuse, offered Thompson a new contract, and did not remove any names from the masthead. Nevertheless, Thompson claimed that the relationship ended with what he described as his firing. "The *attempt* was enough," he told William McKeen in 1990. After Saigon, he added, everything he wrote for *Rolling Stone* was a special assignment. Over the next three decades, he placed fewer than twenty original articles there, but several were among his most memorable from that period. They included his coverage of Jimmy Carter, which raised the Georgia Democrat's profile before his 1976 presidential run; "The Banshee Screams for Buffalo Meat" (1977), his eulogy for Oscar Acosta; "A Dog Took My Place" (1983), which focused on the high-profile Pulitzer divorce in Florida; "Fear and Loathing in Elko" (1992), a fantastical reverie on the occasion of Clarence Thomas's Supreme Court nomination; and Thompson's 1994 obituary for Richard Nixon, a final statement about his chief adversary.

Edited by Love, the Nixon obituary was arguably the last important piece Thompson wrote for *Rolling Stone*. Even two decades after his resignation, Nixon evoked Thompson's finest invective, and readers noticed that his earlier screeds held up surprisingly well. "He was often criticized at the time for having a cartoonish take on Nixon—he literally depicted him as a monster—but then people were surprised to hear that Nixon was, in many ways, acting like that version of him," historian Michael Koncewicz said. "As someone who has listened to a couple hundred hours of the Nixon tapes, I can tell you that Hunter's instincts were more or less spot-on."

By casting Nixon as a uniquely evil figure, however, Thompson may have skewed the public's sense of the political and media landscape. After Nixon's resignation, many observers concluded that the system worked. The press reported on Nixon and his henchmen, the Senate investigated them, Judge John Sirica stood up to the White House, the House of Representatives was prepared to impeach, and the Senate was ready to convict. Yet that outcome easily could have been otherwise. A highly placed whistleblower at the FBI guided Bob Woodward and Carl Bernstein's reporting at the *Washington Post*, and there was no reason to think that they—or anyone else—would have unearthed that story on their own. Only a few years earlier, activists had broken into an FBI field office and sent top-secret counterintelligence files to a few select outlets. Those files revealed that the bureau's longstanding pattern of political harassment served no legitimate law enforcement purpose. Yet only one outlet, the *Washington Post*, even examined the files; the others returned them to the FBI. Despite the contingent nature of these and other stories, many Americans concluded that the proper democratic safeguards, including a vigilant fourth estate, were in place and working well. As Carey McWilliams noted in his memoir, however, the nation "had come much closer to a *coup d'etat* than many cared to admit then or later."

• • •

Even as Wenner placated Thompson after the Saigon debacle, he was ramping up *Rolling Stone*'s celebrity coverage. There were sound commercial reasons to do so. Founded in 1974, *People* magazine pioneered that form and eventually led all magazines in readership and advertising revenue. Thompson and others scorned celebrity journalism, but Wenner had no qualms about it. Having polled his readers, he knew that Ben Fong-Torres, who wrote the gossip column, was the most popular writer after Thompson. In addition to following those commercial incentives, Wenner understood the appeal of celebrity culture. Indeed, he liked celebrities and used his magazine to meet and mix with them. In 1985, he reaffirmed his commitment to celebrity journalism by purchasing *Us Weekly*, which became an important part of Wenner Media LLC.

Thompson was also becoming a celebrity. A 1974 *Playboy* interview conducted by Craig Vetter both reflected and contributed to Thompson's growing notoriety. Certainly much had changed since *Playboy* spiked his Jean-Claude Killy piece four years earlier. Vetter's introduction described Thompson's signature style and included several Gonzo staples—the looming deadline, drug excesses, even a description of the dramatic weather. When combined with reliable information about Thompson's past, those elements consolidated his reputation as an outlaw journalist. The following month, *Playboy* ran "The Great Shark Hunt," a long-delayed piece about a fishing tournament in Mexico. In it, Thompson reflected on his own celebrity. "When I slumped off the plane from Miami," he wrote, "I was greeted like Buffalo Bill on his first trip to Chicago."

One source of Thompson's celebrity arose from an unexpected quarter. His readers included Garry Trudeau, who had created the syndicated comic strip *Doonesbury* in 1970. Later, Trudeau said he especially relished *Fear and Loathing in Las Vegas*.

> I bought a paperback of Las Vegas when I was traveling with my girlfriend in England, and we stayed up all night howling over it. I would devour a few pages, then tear them out of the book and hand them to her. Neither of us had ever read anything remotely like it.

In July 1974, as the Watergate hearings prefigured the end of the Nixon presidency, Trudeau introduced a new character based on Thompson and Raoul Duke. Uncle Duke was bald, wore Hawaiian shirts, and sported a cigarette holder. He wrote for *Rolling Stone*, consumed vast quantities of alcohol and drugs, and was usually armed. His wife's name was Sandy, and they lived in Colorado when he was not serving as governor of American Samoa or later as US Ambassador to China. The year after Uncle Duke's debut, *Doonesbury* became the first comic strip to receive a Pulitzer Prize. In subsequent decades, Uncle Duke took on a life of his own, but he never strayed far from his Gonzo roots.

Thompson detested the character and often denounced Trudeau. Perhaps more than any other single source, however, *Doonesbury* reinforced Thompson's celebrity well after his literary output peaked. "I think at times he's been ambivalent about the strip," Trudeau said in 2004, "because it's had a usefulness in his career, heightening his profile. But mostly I take him at his word that he hates being in the strip and has no love for me." Thompson especially resented his status as cartoon character. When one filmmaker proposed an animated sequence in his version of *Fear and Loathing in Las Vegas*, Thompson angrily rejected the idea. Yet it was completely predictable that the story would be rendered that way. Indeed, that process of visual realization began with Steadman's illustrations.

Although Thompson enjoyed the financial benefits of his celebrity, he described it as a journalistic liability. He could no longer stand in the back of a room and observe, and he was often more famous than the speaker in front of the audience. His public persona also invited constant temptation. In this respect, Abe Peck observed, Thompson resembled John Belushi, whose appetites were almost as famous as his exuberant comedy. When Peck took a short walk in downtown Chicago with Belushi, at least five people offered the comedian drugs. Thompson never complained about such temptations, which he was neither inclined nor equipped to resist.

. . .

In 1977, Wenner moved *Rolling Stone*'s main office to New York City. San Francisco had lost much of its cachet since the Summer of Love ten years earlier, and Wenner reportedly called the city a provincial backwater. The move put Wenner's operation closer to Madison Avenue, but Thompson had misgivings. "*Rolling Stone* began to be run by the advertising and business departments and not by the editorial department," he said later. "It was a financial leap forward for Wenner and *Rolling Stone,* but the editorial department lost any real importance." The move underscored Thompson's estrangement from the magazine.

> Essentially, the fun factor had gone out of *Rolling Stone.* It was an
> outlaw magazine in California. In New York, it became an establishment
> magazine, and I have never worked well with people like that. Today at
> *Rolling Stone,* there are rows and rows of white cubicles, each with its
> own computer. That's how I began to hate computers. They represented
> all that was wrong with *Rolling Stone.* It became like an insurance
> office with people communicating cubicle to cubicle.

Nevertheless, Thompson wrote "The Banshee Screams for Buffalo Meat" that year and sold the film rights for $100,000. He also met Laila Nabulsi, a segment producer at *Saturday Night Live,* the popular comedy program that premiered in 1975. The two became an item, and Nabulsi eventually obtained the rights to *Fear and Loathing in Las Vegas,* thus beginning the long process of bringing that story to the screen. *Where the Buffalo Roam* (1980) premiered the same year Sandy divorced Thompson. Bill Murray inhabited Thompson's persona—the two men shared a home in the Hollywood hills during production—but the Acosta character was unrecognizable. Boyle's radical attorney was neither Chicano nor Samoan, but Bulgarian. Thompson later credited Murray's performance but described the film as a "horrible pile of crap."

After his divorce, Thompson stayed at musician Jimmy Buffett's home in Florida and cowrote an unsold screenplay about drug smuggling. Returning to Woody Creek, he began hiring a series of female assistants and holding court at Owl Farm. As Aspen became a popular destination for celebrities, movie stars and rock musicians visited the fortified compound. Although he did not feel the need to perform for his close friends, he often supervised target practice, staged explosions, and otherwise reinforced his Gonzo reputation. The clubhouse feeling was infectious. Thompson's belligerence was fun to be around, David Felton recalled, and made one feel more powerful for a while. Thompson faced few consequences for his mischief at Owl Farm or even in town. If he took LSD and discharged a shotgun while playing golf, as he did with George Plimpton and Terry McDonell, he had little to fear from law enforcement. His many friends included Bob Braudis, who replaced Dick Kienast as sheriff in 1987. When asked whether he gave Thompson special treatment, Braudis replied:

> I think special treatment is a part of life and when you know the doorman, maybe you don't pay the cover charge, or when you know the doctor, and maybe he's your friend, he doesn't order all of those tests that cost thousands of bucks because he knows it's a waste of your money. So special treatment comes by being special, I believe, and everyone in this county, in a non-derogatory sense, is special.

Aspen was special, too. It had become a magnet for hipsters, beautiful women, drug dealers, and the rich. It was by no means a literary hub, and as Thompson's out-of-town assignments dwindled, Aspen's limitations reshaped his own. The Bay Area ignited *Hell's Angels,* Los Angeles generated "Strange Rumblings in Aztlan," and Las Vegas inspired his Gonzo classic, but Aspen never served as the setting for a major work. Thompson was active in politics, which he defined as the art of controlling your environment, but that was easier to do in Aspen, and few would argue that it broadened him as a writer. Yet when asked whether Thompson liked Aspen because he could be a big fish in a small pond, McDonell was skeptical. Having socialized with Thompson in New York City and elsewhere, he replied, "I never saw him in a room where he wasn't the dominant guy."

In the late 1970s, Thompson found another way to capitalize on his reputation. James Silberman, who had moved from Random House to Simon & Schuster, oversaw the publication of *The Great Shark Hunt: Strange Tales from a Strange Time* (1979). The anthology, which the 42-year-old Thompson regarded as his version of *Advertisements for Myself,* was a critical and commercial success. It included his early journalism, some of which had become difficult to find, and it received positive notices in key outlets. John Leonard's review in the *New York Times* noted Thompson's repeated references to geeks, the circus sideshow performers who bit the heads off chickens. "In a number of ways on various occasions—at the Super Bowl, the Kentucky Derby, and the America's Cup yacht race—Dr. Thompson has behaved like a journalistic geek," Leonard maintained. But he also conceded that some chickens needed their heads bitten off, and he described Thompson's journalism as "surprisingly straight, ungeeky, and often quite moving." The book's reading line billed *The Great Shark Hunt* as "Gonzo Papers, Volume 1," suggesting more anthologies to come. Those that did—*Generation of Swine* (1988), *Songs of the Doomed* (1990), and *Better Than Sex* (1994)—had less impact, but book royalties and advances began to account for a larger portion of Thompson's income.

Another book flowed from Thompson's coverage of the 1981 Honolulu marathon for *Running* magazine. Commissioned by Paul Perry, who later wrote a biography of Thompson, "Charge of the Weird Brigade" led out to *The Curse of Lono* (1983), which Thompson wrote for Alan Rinzler at Bantam. Rinzler offered a $100,000 advance to Thompson and Steadman despite the fact that, several years earlier, Thompson collected a $25,000 advance from Bantam for an unwritten book about Reagan. When the final manuscript for *The Curse of Lono* was due, Rinzler flew to Colorado and once again tape-recorded Thompson in an effort to produce a usable draft. In the end, he secretly retrieved the scattered notes from Thompson's room at the Hotel Jerome and returned to New York City. After assembling the manuscript, he sent it to an irate Thompson for his approval. Rinzler and Bantam parted ways shortly after that, and though Ian Ballantine took over the project, he made no changes to the book.

The Curse of Lono lacked the crackle of Thompson's earlier efforts, but William McKeen thought it might be his most underrated work, and British scholar William Stephenson called it an important part of Thompson's *oeuvre*. After covering the marathon, Thompson's first-person narrator returns from a fishing trip with a large marlin. In the harbor, he exclaims to a crowd that he is Lono, the Hawaiian deity. In addition to offending the locals, the declaration provokes the local realtors who depend on tourism, and Thompson is forced to seek refuge. The book includes passages from Twain's *Letters from Hawaii* and Richard Hough's *The Last Voyage of Captain James Cook*, leading Stephenson to read it as both a critique of neocolonialism and a creative response to Thompson's own celebrity. Stephenson concluded that *The Curse of Lono* was "a self-ironic, reflexive reworking of *Fear and Loathing in Las Vegas* for the era of globalization, by an author who knew he had become trapped by his own brand." The book reportedly sold two hundred thousand copies, suggesting that the brand was alive and well.

The same year, *Rolling Stone* published Thompson's piece on the sensational Pulitzer divorce in Palm Beach. Recently installed as managing editor, Terry McDonell persuaded Thompson to write about the trial, which included lurid tales of drug abuse and kinky sex. Wenner approved the assignment but doubted it would come to fruition. When it did, "A Dog Took My Place" skewered high-society depravity in the early years of the Reagan era. McDonell left *Rolling Stone* before the article appeared, and David Rosenthal replaced him on that piece and as managing editor. McDonell later edited Thompson at *Esquire*, and after Silberman's departure from Simon & Schuster, Rosenthal handled Thompson's books, first at Random House and then at Simon & Schuster, where he signed on as publisher in 1997.

. . .

Even as Ronald Reagan finished his first term, Thompson did not suspect he would become the dominant American politician in the second half of the twentieth century. When interviewed in 1979 about the upcoming presidential race, Thompson had failed to mention Reagan at all. Once in office, Reagan and his administration provided plenty of grist for Thompson's mill, but his output never matched the Nixon screeds for power or influence. Thompson had little interest in returning to the campaign trail, and though he attended the 1984 Democratic National Convention in San Francisco, he did not produce any publishable copy. It was his last attempt at campaign coverage from an actual news site.

In some ways, Reagan preempted Thompson by dishing up his own version of the American Dream. As governor of California, Reagan had ridiculed the counterculture and claimed that the United States could pave Vietnam, put parking stripes on it, and still be home by Christmas. He stuck with Nixon to the bitter end, and once in the White House, Reagan doubled down on the drug war, ramped up military spending, cut taxes for the wealthy, blew up the deficit, cracked down on the unions, and tooted the dog whistle. In his sunny view, even the country's gravest mistakes, crimes, and sins were trivial compared to America's divinely ordained role as leader of the free world. He also shared Nixon's peculiar sense of inculpability. Discussing the president's role in national security, Nixon had famously claimed, "Well, when the president does it, that means that it is not illegal." In effect, Reagan extended that immunity to the nation as a whole. In Reagan's imaginary republic, America could do no wrong. If a person thought that about himself, he would be considered a sociopath.

Yet Thompson had a problem with his main trope. There was only so much he could do with hyperbole. Having called Nixon a werewolf, he had less running room with Reagan, who was the more consequential figure. Another problem was that Thompson predicated his work on an American Dream that never matched the facts on the ground. So did Reagan, whose nostalgic version of that dream sparked a renewed desire to believe in it. That desire itself was true, irrefutable, and politically powerful. Instead of reflecting on the painful lessons of Watergate and Vietnam, Reagan and his supporters started with a received truth about America and ignored all the counter-evidence. It was Hofstadter all over again—not the myth of the happy yeoman, but the American tradition of anti-intellectualism and eventually the paranoid style. Given a chance to grow up after Vietnam and Watergate, Americans chose not to. Instead, they celebrated Reagan and turned Sylvester Stallone's *Rambo* (1982) into a successful film franchise.

As Reagan's myth found purchase, the media landscape continued to shift. In 1985, Australian publisher Rupert Murdoch bought the parent company of 20th Century Fox and began developing a new television network. After launching Sky News in Europe four years later, he hired Nixon's former media advisor to build Fox News, which premiered in 1996. Soon that cable outlet was circulating right-wing fever dreams, some of which predated the modern conservative movement and even the New Deal. Those tropes were echoed and elaborated on AM talk radio, conservative websites, and evangelical outlets of various kinds. Yet if right-wing media was expanding its reach, the counterculture proved to be remarkably durable as well. Over the second half of the twentieth century, the mainstream culture absorbed many of its attitudes, concerns, and values. Eventually no American city was without its yoga studios, farmers market, or recycling center, and marijuana dispensaries began to operate freely in a growing number of states. As counterculture veteran Peter Coyote observed, hippies won all the cultural battles and lost all the political ones.

As Reagan and the counterculture sharpened their visions of America on each other, they had one thing in common: Neither required anyone to grow up. Thompson was skilled at calling out corruption and phoniness, and there was no shortage of either during the Age of Reagan. But Thompson was no help at all when it came to growing up.

· · ·

In 1985, Thompson began writing a weekly column for Will Hearst at the *San Francisco Examiner*. Over the next five years, he churned out 175 pieces, first as the newspaper's media critic, and then as a 1988 campaign observer. Some of the columns appeared in *Generation of Swine* and *Songs of the Doomed*, and many ran in obscure outlets through a syndication deal that met with limited success. Given Thompson's remarks about Hearst newspapers over the years, his arrangement with the *Examiner* was ironic, but so was Will Hearst's relationship with the Bay Area tech industry. As the Internet destroyed what was left of the family's newspaper chain, Hearst profited handsomely from his tech investments. After studying mathematics at Harvard, he worked several jobs in the family business to prepare himself for upper management. But after meeting Wenner during the Patricia Hearst saga, he accepted a position as managing editor of *Outside* magazine, another Wenner venture. When Wenner moved his operation to New York City in 1977, Hearst stayed in San Francisco, and Terry McDonell took over at *Outside* before moving to *Rolling Stone*. After a stint in the cable television business, Hearst returned to the family business, became the *Examiner*'s publisher, and hired Hinckle and Thompson to spice up the newspaper.

Thompson's editor at the *San Francisco Examiner* was David McCumber, whom Hearst described as Thompson's case officer. In "Secret Cables to Willie Hearst," which appeared in *Songs of the Doomed*, Thompson both implored Hearst to fire McCumber and threatened to join his editor if he left the *Examiner*. Thompson also demanded that Hearst reimburse his expenses, just as his grandfather would have done. "When the Old Man sent Jack London and Frederic Remington to cover his war in Cuba," Thompson wrote, "I doubt if he told them to pay their own expenses." Where, he asked Hearst, was his performance bonus, the check for his Phoenix trip, and reimbursement for the television dish he installed at his home? Thompson again compared Hearst unfavorably to his grandfather.

> The Old Man was a monster, but nobody ever accused him of skimming nickels and dimes off his best writers' expense accounts—and it wasn't his cheapjack *accountants* who made him a legend in American journalism and the highest roller of his time.

Those complaints notwithstanding, Hearst said the chief challenge of working with Thompson was obtaining copy, and he commended McCumber for working with the fragments he received from Thompson. Thompson also acknowledged McCumber's efforts in *Generation of Swine, Songs of the Doomed*, and in *Screwjack*, a collection of stories published in 1991 and reissued by Simon & Schuster in 2000.

During his visits to San Francisco, Thompson befriended porn impresarios Jim and Artie Mitchell. After growing up in Antioch, a blue-collar exurb in the East Bay, Jim served in the military before studying film and photography at San Francisco State College. Soon he was selling nude photographs downtown and making short pornographic films. Before long, he and Artie rented a sound stage on Potrero Hill, began turning out feature-length productions, and opened the O'Farrell Theatre in the Tenderloin to screen them. Frequently arrested, the Mitchells were represented by attorney Michael Kennedy, who also defended Huey P. Newton, Cesar Chavez, and Timothy Leary. In 1972, the Mitchell Brothers hit the jackpot with *Behind the Green Door* (1972), and the O'Farrell Theatre developed into what Thompson called the Carnegie Hall of public sex in America. Dancers cavorted on stage while half-naked women gave lap dances to customers. Some of the dancers followed the teachings of Bhagwan Shree Rajneesh, whose community in rural Oregon was stirring controversy. Another performer, Nina Hartley, went on to star in and direct her own pornographic movies; later, she appeared in *Boogie Nights* and delivered sex-positive feminist lectures at Harvard, Berkeley, and Dartmouth.

In 1988, the Mitchells produced a thirty-minute movie called *Hunter S. Thompson: The Crazy Never Die,* which featured Thompson lampooning Reagan and Nixon before live audiences, working with McCumber in the *Examiner* newsroom, and chatting with strippers. During this time, Thompson was purportedly researching a story on feminist pornography for *Playboy* and writing a book for Random House whose title, *The Night Manager,* echoed his self-styled position at O'Farrell Theatre. He never completed either project, but he did write for the *War News,* a publication the Mitchells created to protest the Gulf War. Edited by Warren Hinckle, the paper also included contributions from Daniel Ellsberg, Michael Moore, Paul Krassner, and cartoonist Robert Crumb.

In 1990, the year Thompson's final article ran in the *Examiner,* he was arrested for sexual assault at Owl Farm. Gail Palmer, who directed and acted in pornographic movies, filed the charges. By that time, she was out of the business and living in Michigan, but she wanted to meet Thompson while she and her husband were skiing in Aspen. She came by Owl Farm, mayhem ensued, and her husband paid a visit to the sheriff's office the next day. After a police search turned up drugs and explosives at Owl Farm, charges were filed. To show their support for Thompson, the Mitchells restored a 1971 Chevrolet Caprice convertible, the same model Thompson drove to Las Vegas, and led a caravan with several dancers to Colorado. They timed their arrival to coincide with Thompson's preliminary hearing, but prosecutors finally dropped the charges. Thompson regarded the outcome as a victory for the Fourth Amendment, and he devoted a section of *Songs of the Doomed* to the episode.

When that book appeared in 1990, its flap copy touted Thompson's "long-awaited sex book, *Polo Is My Life.*" In a later interview, Thompson said the story was about "the manager of a sex theater who's forced to leave and flee to the mountains. He falls in love and gets in even more trouble than he was in the sex theater in San Francisco." *Rolling Stone* ran a related short story with the same title, and *Better Than Sex* included an excerpt, but Thompson never completed the book. By that time, the Mitchells had self-destructed. Artie, who admired Hunter but was lost in cocaine and alcohol, threatened Jim's longtime girlfriend on a telephone call to her friend. Jim asked his girlfriend not to call the police, but Artie also left a message on Jim's home telephone threatening to kill him. Jim, who had protected his younger brother for years, drove to Artie's home in Marin County and shot him. Defended by Michael Kennedy, Jim was convicted of voluntary manslaughter, and the following year, Simon & Schuster published McCumber's book about the rise and fall of the Mitchell Brothers.

. . .

Although many Thompson projects were collapsing, others were heading for the finish line. Thompson started working on *Better Than Sex* after Bill Clinton's presidential victory in 1992, and Juan assisted his father in what he called "a wild, chaotic effort." After Random House published the book in 1994, Juan compared the final product to a scrapbook. Thompson dedicated it to his assistant, Nicole Meyer, whom he described as his "vampire in the Garden of Agony," an echo of his earlier work on Big Sur. A brief review in the *New York Times* described *Better Than Sex* as "a collection of mash notes" to Clinton's campaign staffers.

> Such shooting from the hip is Mr. Thompson's forte; what disappoints in this book is its disjointedness. *Better Than Sex* reads like a hodgepodge, a series of dispatches hurriedly lashed together. But in his own cracked, inimitable style, Mr. Thompson proves to be an upbeat Jeremiah, a civic-minded curmudgeon.

Although *Better Than Sex* seemed to demonstrate Thompson's continuing political relevance, it also showed that he was coasting on literary capital he had accrued two decades earlier.

Douglas Brinkley began editing Thompson's vast correspondence and preparing a three-volume series for Simon & Schuster. The first volume, *The Proud Highway*, received strong reviews when it appeared in 1997. "This is the book that launches the reassessment of Hunter Thompson," publisher David Rosenthal said. "And at the same time, it's a big commercial book." The second volume, which appeared in 2000, received even more plaudits. Writing for the *New York Times*, Christopher Buckley concluded that Thompson's reportage had "an impressionistic side—for which his fans, including this one, are profoundly grateful. These untidy letters are welcome, showing us as they do a great American original in his lair." Edited by Marysue Ricci for Simon & Schuster, *The Rum Diary* (1998) did not fare as well. David Kelly's review in the *New York Times* quoted Thompson's observation that a week in Las Vegas was like stumbling into a time warp, a regression to the late 1950s. "The same goes for *The Rum Diary*," Kelly said. "If you're looking for the birthplace of gonzo, you won't find it here."

The same year Thompson's novel appeared, Johnny Depp and Benicio Del Toro starred in Terry Gilliam's *Fear and Loathing in Las Vegas*. Gilliam's style seemed well suited to the material, and there was no shortage of star power. In addition to Depp and Del Toro, the cast included Christina Ricci, Ellen Barkin, Gary Busey, Cameron Diaz, Lyle Lovett, Harry Dean Stanton, and Tobey Maguire. Yet even as Stephen Holden credited the book and Gilliam's fidelity to it, the *New York Times* reviewer dismissed the film as "a gaudy splat of a movie." Part of the challenge was capturing the book's voice. "Even the most precise cinematic realizations of Mr. Thompson's images (and of Ralph Steadman's cartoon drawings for the book) don't begin to match the surreal ferocity of the author's language," Holden observed. Many films, including every version of *The Great Gatsby*, faced the same problem, but some of Holden's criticisms also applied to the source material, not all of which had aged well.

> In the strongest scene, which comes late in the film, Dr. Gonzo insults a waitress (Ellen Barkin) in a greasy spoon who quickly regrets standing up to him. Brandishing a knife, the lawyer reduces the poor woman to a speechless, quivering wreck. The scene is ugly enough to cast a moral shadow over the preceding fun and games and make you dislike these selfish rampaging hipsters, who have spent the best part of the movie stoned out of their gourds, trashing hotel rooms, and intimidating the help.

Holden's concluding observation also extended to the book. Although Thompson noted the counterculture's failures, he also presented the American Dream, Las Vegas style, as the enemy. "As we all know now," Holden wrote, "it was never that simple."

Despite the film's modest reception and *The Rum Diary*'s tepid reviews, Depp labored to bring that novel to the screen as well. When it premiered in 2011, he played Paul Kemp opposite Amber Heard's Chenault. Directed by Bruce Robinson, the film omitted Yeamon, an important Thompson stand-in, and made Chenault the developer's girlfriend. The film received a polite review in the *New York Times* from A. O. Scott. Claiming that Depp seemed to be acting "from behind the mask of his own charisma," Scott credited Giovanni Rispoli's depiction of Moburg, Kemp's degenerate colleague, as "the most interesting and authentic thing in the movie." Throughout his review, Scott balanced his criticisms of the film with respect for Thompson. "The rest is pleasant enough," he concluded about Robinson's effort, "which may sound more damning than I mean it to, given Thompson's reputation."

. . .

In 2000, the same year the second volume of correspondence appeared, Thompson began writing an online column at ESPN. The offer came from John Walsh, the *Rolling Stone* managing editor who handled Thompson's "Fear and Loathing at the Super Bowl" in 1974. In 1988, Walsh began his long career at ESPN, and by the time Thompson signed on, the Hearst Corporation owned a 20 percent stake in what had become a cable television gold mine. Thompson loved the idea of returning to sportswriting, but Walsh said his physical and intellectual decline was painfully obvious. After years of hip pain that restricted his mobility, the 62-year-old Thompson entered the hospital for hip replacement surgery in 1999. Before the operation, he told the surgeon he would not stop drinking, and his nurses were instructed to give him whiskey during his recovery. Immediately after his surgery, however, he was already delirious from alcohol withdrawal, and his doctors induced a coma while he detoxicated. Months later, he was noticeably calmer, which Juan attributed to the absence of chronic pain.

For his new job, Thompson watched the games at home but had trouble completing even short pieces. "We would give him stories and tips and clues, but it rarely registered," Walsh said. Thompson was paid generously by online standards, but only when his pieces appeared. "He was in complete control of his destiny," Walsh said, "which he never wanted." Thompson came to rely on that income, but the results were uneven. "There were some good columns," Walsh said, "and then there were some that the editors had to try to save."

Thompson's ESPN columns slipped into self-imitation, and though he kept up with politics and sports, he had less and less to say that readers could not find elsewhere or figure out on their own. Even so, he produced 128 pieces peppered with political commentary and media criticism. Betting was also a major theme. Walsh thought gambling produced a thrill for Thompson, but it also helped him connect with friends. He did not place bets with bookies; rather, his friends came over to watch the games, and he encouraged betting, including side bets to keep things hopping. His wagers performed the same connective function on the 1972 campaign trail. As an outsider, he used betting to demonstrate his political acumen and to bond with his colleagues. It may have been part of his liberationist project as well. Walsh did not consider Thompson a gambling addict, but some compulsive gamblers are thought to have a deep-seated wish to free themselves from the dominion of money. That wish assorted well with Thompson's general improvidence. A relentless haggler, he routinely spent everything he earned and more.

In 2003, Thompson's physical problems returned. Spinal stenosis immobilized him again, and he entered the hospital again for back surgery. Alcohol withdrawal again led to a drug-induced coma, and two contentious weeks later, he was released from the hospital. Despite his physical challenges, Thompson's personal life was relatively stable. After many years of fraught relations, Thompson and Juan had grown closer. In 2003, he also married 31-year-old Anita Bejmuk, whom he had hired four years earlier as an assistant. Domestic peace did not improve his critical fortunes, however. The same year he remarried, Simon & Schuster published *Kingdom of Fear* to poor reviews. Janet Maslin's notice in the *New York Times* called it "a haphazard journalistic yard sale" but conceded that Thompson turned "his trademark paranoia into something all too legitimate" and could claim "a rare durability." In "Bedtime for Gonzo," Jack Shafer wondered why Thompson darted from digression to digression instead of addressing his past in any sustained or thoughtful way. "You'd think that at this point in his life—Thompson is 65—he'd be more interested in exorcising his demons than in making cartoons out of them."

David Rosenthal presumably had no illusions about *Kingdom of Fear*, but he later said he felt a personal obligation to Thompson. He added that the "fun factor" with Thompson was always high, and that the usual rules did not apply to him. "For an author to get away with some of Hunter's behavior," he said, "he has to be a successful author commercially, because no publisher will tolerate it." In fact, Rosenthal had long ago assigned Marysue Ricci to Thompson's projects. "I think you needed more than one person working with Hunter," he said. "We played good cop, bad cop all the time."

For *Kingdom of Fear*, Thompson also sought editorial help from Alan Rinzler, to whom he sent the manuscript before inviting him to work on it with him in Colorado. When Rinzler asked about a fee, Thompson said he would not pay him because he had already spent the advance. When the book came out, it was exactly the version Rinzler had seen. Later, Rinzler compared editing Thompson to combat. In that sense, his experience was the editorial version of Thompson's feat with *Hell's Angels.* Having ridden with the motorcycle gang and lived to tell the story, Thompson dined out on that experience for the rest of his career. It was the same for Rinzler, who felt he could edit anyone after working with Thompson.

Thompson's final book, *Hey Rube,* repackaged his ESPN columns and was dedicated to two deceased friends, George Plimpton and musician Warren Zevon. Published as George W. Bush's first term came to a close, *Hey Rube* had a strong political dimension. The front matter included two quotations: one from Rudyard Kipling, who noted the foolishness of Christians trying "to hustle the East," and the other from Nixon, who claimed that those who could not produce peace within four years should not be given another chance. Both alluded to the invasions of Afghanistan and Iraq, but Thompson made his meaning even plainer in his author's note. His ESPN columns, he wrote, were a weekly record of "what it was like to be alive and suffering in the first disastrous days of the George W. Bush administration." *New York Times* writer David Streitfeld later observed that Thompson was yelling at the top of lungs during this period but to no great effect.

The most notable piece in *Hey Rube* was "Fear and Loathing in America: Beginning of the End," which originally appeared on September 12, 2001. "When 9/11 happened, we all knew that Hunter would go to a unique place, which he did," Walsh said. After summarizing the destruction of the World Trade Center and damage to the Pentagon, Thompson looked to the future: "Make no mistake about it: we are At War now—with somebody—and we will stay At War with that strange and mysterious Enemy for the rest of our lives." Protracted conflict was certain despite the many questions that still hung in the air the day after the attack.

> We are going to punish somebody for this attack, but just who or where will be blown to smithereens for it is hard to say. Maybe Afghanistan, maybe Pakistan or Iraq, or possibly all three at once. Who knows? Not even the Generals in what remains of the Pentagon or the New York papers calling for *war* seem to know who did it or where to look for them.

Thompson's instant analysis was prophetic. That it originally appeared on a sports website reflected the media's increasingly kaleidoscopic quality as well as his diminished stature. As Internet access burgeoned, the mainstream media's uncritical acceptance of the Iraq invasion sent millions of readers to alternative outlets, many of them online.

Hey Rube appeared in August 2004, and reviews were generally positive but not plentiful. *Kirkus Reviews* described it as "a treat for Thompson's many fans," and *Publishers Weekly* said it displayed "an energy and humor lacking in some of his more recent collections." Nevertheless, it was the only full-length Thompson book that the *New York Times* declined to review at all.

· · ·

That fall, Thompson was despondent. Not only was George W. Bush's re-election a setback, but he was also hobbled again. On a trip to Hawaii, Thompson slipped in the bathroom and broke his leg. Actor Sean Penn immediately chartered a plane that delivered Thompson to a Colorado clinic. Wheelchair bound, Thompson was irritated and depressed but surprisingly sentimental. He contacted dozens of friends during the 2004 holidays, and those who visited Owl Farm received emotional farewells. In January 2005, he traveled to New Orleans to cover the production of *All the King's Men*, which starred Sean Penn, for *Playboy*. He appeared at Arnaud's Restaurant for a private party, but he was unable to reach the second-floor dining room in his wheelchair, and he refused help. In the downstairs bar, he told Douglas Brinkley that his time had come to die.

Back at Owl Farm the following month, Thompson composed a note to himself.

> Football Season is Over. No More Games. No More Bombs. No More Walking. No More Fun. No More Swimming. 67. That is 17 years past 50. 17 more than I needed or wanted. Boring. I am always bitchy. No Fun—for anybody. 67. You are getting Greedy. Act your old age. Relax—This won't hurt.

That weekend, he and Anita hosted Juan and his family. On Sunday, while Anita was at the gym and Juan was in another room, Thompson sat at the kitchen counter in front of his typewriter, put the barrel of a .45 caliber pistol in his mouth, and pulled the trigger.

12 Legacy

When Thompson committed suicide in 2005, he had not written a major book-length work in decades. Nevertheless, his literary reputation improved markedly in the years before his death. Four biographies appeared in the early 1990s, and they combined with several other works to boost Thompson's critical fortunes. In 1996, Modern Library republished *Fear and Loathing in Las Vegas* along with "Strange Rumblings in Aztlan," "The Kentucky Derby Is Decadent and Depraved," and the so-called jacket copy for the Las Vegas book. That publication literally placed Thompson between Jonathan Swift and Henry David Thoreau on the roster of Modern Library authors. The following year, the first volume of edited correspondence appeared, and the year after that, a new edition of *Fear and Loathing in Las Vegas* coincided with the release of Terry Gilliam's film. In 2000, the second volume of correspondence fortified Thompson's reputation as a significant American writer. David Streitfeld, who interviewed Thompson several times, noted that those volumes were especially important to him. Having his letters taken seriously was the biggest dream of his last twenty years. Streitfeld also called the second volume of correspondence "*the* major Thompson work." The third volume of correspondence was announced but never appeared.

In the aftermath of Thompson's suicide, several new efforts consolidated those gains. Chief among them were William McKeen's 2008 biography, an oral history assembled by Jann Wenner and Corey Seymour, and Alex Gibney's documentary film. Other valuable sources from that period were J. C. Gabel and James Hughes's oral history, published by *Stop Smiling* magazine in 2005, and a volume of interviews edited by Beef Torrey and Kevin Simonson that appeared in 2008. Tributes to Thompson took other forms as well. GonzoFest Louisville, an annual literary and musical event, was founded in 2011 and has featured many of the authors cited in this book.

When Simon & Schuster published a fortieth-anniversary edition of the campaign book, Matt Taibbi contributed the introduction. Taibbi's first solo book, *Spanking the Donkey: On the Campaign Trail with the Democrats* (2005), was an updated version of Thompson's campaign book. It was therefore fitting that Taibbi also became a contributing editor at *Rolling Stone*. After winning a National Magazine Award for his political columns in 2008, he wrote a hard-hitting article on Goldman Sachs, the investment bank he described as "a great vampire squid wrapped around the face of humanity, relentlessly jamming its blood funnel into anything that smells like money." But Taibbi did more than impugn the Wall Street giant; he also explained its complicated hustles to general readers, and his work proved difficult to refute or ignore. The following year, Wenner called Taibbi "absolutely the first person to come along since Hunter who could be called Hunter's peer." Taibbi's subsequent work showed less Gonzo influence, but his pointed media criticism also invited comparisons with Thompson.

Taibbi began his introduction to the anniversary edition by claiming that no book meant more to a single professional audience than *Fear and Loathing on the Campaign Trail '72* meant to American political journalists. Much of that book's influence, he maintained, flowed from its staging. Virtually every subsequent campaign book included the hotshot reporter and campaign wizard, the backstage chatter, and candidates who played the roles of villain, sellout, and savior. As Taibbi also noted, however, Thompson's influence stretched well beyond establishing those conventions. Although his style often led readers, including many colleagues, to dismiss him as a party animal and put-down artist, Taibbi argued that Thompson's idealism, outrage, and passionate search for the truth accounted for his influence. Whereas most political journalists tried to impress others with their hard-boiled realism, Thompson "laid out his fragile hopes and awesome disappointments for everyone to see." It was a surprising and important insight, for it suggested that despite Thompson's gift for satire and invective, it was his sincerity, vulnerability, and humanity that distinguished his campaign book from earlier ones and influenced later ones.

Four years later, political scientist Susan McWilliams wrote about Thompson in *The Nation*, which her grandfather had edited for two decades. In that article, she argued that Thompson anticipated the retaliatory right-wing politics of Donald Trump. Her claim resonated with a cohort of younger journalists, who began reading Thompson with an eye for his continuing relevance. The same year, Juan Thompson's memoir appeared and documented his turbulent family life and reconciliation with his father. Shortly after that, several more contributions broadened our understanding of Thompson and his work. They included Warren Hinckle's *Who Killed Hunter S. Thompson?* (2017), an anthology compiled by his former editor, colleagues, and friends; Timothy Denevi's *Freak Kingdom* (2018), which traced Thompson's political odyssey from Kennedy's assassination to Nixon's resignation; and David Streitfeld's *Hunter S. Thompson: The Last Interview and Other Conversations* (2018), which collected key interviews from 1967 to 2004. Later, Streitfeld maintained that Thompson's literary output finally seemed to be emerging from the shadow cast by his own persona. The appearance of Eric Shoaf's *Gonzology: A Hunter Thompson Bibliography* (2018) was a step in that direction. Shortly before his death, Shoaf also contributed his collection of Thompson publications to the University of California, Santa Cruz.

Fifty years after *Fear and Loathing in Las Vegas,* the question remains: How should we understand that body of work and the writer who created it? We cannot ignore Thompson's earliest journalism, but I have argued that his move to San Francisco was the first major step in his literary formation. He was drawn to the city in part by Kerouac, and his debt to the Beat novelist is widely recognized, yet Henry Miller was the more important influence by far. In Kerouac's work, Thompson recognized a blend of autobiography and fiction that appealed to major trade publishers and a new generation of readers. Thompson also adopted Kerouac's use of the road trip and wingman to propel his narratives. In Miller, however, he saw a form of independence that was virtually complete. Many of Miller's favorite topics and themes were alien to Thompson, and the converse was also true. Miller had almost nothing to say about conventional politics except that it was an especially lethal form of madness, and neither drugs nor football interested him in the slightest. Likewise, Thompson steered clear of sexually explicit fiction, mysticism, and the arts. Nevertheless, one feels Miller's influence not only in Thompson's voice, but also in his critique of American culture and distinctive model of authorship.

After moving to Woody Creek, Thompson visited San Francisco and New York City infrequently. That absence kept his person fresh and new, added to his mystique, and reflected his insistence on personal freedom and autonomy. Even as the Bay Area became an occasional stop rather than home base, it remained central in other ways. Hinckle observed that San Francisco and Northern California were a seminal part of Thompson's life, and Wenner added that Thompson had more affection for San Francisco than for any other city. The region furnished the stories that made

Thompson a national figure, hosted the outlets that published his major work, and shaped his unique persona. It is difficult to imagine a comparable development in New York, Boston, Chicago, or Los Angeles, much less Aspen or Louisville. Indeed, it is difficult to imagine that development in San Francisco ten years earlier or later.

The advent of New Journalism also played a key role in Thompson's literary formation. What he saw in Tom Wolfe's work focused his ambitions and literary talents. When Carey McWilliams tapped Thompson to write about the Hell's Angels, the young freelancer had already learned from Wolfe that the West Coast could be mined for publishable stories. Many of Thompson's were centered in the Bay Area, but "Strange Rumblings in Aztlan" was set against the Chicano movement in Los Angeles, and *Fear and Loathing in Las Vegas* played out against that city's unique backdrop. The Las Vegas book's Gonzo predecessor, "The Kentucky Derby Is Decadent and Depraved," was even more attuned to place. I have argued that it was also more powerful. In that piece, Thompson lampooned Louisville's major event, presented it as a synecdoche for the tumultuous American scene during the Nixon era, and recognized his complicity in that lunacy. After its publication and his run for sheriff the same year, Thompson consistently positioned himself as an outsider, albeit one with enviable connections.

As we have seen, New Journalism had its critics. In a 2005 *New York Times* book review, Luke Mitchell claimed, "What was best about what the new journalists did was not new. And what was worst—the celebrity promotion on the parts of their editors, the trend-fetishism, the forced archetyping and false mythologizing—was not journalism." Though sweeping, both claims have merit. One wonders, however, about their importance, especially given the challenges American journalism has faced since that time. In the late 1990s, the US news industry began shedding jobs at an alarming rate, and key outlets botched or failed to anticipate momentous stories. The two events that bookended Thompson's death—the run-up to the US invasion of Iraq and the global economic meltdown—eluded virtually every major news organization, including the *New York Times*. That newspaper's coverage of the first story actively misled its readers, and an army of business journalists failed to detect the housing bubble that crashed the global economy in 2007. In short, mainstream media outlets have faced much more critical problems than the effects of New Journalism, and American letters certainly would be poorer without its contributions.

After his New Journalism phase but before he wrote for *Rolling Stone*, Thompson forged his signature style. I would highlight four separate events during that interval that sparked his creation. The first was his experience in Chicago during the 1968 Democratic National Convention. As we have seen, that trauma transformed his understanding of American politics and his place in it. He would later claim that he arrived in Chicago as a journalist and left a raving beast. Although he wrote nothing about the convention in its immediate aftermath, the experience shifted his personal and professional horizons. After 1968, he no longer showcased socially marginal groups for mainstream audiences. Instead, he targeted mainstream politicians for a growing audience of younger readers.

The second development was his pairing with Ralph Steadman, whose illustrations gave Thompson's hallucinatory prose an effective visual counterpart. "The Kentucky Derby Is Decadent and Depraved" was not his first piece to be illustrated, but Steadman's contributions were an indispensable part of Gonzo journalism and its reception. Thompson recognized the value of that contribution well before the article received widespread acclaim. As William Stephenson has noted, Thompson was especially attuned to the power of visual style. He understood the appeal of Steadman's illustrations, the Freak Power posters, and photography and television more generally. Especially toward the end of their partnership, Steadman's work not only complemented Thompson's output, but also stimulated it. For all these reasons, Gonzo journalism cannot be reduced to Thompson's prose. Rather, the potent combination of verbal and visual effects accounted for the franchise's success and durability.

The third factor was Thompson's decision to produce a string of stories in the mold of the Kentucky Derby piece. In his correspondence with Warren Hinckle, Thompson outlined a series of articles set in high-profile venues. The Thompson-Steadman Report, as Thompson proposed to call it, never came off at *Scanlan's*, but he and Steadman produced the Las Vegas book in its image. Even on the brink of publishing that book, however, Thompson did not fully appreciate the popularity of the franchise he had conceived. In particular, he worried that his "neo-fictional outburst" would undermine his credibility as a journalist. With the publication of *Fear and Loathing in Las Vegas*, however, Thompson's fate—and Gonzo's—was sealed.

The fourth factor was Thompson's decision to write *Fear and Loathing in Las Vegas* in the voice of Raoul Duke. It was his attempt, he later told Tom Wolfe, to prevent the "grey little cocksuckers who run things" from "drawing that line between Journalism and Fiction." That decision seems minor at this remove, but Thompson labored over it, and its significance is still lost on publishing insiders, not to mention the general public. Bookstores continue to stock that book in nonfiction or journalism, despite the fact that its two main characters are fictional. None of this is surprising given Thompson's concerted efforts to blur those generic distinctions. Those efforts, in fact, stand at the center of his project. As William Kennedy noted, Thompson wanted to transcend New Journalism, and he did so with *Fear and Loathing in Las Vegas.* "What he wrote was a singular work that was a mutation of the fictional form, which is why his place is secure, because nobody can ever do that again."

By 1972, Thompson had established himself as a unique talent, and his campaign reporting that year enhanced his reputation. His campaign book, another critical and commercial success, influenced many who had given his previous Gonzo journalism a wide berth. During that period, Thompson's editors became even more central to his success. As early as the Kentucky Derby article, they assembled and polished his key works, and over time, his project depended entirely on his ability to martial their talents. Even with that editorial support, he often failed to deliver copy that could be lashed into publishable form. It was an obvious liability, but it must be balanced against Thompson's gifts. Without his efforts, all the editorial support in the world could not generate a Gonzo masterpiece. That feat depended on what William Kennedy called Thompson's "spectacular roundelay," the fruitful interplay between his life and work. Its generative power, which was rooted in Thompson's personality and stamina, peaked quickly and yielded diminishing literary returns for decades. As Thompson noted, it is difficult to stay up on that wire for long. Yet between 1965 and 1975, he performed his aerial act at a remarkably high level.

On the strength of his major works, Thompson became a durable symbol of the counterculture. By no means a hippie or flower child, Thompson symbolized a new and deeply irreverent approach to American politics and culture. It was not simply a matter of shocking the bourgeoisie, as bohemians had done for generations. Rather, the Baby Boomer iconoclasm that he channeled at *Rolling Stone* reflected a darker suspicion that mainstream culture had lost its way and perhaps its collective mind. Even as traditional outlets portrayed hippies as kooks and reprobates, many young people had concluded that America could not temper its violence, materialism, or environmental rapacity, much less sustain the American Dream as Thompson understood it. It was no coincidence that lunacy became one of his major themes. In his review of *The Great Shark Hunt*, Nelson Algren remarked on that aspect of Thompson's work. "Now that the dust of the '60s has settled," Algren observed, "his hallucinated vision strikes one as having been, after all, the sanest." Although drugs were an important part of that vision, Thompson resisted the counterculture's tendency to associate psychedelics with wisdom or the occult. For him, drugs were never a sacrament but rather a way of life.

If the counterculture accounted for much of Thompson's legacy, his work also can be linked to an older strain of American journalism with a complex relationship to the truth. In that spirit, Tom Wolfe described him as "the only twentieth-century equivalent of Mark Twain." Thompson's diatribes also recalled H. L. Mencken, who railed against the booboisie, Bible-thumpers, and the New Deal. But in the screeds he directed at Nixon, Thompson most resembled Mencken's hero, Ambrose Bierce, whose ferocious invective made him the scourge of San Francisco. Insofar as Thompson channeled Bierce's acerbic spirit, he resembled an old-fashioned scold more than a flower child. Like Bierce, Thompson targeted US imperialism and corporate behemoths, tried his hand at fiction, and was difficult to manage. Will Hearst, Douglas Brinkley, and Jann Wenner also drew the comparison to Bierce. "I always saw him as an Ambrose Bierce–Mark Twain kind of guy," Wenner said. "He had that wit and that acid tongue and that gift of hyperbolic language. He could have continued in that direction. He was deeply involved in what America could be and should be." Thompson also resembled Bierce in his weaknesses. Both writers, for example, forced the note of savage irony to diminishing effect. Unwilling or unable to alter his literary practices, Thompson's output declined in quality and quantity. Although his celebrity exceeded anything he could have imagined early on, many commentators focused on the gap between his aspirations and accomplishments. Some, including his ex-wife, regarded that gap as tragic.

Finally, there is the question of genre, the horizon of expectations against which Thompson's work should be judged. Decades after Gonzo's debut, his effort to blur the lines between fiction and journalism continued to stir controversy. That quarrel was especially apparent in the coverage following his suicide. *Los Angeles Times* media critic Tim Rutten conceded that Thompson was "a social satirist of bitingly comedic power" but claimed that forty years had passed since he had created "a recognizable work of journalism—*The Hell's Angels, a Strange and Terrible Saga* (sic)." Rutten also proposed a new label for Thompson's subsequent output. "If the rest of his work requires a category, it's performance art, not journalism." Rutten's analysis had two chief concerns: to define the boundaries of acceptable journalism, and to place almost all of Thompson's work outside those boundaries. That Thompson was also a formidable media critic went unremarked in Rutten's piece.

In many ways, performance art is an apt description of Thompson's *modus operandi.* The Gonzo method consisted largely of causing a scene and then writing about it. One can quibble, however, with other parts of Rutten's assessment. Thompson's work at the *San Francisco Examiner* and ESPN was nothing if not journalism, which is usually understood to include commentary. Moreover, "The Temptations of Jean-Claude Killy" and "Strange Rumblings in Aztlan" postdate *Hell's Angels* and do not fit comfortably in the category of performance art. Indeed, the latter article is more memorable than the *Los Angeles Times'* coverage of Ruben Salazar's death, despite the hometown newspaper's obvious advantages on that story. Rutten's assessment of Thompson's legacy was also problematic. He argued that Gonzo was "an evolutionary dead end" insofar as it began and ended with Thompson's output. At the same time, he worried that Gonzo exercised too much influence insofar as it "can be misread as permission for so much of the tedious narcissism that now infects our journalism, as it does so many other aspects of our collective lives." That trend, Rutten claimed, was "Gonzo's deformed offspring." One wonders whether Thompson's influence, or Rutten's anxiety about it, inspired Rutten's narrow definition of journalism in the first place.

Marc Cooper, who was then a columnist for *LA Weekly*, responded forcefully to Rutten's assessment. "What Thompson accomplished has led us into a dead end," he remarked sarcastically on his blog. "All that posturing, that sneering at authority, all the capacity to write circles around the short-sleeved dullards that populate your average city desk—well—that has apparently led us only to the intellectual graveyard." Cooper then railed against corporate journalism generally.

> Rutten's right that much of American journalism, and certainly that of his fluffy home paper, is indeed infected with a "tedious narcissism." Tedious as hell—as the *Times* and just about every other paper in the country adheres to the obsolete he-said/she-said language of insurance company reports to fill their news columns. So deathly afraid that any trace of human bias or insight (God Forbid) might actually appear in one of these news reports, they are dutifully scrubbed by squads of Newsroom Elders who guarantee every rough edge and every stitched seam will be filed off and sealed up before being pushed out to the public as perfectly symmetrical ingots of composite and inert News Product.

Cooper also addressed the question of Thompson's influence among journalism students.

> Maybe Rutten should spend some more time in a Journalism School and judge for himself: are the majority of students drawn recklessly toward the deformed, narcissistic, outlaw standard set by Gonzo? Or do

they, instead, spend their nights sleepless, wetting their beds, worried they won't be hired on as fully compliant clogs [*sic*] by some gargantuan corporate employer like Gannett and then assigned for the next 10 years as junior assistant deputy to the assistant suburban lifestyle editor—a post whose stability and predictability they deeply, oh so deeply, yearn for?

Cooper's rebuttal implied that Thompson's influence over young journalists was negligible, perhaps unfortunately so. It also suggested that nerve and audacity were more important than outdated notions of objectivity, at least for the kind of journalism Cooper valued. But one need not endorse Thompson's Gonzo example to reach Cooper's conclusion about journalistic objectivity. Indeed, Ruben Salazar drew a similar one in 1968.

The Thompson retrospectives took a historical turn in David Weir's piece for the *San Francisco Chronicle*. He began by noting that much of the mainstream press "more or less politely dismissed" Thompson as the father of New Journalism. That honor, Weir claimed, "doesn't begin to tell his story or describe his place in history." Instead, it was more accurate to view Thompson as part of an older strain of American muckraking.

The kinds of stories Thompson did were much like those of the early 20th-century writers Upton Sinclair, Lincoln Steffens, or Ida Tarbell (or even further back—Mark Twain). Those writers, too, spoke in a fearless, passionate voice, occasionally blended fact with fiction and, like Thompson, refused to bow before the God of objectivity that seems to act as a constraint on so many young journalists today. The muckrakers saw through society's hypocritical veneer and wasted no time sharing their view with us. Far from being "objective," they breathed outrage. At their best, the muckrakers were fair, but they took no prisoners along the way. They never apologized for telling it as they saw it— which was, in retrospect, proved to be pretty much the way it was.

To underscore his point, Weir offered an anecdote from the more recent past: "I always liked what the Bay Area's own Jessica Mitford, the 'Queen of the Muckrakers,' had to say much later in the 20th century. 'Objectivity?' she quipped. 'Sure, I believe in objectivity. I've always got an objective!'" Mitford, who also served on the editorial board of *Ramparts* magazine, indirectly but freely conceded what many traditional journalists would not—that the standard of strict objectivity did not hold up well to scrutiny. There were no purely objective grounds for selection, emphasis, diction, tone, or other basic elements in any story. Quite aside from that debate, however, Weir was correct that American journalism had traditionally made a place for more pointed writing and even crusading.

As these eulogies suggested, Thompson triggered a larger argument within the profession, but that debate shed little light on Thompson's unique talent. He was not a traditional journalist, much less a reporter. Nor was he a traditional novelist, though he worked the crease between fiction and journalism vigorously. Rather, he was a writer, satirist, and stylist whose major works created the standards by which they should be judged. That point was acknowledged, if not fully explored, in another *San Francisco Chronicle* piece that ran the same day as Weir's. The paper's foreign and national editor, A. S. Ross, opened with an overheated repudiation of Thompson and his eulogists.

> Not since the death of Princess Diana has so much worshipful ink been spilled on the occasion of a mere mortal's passing. He was a giant among men. Who cared that for years he had been a largely burned-out case, more of a circus act than a serious writer, reveling in adolescent stunts with firearms, alcohol, narcotics—the predictable paraphernalia of the self-styled outlaw who wowed the chattering classes and other assorted rubes and poseurs long after his appeal had worn off for almost everybody else?

After mocking the journalists who identified with Thompson and his persona, Ross pivoted unexpectedly to a literary perspective.

> The drooling eulogies also do Thompson a disservice because they ultimately fail in the one thing he presumably would want, and based on his early work—especially his Kentucky Derby piece in *Scanlan's* and the book *Hell's Angels: The Strange and Terrible Saga of Outlaw Motorcycle Gangs* [sic]—deserves to be examined critically as a writer who is part of a rich American literary tradition.

Again, one need not endorse Ross's denunciations to agree with his awkwardly worded conclusion. Critical examinations of Thompson's work were long overdue, and for exactly the reason Ross suggested.

Other appraisals of Thompson have targeted his personal conduct and its pernicious influence. Many of those appraisals fall outside the scope of this project, but one is especially relevant. A 2017 *Denver Post* article quoted local writer Laura Bond, a former music editor at a Denver outlet called *Westword*. "I think it's preferable and possible to be a good person and a good artist," Bond said, adding that Thompson was neither. "His destructive tendencies were so romanticized, and he did a lot to perpetuate the idea that creativity and freedom are fueled by drugs and alcohol. That idea has taken a lot of people down dangerous roads." As a former music editor, Bond faced many "incoherent first drafts from wannabe gonzo journalists." That legacy, along with Thompson's misogyny, "just feels totally outmoded, uninteresting, and sad to me today."

There is much to agree with in Bond's remarks. It is a pity, if not a surprise, that more artists are not better people. Drug and alcohol abuse are dangerous, Thompson's destructive tendencies were romanticized, and incoherent first drafts are irksome for any editor. Finally, it is notable and refreshing that Bond considered Thompson an artist in the first place. Both the dismissal of his work and the remark about his misogyny might very well reflect careful study. Worse has been said about Thompson's conduct, and I do not regard the question of his artistic achievement as settled.

Nevertheless, Bond's judgments miss the mark in other ways. Insofar as they are grounded in her professional experience, the arc of her career may help us understand her critique. In 2005, she left her position at *Westword*, which is now part of the Voice Media Group. It describes itself as "the voice of Denver for faithful readers who appreciate hard-hitting journalism. And better beer." It also "gives back to the city" by presenting, among other things, "High Style, a cannabis-inspired fusion of fashion, education, and wellness." Although *Westword* is not connected to *Rolling Stone*, it is difficult to imagine its self-description, or perhaps even its existence, were it not for *Rolling Stone*'s success and Thompson's contributions to it. After leaving *Westword*, Bond landed at the Denver Foundation, which "currently assists Metro Denver individuals, families, and businesses accomplish their charitable goals by helping them design personalized charitable giving strategies and establishing customized, flexible donor funds." Bond now describes herself as "a mission-driven leader, writer, editor, and communications specialist." In my own efforts to remain employed, I have almost certainly described myself in similar terms. I would be remiss, however, if I did not admit that such language now feels outmoded, uninteresting, and sad to me today. Thompson is a vivid reminder that other ways of living and writing are possible, even if most of us do not choose them. Indeed, the entire counterculture is that reminder writ large. As Curtis White has argued, we lose something important when the counterculture's spirit of impertinence is proscribed or absent.

If Bond's dismissal of Thompson and his work seems precipitous, her point about wannabe Gonzo journalists also flags a key misconception. Equating Thompson's style with his appetites is the surest way to misunderstand it. Although Thompson's life and work were inextricably linked, I have tried to show that he found his voice after a long apprenticeship, complete with failed experiments and false starts that would have discouraged many writers. Even after producing his first bestseller, which demanded journalistic resourcefulness as well as physical courage, he struggled to invent a new form for the Las Vegas book. The campaign book that followed blended participatory reporting with the Gonzo approach, but it also required Thompson to master the details of political campaigns and to overcome significant institutional challenges, most notably the perceived irrelevance of his employer. Despite the hopes of wannabe Gonzo journalists, there was no shortcut, pharmaceutical or otherwise, to Thompson's success.

Although that success was hard won, we should not regard it as the inevitable result of isolated genius. Thompson's talent was undeniable, but much of his work was inspired and shaped by skilled editors. Even more important were the contributions of Ralph Steadman, a gifted visual artist who responded sympathetically and creatively to his project. Having combined his unique voice with Steadman's illustrations, Thompson did not waste that powerful instrument on forgettable topics. Rather, he used it to tell unsettling truths, expose lies, and ridicule hypocrites. His targets included a sitting US president, the leaders of both major political parties, a misbegotten war, unchecked and dishonest law enforcement, and a docile mainstream media. If Thompson's high white note was difficult to reach, it was even harder to sustain. Once heard, however, it was impossible to forget.

Acknowledgments

Many colleagues, friends, and loved ones have earned my gratitude for their direct and indirect help with this project. For their willingness to share their memories and expertise, I wish to thank Jon Carroll, Judy Clancy, David Felton, Elisa Florez, Joe Hagan, Margaret Harrell, Will Hearst, Denise Kaufman, Sarah Lazin, Jacques Leslie, Greil Marcus, Terry McDonell, Michael Murphy, Abe Peck, Charles Perry, Alan Rinzler, Phillip Rodriguez, David Streitfeld, Juan Thompson, David Weir, and Jann Wenner. I should emphasize my gratitude to Joe Hagan, William McKeen, Abe Peck, and David Streitfeld— not only for their own excellent work, but also for their support on this project.

The bibliography is a master list of my other intellectual debts, but some sources were especially important. The two volumes of correspondence edited by Douglas Brinkley were indispensable, as was Jann Wenner and Corey Seymour's oral biography of Thompson. From the moment I saw it in Tower Records in San Rafael, I was riveted by the 2005 issue of *Stop Smiling*, which featured many of Thompson's editors. Many years later, I misplaced my copy; receiving a new one long after the publication had folded was an unexpected gift.

In some ways, my interest in this project began with my biography of Carey McWilliams, which was sponsored by Jim Reische at the University of Michigan Press and later reissued by the University of California Press. My book on *Ramparts* magazine, which Ellen Adler published at The New Press, reinforced my interest in Thompson and introduced me to Warren Hinckle and Jann Wenner. My subsequent book about the Grateful Dead, which Marc Resnick sponsored at St. Martin's Press, also drew me back to Thompson and his San Francisco milieu. In each case, I had to pull myself away from Thompson's story and return to the work at hand. I took that as a signal that Thompson should be my next subject.

My agent, Andy Ross, helped me place this project, and Reed Malcolm deserves much credit for his editorial guidance. His friendship, and that of editorial director Kim Robinson, is another blessing. For their skill and good temper, I'm grateful to Lynda Crawford, who edited the manuscript, and to Julie Van Pelt, who guided it through production. In addition to writing about Thompson's time in Sonoma County, Patrick Joseph commissioned my article on the early years of *Rolling Stone* for *California* magazine. Likewise, Jason Sexton sponsored my piece on Thompson for *Boom: A Journal of California*. Nicholas Meriwether invited me to deliver a paper on Thompson to the Grateful Dead Scholars Caucus, to which I belong. Another member of that happy few, Jay Williams, called my attention to Jack London and his distinctive model of authorship. As my manuscript took shape, I participated in an online celebration of Margaret Harrell's *The Hell's Angels Letters* with Margaret, William McKeen, Rory Patrick Feehan, Ron Whitehead, and moderator Alice Osborne. I am grateful to them for including me in that discussion.

Before the pandemic shut the archives I hoped to visit in person, I examined Eric Shoaf's collection of Thompson's work at the University of California, Santa Cruz. For their help at the library, I thank Jessica Pigza and Teresa Mora. I also relished my visit with Magnus Toren, proprietor of the Henry Miller Library in Big Sur. On the same trip, I visited the Esalen Institute courtesy of Michael Murphy, its cofounder. Soaking in the hot baths was a dirty job, but someone had to do it. Carol Pogash shared unpublished correspondence from Thompson's early days. Mark Ettlin, whose friendship I have valued for almost half a century, called my attention to sportswriter Furman Bisher. Selah.

My father, Douglas Richardson, introduced me to the work of George Plimpton, who played a larger role in this project than I expected. I am grateful for that introduction as well as all the others. Finally, I thank Ashley Richardson, Gladys Richardson, Mary Grace Richardson, and Beth Tudor for their love and support in a world of fear and loathing.

Notes

INTRODUCTION

1 **Although Thompson's books:** Gabel & Hughes 2005; see also Feehan 2018.
   "I'm really in the way": Finch 1978.
   In this sense: Streitfeld 2018, p. xi.
   "You could strike sparks": Thompson 1972, p. 68 (*Fear and Loathing in Las Vegas*).

2 **Exactly *how* they were going to:** Crouse 2003, p. ix.
   "A good writer stands above movements": Thompson 1997, p. 129.
   Few critics hold that novel: Thompson 1997, p. 70.

4 **In 1975, for example:** Thompson 2000, p. 613 (*Fear and Loathing in America*).

5 **"The true voice of Thompson":** Kunzru 1998.

CHAPTER 1. BROODING

7 **Thompson claimed to welcome the reminder:** Thompson 2000, p. 258 (*Fear and Loathing in America*).

8 **Rather, it was:** Adams 1931, p. 415.
   In his seminal 1956 article: Hofstadter 1956.

9 **He chose not to work for others:** Quoted in Weingarten 2006, p. 128.
   "My only faith": Thompson 1997, p. 322.
   He immediately wrote to Silberman: Thompson 1997, p. 610.
   Like most others: Thompson 1998, p. 5 (*The Rum Diary*).

10 **"I loathe the fucking memory":** Thompson 2000, p. 263 (*Fear and Loathing in America*).
   "You might as well have told me": Thompson 2000, p. 205 (*Fear and Loathing in America*).

"Why in the name of stinking Jesus": Thompson 2000, p. 263 (*Fear and Loathing in America*).

He called one of them: Schlesinger 1952.

11 **Shortly after signing a contract:** Thompson 1997, p. 529.

"God only knows": Thompson 2000, p. 261 (*Fear and Loathing in America*).

12 **Norman Mailer's *Advertisements for Myself*:** Wenner & Seymour 2007, p. 435.

He didn't consider Exley: Thompson 2000, p. 184 (*Fear and Loathing in America*).

That way, he explained: Thompson 2000, p. 264 (*Fear and Loathing in America*).

As he wrote to Silberman: Thompson 2000, p. 164 (*Fear and Loathing in America*).

"Hell, you're an editor": Thompson 2000, p. 269 (*Fear and Loathing in America*).

13 **Having learned that Thompson:** Vetter 1974.

"This whole thing": Steadman 2006, p. 31.

Later, he confided that: Thompson 2000, p. 310 (*Fear and Loathing in America*).

No one was more surprised: Vetter 1974.

14 **The idea, he explained to Steadman:** Thompson 2000, p. 320 (*Fear and Loathing in America*).

CHAPTER 2. THE STORM OF LIFE

15 **"Hunter was always where":** Perry 1992, p. 6.

It was Jackie Robinson: Whitmer 1993, p. 33.

"I've always felt like a Southerner": Carroll 1993, p. 25.

16 **As one longtime friend said:** Wenner & Seymour 2007, p. 70.

Another friend remarked: Wenner & Seymour 2007, p. 72.

Privately, Thompson said: Thompson 1997, p. 185.

17 **"Athenaeum was tied into the Louisville elite":** Wenner & Seymour 2007, p. 13.

I was always amazed: Wenner & Seymour 2007, p. 13

Although one childhood friend: Carroll 1993, p. 22.

"But you really didn't even need them": Wenner & Seymour 2007, p. 14.

"I think Hunter always *hated*": Carroll 1993, p. 57.

Let us visualize the secure man: Perry 1992, pp. 16–17.

18 **Hunter represents freedom:** Carroll 1993, p. 278.

"He was fearless": Carroll 1993, p. 19.

One friend observed: Carroll 1993, p. 57.

When Hunter started getting into trouble: Carroll 1993, p. 51.

19 **"Everybody else had money":** Carroll 1993, p. 58.

On two consecutive nights: Whitmer 1993, p. 72.

Toward the tail end: McKeen 1991.

Brown had been killed: Wenner & Seymour 2007, p. 32.

As Thompson biographer: McKeen 2008, p. 50.

McKeen also observed: Gates 2017.

20 **Critics described Dangerfield:** Gates 2017.

Reading *The Ginger Man*: Allen 1972.

Thompson also cast: Wenner & Seymour 2007, p. 47.

21 **He was reading voluminously:** Wenner & Seymour 2007, p. 45.

According to Kennedy: Wenner & Seymour 2007, p. 45.

Much later in life: McKeen 1990.

22 **"This never happened in Puerto Rico":** Perry 1992, p. 51.

A Kentucky native: Thompson 1998, p. 109.

"I was a young writer": Kerouac 1957, p. 8.

23 **Thompson wasn't a Kerouac fan:** Thompson 1997, p. 140.

Writing to Silberman in 1971: Thompson 2000, p. 421 (*Fear and Loathing in America*).

"I wasn't trying to write like him": Brinkley & McDonell 2000.

"The most important thing about Kennedy": Thompson 2000, p. 260 (*Fear and Loathing in America*).

"With John Kennedy and Bobby Kennedy": Gibney 2008.

24 **That was when I first understood:** Thompson 2000, p. 260 (*Fear and Loathing in America*).

Thompson followed the presidential campaign: Thompson 2000, p. 260 (*Fear and Loathing in America*).

CHAPTER 3. ROUGHING IT

26 **When railroad magnate:** McWilliams 1929, p. 240.

"I don't like the job": McWilliams 1929, p. 295.

Poet Kenneth Rexroth: Davidson 1989, p. 11.

"In the spiritual and political loneliness": Snyder 1977, p. 45.

27 **City of hills and fog and water:** Thompson 1997, p. 237.

Say "no" to San Francisco: Thompson 1997, p. 238.

28 **Both were banned in the United States:** Orwell 1940.

Largely through his letters: Hoyle 2014, p. 89.

The early settlers are dying off: Miller 1957, p. 11.

29 **"If an art colony is established here":** Miller 1957, p. 13.

"Everyone who has come here": Miller 1957, p. 25.

Edited by Lawrence Durrell: Mailer 1976, p. ix.

Nor did he envision: Miller 1959, p. 358 (*The World of Sex*).

More than any other single figure: Kripal 2007, p. 37.

"This little black book of Miller's": Thompson 1997, p. 256.

In his review of that work: Crews 1977.

30 **"There ain't much to do here":** Thompson 1997, p. 256.

The Rum Diary, **Thompson wrote Kennedy:** Thompson 1997, p. 278.

I have tonight begun reading: Thompson 1997, p. 358.

31 **"I was shocked by it":** Perry 1992, pp. 55–56.

Decades later, Sandy alluded to: Carroll 1993, pp. 192–93.

"He was loving, he was generous": Gibney 2008.

Hunter had two extremes in him: Gibney 2008.

32 **"Hunter had studied my book like a Bible":** Whitmer & VanWyngarden 1987, p. 78.

"We were not trying to pass judgment": Whitmer & VanWyngarden 1987, p. 78.

"Yes, there are queers here": Thompson 1997, p. 253

33 **"Hunter had a lot of aggression":** Whitmer & VanWyngarden 1987, p. 78.

I am surrounded by lunatics here: Thompson 1997, p. 280.

"If half the stories about Big Sur were true": Thompson 1961 ("Big Sur").

As his fame spread: Thompson 1961 ("Big Sur").

34 **What will happen when this world of neuters:** Thompson 1961 ("Big Sur").

I knew that if I had a baby: Wenner & Seymour 2007, p. 55.

35 **He could never forget the horror:** Thompson 1961 ("Burial at Sea").

He wondered what his friends would say: Thompson 1961 ("Burial at Sea").

In this indirect way: Author interview with Michael Murphy.

CHAPTER 4. OBSERVER

36 **It was "full of digressions":** Wenner & Seymour 2007, p. 63.

This is sharp, witty, participatory: Kevin 2015.

"The Thompson who left for the continent": Kevin 2014, p. 12.

37 **Years later, however:** Wenner & Seymour 2007, p. 62.

   He called the first piece: Thompson 1997, p. 402.

   "It is a goddamned abomination": Thompson 1997, p. 367.

   "I'm beginning to think you're a phony": Thompson 1997, p. 368.

   Thompson was amazed: Thompson 1997, p. 368.

38 **Failing monetary satisfaction:** Thompson 1997, p. 415.

   Too many people in this gutless world: Thompson 1997, p. 416.

39 **I suppose your boys over there:** Thompson 1997, p. 418.

40 **"All of you cheap bookstore Marxists":** Thompson 1997, p. 418.

   We now enter the era of the shit-rain: Thompson 1997, p. 420.

   "Mailer is an antique curiosity": Thompson 1997, p. 421.

41 **"If I were Fanon":** Thompson 1997, p. 436.

   For nearly a year: Thompson 1997, p. 438.

   "It was actually a shack": Wenner & Seymour 2007, p. 67.

42 *The People of the Abyss:* Weingarten 2006, p. 15.

   Similarly, *The Road*: Labor 2013, p. 243.

   "I have been forced to conclude": London 1903.

   As a literary celebrity: Williams 2014, p. 45.

   "IT WAS MY REFUSAL": Williams 2014, p. 15.

   His key issue was justice: Labor 2013, p. 151.

43 **I am not too worried:** Thompson 1997, p. 449.

   "Once it turns into power politics": Thompson 1997, p. 449.

   His dream panel: Thompson 1997, pp. 458–59.

   In the event of various: Thompson 1997, pp. 458–59.

44 **The article described the saloon's proprietor:** Thompson 1967.

45 **In Idaho, Thompson maintained:** Thompson 1964.

46 **He was depressed:** Thompson 1997, p. 451.

   "I would wander in off-hours": McKeen 1990.

   The raucous event: Skipper 2016, p. 2.

47 **Reporting for NBC:** Clark 1993.

   Jackie Robinson, the GOP delegate: Robinson 1972, p. 340.

   "You know, these nighttime news shows": Perlstein 2001, p. 378.

   "Suddenly Louis and I heard a voice": Davis 2010, p. 4.

   As historian Rick Perlstein noted: Perlstein 2001, p. 392.

48 **The Goldwater delegates went completely amok:** Thompson 1972 ("More Fear and Loathing in Miami").

   Equally formative was Norman Mailer's coverage: Aldridge 1966.

Douglas Brinkley claimed that Mailer's work: Wenner & Seymour 2007, p. 435.

He still had much to learn: Thompson 1997, p. 463.

49 "The Free Speech Movement": McKeen 1990.

The book drew its title: Wolfe 1965, p. 5.

50 When I started writing: Weingarten 2005, p. 95.

The title essay: McDonell 2016, p. 367.

"Jack London of all people": Dundy 1966.

51 "Entertainment rather than information": Macdonald 1965.

CHAPTER 5. NEW JOURNALIST

52 He was later described: Starr 2002, pp. 257, 103.

Radical writer Mike Davis: Davis 2005.

53 In 1950, he ran for the US Senate: Mitchell 1998, p. xvi.

Writing for *The Nation* that year: McWilliams 1950.

54 Where Mr. Hoover got his figure: Thompson 1965 ("The Nonstudent Left").

When contacted about this project: Email message to author.

"I am long past the point of simple poverty": Thompson 1997, p. 481.

56 Jarvis was "the only guy": Thompson 1997, p. 499.

After recounting Jarvis's violent past: Thompson 1967, p. 61 (*Hell's Angels*).

After a tense introduction: Thompson 1997, p. 499.

57 Although the magazine did not pay well: Thompson 1997, p. xxvii.

In 1966, he told McWilliams: Thompson 1997, p. 573.

Borrowing a trope from H. L. Mencken: McWilliams 1946, p. 376.

"I didn't know if he was a Hell's Angel": Perry 1992, pp. 101–2.

58 "He didn't need any help writing the book": Wenner & Seymour 2007, p. 86.

As Harrell recalled: Author interview with Margaret Harrell.

There was just enough explosiveness: Author interview with Margaret Harrell.

He asked Harrell to remind the publicity department: Harrell 2011, p. 96.

59 "I should have dedicated the book": Harrell with Whitehead 2020, p. 50.

He described them as: Harrell 2011, p. 88.

60 "That night we started the tradition": Harrell 2011, p. 103.

"Everybody I knew had read *On the Road*": Gibney & Ellwood 2011.

Writing to Lionel Olay: Thompson 1997, p. 400.

61 **"We had been accepted by the old gunfighters":** Gibney & Ellwood 2011.

"I could see that it was a love affair": Perry 1992, p. 105.

"I met Allen in San Francisco": Plimpton 2000, p. 53.

62 **According to Thompson:** Gibney 2008.

In a Merry Prankster publication: Babbs 1981.

Years earlier, Michael Murphy had advised him: Whitmer & VanWyngarden 1987, p. 83.

"When we left," Sandy recalled: Gibney 2008.

Wolfe did not take LSD: Weingarten 2006, p. 105.

"Wolfe's problem is that he's too crusty": Thompson 1979, p. 108.

63 **His author's note explained:** Wolfe 1968, p. 415.

Nevertheless, Mayor Sam Yorty had declined: Davis & Wiener 2020, p. 208.

"Nobody told me there was an explosive situation in Los Angeles": Theoharris 2005; Kennedy 2018.

LA police chief William Parker: Joseph 2006, p. 121.

He also claimed that the trouble started: Buntin 2008, p. 310.

Regarding his department's success in suppressing violence: Rutten 2009.

64 **"It Ain't Hardly That Way No More":** Thompson 1965.

In the Hell's Angels book, however: Thompson 1967, p. 205.

65 **"There will be more of this kind of demagogy":** McWilliams 1966.

"We completely decorated the place": Sculatti & Seay 1985, p. 33.

"About 400 or 500 people showed up": Weller 2012.

Covering the event for the *San Francisco Chronicle*: Gleason 1969, p. 6.

66 **In September 1965, he shared his enthusiasm:** Thompson 1997, p. 542.

"After Ralph Gleason did that column": Tamarkin 2003, p. 41.

He later described it as: Graham 1992, p. 121.

"We went to get this chopped liver sandwich": Graham 1992, p. 123.

67 **According to one scholar, it was:** Bernstein 2008, p. 5.

Jerry Garcia described the event as: Lydon 1969.

"When the dull projections took over": Gleason 1969, p. 18.

I got terrified about the deadline: Vetter 1974.

68 **The daily press is the evil principle:** Thompson 1967, p. 21 (*Hell's Angels*).

Weird as it seems: Thompson 1967, p. 13 (*Hell's Angels*).

"If the 'Hell's Angels Saga' proved any one thing": Thompson 1967, p. 34 (*Hell's Angels*).

He was especially critical of the *Times*: Thompson 1967, p. 34 (*Hell's Angels*).

He called one of its stories: Thompson 1967, p. 35 (*Hell's Angels*).

69 **Writing to his editor at the *National Observer*:** Thompson 1997, p. 502.

The *New York Times Book Review* echoed Thompson's remark: Litwak 1967.

If Barger *had been stomped* by the locals: Thompson 1967, pp. 141–42 (*Hell's Angels*).

70 **"The case never came to court":** Thompson 1967, p. 241 (*Hell's Angels*).

"Every time I talked to the Angels": Thompson 1967, p. 241 (*Hell's Angels*).

71 **After describing the motorcycle gang's assault:** Thompson 1967, p. 245 (*Hell's Angels*).

"What's truly shocking about reading the book today": McWilliams 2016.

"The old way of life was scattered back along Route 66": Thompson 1967, p. 153 (*Hell's Angels*).

"Ten years later," Thompson maintained: Thompson 1967, p. 153 (*Hell's Angels*).

72 **Algren's most famous novels:** Lombardi 2008.

"Much of what happens in the story": Asher 2019, p. 372.

Finally, Algren subscribed to *Police Chief* magazine: Asher 2019, p. 423.

"You have got to get over the idea": Thompson 1997, pp. 557–58.

Six days later, Algren replied: Thompson 1997, pp. 558–59.

73 **"Regardless of what you think":** Thompson 1997, p. 559.

74 **"I admired Algren and still do":** Whitmer 1984.

"It was about this time that my longstanding rapport": Thompson 1967, pp. 253–54 (*Hell's Angels*).

"He needed that ending": Weingarten 2005, p. 141.

Anyway, I'm off on another book now: Thompson 1997, p. 586.

Several months after that, Thompson wrote: Thompson 1997, p. 605.

75 **Hunter found out I was upset with him:** Barger 2000.

"Hunter turned out to be a real weenie": Barger 2000, p. 125.

"I read the book, *Hell's Angels: A Strange and Terrible Saga*": Barger 2000, p. 127.

He generally liked hippies: Barger 2000, p. 130.

"That book made him realize that there was a market": Gibney 2008.

Until he took on that project: Thompson 1990, p. 109.

76 **I noted the transformation of Hunter:** Wenner & Seymour 2007, p. 90.

"He never responded," Jim noted later: Carroll 1993, p. 118.

77 **Says Hunter Thompson about Hunter Thompson:** Thompson 1967 ("Why Boys Will Be Girls").

CHAPTER 6. HASHBURY

78 *Ramparts* **staff writer Adam Hochschild:** Richardson 2009, p. 97.

79 **I met [Hinckle] through his magazine:** Brinkley & McDonell 2000.

Boozing with Hinckle: Richardson 2009, p. 55.

"Cookie's was a narrow dim room": Hinckle 2017, p. 10.

80 **"That fucking monkey should be killed":** Thompson 1997, p. 641.

Ramparts **is slick enough to lure the unwary:** *Time* 1967 ("A Bomb in Every Issue").

82 **In an open society like the U.S.:** *Time* 1967 ("The Silent Service").

One CIA director privately referred to this influence: Wilford 2008, p. 7.

The media coverage tilted toward drugs: Gitlin 1987, p. 215.

"The hippies grew up in my backyard": Hinckle 1974, p. 138.

The danger in the hippie movement: Hinckle 1967.

83 **Now, in 1967, there is not much doubt:** Thompson 1967.

84 **There had to be a whole new scene:** Thompson 1967.

85 **"Call it the weather," she wrote:** Didion 1960.

86 **In 1960, Didion began contributing:** Menand 2015.

"She seemed to be the only sensible person in the world": Daugherty 2015, p. 235.

In fact, her descriptions bore a strong resemblance: *Time* 1967 ("The Hippies").

The center was not holding: Didion 1968, p. 85.

87 **She spoke to Arthur Lisch:** Didion 1968, pp. 99–100.

At some point between 1945 and 1967: Didion 1968, p. 123.

Anybody who thinks this is all about drugs: Didion 1968, p. 120.

According to Didion's biographer: Daugherty 2015, p. 230.

88 **I was in fact as sick as I have ever been:** Didion 1968, p. xiii.

Yet many of her encounters in those years: Didion 1979, p. 19.

The only problem was that my entire education: Didion 1979, pp. 12–13.

89 **Because police routinely ignored the drug use:** Hartlaub 2017.

There is no such thing as a hippy: Freeman & Meyer 1967.

90 **"There has been no point in American history that I know of":** Richardson 2015, p. 87.

91 **"Something like 15 out of the first 19 albums":** Gleason 1969, p. 68.

"You make the social revolution first": Richardson 2015, pp. 92–93.

"It was the only place I knew": Gleason 2016, p. xi.

92 **"They were oblivious to the cultural changes":** Richardson 2009, p. 108.

He resigned from *Ramparts* magazine: Gleason 2016, p. 259.

"The Free Speech Movement had an enormous effect": Richardson 2017.

93 **The San Francisco Bay Area was a hotbed:** Gibney 2008.

What I found objectionable about the hippies: Hinckle 1974, pp. 144–45.

We didn't want to be part of that hippie way of life: Hagan 2017, p. 87.

94 **Many hippies abandoned the Haight:** Thompson 1970 ("The Battle of Aspen").

In his Hashbury piece: Thompson 1967.

The profile noted that Snyder: Goodyear 2008.

95 **"His utopia, which he had experienced before":** Gibney 2008.

The hippies threatened the establishment: Thompson 2000, p. 7 (*Fear and Loathing in America*).

Any thinking hippie, he wrote: Thompson 2000, p. 7 (*Fear and Loathing in America*).

96 **Reflecting on his arrangement and its costs:** Rosenbaum 1977.

In a letter to Lord: Thompson 1997, p. 264.

In a long letter to Paul Krassner: Thompson 1997, p. 647.

He'd come blundering into our offices: Wenner & Seymour 2007, pp. 89–90.

"The arguments we had about money went on and on": Wenner & Seymour 2007, p. 89.

97 **Hippies, he wrote, were "in part a hoax of American journalism":** Harris 1967.

"Five years of madness in this hideout": Acosta 1972, p. 66.

"In terms of style," one critic observed: Stavans 1995, p. 19.

Born four years apart, both men: Calderon 2004, p. 89.

98 **As you well know, I have been at war with myself and the universe:** Calderon 2004, p. 94.

CHAPTER 7. TOTALLY GONZO

99 **"All I really want to do":** Thompson 2000, p. 50 (*Fear and Loathing in America*).

"It was a very weird trip": Thompson 1973, p. 44.

100 **For years I've regarded his very existence:** Thompson 1968.

That terse formulation: Wenner & Seymour 2007, p. 99.

"I just wanted to *be there*": Thompson 2003, p. 15.

He told Silberman that Peter Collier: Thompson 2000, p. 15 (*Fear and Loathing in America*).

101 Reporting for *Harper's* magazine, Norman Mailer observed: Mailer 1968, p. 162 (*The Armies of the Night*).

As he later recalled: Thompson 2003, p. 80.

When he submitted his expenses to Silberman: Thompson 2000, p. 119 (*Fear and Loathing in America*).

That week at the Convention changed everything: Thompson 2003, p. 78.

102 "The idea sprang fully formed from his head": Richardson 2009, p. 135.

Hinckle's mentor, . . . Howard Gossage: Hinckle 1974, p. 358.

A fixture at New York's celebrity watering holes: McFadden 2009.

A beatnik detractor, Hefner preferred to tout: Draper 1990, pp. 59–60.

103 In an internal discussion, another *Playboy* editor: Thompson 2000, p. 222 (*Fear and Loathing in America*).

Hunter's such an amazingly brutish physical specimen: Carroll 1993, p. 124.

One of Thompson's editors, Alan Rinzler: Whitmer 1993, p. 177.

"So Hunter could be really sweet and everything": Harrell 2011, p. 66.

"I was afraid of the guy": Carroll 1993, p. 20.

"I used to dread Hunter getting up in the afternoon": Carroll 1993, pp. 121–22.

104 Chevrolet doesn't pay him to say what he thinks: Thompson 1970 ("The Temptations of Jean-Claude Killy").

105 "Don't you understand?" he said: Edelman 2016.

"Well," he replied, "I'm just sitting here smoking marijuana": Thompson 1970 ("The Temptations of Jean-Claude Killy").

106 "On lesser fronts, I want to impose a condition": Thompson 2000, p. 283 (*Fear and Loathing in America*).

107 "We young students did not read the newspapers in those years": Gay 1968, p. 70.

Drawing on the Art Nouveau, Dada, and Pop traditions: Guffey 2014, p. 167.

"The only thing of value": Perry 2013.

In 1969, Steadman visited New York City: Paul 2013.

"I don't think he even liked the idea of this country": Thompson 1979, p. 112.

"They were the ultimate in assimilated flesh color": Steadman 2006, p. 9.

"You scumbag!" Thompson said over breakfast: Steadman 2006, p. 31.

"He catches things," Thompson noted: Thompson 1979, pp. 11ff.

108 **"I think what he saw in our connection":** Paul 2013.

"And I mean that quite literally," Rubin said: Perlstein 2008, p. 475.

"If it's to be a bloodbath, let it be now": Perlstein 2014, p. 90.

"You know, you see these bums": Perlstein 2008, p. 482.

109 **After Kent State, Nixon's top aide:** Cohen & Koncewicz 2020.

"I would lie in the bathtub in this weird hotel": Rosenbaum 1977.

He later compared his editorial task: Hinckle 2017, p. 91.

Thompson made his deadline: Rosenbaum 1977.

110 **What distinguished the Kentucky Derby piece:** Hinckle 2017, p. 92.

When those arrived the next morning: Hinckle 2017, p. 91.

"Look." The man tapped me on the arm: Thompson 1970 ("The Kentucky Derby Is Decadent and Depraved").

113 **Well after submitting the piece:** Thompson 2000, p. 304 (*Fear and Loathing in America*).

The article is useless: Thompson 2000, pp. 309–10 (*Fear and Loathing in America*).

114 **"People were calling it a tremendous breakthrough":** Rosenbaum 1977.

It was a wonderful story and departure piece: Wenner & Seymour 2007, p. 124.

"In time he found a way to turn himself": Wenner & Seymour 2007, p. 127.

"This was no longer the Hunter who would sit down": Wenner & Seymour 2007, p. 123.

And that's what he did: Wenner 2005, p. 52.

115 **In London's case, the constructed nature of that character:** Williams 2014, p. 9.

CHAPTER 8. ROLLING STONE

117 **"The peace and love generation was smashing itself to bits":** Cutler 2010, p. 170.

"If the name 'Woodstock' has come to denote": Gleason 1970.

In a letter to Silberman: Thompson 2000, pp. 261–62 (*Fear and Loathing in America*).

118 **Behind the scenes:** Draper 1990, p. 114.

"Having once read your Angels book in galley proof": Thompson 2011, pp. 9–10.

119 **He was wearing his famous "gook" Hawaiian shirt:** Whitmer 1993, pp. 170–71.

"I didn't like their particular politics": Hagan 2017, p. 161.

One described the situation as: Hagan 2017, p. 162.

120 As the Altamont coverage showed: Thompson 2000, p. 502 (*Fear and Loathing in America*).

Yet each man was happy to use the other: Hagan 2017, p. 280.

"What happened in the Haight": Thompson 1970 ("The Battle of Aspen").

I'm still not sure what launched me: Thompson 1970 ("The Battle of Aspen").

Hunter Thompson is a moralist: Watkins 2015, p. 3.

121 He also proposed that Aspen be renamed: Thompson 1970 ("The Battle of Aspen").

In a post-election letter to Carey McWilliams: Thompson 2000, p. 336 (*Fear and Loathing in America*).

"It was wonderful," Benton said: Wenner & Seymour 2007, p. 104.

122 "And if the Wallposter name rings a bell": Thompson 2000, p. 283 (*Fear and Loathing in America*).

He later explained that he employed it regularly: Finch 1978.

In the final issue of *Scanlan's*: Thompson 1971 ("Aspen Wallposter").

In his concession speech: Thompson 2000, p. 332 (*Fear and Loathing in America*).

123 Thompson refused to endorse: Thompson 2000, p. 145.

He communicated some of that excitement: Thompson 2000, p. 332 (*Fear and Loathing in America*).

Maybe "The Battle of Aspen" might be a working title: Thompson 2000, p. 334 (*Fear and Loathing in America*).

124 If you want to go with "The Battle for Aspen": Thompson 2000, p. 334 (*Fear and Loathing in America*).

125 Later, Mailer described "the land of Millett": Mailer 1971, p. 93.

So her land was a foul and dreary place to cross: Mailer 1971, p. 95.

"It was a guy's magazine": Hopper 2018.

126 Staff member Sarah Lazin: Author interview with Sarah Lazin.

"There are those who see Hunter's destructive tendencies as cute": Hagan 2017, p. 280.

Ruiz committed himself to *el movimiento*: Garcia 2015, p. 41.

127 He could sell the movement book: Thompson 2000, p. 37 (*Fear and Loathing in America*).

When Acosta furnished an outline: Thompson 2000, p. 47 (*Fear and Loathing in America*).

If McWilliams ran the piece in *The Nation*: Thompson 2000, p. 56 (*Fear and Loathing in America*).

Hunter, I came here to blow minds: Thompson 2000, p. 53 (*Fear and Loathing in America*).

"Get hold of a good green hillside": Thompson 2000, p. 156 (*Fear and Loathing in America*).

128   **"Oscar said he took off his apron":** Sahagun 2018.

"He was the only one who was offering": Rodriguez 2017.

129   **"Oscar didn't want to be a lawyer":** Garcia 2015, p. 67.

Instead of fleeing: Thompson 1977.

The history of Los Angeles County: Acosta 1996.

This marks the transformation: Calderon 2004, p. 96.

130   **When asked why he was leaving objective journalism:** *Democracy Now* 2010.

131   **"I'm still trying to find the water fountains":** Dean 1976, p. 34.

"The malignant reality of Ruben Salazar's death": Thompson 1971 ("Strange Rumblings in Aztlan").

CHAPTER 9. LAS VEGAS

133   **As Thompson would note later:** Thompson 1979, p. 105.

134   **"When these guys came here":** Ives 2005.

"He was a success": Hyman 1989.

I think this notion that Vegas: Ives 2005.

"It's the middle of the desert": Peters 2019.

135   **Hunter was absolutely obsessed with the Senate hearings:** Whitmer 1993, p. 86.

Kennedy's zeal pushed Hoffa into the arms of the GOP: Warren 2001.

"He was the spark that changed Vegas": Fedrizzi 2013.

When Korshak arrived in Las Vegas: Thomas 1996.

136   **As his narrator notes in *Fear and Loathing in Las Vegas*:** Thompson 1972, p. 156.

"The rejection by *Sports Illustrated* infuriated him": Gibney 2008.

137   **One day Hunter came in:** Wenner & Seymour 2007, p. 133.

138   **But this time our very presence:** Thompson 1972, p. 110 (*Fear and Loathing in Las Vegas*).

"They're all a bunch of lily-covered liverworts": Denevi 2018, p. 200.

139   **He intended to satisfy his contractual obligations:** Thompson 2000, p. 406–7 (*Fear and Loathing in America*).

In the days before the Freak Power spirit: Truscott 1972.

140   **The Nixon campaign in 1968:** Baum 2016.

"We were really going to clean up this town": Jackovich 1980.

141 **When "Fear and Loathing in Las Vegas" appeared:** Thompson 1997, p. 209.

Who else would have given Hunter the encouragement?: Carroll 1993, p. 273.

As Duke notes in *Fear and Loathing in Las Vegas*: Thompson 1972, p. 67.

142 **The problem was that Wenner:** Wenner & Seymour 2007, p. 134.

You scurvy pig-fucker: Thompson 2000, p. 386 (*Fear and Loathing in America*).

Let's keep in mind: Wenner & Seymour 2007, p. 135.

My idea was to buy a fat notebook: Thompson 1979, p. 106.

143 **In the end, he found himself:** Thompson 1979, p. 106.

He later called the Las Vegas book: McKeen 1990.

144 **Thompson certainly had that tradition in mind:** Thompson 1979, p. 110.

We were somewhere around Barstow: Thompson 1972, p. 3 (*Fear and Loathing in Las Vegas*).

At that point, there was still kind of that Timothy Leary approach: Gibney 2008.

"I've never believed in that guru trip": Vetter 1974.

145 **A very painful experience in every way:** Thompson 1972, pp. 22–23 (*Fear and Loathing in Las Vegas*).

We had two bags of grass: Thompson 1972, p. 4 (*Fear and Loathing in Las Vegas*).

His editors at *Rolling Stone*: Thompson 2000, p. 406 (*Fear and Loathing in America*).

146 **In these circumstances, hyperbole is called for:** Klein 1993, pp. 17–18.

But our trip was different: Thompson 1972, p. 18 (*Fear and Loathing in Las Vegas*).

"Hallucinations are bad enough": Thompson 1972, p. 47 (*Fear and Loathing in Las Vegas*).

What's happening here?: Thompson 1972, p. 45 (*Fear and Loathing in Las Vegas*).

Mistaken for a drunk at the door: Thompson 1972, p. 46 (*Fear and Loathing in Las Vegas*).

147 **"There was madness in any direction":** Thompson 1972, pp. 67–68 (*Fear and Loathing in Las Vegas*).

When the agency offers a Mercedes: Thompson 1972, p. 194 (*Fear and Loathing in Las Vegas*).

"If Charlie Manson checked into the Sahara": Thompson 1972, p. 106 (*Fear and Loathing in Las Vegas*).

"A sort of huge under-financed Playboy Club": Thompson 1972, p. 109 (*Fear and Loathing in Las Vegas*).

148   **It was bad enough if she were only:** Thompson 1972, pp. 115–16 (*Fear and Loathing in Las Vegas*).

"It just occurred to me": Thompson 1972, p. 118 (*Fear and Loathing in Las Vegas*).

Another drug binge ensues: Thompson 1972, p. 135 (*Fear and Loathing in Las Vegas*).

"These poor bastards didn't know mescaline from macaroni": Thompson 1972, p. 143 (*Fear and Loathing in Las Vegas*).

149   **"You sonofabitch!":** Thompson 1972, p. 159 (*Fear and Loathing in Las Vegas*).

"The waitress was clearly in shock": Thompson 1972, p. 160 (*Fear and Loathing in Las Vegas*).

That reflection gives way to a broader rumination: Thompson 1972, p. 178 (*Fear and Loathing in Las Vegas*).

Leary, Barger, Ginsberg, Kesey: Thompson 1972, pp. 180–81 (*Fear and Loathing in Las Vegas*).

"Here we were," Duke says: Thompson 1972, p. 182 (*Fear and Loathing in Las Vegas*).

150   **It is not a comical version of *Heart of Darkness*:** Spender 1965, p. xi.

Duke describes the conference: Thompson 1972, p. 201 (*Fear and Loathing in Las Vegas*).

Duke concludes that the prosecutors: Thompson 1972, p. 201 (*Fear and Loathing in Las Vegas*).

"Not everybody loves you, man": Thompson 1972, p. 193 (*Fear and Loathing in Las Vegas*).

151   **"A few years ago," Thompson told O'Brien:** Thompson 1997, p. 623.

152   **"Like, did you even so much as ask me":** Thompson 2000, p. 447 (*Fear and Loathing in America*).

For these and other reasons: Author interview with Phillip Rodriguez.

Oscar was suave in a weird way: Gilliam 1998.

153   **You don't know how fucking lucky you are:** Thompson 2000, pp. 448–50 (*Fear and Loathing in America*).

"Dear Oscar," he wrote in April 1972: Thompson 2000, pp. 476–77 (*Fear and Loathing in America*).

The next year, Acosta told Lynn Nesbit: Thompson 2000, p. 526 (*Fear and Loathing in America*).

I've been silent on the subject: Thompson 2000, pp. 542–43 (*Fear and Loathing in America*).

154   **In a letter to his mother:** Thompson 2000, p. 554 (*Fear and Loathing in America*).

"I am still looking to you": Thompson 2000, pp. 561–62 (*Fear and Loathing in America*).

"**What in the fuck would cause you to ask me for** *money*": Thompson 2000, p. 562 (*Fear and Loathing in America*).

155 "**So he decided to get another business**": Felton 1980 ("Hunter Thompson Has Cashed His Check").

"**Oscar was one of God's own prototypes**": Thompson 1979, p. 515.

In the *New York Times,* **Christopher Lehmann-Haupt**: Lehmann-Haupt 1972.

He never fully recovered: Martin 2001.

156 **Another reviewer for the** *New York Times*: Woods 1972.

He has permanently altered the landscape: Truscott 1972.

The *New Republic* **was less impressed**: *New Republic*, Oct. 14, 1972.

Fear and Loathing in Las Vegas **made Thompson**: Browne 2017.

He even converted his office: Draper 1990, p. 181.

"**He inherited Hunter**," **Hinckle said of Wenner**: Hagan 2017, p. 180.

"**The reinvention of** *Rolling Stone* **around Hunter Thompson**": Hagan 2017, p. 180.

157 **More and more, he expected his contributors**: Draper 1990, p. 178.

"**The leader of the pack in the office**": Wenner and Seymour 2007, p. 142.

He was no longer Jann Wenner: Hagan 2017, p. 249.

Some began to see the magazine: Draper 1990, p. 180.

Thompson was "so belligerent and stubborn": Draper 1990, p. 180.

"**The Gonzo journalist was the star of the conference**": Draper 1990, p. 183.

"**Everybody was poking the elephant with a stick**": Hagan 2017, p. 203.

The hot baths, staff writer Robin Green noted: Hagan 2017, p. 204.

158 "**That's what I saw," Crouse said**: Hagan 2017, p. 204.

CHAPTER 10. CAMPAIGN TRAIL

160 "**There is an inverse proportion**": Crouse 1973, p. 19.

Here was this awful little POW camp: Crouse 1973, p. 217.

The White House preferred: Crouse 1973, p. 218.

Carl Bernstein, whose reporting: Crouse 1973, p. 300.

161 **When that reporter's enthusiasm**: Crouse 1973, p. 257.

They shouldn't try to be objective: Crouse 1973, p. 305.

It was his colleague: Crouse 1973, p. 311.

162 **Its founder, Henry Luce, believed that**: Hoffman 1995, p. 34.

Years later, President Johnson pointed to a manila folder: Hoffman 1995, p. 84.

It would be written as a novel is written: Pace 1986.

"A book, to be a great book": Hoffman 1995, p. 110.

163   **"I don't disagree with the accuracy":** Tolchin 1990.

  "In 1968," White wrote: Crouse 1973, p. 36.

  Political journalist Richard Rovere: Hoffman 1995, p. 6.

  When asked about his critics: Pace 1986.

164   **White consented but later described his piece for *Life*:** Pace 1986.

  For historian Rick Perlstein: Perlstein 2013.

  Unlike most other correspondents: Thompson 1973, p. 4.

165   **Hunter worked his ass off:** Wenner & Seymour 2007, p. 164.

  Instead, his "jangled campaign diary": Thompson 1973, p. 8.

  He was viewed with a combination of love and fear: Wenner & Seymour 2007, p. 161.

166   **Some people will say that words like *scum* and *rotten*:** Thompson 1994 ("He Was a Crook").

167   **"What wish is enacted":** White 1990, p. 215.

  "We tell ourselves stories in order to live": Didion 1979, p. 11.

  Working for Big Ed, he wrote: Thompson 1973, p. 238.

  "This was bullshit, of course": Thompson 1973, p. 142.

  Not much has been written about The Ibogaine Effect: Thompson 1973, pp. 134–35.

168   **Humphrey's resume cut no ice with Thompson:** Thompson 1973, p. 118.

  His insult, Thompson noted with satisfaction: Thompson 1973, p. 413.

  Remember me, Hubert?: Thompson 1973, p. 170.

169   **There is no way to grasp:** Thompson 1973, p. 190.

  I have never been one to hold a grudge: Thompson 1973, p. 170.

  As a result, however, the few friends he had: Thompson 1973, pp. 4–5.

  Locals knew that Washington journalists: Herken 2014.

170   **"He had better access to our campaign":** Wenner & Seymour 2007, p. 163.

  Granted, they are both white men: Thompson 1973, p. 372.

  The McGovern campaign resembled a Grateful Dead tour: Thompson 1973, p. 376.

  "McGovern made some stupid mistakes": Thompson 1973, p. 389.

  I am suddenly facing the very distinct possibility: Thompson 1973, p. 208.

171   **Even if that figure:** Thompson 1973, p. 470.

  People who describe Thompson's dark and profane jokes: Thompson [1973] 2012, p. xx (*Fear and Loathing on the Campaign Trail '72*).

172   **My own theory, which sounds like madness:** Thompson 1973, p. 464.

It is Nixon himself who represents: Thompson 1973, pp. 391–92.

173 "Ominous" is not quite the right word: Thompson 1973, p. 392.

This may be the year: Thompson 1973, p. 289.

"Again and again," he wrote in his memoir: McWilliams 1979, pp. 304–5.

174 Richard Nixon represents the dark side of the American Dream: Finch 1978.

"Richard Nixon was an evil man": Thompson 1994 ("He Was a Crook").

175 Having faced that fact: Thompson 1973, p. 2.

Food was brought in constantly: Hicklin & Robertson 2006.

Almost every paragraph of that coverage: Thompson 1973, p. 2.

"He tried to tune up his mind": Hicklin & Robertson 2006.

176 "A reporter covers an institution": Bouton 1990, p. xi.

But behold—we find here a Hunter Thompson: Lehmann-Haupt 1973.

177 Two months later, another *New York Times* review: Seligson 1973.

Even *Time* magazine: Quoted in Perlstein 2014, p. 77.

The vultures are coming home to roost: Thompson 1979, p. 238.

"This is a matter of journalistic ethics": Thompson 1979, p. 240.

178 Noting that he was underwhelmed: Thompson 1979, p. 250.

"Within hours of Nixon's departure": Thompson 1979, p. 319.

"My interest in national politics": Thompson 1979, p. 305.

After more than ten years of civil war: Thompson 1979, p. 305.

CHAPTER 11. AFTER NIXON

179 "Being the premier rock magazine": Richardson 2017.

"We were hipper than anyone better": Author interview with Abe Peck.

180 Little was accomplished: Draper 1990, p. 210.

What their readers wanted: Draper 1990, p. 281.

181 "He kept the sparks flying": Author interview with Abe Peck.

That approach, one of his friends noted: McKeen 2008, p. 225.

182 In short order, however: Gabel & Hughes 2005.

"When Hunter had problems": Author interview with David Felton.

Gesturing to the drugs, Thompson replied: Hagan 2017, p. 286.

By way of reply: Whitmer 1993, p. 219.

He later admitted: McKeen 2008, p. 224.

Generally the lede was easy: Wenner & Seymour 2007, p. xiv–xv.

183 Thompson was usually grateful: Author interview with Sarah Lazin.

Other writers more or less: Love 2005.

"I don't think there's an editor": Gabel & Hughes 2005.

184   **Love learned that such threats:** Love 2005.

"People have worked on stories with him": Gabel & Hughes 2005.

"He had a riff about it": McDonell 2016, p. 240.

"When Hunter paid attention to you": McDonell 2016, p. 239.

This happened more often: McDonell 2016, p. 249.

"Do you need any money?": Wenner & Seymour 2007, p. 173.

185   **Privately, Mailer expressed misgivings:** Plimpton 1990, pp. 123–24.

According to Sandy: Gibney 2008.

"But there he was": Whitmer 1993, p. 232.

186   **His colleague, Nick Proffitt:** Whitmer 1993, p. 233.

"You are not in Las Vegas now": Whitmer 1993, p. 234.

"Laos was the middle of nowhere": Wenner & Seymour 2007, p. 204.

Jacques Leslie, who was covering the war: Author interview with Jacques Leslie.

While in Saigon: McKeen 1990.

187   **As Lynn Nesbit recalled:** Wenner & Seymour 2007, p. 202.

"Jann was always good at picking a horse": Author interview with Abe Peck.

"If you rolled over with Hunter": Author interview with Terry McDonell.

Thompson was said to hate Wenner: Hagan 2017, p. 290.

"The *attempt* was enough": McKeen 1990.

"He was often criticized at the time": Anderson 2020.

188   **As Carey McWilliams noted in his memoir:** McWilliams 1979, p. 304.

189   **"When I slumped off the plane":** Thompson 1979, p. 424.

I bought a paperback: Hagan 2017, p. 197.

"I think at times he's been ambivalent about the strip": Bates 2004.

190   **When Peck took a short walk:** Author interview with Abe Peck.

"*Rolling Stone* began to be run": McKeen 1990.

Thompson later credited Murray's performance: Nelson 1996.

191   **Thompson's belligerence was fun to be around:** Gabel & Hughes 2005.

I think special treatment: Carroll 2010.

Having socialized with Thompson: Author interview with Terry McDonell.

192   **"In a number of ways on various occasions":** Leonard 1979.

Rinzler and Bantam parted ways: Author interview with Alan Rinzler.

The *Curse of Lono* lacked the crackle: McKeen 1991, p. 88; Stephenson 2012, p. 144.

The book includes passages: Stephenson 2012, p. 145.

Stephenson concluded that: Stephenson 2012, p. 151.

193 **When interviewed in 1979:** Perlez 1979.

As governor of California: Cannon 2008, p. 163.

194 **As counterculture veteran Peter Coyote observed:** Bingham 2017.

195 **Thompson's editor at the *San Francisco Examiner*:** Author interview with Will Hearst.

The Old Man was a monster: Thompson 1990, pp. 252–53.

197 **In a later interview:** Nelson 1996.

Thompson started working on *Better Than Sex*: Thompson J. 2016, p. 229.

Such shooting from the hip: "In Short," *New York Times*, Oct. 23, 1994.

"This is the book that launches the reassessment": Quoted in McKeen 2008, p. 335.

198 **Writing for the *New York Times*:** Buckley 2000.

"The same goes for *The Rum Diary*": Kelly 1998.

"Even the most precise cinematic realizations": Holden 1998.

199 **"The rest is pleasant enough":** Scott 2011.

Months later, he was noticeably calmer: Thompson J. 2016, p. 191.

"We would give him stories and tips and clues": Wenner & Seymour 2007, p. 385.

"He was in complete control of his destiny": Gabel & Hughes 2005.

"There were some good columns": Wenner & Seymour 2007, p. 385.

He did not place bets with bookies: Gabel & Hughes 2005.

200 **Janet Maslin's notice:** Maslin 2003.

"You'd think that at this point in his life": Shafer 2003.

"For an author to get away with some of Hunter's behavior": Gabel & Hughes 2005.

Later, Rinzler compared editing Thompson to combat: Author interview with Alan Rinzler.

201 **His ESPN columns, he wrote:** Thompson 2004, p. xx.

Streitfeld later observed: Author interview with David Streitfeld.

"When 9/11 happened": Gabel & Hughes 2005.

After summarizing the destruction: Thompson 2004, p. 90.

202 **In the downstairs bar:** McKeen 2008, p. 349.

CHAPTER 12. LEGACY

203 **Streitfeld also called the second volume:** Author interview with David Streitfeld.

204 **After winning a National Magazine Award:** Taibbi 2009.

The following year, Wenner called Taibbi: Verini 2010.

Taibbi began his introduction: Thompson [1973] 2012, p. xvii.

Whereas most political journalists tried to impress others: Thompson [1973] 2012, p. xxiv.

In that article, she argued that Thompson: McWilliams 2016.

205 **Later, Streitfeld maintained:** Author interview with David Streitfeld.

Hinckle observed that San Francisco: Hinckle 2017, p. 6; Stein 2008.

206 **In a 2005 *New York Times* book review:** Mitchell 2005.

That newspaper's coverage of the first story: Starkman 2014.

207 **He understood the appeal of Steadman's illustrations:** Stephenson 2012, p. 88.

It was his attempt, he later told Tom Wolfe: Thompson 2000, p. 376 (*Fear and Loathing in America*).

208 **"What he wrote was a singular work":** Wenner & Seymour 2007, pp. 143, 141.

"Now that the dust of the '60s has settled": Algren 1979.

209 **In that spirit, Tom Wolfe described him:** Wenner & Seymour 2007, p. 436.

"I always saw him as an Ambrose Bierce–Mark Twain": McKeen 2008, p. 357.

***Los Angeles Times* media critic Tim Rutten:** Rutten 2005.

210 **Rutten's right that much of American journalism:** Cooper 2005.

211 **The kinds of stories Thompson did:** Weir 2005.

212 **Not since the death of Princess Diana:** Ross 2005.

That legacy, along with Thompson's misogyny: Wenzel 2017.

213 **As Curtis White has argued:** White 2019.

Bibliography

Acosta, Oscar. *Oscar "Zeta" Acosta: The Uncollected Works.* Edited by Ilan Stavans. Arte Publico, 1996.

———. *The Revolt of the Cockroach People.* Straight Arrow Books, 1973; rpt. Vintage Books, 1989.

———. *The Autobiography of a Brown Buffalo.* Straight Arrow Books, 1972; rpt. Vintage Books, 1989.

Adams, James Truslow. *The Epic of America.* Little, Brown & Co., 1931; rpt. Routledge, 1945.

Aldridge, John W. "*Cannibals and Christians,* by Norman Mailer." *Commentary,* Oct. 1966.

Algren, Nelson. Review of *The Great Shark Hunt* by Hunter S. Thompson. *Chicago Tribune,* July 15, 1979.

Allen, Henry. "Your Worst Fears *Always* Come True." *Washington Post Book Week,* July 23, 1972; rpt. in Streitfeld 2018.

Anderson, Scott Thomas. "Hunter S. Thompson's Longtime Editor Ponders *Fear and Loathing* in 2020." *San Francisco Chronicle,* July 16, 2020.

Asher, Colin. *Never a Lovely So Real: The Life and Work of Nelson Algren.* W.W. Norton, 2019.

Babbs, Ken, ed. *Spit in the Ocean.* Vol. 6. 1981.

Barger, Ralph "Sonny." "Life in the Hell's Angels." *Washington Post,* July 19, 2000.

Barger, Ralph, with Keith Zimmerman and Kent Zimmerman. *Hell's Angel: The Life and Times of Sonny Barger and the Hell's Angels Motorcycle Club.* HarperCollins, 2000.

Bates, Eric. "The Rolling Stone Interview: Garry Trudeau." *Rolling Stone,* Aug. 5, 2004.

Baum, Dan. "Legalize It All." *Harper's Magazine,* Apr. 2016.

Bernstein, David W. *The San Francisco Tape Music Center: 1960s Counterculture and the Avant-Garde.* University of California Press, 2008.

Bernstein, Richard. "Letters of the Young Author (He Saved Them All)." *New York Times,* July 25, 1997.

Bingham, Clara. "Peter Coyote: Voice of the Vietnam Generation." *Literary Hub,* Oct. 20, 2017. https://lithub.com/peter-coyote-voice-of-the-vietnam-generation/.

Brady, Mildred Edie. "The New Cult of Sex and Anarchy." *Harper's,* Apr. 1947.

Brinkley, Douglas, and Terry McDonell. "The Art of Journalism: An Interview with Hunter S. Thompson." *Paris Review* 156 (Fall 2000).

Browne, David. "*Rolling Stone* at 50: Shaping Contrasting Narratives of Woodstock, Altamont." *Rolling Stone,* Feb. 7, 2017.

Bouton, Jim. *Ball Four: Twentieth Anniversary Edition.* Collier Books, 1990.

Buckley, Christopher. "You Thieving Pile of Albino Warts." *New York Times,* Dec. 10, 2000.

Buntin, John. *L.A. Noir: The Struggle for the Soul of America's Most Seductive City.* Three Rivers Press, 2009.

Calderon, Hector. *Narratives of Greater Mexico: Essays on Chicano Literary History, Genre, and Borders.* University of Texas Press, 2004.

Cannon, Lou. *President Reagan: The Role of a Lifetime.* PublicAffairs, 2008.

Carroll, E. Jean. *Hunter: The Strange and Savage Life of Hunter S. Thompson.* Dutton, 1993.

Carroll, Rick. "Pitkin County's Bob Braudis Reflects on 24 Years as Sheriff." *Aspen Times,* Dec. 10, 2010.

Clark, Kenneth. "NBC's John Chancellor Leaving TV after 43 Years of Globetrotting." *Chicago Tribune,* June 20, 1993.

Cohen, Robert, and Michael Koncewicz. "'Tin Soldiers and Nixon's Coming': The Shootings at Kent State and Jackson State at 50." *The Nation,* May 4, 2020.

Cooper, Marc. "Ruttin' Tim Rutten." Feb. 28, 2005. https://marccooper.typepad.com/marccooper/2005/02/ruttin_tim_rutt.html.

Crews, Frederick. "Stuttering Giant." *New York Review of Books,* Mar. 3, 1977.

Crouse, Timothy. *The Boys on the Bus.* Random House, 1973; rpt. Random House Trade Paperback Edition, 2003.

Cutler, Sam. *You Can't Always Get What You Want: My Life with the Rolling Stones, the Grateful Dead and Other Wonderful Reprobates.* Random House Australia, 2008; rpt. ECW Press, 2010.

Daugherty, Tracy. *The Last Love Song: A Biography of Joan Didion.* St. Martin's Press, 2015.

Davidson, Michael. *The San Francisco Renaissance: Poetics and Community at Mid-century.* Cambridge University Press, 1989.

Davis, Belva, with Vicki Haddock. *Never in My Wildest Dreams: A Black Woman's Life in Journalism.* PoliPoint Press, 2010.

Davis, Mike. "Optimism of the Will." *The Nation,* Sept. 1, 2005.

Davis, Mike, and Jon Wiener. *Set the Night on Fire: L.A. in the Sixties.* Verso, 2020.

Dean, John. *Blind Ambition: The White House Years.* Simon & Schuster, 1976.

Democracy Now. "Slain Latino Journalist Rubén Salazar, Killed 40 Years Ago in Police Attack, Remembered as Champion of Chicano Rights." Aug. 31, 2010.

Denevi, Timothy. *Freak Kingdom: Hunter S. Thompson's Manic Ten-Year Crusade against American Fascism*. PublicAffairs, 2018.

Didion, Joan. *The White Album*. Simon & Schuster, 1979.

———. *Slouching Towards Bethlehem*. Farrar, Straus and Giroux, 1968.

———. "Berkeley's Giant: The University of California." *Mademoiselle*, Jan. 1960.

Doyle, Patrick. "How Hunter S. Thompson Became a Legend." *Rolling Stone* website, July 18, 2019. https://www.rollingstone.com/culture/culture-news/rolling-stone-at-50-how-hunter-s-thompson-became-a-legend-115371/.

Draper, Robert. *Rolling Stone Magazine: The Uncensored History*. Doubleday, 1990.

Dundy, Elaine. "Tom Wolfe . . . But Exactly, Yes!" *Vogue*, Apr. 15, 1966.

Edelman, Ezra. *O. J.: Made in America*. ESPN, 2016.

Fedrizzi, Nina. "How to Tour Frank Sinatra's Las Vegas." *Smithsonian*, Mar. 31, 2013.

Feehan, Rory Patrick. "The Genesis of the Hunter Figure: A Study of the Dialectic between the Biographical and the Aesthetic in the Early Writings of Hunter S. Thompson." PhD dissertation, University of Limerick, 2018.

Felton, David. "Hunter Thompson Has Cashed His Check." *Rolling Stone College Papers*, Spring 1980.

———. "Hunting the Great Shark." *Rolling Stone College Papers*, Spring 1980.

Finch, Nigel. *Fear and Loathing in Gonzovision*. BBC Omnibus, 1978.

Freeman, Cort, and Marjorie Meyer. "How Aspen Feels about the Hippies." *Aspen News*, Aug. 10, 1967; rpt. in Watkins 2015.

Gabel, J. C., and James Hughes. "Long Live the High Priest of Gonzo: An Oral History of Dr. Hunter S. Thompson." *StopSmiling*, no. 22 (2005).

Garcia, Mario T. *The Chicano Generation: Testimonios of the Movement*. University of California Press, 2015.

Garrow, David J. *Bearing the Cross: Martin Luther King, Jr., and the Southern Christian Leadership Conference*. William Morrow, 1986.

Gates, Anita. "J. P. Donleavy, Acclaimed Author of *The Ginger Man*, Dies at 91." *New York Times*, Sept. 13, 2017.

Gay, Peter. *Weimar Culture: The Outsider as Insider*. Harper & Row, 1968: rpt. W. W. Norton, 2001.

Gibney, Alex. *Gonzo: The Life and Work of Dr. Hunter S. Thompson*. Magnolia, 2008.

Gibney, Alex, and Alison Ellwood. *Magic Trip: Ken Kesey's Search for a Kool Place*. Magnolia Entertainment, 2011.

Gilliam, Terry. *Fear and Loathing in Las Vegas*. Universal Pictures Home Entertainment, 1998.

Gitlin, Todd. *The Sixties: Years of Hope, Days of Rage*. Bantam, 1987.

Gleason, Ralph J. *Music in the Air: The Selected Writings of Ralph J. Gleason*. Edited by Toby Gleason. Yale University Press, 2016.

———. "Aquarius Wept." *Esquire*, Aug. 1970.

———. *The Jefferson Airplane and the San Francisco Sound.* Ballantine, 1969.

Goodyear, Dana. "Zen Master: Gary Snyder and the Art of Life." *New Yorker,* Oct. 13, 2008.

Graham, Bill, and Robert Greenfield. *Bill Graham Presents: My Life Inside Rock and Out.* Doubleday, 1992.

Green, Robin. *The Only Girl: My Life and Times on the Masthead of Rolling Stone.* Little, Brown and Company, 2018.

Guffey, Elizabeth E. *Posters: A Global History.* Reaktion Books, 2014.

Hagan, Joe. *Sticky Fingers: The Life and Times of Jann Wenner and Rolling Stone Magazine.* Alfred E. Knopf, 2017.

Halberstam, David. "Baseball and the National Mythology." *Harper's,* Sept. 1970.

Harrell, Margaret A. *Keep This Quiet! My Relationship with Hunter S. Thompson, Milton Klonsky, and Jan Mesaert.* Saeculum University Press, 2011.

Harrell, Margaret A., with Ron Whitehead. *The Hell's Angels Letters: Hunter S. Thompson, Margaret Harrell, and the Making of an American Classic.* Norfolk Press, 2020.

Harris, Mark. "The Flowering of the Hippies." *Atlantic Monthly,* Sept. 1967.

Hartlaub, Peter. "Grateful Dead at 50: Nothing Left to Do But Smile." *San Francisco Chronicle,* Mar. 10, 2017.

Herken, Gregg. *The Georgetown Set: Friends and Rivals in Cold War Washington.* Alfred A. Knopf, 2014.

Hicklin, William, and Ian Robertson. *The Final 24: Hunter S. Thompson.* Cineflex Productions, 2006.

Hinckle, Warren. *Who Killed Hunter S. Thompson? The Picaresque Story of the Birth of Gonzo Journalism.* Last Gasp, 2017.

———. *If You Have a Lemon, Make Lemonade: An Essential Memoir of a Lunatic Decade.* G. P. Putnam's Sons, 1974.

———. "The Social History of the Hippies." *Ramparts,* Mar. 1967.

Hoffman, Joyce. *Theodore H. White and Journalism as Illusion.* University of Missouri Press, 1995.

Hofstadter, Richard. "The Myth of the Happy Yeoman." *American Heritage 7,* no. 3 (Apr. 1956).

Holden, Stephen. "A Devotedly Drug-Addled Rampage through a 1971 Vision of Las Vegas." *New York Times,* May 22, 1998.

Hopper, Jessica. "'It Was Us against Those Guys': The Women Who Transformed *Rolling Stone* in the Mid-70s." *Vanity Fair,* Aug. 28, 2018.

Hoyle, Arthur. *The Unknown Henry Miller: A Seeker in Big Sur.* Arcade Publishing, 2014.

Hyman, Harold. "Las Vegas Gaming Pioneer 'Moe' Dalitz Dies at 89." *Las Vegas Sun,* Sept. 1, 1989.

Ives, Stephen. *Las Vegas: An Unconventional History.* American Experience, 2005.

Jackovich, Karen G. "Aspen Sheriff Richard Kienast's Hip Town Backs Him, but Federal Narcs Claim He's a Bust." *People,* June 23, 1980.

Joseph, Peniel E. *Waiting 'til the Midnight Hour: A Narrative History of Black Power in America.* Henry Holt and Company, 2006.

Kaiser, Charles. "Books in Brief: Nonfiction." *New York Times,* July 13, 1997.

Kelly, David. "Fear and Loathing in San Juan." *New York Times,* Nov. 29, 1998.

Kennedy, Randall. "Has America Created a Misleading Fable about the Civil Rights Movement?" *Washington Post,* Feb. 2, 2018.

Kerouac, Jack. *On the Road.* Viking Press, 1957.

Kevin, Brian. "Read 18 Lost Stories from Hunter S. Thompson's Forgotten Stint as a Foreign Correspondent." *Open Culture,* June 15, 2015. http://www.openculture.com/2015/06/read-18-lost-stories-from-hunter-s-thompsons-forgotten-stint-as-a-foreign-correspondent.html.

———. *The Footloose American: Following the Hunter S. Thompson Trail across South America.* Broadway Books, 2014.

Klein, Richard. *Cigarettes Are Sublime.* Duke University Press, 1993.

Kohn, Howard, and David Weir. "The Inside Story." *Rolling Stone,* Oct. 23 and Nov. 20, 1975.

Kripal, Jeffrey J. *Esalen: America and the Religion of No Religion.* University of Chicago Press, 2007.

Kunzru, Hari. "The First Person, Steroid-Enhanced." *London Review of Books,* Oct. 15, 1998.

Kuralt, Charles. *A Life on the Road.* G.P. Putnams, 1990.

Labor, Earle. *Jack London: An American Life.* Farrar, Straus and Giroux, 2013.

Lamantia, Philip. *The Collected Poems of Philip Lamantia.* University of California Press, 2013.

Lehmann-Haupt, Christopher. "Fear, Loathing and Fun on the Thompson Trail." *New York Times,* Jan. 25, 1993.

———. "Hunter S. Thompson Going Sane." *New York Times,* May 18, 1973.

———. "Heinous Chemicals at Work." *New York Times,* June 22, 1972.

Leonard, John. "Books of the Times." *New York Times,* Aug. 10, 1979.

Litwak, Leo E. "On the Wild Side." *New York Times,* Jan. 29, 1967.

Lombardi, John. "Death by Gonzo." *New York,* 2008.

London, Jack. "Stranger than Fiction." *The Critic,* Aug. 1903.

Love, Robert. "A Technical Guide for Editing Gonzo: Hunter S. Thompson from the Other End of the Mojo Wire." *Columbia Journalism Review,* May/June 2005.

Lydon, Michael. "May 1969: Three Days with the Dead." *Rolling Stone,* August 23, 1969.

Macdonald,, Dwight. "Parajournalism, or Tom Wolfe and His Magic Writing Machine." *New York Review of Books,* Aug. 26, 1965.

Mailer, Norman. *Genius and Lust: A Journey through the Major Writings of Henry Miller.* Grove Press, 1976.

———. "The Prisoner of Sex." *Harper's,* Mar. 1971.

———. *Miami and the Siege of Chicago.* D.I. Fine, 1968; rpt. New York Review of Books, 2008.

———. *The Armies of the Night: History as a Novel, the Novel as History*. New American Library, 1968.

Martin, Douglas. "Sandy Lehmann-Haupt, 59, One of Ken Kesey's Busmates." *New York Times*, Nov. 3, 2001.

Maslin, Janet. "Reflections on a World Gone Gonzo, from an Expert." *New York Times*, Jan. 14, 2003.

McCumber, David. *X-Rated: The Mitchell Brothers: A True Story of Sex, Money, and Death*. Simon & Schuster, 1992.

McDonell, Terry. *The Accidental Life: An Editor's Notes on Writing and Writers*. Alfred A. Knopf, 2016.

McFadden, Robert D. "Sidney Zion, Writer Who Crusaded to Reduce Doctors' Hours, Dies at 75." *New York Times*, Aug. 2, 2009.

McKeen, William. *Outlaw Journalist: The Life and Times of Hunter S. Thompson*. W.W. Norton, 2008.

———. *Hunter S. Thompson*. Twayne Publishers, 1991.

———. Interview with Hunter S. Thompson, Mar. 1990; rpt. in McKeen 1991, Torrey & Simonson 2008, Streitfeld 2018.

McMillian, John. *Smoking Typewriters: The Sixties Underground Press and the Rise of Alternative Media in America*. Oxford University Press, 2011.

McWilliams, Carey. *The Education of Carey McWilliams*. Simon & Schuster, 1979.

———. "How to Succeed with the Backlash." *The Nation*, Aug. 24, 1966.

———. "Bungling in California." *The Nation*, Nov. 4, 1950.

———. *Ambrose Bierce: A Biography*. Albert & Charles Boni, 1929.

McWilliams, Susan. "This Political Theorist Predicted the Rise of Trumpism. His Name Was Hunter S. Thompson." *The Nation*, Dec. 15, 2016.

Meltzer, David, ed. *San Francisco Beat: Talking with the Poets*. City Lights Publishers, 2001.

Menand, Louis. "Out of Bethlehem: The Radicalization of Joan Didion." *New Yorker*, Aug. 17, 2015.

Miller, Henry. *The Henry Miller Reader*. Edited by Lawrence Durrell. New Directions, 1959.

———. *The World of Sex*. Olympia Press, 1959.

———. *Big Sur and the Oranges of Hieronymus Bosch*. New Directions Press, 1957.

———. *The Air-Conditioned Nightmare*. New Directions Press, 1945.

Millett, Kate. *Sexual Politics*. Doubleday, 1970.

Mitchell, Greg. *Tricky Dick and the Pink Lady: Richard Nixon vs. Helen Gahagan Douglas—Sexual Politics and the Red Scare, 1950*. Random House, 1998.

Mitchell, Luke. "Army of the Night." *New York Times*, Dec. 18, 2005.

Nelson, Sara. "Interview with Hunter Thompson." *The Book Report*, 1996. http://www.fargonebooks.com/hunter.html.

Orwell, George. *Inside the Whale and Other Essays*. Victor Gollancz, 1940; rpt. Penguin 1957, 1991.

Pace, Eric. "Theodore White, Chronicler of U.S. Politics, Is Dead at 71." *New York Times,* May 16, 1986.

Paul, Charlie. *For No Good Reason.* Mongrel Media/Metropole Films Distribution/Sony Pictures Classics, 2013.

Penman, Ian. "Night of the Hunter." *The Guardian,* Dec. 15, 2000.

Perlez, Jane. "Political Highs and Lows." *Washington Journalism Review,* Nov./Dec. 1979; rpt. in Streitfeld 2018.

Perlstein, Rick. *The Invisible Bridge: The Fall of Nixon and the Rise of Reagan.* Simon & Schuster, 2014.

———. "Kennedy Week: The Myth of Camelot and the Dangers of Sycophantic Consensus Journalism." *The Nation,* Nov. 23, 2013.

———. *Nixonland: The Rise of a President and the Fracturing of America.* Simon & Schuster, 2008.

———. *Before the Storm: Barry Goldwater and the Unmaking of the American Consensus.* Hill and Wang, 2001.

Perry, Kevin EG. "Drawing Became a Weapon." *GQ,* Mar. 4, 2013. https://kevinegperry.com/2013/03/04/ralph-steadman-interview-drawing-became-a-weapon/.

Perry, Paul. *Fear and Loathing: The Strange and Terrible Saga of Hunter S. Thompson.* Thunder's Mouth Press, 1992.

Peters, Frederick. "The Brave New World of Las Vegas Architecture." *Forbes,* July 31, 2019.

Plimpton, George. *The Best of Plimpton.* Atlantic Monthly Press, 1990.

Plimpton, George, and Terry McDonell. "Hunter S. Thompson: The Art of Journalism No. 1." *Paris Review,* no. 156 (Fall 2000).

Richardson, Peter. "Roots Music: The Beginnings of *Rolling Stone.*" *California,* Winter 2017.

———. "Between Journalism and Fiction: Hunter S. Thompson and the Birth of Gonzo." *BOOM: Journal of California* 6, no. 4 (2016), pp. 48–57.

———. *No Simple Highway: A Cultural History of the Grateful Dead.* St. Martin's Press, 2015.

———. *A Bomb in Every Issue: How the Short, Unruly Life of Ramparts Magazine Changed America.* The New Press, 2009.

———. *American Prophet: The Life and Work of Carey McWilliams.* University of Michigan Press, 2005; rpt. University of California Press, 2019.

Robinson, Jackie. *I Never Had It Made.* Fawcett Press, 1972.

Rodriguez, Phillip, dir. *The Rise and Fall of the Brown Buffalo.* City Projects LLC, 2017.

Rosenbaum, Ron. "Hunter Thompson: The Good Doctor Tells All . . . about Carter, Cocaine, Adrenaline, and the Birth of Gonzo Journalism." *High Times,* Sept. 1977.

Ross, A.S. "Hunter S. Thompson: Death of an American Original." *San Francisco Chronicle,* Feb. 27, 2005.

Rustin, Bayard. "The Watts." *Commentary,* Mar. 1966. https://www.commentarymagazine.com/articles/the-watts/.

Rutten, Tim. "Leave Chief Parker Behind." *Los Angeles Times,* Apr. 11, 2009.
———. "Gonzo, but No Journalist." *Los Angeles Times,* Feb. 26, 2005.
Sahagun, Louis. "They Faced 66 Years in Prison. The 'Eastside 13' and How They Helped Plan the East L.A. Walkouts." *Los Angeles Times,* Mar. 8, 2018.
Salter, James. *Burning the Days: Recollection.* Random House, 1997.
Schlesinger, Arthur, Jr. *A Life in the Twentieth Century: Innocent Beginnings, 1917–1950.* Houghton Mifflin Harcourt, 2000.
———. "History of the Week." *New York Post,* May 4, 1952.
Scott, A.O. "In San Juan, on the Road to Gonzo." *New York Times,* Oct. 27, 2011.
Sculatti, Gene, and Davin Seay. *San Francisco Nights: The Psychedelic Music Trip, 1965–1968.* St. Martin's Press, 1985.
Seligson, Tom. "The Tripping of the President." *New York Times,* July 15, 1973.
Shafer, Jack. "Bedtime for Gonzo." *New York Times,* Feb. 23, 2003.
Silverman, Al. *The Times of Their Lives: The Golden Age of the Great American Book Publishers, Their Editors and Authors.* St. Martin's Press, 2008.
Skipper, John C. *The 1964 Republican Convention: Barry Goldwater and the Beginning of the Conservative Movement.* McFarland and Company, 2016.
Snyder, Gary. *The Old Ways: Six Essays.* City Lights, 1977.
Southern, Terry. "Twirling at Ole Miss." *Esquire,* Feb. 1, 1963.
Spender, Stephen. Introduction to *Under the Volcano* by Malcolm Lowry, xi. Harper & Row, 1965,
Starkman, Dean. *The Watchdog That Didn't Bark: The Financial Crisis and the Disappearance of Investigative Journalism.* Columbia University Press, 2014.
Starr, Kevin. *Embattled Dreams: California in War and Peace, 1940–1950.* Oxford University Press, 2002.
Stavans, Ilan. *Bandido: Oscar "Zeta" Acosta and the Chicano Experience.* HarperCollins, 1995.
Steadman, Ralph. *The Joke's Over: Bruised Memories, Gonzo, Hunter S. Thompson, and Me.* Harcourt, 2006.
Stein, Ruthe. "Hunter S. Thompson Documentary Closes Festival." *San Francisco Chronicle,* Apr. 20, 2008; updated Feb. 11, 2012.
Stephenson, William. *Gonzo Republic: Hunter S. Thompson's America.* Continuum, 2012.
Streitfeld, David. *Hunter S. Thompson: The Last Interview and Other Conversations* Melville House, 2018.
Taibbi, Matt. "The Great American Bubble Machine." *Rolling Stone,* July 13, 2009.
Tamarkin, Jeff. *Got a Revolution! The Turbulent Flight of Jefferson Airplane.* Simon & Schuster, 2003.
Theoharris, Jeanne. "50 Years Later, We Still Haven't Learned from Watts." *New York Times,* Aug. 11, 2005.
Thomas, Robert Mcg. "Sidney Korshak, 88, Dies; Fabled Fixer for the Chicago Mob." *New York Times,* Jan. 22, 1996.
Thompson, Hunter S. *Fear and Loathing at Rolling Stone: The Essential Writings of Hunter S. Thompson.* Edited by Jann S. Wenner. Simon & Schuster, 2011.

————. *Hey Rube: Blood Sport, the Bush Doctrine, and the Downward Spiral of Dumbness.* Simon & Schuster, 2004.

————. *Kingdom of Fear: Loathsome Secrets of a Star-Crossed Child in the Final Days of the American Century.* Simon & Schuster, 2003.

————. *Fear and Loathing in America: The Brutal Odyssey of an Outlaw Journalist.* Edited by Douglas Brinkley. Simon & Schuster, 2000.

————. *Screwjack: A Short Story.* Simon & Schuster, 2000.

————. *The Rum Diary: A Novel.* Simon & Schuster, 1998.

————. *The Proud Highway: Saga of a Desperate Southern Gentleman.* Edited by Douglas Brinkley. Simon & Schuster, 1997.

————. "He Was a Crook." *Rolling Stone,* June 16, 1994.

————. *Better than Sex: Confessions of a Political Junkie.* Random House, 1994.

————. *Songs of the Doomed: More Notes on the Death of the American Dream.* Summit Books, 1990.

————. *The Great Shark Hunt: Strange Tales from a Strange Time.* Summit Books/Simon & Schuster, 1979; rpt. 2003.

————. "The Banshee Screams for Buffalo Meat." *Rolling Stone,* Dec. 15, 1977.

————. *Fear and Loathing: On the Campaign Trail '72.* Straight Arrow Books, 1973; rpt. Simon & Schuster, 2012.

————. *Fear and Loathing in Las Vegas: A Savage Journey to the Heart of the American Dream.* Random House, 1972.

————. "More Fear and Loathing in Miami: Nixon Bites the Bomb." *Rolling Stone,* Sept. 28, 1972.

————. "Strange Rumblings in Aztlan." *Rolling Stone,* Apr. 29, 1971.

————. "Aspen Wallposter" (advertisement). *Scanlan's Monthly,* Jan. 1971.

————. "The Battle of Aspen." *Rolling Stone,* Oct. 1, 1970.

————. "The Kentucky Derby Is Decadent and Depraved." *Scanlan's Monthly,* June 1970.

————. "The Temptations of Jean-Claude Killy." *Scanlan's Monthly,* Mar. 1970.

————. "Presenting: The Richard Nixon Doll." *Pageant,* July 1968.

————. "The Ultimate Freelancer." *The Distant Drummer,* Nov. 1967.

————. "Why Boys Will Be Girls." *Pageant,* Aug. 1967.

————. "Nights in the Rustic." *Cavalier,* Aug. 1967.

————. "The 'Hashbury' Is the Capital of the Hippies." *New York Times Magazine,* May 14, 1967.

————. *Hell's Angels: A Strange and Terrible Saga.* Random House, 1967.

————. "The 450-Square-Mile Parking Lot." *Pageant,* Dec. 1965.

————. "The Nonstudent Left." *The Nation,* Sept. 27, 1965.

————. "It Ain't Hardly That Way No More." *Pageant,* Sept. 1965.

————. "Motorcycle Gangs: Losers and Outsiders." *The Nation,* May 17, 1965.

————. "What Lured Hemingway to Idaho?" *National Observer,* May 25, 1964.

————. "A Southern City with Northern Problems." *The Reporter* 29, Dec. 19, 1963.

———. "Burial at Sea." *Rogue,* Dec. 1961.

———. "Big Sur: The Tropic of Henry Miller." *Rogue,* Oct. 1961.

Thompson, Juan. *Stories I Tell Myself: Growing Up with Hunter S. Thompson.* Penguin Random House, 2016.

Time magazine. "The Hippies." *Time,* July 7, 1967.

———. "The Silent Service." *Time,* Feb. 24, 1967.

———. "A Bomb in Every Issue." *Time,* Jan. 6, 1967.

Tolchin, Martin. "How Johnson Won Election He'd Lost." *New York Times,* Feb. 11, 1990.

Torrey Beef, and Kevin Simonson, eds. *Conversations with Hunter S. Thompson.* University of Mississippi Press, 2008.

Truscott, Lucian K., IV. "The American Dream and Hunter Thompson's *Fear and Loathing.*" *Village Voice,* July 13, 1972.

Verini, James. "Lost Exile: The Unlikely Life and Sudden Death of *The Exile,* Russia's Angriest Newspaper." *Vanity Fair,* Feb. 24, 2010.

Vetter, Craig. "Playboy Interview: Hunter Thompson." *Playboy,* Nov. 1974.

Warren, James. "Nixon's Hoffa Pardon Has an Odor." *Chicago Tribune,* Apr. 8, 2001.

Watkins, Daniel Joseph. *Freak Power: Hunter Thompson's Campaign for Sheriff.* Meat Possum Press, 2015.

Weingarten, Marc. *The Gang That Wouldn't Write Straight: Wolfe, Thompson, Didion, and the New Journalism Revolution.* Crown Publishers, 2005.

Weir, David. "Hunter S. Thompson: Death of an American Original." *San Francisco Chronicle,* Feb. 27, 2005.

Weller, Sheila. "LSD, Ecstasy, and a Blast of Utopianism: How 1967's 'Summer of Love' All Began." *Vanity Fair,* July 2012.

Wenner, Jann S., ed. *Rolling Stone,* Mar. 24, 2005.

Wenner, Jann S., and Corey Seymour. *Gonzo: The Life of Hunter S. Thompson.* Little, Brown and Company, 2007.

Wenzel, John. "Hunter S. Thompson, Back in the Spotlight: Should His Gonzo Lifestyle Overshadow His Work?" *Denver Post,* Feb. 5, 2017.

White, Curtis. *Living in a World That Can't Be Fixed: Reimagining Counterculture Today.* Melville House, 2019.

White, Hayden. *The Content of the Form: Narrative Discourse and Historical Representation.* Johns Hopkins University Press, 1990.

White, Theodore. *The Making of the President 1960.* Atheneum House, 1961.

Whitmer, Peter O. *When the Going Gets Weird: The Twisted Life and Times of Hunter S. Thompson.* Hyperion, 1993.

———. "Hunter Thompson: Still Crazy After All These Years?" *Saturday Review,* Jan.–Feb. 1984; rpt. in Torrey & Simonson 2008, pp. 48–56.

Whitmer, Peter O., with Bruce VanWyngarden. *Aquarius Revisited: Seven Who Created the Sixties Counterculture.* Macmillan, 1987.

Wilford, Hugh. *The Mighty Wurlitzer: How the CIA Played America.* Harvard University Press, 2008.

Williams, Jay. *Author Under Sail: The Imagination of Jack London, 1893–1902.* University of Nebraska Press, 2014.

Wolfe, Tom. *The Electric Kool-Aid Acid Test.* Farrar, Straus and Giroux, 1968.

———. *The Kandy-Colored Tangerine-Flake Streamline Baby.* Farrar, Straus and Giroux, 1965.

Woods, Crawford. "The Best Book on the Dope Decade." *New York Times,* July 23, 1972.

Yehling, Robert. "The High Times Interview: Marty Balin." *High Times,* Mar. 2000.

Index

Acosta, Oscar "Zeta," 97–98, 121, 155; Las Vegas road trips with Thompson, 133, 136, 137–38; in Los Angeles, 123, 126–30, 133, 152; response to *Fear and Loathing in Las Vegas* publication, 151, 152–55; Thompson on, 152–53, 154–55; Thompson's *Rolling Stone* obituary, 155, 187, 190

Adams, James Truslow, 8

Adler, Lou, 91

Advertisements for Myself (Mailer), 12, 21, 30, 191

Afghanistan war, 201

Africa, Thompson on assignment in, 184–85

Agee, James, 21

Agnew, Spiro, 150

Air-Conditioned Nightmare, The (Miller), 28

Albert, Stew, 123

alcohol use. *See* drinking

Alger, Horatio, 8

Algren, Nelson, 21, 71–74, 208

Ali, Muhammad, 15, 145, 147, 185

Alpert, Richard, 61

Altamont festival, 106, 116–18, 145, 149

American culture: Thompson as cultural critic, 5, 6, 36, 201, 208, 209. *See also* American Dream; counterculture; media *entries*; politics

American Dream: death of, as Thompson preoccupation, 40, 57, 104, 194, 208; as motif in Thompson's work, 17, 22, 40, 72, 104, 145–46, 147, 156, 174, 194; Nixon and, 174; Reagan and, 193–94; Thompson's planned "death of the American Dream" book, 8–10, 14, 123–24, 136–37, 139; Thompson's version of, 8–9, 22. *See also* American culture

American Dream, An (Mailer), 155

American Samoa, Thompson's preoccupation with, 151

Animal Farm (Orwell), 10

Arendt, Hannah, 107

Argosy, 37–38

Armies of the Night, The (Mailer), 12, 156

Aspen, 89, 95–96, 191; Acosta in, 97, 98, 128; Aspen politics and Thompson's county sheriff run, 14, 120–24; Nixon-era drug enforcement in, 140–41; Thompson on, 40; Thompson's Aspen politics piece, 118, 120, 123. *See also* Woody Creek

Aspen Illustrated News, 121

Aspen News, 89

Aspen Wallposter, 121–22

Aspinall, Owen, 151

Athenaeum Literary Association (Louisville), 16, 17–18

Atlantic Monthly, 97

authoritarianism/fascism, 82, 83, 87
*Autobiography of a Brown Buffalo,
The* (Acosta), 97

Babitz, Eve, 86
back-to-the-land movement, 94–95
Baez, Joan, 32
Baldwin, James, 21
Balin, Marty, 66
Ballantine, Ian, 57–58, 192
Ballantine Books, 7, 11, 57, 58
Ball Four (Bouton), 176
Banks, Russell, 73
"Banshee Screams for Buffalo Meat,
The" (Thompson), 155, 187, 190
Bantam, 3, 192
Barger, Ralph "Sonny," 69–70, 74–75,
117, 149, 171
baseball, 15
"Battle of Aspen, The" (Thompson),
118, 120, 123
Baxter, Tiny, 69
Beatles, The, 66, 85
Beats, 26–27, 83, 97; the Merry Prank-
sters and, 60, 61; Miller as precursor,
29; as precursors to the hippies, 65,
82, 84, 85; Thompson piece on, 44.
*See also specific individuals and
works*
Beauvoir, Simone de, 72
Behind the Green Door (film), 196
Bejmuk, Anita. *See* Thompson, Anita
Bejmuk
Bellow, Saul, 21
Belushi, John, 190
Benton, Tom, 121
Berkeley: Didion at UC Berkeley, 85,
86; links to the hippie movement,
83–84, 85; political activism in, 49,
53, 54, 83–84, 91–92, 108; and *Ram-
parts* staff, 78, 79; *Spider* magazine,
54; Thompson's Berkeley activism
piece, 49, 53–54, 64; UC Berkeley
and *Rolling Stone*, 92, 93; Wenner at
UC Berkeley, 91–92
Bermuda, the Thompsons' trip to, 35
Bernstein, Carl, 160–61, 188

Better Than Sex (Thompson), 192, 197
Bibb, Porter, 17, 141
Bierce, Ambrose, 26, 78, 209
Big Sur, 93; Miller in, 28–29, 33, 95,
96; *Rolling Stone* editorial meeting
in (1971), 157, 158; Thompson in,
27, 29–35; Thompson's writing on,
2, 9, 33–35, 64
Big Sur (Kerouac), 27, 30, 31
*Big Sur and the Oranges of Hierony-
mus Bosch* (Miller), 28–29
"Big Sur: The Tropic of Henry Miller"
(Thompson), 33–35
Bisher, Furman, 19
Black Panther Party, 53–54, 80, 88, 110
Blacks: and the Hell's Angels, 70–71;
and Nixon's drug war, 140; in the
San Francisco Bay Area, 25, 59;
Thompson on O. J. Simpson, 105;
the Watts Riots, 44, 63–64. *See also*
Black Panther Party; race and racial
politics
Bocaccio, 21
Boise, Ron, 59
Bond, Laura, 212–13
Boston Phoenix, 123
Bourjaily, Vance, 30–31
Bouton, Jim, 176
Boys on the Bus, The (Crouse), 2, 159–
61
Brady, Mildred Edie, 28
Braudis, Bob, 124, 191
Breach of Faith (White), 163
Brett, George, 42
Bridges, Harry, 91
Brinkley, David, 47, 48, 75
Brinkley, Douglas, 23, 136–37, 202; on
the Gonzo persona as Thompson's
chief legacy, 1, 4; Thompson corre-
spondence publication, 197–98, 203;
on Thompson's literary influences,
12, 48, 209
Brown, Pat, 48, 55, 56, 63, 64, 83, 85
Brown, Welburn, 19
Bruce, Lenny, 32, 90
Brundage, Avery, 104
Buchanan, Pat, 99, 151

Buckley, Christopher, 198
Buffett, Jimmy, 191
Bull, Sandy, 59, 95
Bureau of Narcotics and Dangerous Drugs, 138
"Burial at Sea" (Thompson), 35, 44
Burks, John, 137
Burton, Phil, 101
Bush (George W.) administration, 201, 202

Caddell, Pat, 165, 171
Caen, Herb, 121
Cahill, Tim, 18
Calderon, Hector, 97–98, 129–30
California: civil rights and racial justice legislation, 55, 64; Didion's writing on, 85–89; gubernatorial politics and races, 48, 64–65, 83; 1930s–1940s immigrants and the roots of the Hell's Angels, 71–72; Northern California's importance to Thompson, 205–6; racial politics of the 1960s, 44, 53–55, 63–65, 80. *See also* Berkeley; Big Sur; Glen Ellen; Los Angeles; San Francisco; University of California
California School of Fine Arts, 26
Cameron, Angus, 10, 11
Camus, Albert, 21
Capitol insurrection (2021), 5
Caputo, Philip, 186
Cardoso, Bill, 103, 114, 185
Caro, Robert, 163
Carter, Jimmy, 187
Cassady, Neal, 27, 58, 60, 61, 62, 75
Castro, Fidel, 15
Catcher in the Rye, The (Salinger), 21
Catolicos por La Raza, 128–29
Cavalier, 44, 72
celebrity, Thompson's, 1, 2, 4, 188–90, 209
celebrity journalism, 188
Chambers, Whittaker, 162
Chancellor, John, 47
"Charge of the Weird Brigade" (Thompson), 192

Charlatans, 65
Chavez, Cesar, 196
Chenault (character), 21–22, 199
Chevrolet: and Jean-Claude Killy, 102, 104, 105; and O. J. Simpson, 105
Chicago: 1968 Democratic Convention in, 100–102, 104, 120, 159, 168, 171, 206–7; Thompson on, 104–5
Chicago Sun-Times, 161
Chicago Tribune, 74
Chicano movement, 126–27; Acosta and his activities in Los Angeles, 126–30, 133, 152. *See also* "Strange Rumblings in Aztlan"
China, White's reportage on, 162
CIA, 81
City Lights, 26, 27
civil rights movement, 16, 43–44. *See also* race and racial politics
Clancy, John, 121
Cleaver, Eldridge, 80, 145
Clinton, Bill, 197
cocaine, 181–82, 183
Cohan, George M., 78
Cohelan, Jeffery, 79
Cohn, Roy, 102
"Collect Telegram From a Mad Dog" (Thompson), 54
Collier, Barnard, 37
Collier, Peter, 100
Colorado. *See* Aspen; Woody Creek
Columbia University, Thompson's studies at, 19
Communism: Algren's Party membership, 72; anticommunism in the US, 46–47, 52, 53, 55; the Kennedy assassination seen as victory for, 39–40; the Party and the Chicano movement, 131; Thompson's *People's World* subscription, 122; Wolfe's dissertation on Communist writers, 50. *See also* FBI/FBI investigations and surveillance
Conklin, Sandra. *See* Thompson, Sandra Conklin
Conrad, Joseph, 21, 74, 143, 150
consensus journalism, 162, 164, 169

conservatism, 6, 48, 83, 194, 204; hippie movement viewed as response to, 84–85. See also politics; specific politicians
Cooper, Marc, 210–11
counterculture: the back-to-the-land movement, 94–95; Miller as grandfather figure, 29; Roszak's coinage of the term, 90; Thompson as countercultural figure, 208–9. See also Beats; hippie counterculture
COVID-19 pandemic, 5
Coyote, Peter, 194
Crews, Frederick, 29
Crosby, Stills, Nash & Young, 117
Crosby, Stills & Nash, 94–95
Crouse, Timothy, 2, 95, 158, 159–61, 180
Crumb, Robert, 196
Curse of Lono, The (Thompson), 192–93
Cutler, Sam, 117

Daily Californian, 91, 92
Daley, Richard J., 104, 171
Dalitz, Morris "Moe," 134, 135
Dante, 21
Davis, Belva, 47
Davis, Ed, 131
Davis, Mike, 52
DEA (Drug Enforcement Agency), 140
Dean, John, 131, 177
DeCanio, Stephen, 54
Delaney, Robert, 121
DeLillo, Don, 73
Dellums, Ron, 79, 124
DeLorean, John, 105
Del Toro, Benicio, 152, 198
Democratic Party, 47; 1968 National Convention (Chicago), 100–102, 104, 120, 159, 168, 171, 206–7. See also political campaigns; specific politicians
Denevi, Timothy, 205
Denver Post, 212
Depp, Johnny, 198–99
Desert Inn (Las Vegas), 134, 135, 136

Dharma Bums, The (Kerouac), 26, 94
Didion, Joan, 85–89, 97, 112, 167
Diggers, 84, 87, 89
Dinesen, Isak, 21
Distant Drummer, 32, 118
"A Dog Took My Place" (Thompson), 187, 193
Donadio, Candida, 73
Donleavy, J. P., 19–20, 21
Don Quixote (Cervantes), 21
Doonesbury, 189
Doors, The, 88
Dos Passos, John, 21
Doudna, Christine, 125–26
Douglas, Helen Gahagan, 53
Down and Out in Paris and London (Orwell), 11
"Down and Out in San Francisco" (Thompson), 27
Downey, Barbara, 126
Draper, Robert, 157
Dr. Gonzo (character), 130, 137, 138, 143, 208. See also Acosta, Oscar "Zeta"; Fear and Loathing in Las Vegas
drinking: Didion's, 88; Hinckle's, 79–80; in the Kentucky Derby piece, 110, 112–13; London's, 42; Thompson's, 17, 18, 42, 46, 165, 175, 182, 199, 200
Drug Enforcement Agency (DEA), 140
drugs and drug use: Acosta's drug use, 136, 153, 154; among the Hell's Angels, 71; California cannabis cultivation, 94; Cassady's drug conviction, 27; and Didion's "Slouching Towards Bethlehem," 87–88; drug enforcement, 120, 121, 138, 139–41; in the hippie counterculture, 65, 67, 82, 84, 85, 87, 89, 93, 94, 208–9; in Kerouac's work, 23; LSD and the Merry Pranksters, 25, 60–63, 65, 93, 155; and the Thompson-Acosta Las Vegas trips, 136, 137–38; Thompson's drug use, 42, 46, 59, 61, 62, 121, 144, 175, 181–82, 183–84, 208;

in Thompson's work, 144, 145, 146–48, 167–68; the Trips Festival, 67
Duke, Raoul (character, pseudonym, and alter ego), 1–2, 14, 181, 207–8; before *Fear and Loathing in Las Vegas*, 12, 14, 122; Trudeau's "Uncle Duke" character, 189. See also *Fear and Loathing in Las Vegas*
Duncan, Donald, 81
Durocher, Larry, 180
Durrell, Lawrence, 29
Dylan, Bob, 15, 95, 145

Eagleton, Thomas, 170
East Bay Dragons, 71
Eastside 13 (Los Angeles), 128
economic crash of 2008, 204, 208
Edwards, Joe, 120
Ehrlichman, John, 140, 141
Eisenhower, Dwight D., 23, 47
Electric Kool-Aid Acid Test, The (Wolfe), 62–63, 155
Ellsberg, Daniel, 102, 141, 196
Ertegun, Ahmet, 90–91
Esalen Institute, 35, 43; *Rolling Stone* editorial meeting at, 157, 158
Esparza, Moctesuma, 128
ESPN, Thompson's columns for, 19, 199–200, 201–2, 210
Esquire, 30, 48, 50, 103, 193
Eszterhas, Joe, 157
Evers, Medgar, 44
Exley, Frederick, 12

Factories in the Field (McWilliams), 10, 52–53
Family Dog commune, 65
Fanon, Frantz, 40–41
Fan's Notes, A (Exley), 12
Farr, Fred S., 55
fascism/authoritarianism, 82, 83, 87
Faulkner, William, 21
FBI/FBI investigations and surveillance: Algren and, 72; civil rights movement and, 43; FBI whistleblower as Watergate reporting source, 188; Free Speech Movement

and, 54; Hemingway and, 45; Kerr and, 83; McWilliams and, 53; *Scanlan's Monthly*, 130; Thompson's file, 122; White and, 162
Fear and Loathing in America (ed. Brinkley), 197–98, 203
"Fear and Loathing in America: Beginning of the End" (Thompson), 201
Fear and Loathing in Las Vegas (film), 152, 153–54, 190, 198, 203
Fear and Loathing in Las Vegas (Thompson), 133–39, 141–56, 165, 214; Acosta's response and disappearance, 151, 152–55; critical reception and influence on Thompson's career, 155–57, 207; the dedication, 42; film rights and adaptation, 152, 153–54, 198, 203; generic ambiguity of, 4, 142–43, 207–8; genesis of/literary influences on, 7, 8–14, 19, 143, 207; Las Vegas investigative trips, 133, 136–38; the Las Vegas setting, 133–36, 206; 1990s editions of, 203; *Rolling Stone* and, 136–37, 141–43, 145, 153, 156–57; Steadman's illustrations, 143; summary and themes, 144–51; Thompson on, 12–14, 142–43, 150; Thompson's conception and approach, 136–37, 165, 207; the title, 143; Trudeau on, 189; the writing and editorial processes, 137, 139, 142–43. See also Dr. Gonzo; Duke, Raoul
Fear and Loathing on the Campaign Trail '72 (Thompson), 159, 164–77, 214; book's completion and appearance, 174–77; Crouse and, 158, 159; fortieth anniversary edition, 204; genesis of, 157–58; journalistic approach and methods, 159, 164–69, 200; media context for, 162–64; reporting challenges, 169–71; significance and influence of, 204, 208; Thompson and the McGovern campaign, 165, 169–71, 172; Thompson's reflections on Nixon and his win, 172–73, 174, 177–78

Felton, David, 137, 142, 155, 157, 182, 183–84, 191
feminist literary criticism, 124–26, 155
Ferlinghetti, Lawrence, 26, 27, 31
Ferris, Timothy, 184
fiction: feminist literary critiques, 124–26, 155; fiction/fact blending in Thompson's work, 3–4, 10, 12, 14, 24, 50, 109–10, 114–15, 142–43, 207–8; London's views on, 42; Thompson as novelist, 11, 12, 24, 30, 40; Thompson's views on, 11, 40. *See also* "Burial at Sea"; *Prince Jellyfish*; *Rum Diary, The*; *other specific works and authors*
Fiedler, Leslie, 76
financial crisis of 2008, 204, 208
"First Party at Ken Kesey's with Hell's Angels" (Ginsberg), 61
Fitzgerald, F. Scott, 16, 17, 21, 45; *The Great Gatsby*, 12, 16–17, 22, 89, 104, 134, 198
Flamingo Hotel & Casino (Las Vegas), 138, 147
Florida, Thompson in, 191
folk music, 94–95
Fong-Torres, Ben, 188
Ford, Gerald, 178
Foreman, George, 185
Fountainhead, The (Rand), 2
Fox Broadcasting Company/Fox News, 194
Frazier, Joe, 145, 185
freedom. *See* independence/self-reliance
Freeman, Louis, 47
Free Speech Movement, 49, 54, 83, 91–92
Fritsch, Billy "Sweet William," 32

Gabel, J. C., 203
gambling: in Las Vegas, 133–35; Thompson's, 165, 199–200
Garcia, Jerry, 67, 75, 86–87, 88
Gardner, Fred, 101, 102
Geiger, Bob, 42
Generation of Swine (Thompson), 192, 195

Gilliam, Terry, 198
Ginger Man, The (Donleavy), 19–20, 21
Ginsberg, Allen, 19, 26, 61, 82, 149
Girodias, Maurice, 123
Gitlin, Todd, 82
Gleason, Ralph J., 90–92; and Altamont, 117, 118; and Olay's obscenity arrest, 32; and *Rolling Stone's* founding and staff, 91–92, 93; and the San Francisco counterculture music scene, 65, 66, 67, 90–91, 92; and Thompson's work, 120
Glen Ellen (California): Rustic Inn piece, 44–45; Thompson's time in, 39, 41–48
Goddard, Donald, 107, 113
Goldman Sachs, Taibbi's coverage of, 204
Goldwater, Barry, 43, 46–47, 48, 64, 83, 178
Gonzofest Louisville, 203–4
Gonzo journalism: "Gonzo" as term, 114; the Gonzo persona's evolution and role, 1, 76, 114–15, 181–82, 186, 189–90, 191; as a label, 3, 13; Miller as precursor, 34; as performance art, 209–10; the persona as Thompson's key legacy, 1, 4; the role of Steadman's illustrations, 3, 107–8, 143, 207, 214; stylistic and thematic hallmarks of, 110, 111, 145–46, 166, 167, 209–10. *See also* Thompson, Hunter S., —LITERARY FORMATION, STYLE, AND METHODS; *specific Thompson works*
Gonzo Letters (Thompson's published correspondence), 3, 197–98, 203
Gonzo Papers (Thompson anthologies), 75–76, 191–92, 195, 196–97, 201–2. *See also specific titles*
Goodwin, Doris Kearns, 163
Goodwin, Richard, 162, 178, 180
Gossage, Howard, 102
Graham, Bill, 66–67, 94
Grateful Dead, 66, 67, 71, 86–87, 93; at Altamont, 117; drug arrests and

move to Marin, 89, 94; *Working-man's Dead*, 95
Great Gatsby, The (Fitzgerald), 12, 16–17, 22, 89, 104, 134, 198
Great Shark Hunt, The (Thompson; book), 74, 191–92, 208
"Great Shark Hunt, The" (Thompson; magazine piece), 189
Great Society, 65
Green, Robin, 157
Greene, Bob, 161
Greenfield, Robert, 157
Greer, Germaine, 161
Gregory, Dick, 43
Griffin, Rick, 94
Grosz, George, 107
Grove Press, 20
Gulf War, 196
guns: gun rights and legislation, 53–54, 63, 80; Thompson and, 2, 16, 30–31, 57, 103, 121, 191

Hagan, Joe, 118, 156–57
Haight-Ashbury, 46, 65–67; birth of the hippie scene, 65, 84; decline of, 94; music and art scene, 65–67, 85, 86–87, 89, 90–91; as Thompson's backyard, 46, 66; Thompson's "Hashbury" piece, 2, 83–85, 89–90, 94. *See also* hippie counterculture
Halberstam, David, 176
Hamill, Pete, 125
Harper's, 125
Harrell, Margaret, 58–60
Harris, Mark, 97, 137
Harrison, George, 85
Hart, Gary, 168
Harte, Bret, 25, 78
Harvey, Bob, 66
"'Hashbury' Is the Capital of the Hippies, The" (Thompson), 2, 83–85, 89–90, 94
Hawken, Paul, 86
Hearst, Patricia, 180
Hearst, Will, 180, 194, 195, 209. See also *San Francisco Examiner*
Hearst, William Randolph, 26, 195

Hearst Corporation, 199. *See also* Hearst, Will; *San Francisco Examiner*
Heart of Darkness (Conrad), 74, 143, 150
Hefner, Hugh, 102–3
Hell's Angels, 2, 59, 68–74; at Altamont, 117–18; Hinckle on, 83; the Lynch report, 55–56; in the media, 67–69, 70; and the Merry Pranksters/hippies, 61, 71, 75; Thompson's beating and disillusionment, 74. *See also* Barger, Ralph "Sonny"
Hell's Angels project, 6, 54, 64, 67–75, 77, 143, 214; Barger on the book, 75; book contract, preparation, and publication, 7–8, 57–60, 67; the book's content summarized, 67–72, 74; the book's critical reception, 69, 71, 74, 209; contretemps over Algren quotation, 72–74; influence on Thompson's career, 75–76; magazine piece for *The Nation*, 7–8, 11, 56–57, 68, 75; Wenner and, 92
Hell's Angels: The Strange and Terrible Saga of the Outlaw Motorcycle Gangs (Thompson). *See* Hell's Angels project
Helms, Chet, 67, 87, 94
Helms, Richard, 81
Hemingway, Ernest, 29, 39, 72; as catalyst for Thompson's friendship with Acosta, 97, 98; *The Sun Also Rises*, 8, 21, 22; as Thompson enthusiasm/influence, 9, 16, 21, 29; Thompson's piece on Hemingway in Idaho, 45
Hendrix, Jimi, 91
Henry Miller Reader, The, 29
Hey Rube (Thompson), 202–3
Hinckle, Warren, 78–80; and the *Aspen Wallposter*, 121–22; and Gleason, 92, 93; posthumous Thompson compilation by, 205; at *Ramparts*, 11, 78–79, 101–2, 125; at the *San Francisco Examiner*, 195; at *Scanlan's Monthly*, 3, 102, 103, 106, 109–10, 125, 130; and Steadman, 106; and Thompson, 3, 11, 79, 80,

Hinckle, Warren (continued)
156; views on the hippie counterculture, 82–83, 93, 117; and Wenner/
Rolling Stone, 92, 93, 156. See also
Ramparts; Scanlan's Monthly
hippie counterculture, 65–67, 82–91,
194; Acosta on, 97; Altamont and its
legacy, 106, 116–18, 144–45, 149; in
Aspen, 89, 95; the Beats as precursors, 65, 82, 84, 85; conventional
media portrayals and critiques of,
86–88, 89; Didion on, 86–88; the
Diggers, 84, 87; drugs and, 65, 67,
82, 84, 85, 87, 89, 93, 94, 208–9; Fear
and Loathing in Las Vegas as elegy
for, 145–46, 147, 155; the Haight-
Ashbury's decline, 94; the Hell's
Angels and, 61, 71, 75; Hinckle's
views on, 82–83, 93, 117; the Merry
Pranksters, 60–63, 65, 93, 155; and
Nixon's drug war, 140; politics and,
82–83, 84–85, 86, 87, 91, 117; Rolling Stone as product of, 92; the San
Francisco music scene, 65–67, 85,
86–87, 89, 90–91; seen as a media
invention, 89–90, 97; as a social
movement, 87, 88, 90, 91; the Summer of Love and its impacts, 82, 85,
89; sympathetic media observers,
90–91; Thompson's views and writ-
ing on, 83–85, 87, 89–90, 94, 95. See
also Haight-Ashbury
Hobsbawm, Eric, 91
Hochschild, Adam, 78
Hoffa, Jimmy, 135
Hoffman, Abbie, 179
Hoffmann, Joyce, 164
Hofstadter, Richard, 8, 194
Holden, Stephen, 198
homosexuality: references in "Howl,"
26; Thompson's views on, 32–33,
76–77
Honolulu marathon piece, 192
Hoover, J. Edgar, 53, 54, 83. See also
FBI/FBI investigations and surveil-
lance
Hough, Richard, 192

House Committee on Un-American
Activities (HUAC), 53, 55
"Howl" (Ginsberg), 26
HUAC (House Committee on Un-
American Activities), 53, 55
Hudson, William "Jo," 30, 31, 32
Hughes, Howard, 134
Hughes, James, 203
Human Be-In, 82
Hume, Brit, 161
Humphrey, Hubert, 168–69
Hunter, George, 65
Hunter, Meredith, 117
Hunter S. Thompson: The Crazy
Never Die (film), 196
Huntley, Chet, 47, 48

illustrations. See Steadman, Ralph
independence/self-reliance: as literary
motif, 22, 23; London as model of,
42, 45; Thompson's valorization of,
8–9, 18, 22, 27, 95
Innes, Bruce, 136, 150
intellectual property rights, 73
International Creative Management, 96
Iowa Writer's Workshop, 73, 123
Iraq war, 201, 206
Islands in the Stream (Hemingway),
39
"It Ain't Hardly That Way No More"
(Thompson), 64

Jagger, Mick, 118
James, Harry, 136, 146
January 6 (2021) Capitol insurrection,
5
Japanese-American internment, 52
Jarvis, Birney, 56, 69
Jefferson, Thomas, 21, 95
Jefferson Airplane, 65, 66, 90, 117
Jenkins, Loren, 121, 186
Johnson, Lyndon B., 40, 48, 49, 83,
162; and Kennedy's 1960 win, 163;
Thompson's letter offering to serve
as governor of American Samoa,
151; Thompson's planned 1968 cam-
paign book, 99

Johnson, Samuel, 150

Joplin, Janis, 91, 94

journalism. *See* Gonzo journalism; media and media critiques; New Journalism; participatory journalism; *specific topics*

journalistic objectivity and norms: critiques of objectivity, 161, 166–67, 169, 211; Salazar's work and, 130; Thompson's work and, 106, 132, 166, 167, 169, 211

Joyce, James, 21

Kalb, Marvin, 163

Kandel, Lenore, 32

Kandy-Kolored Tangerine-Flake Streamline Baby, The (Wolfe), 49–50

Keating, Edward, 79

Kelley, Alton, 65

Kelly, David, 198

Kemp, Paul (character), 21–22

Kemp, Penny, 19

Kemp, Welburn (character), 19

Kennedy, Anthony, 86

Kennedy, Jacqueline, 164, 180

Kennedy, John F., 23, 39–40, 47, 85, 145, 168; White's account of the 1960 campaign, 162–63

Kennedy, Michael, 196, 197

Kennedy, Robert F., 23, 99, 100, 135, 145

Kennedy, William, 20, 30, 37, 121; on the campaign '72 book, 4; on the Kentucky Derby piece, 114; on *The Rum Diary*, 36; on Thompson's literary development, 114, 208; on Thompson's public persona, 76, 208; on Thompson's reading habits, 20–21

Kent State protest and shootings (1970), 108–9, 111, 113, 119

Kentucky. *See* Kentucky Derby entries; Louisville

Kentucky Derby, Algren piece on, 72

"Kentucky Derby is Decadent and Depraved, The" (Thompson), 13, 106–15, 147, 151, 203, 206; background, 13, 106–10; Modern Library republication of, 203; reception and influence of, 114–15; summary, 110–13; Thompson's opinion of, 113–14

Kerouac, Jack, 26–27, 31, 82; *Big Sur*, 27, 30, 31; *The Dharma Bums*, 26, 94; as influence on Acosta, 97; as influence on Thompson, 19, 21, 22–23, 144, 205; Kesey and, 60, 61; *On the Road*, 22–23, 60, 144, 146, 156; Thompson's work compared to, 156

Kerr, Clark, 49, 83, 85

Kesey, Ken, 60–63, 67, 75, 88, 94, 149

Kevin, Brian, 36

Kienast, Dick, 124, 140–41, 191

Kierkegaard, Søren, 68

Killy (Jean-Claude) profile, 11, 102–6, 210

Kimball, George, 123

King, Martin Luther, Jr., 79, 99, 127, 145

Kingdom of Fear (Thompson), 200–201

Kipling, Rudyard, 201

Kirkus Reviews, 201–2

Klein, Joe, 182

Klein, Richard, 146

Knopf, 11

Kohn, Howard, 180

Koncewicz, Michael, 188

Korematsu v. United States, 52

Korshak, Sidney, 135

Krassner, Paul, 96, 118, 196

Kunkin, Art, 118

Kunzru, Hari, 5

Kuralt, Charles, 7, 99

Laos, Thompson in, 186

La Raza, 126–27, 131

Last Tycoon, The (Fitzgerald), 45

Las Vegas: history of, 133–36; Thompson and Acosta in, 133, 136, 137–38; Thompson on, 50; Thompson's first visit, 39; Wolfe on, 50. See also *Fear and Loathing in Las Vegas*

LA Weekly, 210

Lawrence, D. H., 21, 124

Lazin, Sarah, 149
Leary, Timothy, 144, 145, 149, 196
Lehmann-Haupt, Christopher, 125, 155, 176
Lehmann-Haupt, Sandy, 155
Leibovitz, Annie, 157
Lennon, John, 85
Leonard, John, 192
Leslie, Jacques, 186
Lewis, Grover, 137
Lewis, Huey, 32
liberalism: racial politics and, 43–44; *Ramparts*'s critiques of, 83. *See also* conservatism; politics; *specific politicians*
Life, 164
Lipsyte, Robert, 105
Lisch, Arthur, 87
Liston, Sonny, 39
Little, Brown and Company, 10
Lomax, Louis, 43
Lombardi, John, 32, 118, 119
London, Jack, 26, 41–42; parallels with Thompson, 42, 45, 114–15; as participatory journalism pioneer, 36, 42, 51; Thompson's Rustic Inn piece, 44–45
Lord, Sterling, 96
Los Angeles: Acosta's run for sheriff, 129; the Chicano movement and the 1968 school blowouts, 126–30; McWilliams and, 52–53, 57; Thompson archive in, 4; the Watts Riots, 44, 63–64
Los Angeles Free Press, 118
Los Angeles Herald-Examiner, 131
Los Angeles Times, 130, 137, 157, 209, 210
Louisville: and/in the Kentucky Derby piece, 107, 110; echoes of, in *The Rum Diary*, 22; Gonzofest Louisville, 203–4; as the home of Daisy Buchanan, 17; Thompson's childhood and teen years in, 15–19, 122; Thompson's feelings about/reportage on, 16, 17, 44
Louisville Courier-Journal, 20

Love, Robert, 183, 184, 187
LSD, 25, 60, 93, 182; the Merry Pranksters, 60–63, 65, 93, 155; the Trips Festival, 67. *See also* drugs and drug use
Luce, Henry, 80, 162
Lynch, Thomas C., and the Lynch report, 55–56, 67, 69

Macdonald, Dwight, 51
Mademoiselle, 85
Mailer, Norman, 12, 19, 21, 43, 96; *Advertisements for Myself*, 12, 21, 30, 191; *An American Dream*, 155; *Armies of the Night*, 12, 156; *Fear and Loathing in Las Vegas* compared to, 155, 156; and Millett's feminist criticism, 124, 125, 155; New York City mayoral campaign, 124; political journalism, 30, 48, 161; Thompson on, 40, 46; Thompson's 1961 letter to, 29–30; and Thompson's Foreman-Ali fight assignment, 185
Making of a Counter Culture, The (Roszak), 90
Making of the President 1960, The (White), 162–63, 176
Malcolm X, 43
Mankiewicz, Frank, 157–58, 171
Manson Family, 88, 116, 118, 137, 144–45, 147
Man with the Golden Arm, The (Algren), 72, 73, 74
Marcus, Greil, 92–93
Maslin, Janet, 200
MCA (entertainment agency), 135
McCarthy, Joseph, 102
McCumber, David, 195, 197
McDonell, Terry, 184, 187, 191, 193, 195
McGinniss, Joe, 162
McGovern, George: Thompson and the McGovern campaign (1972), 165, 169–71, 172
McKeen, William, 4, 19, 174, 187, 192, 203
McWilliams, Carey, 10–11, 52–55, 59, 69, 121; background and antidiscrim-

ination work, 10, 52–53, 55; *Factories in the Field,* 10, 52–53; and Nixon/the 1972 presidential campaign, 169, 173–74; *North from Mexico,* 126; on Reagan, 64, 65; at *The Nation,* 11, 52, 127; Thompson and, 3, 11, 53–55, 57; on Watergate, 188
McWilliams, Susan, 71, 204
Meat Possum Press, 121
media and media critiques: celebrity journalism, 188; consensus journalism, 162, 164, 169; critical debates over Thompson's journalistic legacy, 209–12; critiques of journalistic objectivity, 161, 166–67, 169, 211; hippie movement viewed as media invention, 89–90, 97; mainstream media's recent limitations and challenges, 206; the media and the 1964 GOP convention, 47, 48; objectivity and its limitations, 6, 130, 132, 161, 166, 167, 169, 211; in the Reagan era, 194; *Rolling Stone* in the media landscape, 92, 94, 179, 180; the significance of countercultural media, 213; Thompson as media critic, 37–38, 67–69, 89–90, 131, 166, 169, 173, 178, 194, 209; *Time's* critiques of *Ramparts,* 80, 81–82; Watergate coverage, 160–61, 177–78, 188. *See also* music journalism; political journalism; sports journalism; *specific media outlets*
Melville, Herman: *Moby-Dick,* 147
Mencken, H. L., 10, 53, 57, 209
men's magazines: and feminist criticism, 125–26. *See also specific magazines*
Meredith, Scott/Meredith Literary Agency, 96, 123
Merry Pranksters, 60–63, 65, 93, 155
Meyer, Nicole, 197
Miller, Henry, 28–29, 33, 95, 96; as influence on Thompson and others, 21, 29, 34, 45, 205; work of, 28–29, 34, 124
Millett, Kate: *Sexual Politics,* 124–25, 155

Mingus, Charles, 43
Mint 400 Off-Road Rally, 133, 136. See also *Fear and Loathing in Las Vegas*
Mitchell, Artie, 195–96, 197
Mitchell, Jim, 195–96, 197
Mitchell, John, 108, 130, 150
Mitchell, Joni, 94–95
Mitchell, Luke, 206
Mitford, Jessica, 211
Moby-Dick (Melville), 147
Mohr, Don, 70
Monterey Jazz Festival, 90
Monterey Pop Festival, 91, 116
Moore, Michael, 196
Morrison, Jim, 88
Mother Jones, 78
motorcycle gangs, 25, 55–56, 71, 116. *See also* Hell's Angels *entries*
Mulford, Don, 53–54
Murdoch, Rupert, 194
Murphy, Anne, 62
Murphy, Dennis, 31–32
Murphy, Michael, 32, 35, 43, 62
Murphy, Vinnie "Bunnie" MacDonald, 31, 32, 35
Murray, Bill, 190
music: Altamont and its violence, 116–18, 145, 149; folk's emergence, 94–95; in Las Vegas, 135, 136, 138; the San Francisco music scene of the 1960s–1970s, 65–67, 85, 86–87, 89, 90–91; Thompson's musical enthusiasms, 59, 66, 95
music journalism: documentary films, 116; Gleason's work, 65, 66, 67, 90–91, 117; as *Rolling Stone's* core mission, 92, 93–94, 119
Muskie, Edmund, 101, 167–68, 169, 171

Nabulsi, Laila, 190
Nation, The, 10–11, 78, 79; Hell's Angels piece, 7–8, 11, 56–57, 68, 75; McWilliams's editorship, 11, 52, 127; 1972 campaign coverage, 169; Roszak's series on the counterculture,

Nation, The (continued)
  90; Thompson and, 3, 52, 53–55, 57;
  2016 piece on Thompson, 204. *See
  also* McWilliams, Carey
National Chicano Moratorium March,
  130
National Observer, 30–31, 39, 44, 45,
  46, 48–50, 69, 72; Thompson's South
  American assignment, 36–37, 39
National Rifle Association, 2
National Student Association (NSA),
  81–82
Nesbit, Lynn, 96, 108, 139, 153, 187
New American Review, 125
"New Cult of Sex and Anarchy, The"
  (Brady), 28
New Directions, 28, 29
New Journalism, 2, 3, 42, 50–51, 72,
  100, 206, 208. *See also* participatory
  journalism; *specific writers*
New Republic, 156
Newsweek, 37, 68, 181, 186
Newton, Huey P., 54, 196
New York magazine, 50, 62
New York Review of Books, 51
New York Times, 102; film adaptations
  of Thompson's work reviewed, 198,
  199; Iraq invasion coverage, 206; on
  the Lynch Report, 56; on Millett's
  Sexual Politics, 125; 1972 Nixon editorial, 173; Pentagon Papers publication, 141; reviews of Thompson's
  work, 69, 74, 155–56, 176–77, 192,
  198, 200, 202; Thompson as critic of,
  68; Thompson's Haight-Ashbury
  piece for, 2, 83–85, 89–90, 94
Night Manager project (uncompleted),
  5, 196, 197
"Nights in the Rustic" (Thompson),
  44–45
9/11 attacks, 201
1960 presidential campaign, 23–24, 30,
  162–63
1964 presidential campaign, 46–48,
  83, 159
1968 presidential campaign, 99–101,
  140, 159, 163

1972 presidential campaign, 3–4, 139–
  40, 159–61, 163–64, 172–73. *See also
  Fear and Loathing on the Campaign
  Trail '72*
Nixon, Richard: California gubernatorial defeat (1962), 48; and campus
  activism, 108–9; on the de facto
  legality of a president's actions, 193;
  the Enemies List, 91, 177; and
  Jimmy Hoffa, 135; McWilliams on,
  53, 173–74; and the 1960 loss to
  Kennedy, 163; at the 1964 GOP convention, 47, 48; the 1968 presidential
  campaign, 99–101, 163; the Nixon
  drug war, 139–41; the Nixon White
  House's media relations, 160–61,
  177; and Elvis Presley, 138; and Reagan, 193; resignation, 178, 179; and
  Scanlan's, 130–31; Watergate and its
  media coverage, 160–61, 163, 177–
  78, 188; the White House Plumbers
  and their activities, 141, 173; White's
  accounts of Nixon's presidential
  campaigns, 163–64
—THOMPSON'S VIEWS ON/WRITING
  ABOUT, 23–24, 30, 172–73, 174, 177,
  178; 1968 profile for *Pageant*,
  99–100, 101, 159; Nixon and
  Thompson's county sheriff run, 120,
  121, 122–23; obituary for *Rolling
  Stone*, 187–88; portrayal in *Fear and
  Loathing in Las Vegas*, 150, 151;
  portrayal in *Fear and Loathing on
  the Campaign Trail '72*, 166, 167,
  169, 170; Thompson on Watergate
  and its aftermath, 177, 178. *See also
  Fear and Loathing on the Campaign
  Trail '72*
"Nonstudent Left, The" (Thompson),
  49, 53–54, 64
Noonan, Bill, 123
North from Mexico (Carey), 126
NRA (National Rifle Associaton), 2
Nutt, Jim, 106

objectivity. *See* journalistic objectivity
  and norms

O'Brien, Larry, 151
obscenity charges and trials, 26, 32, 59, 66, 196
O'Connor, Flannery, 21
O'Farrell Theatre (San Francisco), 5, 196
Olay, Lionel, 32, 60, 118
Oliphant, Pat, 106
Olympia Press, 20
Onassis, Jacqueline Kennedy. *See* Kennedy, Jacqueline
One Flew Over the Cuckoo's Nest (Kesey), 60
Only Skin Deep (Kimball), 123
Ono, Yoko, 85
On the Road (Kerouac), 22–23, 60, 144, 146, 156
Orwell, George, 10, 11, 36, 51
Oswald, Lee Harvey, 40
Outside, 195
Owl Farm (Colorado home). *See* Woody Creek
Owl House (Glen Ellen), 41

Pageant, 100; Nixon profile for, 99–100, 101, 159; other Thompson proposals and pieces, 43, 44, 64, 76, 77
Palevsky, Max, 119, 157–58
Palmer, Gail, 196
Paris Review, 13, 51, 61
Parker, William, 63, 64
participatory journalism, 41–42, 51, 62–63; Thompson's work as, 36, 51, 69, 100, 105–6, 165. *See also* New Journalism
Partridge, Marianne, 126
Patterson, Floyd, 39
Peck, Abe, 179, 181, 187, 190
Penn, Sean, 202
Pentagon Papers, 102, 141
People, 188
People's World, 122
performance art, Thompson's work as, 209–10
Perlstein, Rick, 47, 164
Perry, Charles, 93, 137, 144
Perry, Paul, 192

Petitclerc, Denne, 39, 41, 56
Phillips, John, 91
Pierce, David, 59, 103, 120
Pileggi, Nicholas, 134
Pitkin County. *See* Aspen; Woody Creek
Playboy, 72, 196, 202; and the Killy profile, 11, 102–3, 105, 106; late Thompson projects for, 189, 196, 202; Thompson interviewed in, 144, 188–89
Plimpton, George, 13, 51, 185, 191, 201
Police Chief, 72, 122
police violence, 101, 108, 130, 131, 168, 171
political activism: at the 1968 Democratic National Convention, 100–101; campus activism of the 1960s and 1970s, 49, 53, 54, 83–84, 88, 91–92, 108–9; the Los Angeles Chicano movement, 126–30. *See also* race and racial politics
political campaigns: California gubernatorial races, 48, 64–65, 83; countercultural/protest campaigns of the 1960s and 1970s, 79, 120–24, 129; 1960 presidential campaign, 23–24, 30, 162–63; 1964 presidential campaign, 46–48, 83, 159; 1968 presidential campaign, 99–101, 140, 159, 163; 1972 presidential campaign, 3–4, 139–40, 159–61, 163–64, 172–73; Nixon's House and Senate races, 53. See also *Fear and Loathing on the Campaign Trail '72*
political journalism: coverage of the 1972 presidential campaign, 159–61, 163, 169, 172; coverage of Watergate and its aftermath, 160–61, 163, 177–78, 188; GOP criticism of (1964), 48; influence of *Fear and Loathing on the Campaign Trail '72* on, 204; Mailer's reportage, 30, 48, 161; in the 1970s media landscape, 180–81; norms and conventions of, 160–61, 162, 168; presidential campaign books of the 1960s and 1970s, 162–64; in

political journalism (continued)
  Ramparts, 79, 80–81; in Rolling
  Stone, 118, 119, 157–58, 159–60, 164,
  179–80, 204; Salazar's work, 130;
  Thompson's early critiques of, 37;
  Thompson's interest in, 119, 159, 193
—THOMPSON'S WORK: Aspen politics
  piece, 118, 120, 123; Berkeley activ-
  ism piece, 49, 53–54, 64; Better Than
  Sex, 197; "Fear and Loathing in
  America: Beginning of the End,"
  201; in Hey Rube, 201; proposed
  LBJ/1968 campaign book, 99–101;
  Reagan and, 193–94; "Strange Rumblings in Aztlan," 126–32, 133, 137,
  203, 206; Vietnam assignment, 185–
  87; writing on Nixon and Watergate,
  99–100, 101, 159, 177–78, 187–88.
  See also Fear and Loathing on the
  Campaign Trail '72; Nixon, Richard
politics: Aspen politics, 120–24, 140–
  41; political views among the Hell's
  Angels, 71; politics and the hippies,
  82–83, 84–85, 86, 87, 91, 117. See
  also political activism; political campaigns; political journalism; race and
  racial politics; specific politicians
—THOMPSON'S POLITICAL VIEWS, EDU-
  CATION, AND PARTICIPATION, 8, 119,
  170–71; on Goldwater and the 1964
  campaign, 43, 48; on Hemingway's
  political disengagement, 45; impact
  of the Kennedy assassination, 39–40;
  impact of the 1964 Republican
  National Convention, 48; impact of
  the 1968 Democratic National Convention, 100–101, 120, 159, 206–7;
  liberalism and the civil rights movement, 43–44; the 1960 presidential
  campaign, 23–24; Pitkin County
  sheriff campaign, 14, 120–24. See
  also Fear and Loathing on the Campaign Trail '72; Nixon, Richard;
  political journalism
Polo Is My Life (Thompson; uncompleted project), 196, 197
poster art, 66, 67

"Presenting: The Richard Nixon Doll"
  (Thompson), 99–100, 101, 159
presidential campaigns. See political
  campaigns
Presley, Elvis, 138
Price, Ray, 99
Price, Richard, 32–33
Prince Jellyfish (Thompson), 11, 19
"Prisoner of Sex, The" (Mailer), 125
Private Eye, 106
Proffitt, Nick, 186
Proud Highway, The (ed. Brinkley),
  197, 203
Proust, Marcel, 21
Publishers Weekly, 202
Puerto Rico: as setting for The Rum
  Diary, 21–22; Thompson in, 20–21
Pulitzer, Roxanne, 187, 193

Raborn, William, 81
race and racial politics: the Black Panther Party, 53–54, 80, 88, 110; Blacks
  in the San Francisco Bay Area, 25,
  59; the Chicano movement and
  Thompson's "Strange Rumblings in
  Aztlan," 126–32, 133; the civil rights
  movement, 16, 43–44; the Hell's
  Angels and, 70–71; in Louisville, 16;
  McWilliams's antidiscrimination
  work, 52, 55; in 1960s California, 44,
  53–55, 63–65, 80; the 1964 presidential race and, 47; Thompson and,
  15–16, 21–22, 41–44
Ragged Dick (Alger), 8
Rajneesh, Bhagwan Shree, 196
Rambo films, 194
Ramparts, 11, 78–83, 125; CIA and NSA
  exposés, 81–82; contributors, advisors,
  and staff, 72, 78, 79, 100, 106, 124, 161,
  180, 211; failure and shortcomings of,
  11, 83, 102, 180; founding and editorial formula, 78–79; Hinckle's "Social
  History of the Hippies," 82–83; the
  Ramparts Wall Poster, 101–2; and
  Rolling Stone, 92, 119–20; Thompson
  and, 2, 79–80; Vietnam War coverage,
  80. See also Hinckle, Warren

Rand, Ayn, 2

Random House, Thompson and, 3, 7–8, 197; and *Fear and Loathing in Las Vegas* (Thompson), 152, 153; the Hell's Angels book, 7, 58–60; planned "death of the American Dream" book, 8–10, 14, 123–24, 136–37, 139; planned *Night Manager* project, 196, 197. *See also* Silberman, James

rape and rape culture. *See* sexual violence

Reagan, Ronald, 135; California gubernatorial campaign, 64–65, 83; as governor, 54, 83, 108, 128, 193; as president, 86, 193–94; proposed Thompson book about, 192

Realist, 118

Rector, James, 108

Redding, Otis, 91

Reich, Wilhelm, 28

Reporter, The, 16, 44

Republican Party: 1964 National Convention (San Francisco), 46–48. *See also* political campaigns; *specific politicians*

Revolt of the Cockroach People, The (Acosta), 154

Rexroth, Kenneth, 26, 28, 94

Reynolds, Debbie, 136, 146

Ricci, Marysue, 3, 198, 200

Richmond, California, 59, 120

Ricks, Glen, 122

Rifkin, Danny, 89

Rinzler, Alan, 3, 94, 103, 174–75, 192, 200–201

Rise and Fall of the Brown Buffalo, The (film), 152

Rispoli, Giovanni, 199

road literature, 28, 42, 97; *Fear and Loathing in Las Vegas* and, 144, 146. *See also* Kerouac, Jack

Robinson, Bruce, 198, 199

Robinson, Jackie, 15, 47

Rodriguez, Phillip, 152

Rogue, 33, 34, 35, 72, 102

Rolling Stone: advertising and finances, 157, 181; editorial formula and sensibility, 93–94, 118, 119–20, 125–26, 157, 180, 181, 188; founding of, 92–94; in the media landscape, 92, 94, 179, 180; in the mid-1970s, 179–81; move to New York, 190, 195; political/current affairs journalism in, 117–18, 119, 120, 137, 157–58, 159–60, 164, 179–80, 204; staff culture and tensions, 119, 125–26; Taibbi at, 204; Wolfe and, 51. *See also* Wenner, Jann; *other editors and contributors*

—THOMPSON'S ASSIGNMENTS AND PUBLISHED ARTICLES: Acosta obituary, 155, 187, 190; Ali-Foreman fight assignment, 184–85; Ali interview, 15; Aspen politics piece, 118, 120, 123; 1972 campaign reflections, 172–73; Nixon obituary, 187–88; "Polo Is My Life," 197; Pulitzer divorce piece, 187, 193; Salazar piece, 126–32, 133, 137, 203, 206; Vietnam assignment, 185–87. See also *Fear and Loathing in Las Vegas*; *Fear and Loathing on the Campaign Trail '72*

—THOMPSON'S ASSOCIATION WITH, 2, 126, 132, 141–42, 156–58, 159, 181–88; beginnings of, 118–20; editorial support, 142, 182–84; haggles over money, 142, 187; the 1971 Esalen editorial meeting, 157–58; significance of the relationship, 3, 119, 141, 156–57, 179, 181; souring of, 187, 190

Rolling Stones, The, 116–17, 118

Roosevelt, Franklin, 168

Rosenbaum, Ron, 161

Rosenthal, David, 3, 193, 197, 200

Ross, A. S., 212

Roszak, Theodore, 90, 97

Rovere, Richard, 163

Rubin, Jerry, 108

Ruiz, Raul, 126, 129, 130

Rum Diary, The (film), 198–99

Rum Diary, The (Thompson), 4, 9, 11, 30, 31–32, 77, 99; characters, setting, and themes, 8, 21–22, 35; other writers' opinions about, 32, 36; publication and critical reception of, 22, 198
Running, 192
Rustic Inn piece, 44–45
Rutten, Tim, 209–10

Saigon, Thompson on assignment in, 185–86
Salazar, Ruben, 130, 131, 210, 211. *See also* "Strange Rumblings in Aztlan"
Salinger, J. D., 21
Salter, James, 5, 13, 106, 120–21
Samoa, Thompson's preoccupation with, 151
Sands Hotel and Casino (Las Vegas), 135
San Francisco: the Beatles in, 85; at the beginning of the Sixties, 25, 26–27; early Bay Area literary and arts scene, 25–27; the 1964 Republican National Convention, 46–48; *Rolling Stone* moves away, 190; the Summer of Love and the Human Be-In, 82, 85, 89. *See also* Haight-Ashbury; hippie counterculture; *specific San Francisco media outlets*
—THOMPSON AND: influence on his literary development, 1, 2, 205–6; the Mitchell brothers and the *Night Manager* project, 5, 195–97; proposed story on the city's decline, 54–55; Thompson's move to, 25–27, 46, 48–49, 205; work sessions for the '72 campaign book at the Seal Rock Inn, 174–75
San Francisco Chronicle, 27, 32, 56, 89, 121; assessments of Thompson's work, 211, 212; Gleason's music journalism, 65, 66, 67, 90–91, 117
San Francisco Examiner, 26, 28, 54, 97; Thompson's columns for, 194–95, 196, 210
San Francisco Mime Troupe, 66

San Francisco State College, 137
San Juan Star, 20
Sartre, Jean-Paul, 40–41
Saturday Evening Post, 86
Saturday Review, 37
Savio, Mario, 91–92
Scanlan's Monthly, 3, 125, 126, 131–32; the Kentucky Derby piece, 13, 106–15, 147, 151, 206; the Killy profile, 11, 102–6, 210; *Police Chief* review, 122; proposed "Thompson-Steadman Report," 13–14, 207; Salazar piece and, 130, 131
Scanlon, Paul, 137, 182
Scheer, Robert, 66, 78, 79, 92, 124
Schirra, Wally, 150
Schlesinger, Arthur, Jr., 10–11
Scott, A. O., 199
Scott, Jack, 180
Screwjack (Thompson), 195
"Secret Cables to Willie Hearst" (Thompson), 195
self-reliance. *See* independence/self-reliance
Selling of the President 1968, The (McGinniss), 162
Semonin, Paul, 17, 20, 22, 23, 35, 39–40, 40–41, 100
September 11 attacks, 201
Sergeant, The (Murphy), 31–32
sex: in Beat literature and Henry Miller, 26, 28, 29, 124; in fiction, feminist critiques of, 124–25, 155; Hell's Angels sexual practices and abuses, 55, 56, 62, 68, 69, 70; the hippies' sexual nonconformity, 76; the Mitchell brothers and the O'Farrell Theatre, 5, 195–96, 197; Thompson's views on sexual freedom, 29; in Thompson's writing, 33, 34, 35, 147–48. *See also* homosexuality; obscenity charges and trials; sexual violence
Sexual Politics (Millett), 124–25, 155
sexual violence: in the Lynch Report, 56; the Merry Pranksters–Hell's Angels party, 62; Thompson's sexual

assault arrest, 196; in Thompson's writing, 22, 68, 69, 70, 148
Seymour, Corey, 203
Shafer, Jack, 200
Sheinbaum, Stanley, 79
Shoaf, Eric, 205
Silberman, James, 3, 10, 11, 23; and the American Dream book/*Fear and Loathing in Las Vegas*, 7, 9–10, 11–13, 14, 123–24, 139; excerpts of Thompson letters to, 7, 9–10, 23, 96, 100, 101, 117–18, 123–24, 139; and *The Great Shark Hunt*, 191; and the Hell's Angels book, 7, 58, 74
Simon & Schuster, 3, 191, 197, 198, 200
Simonson, Kevin, 203
Simpson, O. J., 105
Sinatra, Frank, 135, 136, 138
Sinclair, Upton, 211
6 Gallery (San Francisco), 26
Sixties counterculture. *See* counterculture; hippie counterculture
60 Minutes, 181
SLATE, 91
Slate's Hot Springs (Big Sur), 28, 31–32, 32–33
Slick, Grace, 65
"Slouching Towards Bethlehem" (Didion), 86–88, 89
Snyder, Gary, 26, 94
Solheim, Michael, 97
Songs of the Doomed (Thompson), 75–76, 192, 195, 196–97
Sonoma County (California), Thompson's time in, 39, 41–48
Sorensen, Ted, 99
Sorrels, Rosalie, 59
Soul on Ice (Cleaver), 80
South America, Thompson in, 36–37, 39
Southern, Terry, 50, 110
Spanking the Donkey (Taibbi), 204
Spider magazine, 54
Sport and a Pastime, A (Salter), 13
sports: Ali as Thompson's personal hero, 15; the Ali-Frazier championship fight (1971), 145, 185; Thompson and, 15, 19, 46. *See also* sports journalism
Sports Illustrated, 72, 133, 136
sports journalism, 19, 51, 72, 176, 185
—THOMPSON'S ASSIGNMENTS AND REPORTAGE, 39, 133, 136, 184–85, 189; *The Curse of Lono*, 192–93; ESPN columns, 19, 199–200, 201–2, 210; Kentucky derby piece, 13, 106–15, 147, 151, 203, 206; "The Temptations of Jean-Claude Killy," 11, 102–6, 210. See also *Fear and Loathing in Las Vegas*
Stanley, Owsley, 93, 145
Steadman, Ralph, 106–8, 143, 171, 174, 185, 192, 207, 214; the importance of the Thompson-Steadman collaborations, 3, 13–14, 107–8, 207, 214; the proposed "Thompson-Steadman Report," 13–14, 207; as sidekick in the Kentucky Derby piece, 111–13; Thompson on Steadman's work, 107–8, 113–14
Steffens, Lincoln, 211
Stephenson, William, 192, 207
Stermer, Dugald, 78, 92
Stone, I. F., 91
Straight Arrow Books, 3, 94, 152, 154–55, 174, 186
"Strange Rumblings in Aztlan" (Thompson), 126–32, 133, 137, 203, 206
Streitfeld, David, 1, 201, 203, 205
Streshinsky, Ted, 86
Styron, William, 46
suicide: Hemingway's, Thompson on, 45; Thompson's death, 1, 202
Summer of Love, 82, 85, 89
Sun Also Rises, The (Hemingway), 8, 21, 22
Sunday Ramparts, 92
Swift, Jonathan, 156
Symbionese Liberation Army, 180

Taibbi, Matt, 171, 204
Tarbell, Ida, 211
Taylor, Derek, 91

Teamsters union, 135
"Temptations of Jean-Claude Killy, The" (Thompson), 11, 102–6, 210
Tenney, Jack, 55
Thomas, Clarence, 187
Thompson, Anita Bejmuk, 31, 200, 202
Thompson, Hunter S.
—CORRESPONDENCE, 2–3, 4; publication of, 197–98, 203. *See also specific correspondents*
—EARLY LIFE AND CAREER, 15–24; background and childhood, 15–16; college courses, 19; father's death and teenage years, 16–19, 122; military service and early writing jobs, 19–21
—LIFE AND CAREER 1960–1974: Aspen politics piece and Thompson's county sheriff run, 14, 118, 120–24; Berkeley activism piece, 49, 53–54, 64; Bermuda trip, 35; Big Sur residence and articles, 2, 27–35, 64; "Collect Telegram From a Mad Dog" (poem), 54; FBI's file on Thompson, 122; friendship with Acosta and Salazar piece, 97–98, 126–32, 133, 137, 203, 206; Hinckle and *Ramparts*, 78–83, 101–2; impact of Altamont and Kent State, 116–18; impact of the Kennedy assassination, 40; Kentucky Derby piece, 13, 106–15, 147, 151, 203, 206; Kesey and the Merry Pranksters, 60–63; Killy profile, 11, 102–6, 210; McWilliams and *The Nation*, 3, 10–11, 52–55, 57; move to Glen Ellen and Rustic Inn piece, 39, 41–48; move to San Francisco, 25–27, 46, 48–49, 205; move to Woody Creek, 1, 39, 94–96; New York–Seattle road trip (1960), 22–23; Nixon profile and the 1968 Democratic Convention, 99–101, 159; Nixon's drug war and Aspen drug enforcement, 139–41; the planned "death of the American Dream" book, 8–10, 14, 123–24, 136–37, 139; productiveness difficul-

ties, 114, 174–75; *The Rum Diary*, 8, 9, 11, 21–22, 30, 31–32, 57, 77; San Francisco hippie scene and Haight-Ashbury piece, 65–67, 83–85, 89–90, 94; South America assignment, 36–37, 39; Wenner and *Rolling Stone*, 118–20, 125–26, 156–58. *See also Fear and Loathing in Las Vegas; Fear and Loathing on the Campaign Trail '72*; Hell's Angels project; hippie counterculture
—LIFE AND CAREER POST–1974, 179–202; Acosta obituary, 155, 187, 190; anthologies (the Gonzo Papers), 75–76, 191–92, 195, 196–97, 201–2; on assignment in Vietnam, 185–86; on assignment in Zaire, 184–85; campus lectures, 181; celebrity status, 1, 2, 4, 188–90, 209; *The Curse of Lono*, 192–93; divorce, 190, 191; ESPN columns, 199–200, 201–2, 210; the impact of Nixon's resignation, 178, 179; life in Woody Creek, 191; Nixon obituary, 187–88; physical decline and death, 1, 199, 200, 202; Pulitzer divorce piece, 187, 193; Reagan presidency and book contract, 192, 193–94; the *Rolling Stone* collaboration in the late 1970s, 181–88, 190; *San Francisco Examiner* columns, 194–95, 196, 210; San Francisco's Mitchell brothers and the *Night Manager* project, 5, 195–97; second marriage, 200; sexual assault arrest, 196; writing process/ difficulties and professional decline, 5, 181–83, 185, 192, 199–200, 208, 209
—LITERARY FORMATION, STYLE, AND METHODS, 1–4, 205–8, 213–14; the American Dream motif, 17, 22, 40, 72, 104, 145–46, 147, 156, 174, 194; the cuckold motif, 35, 44; fiction/fact blending and generic ambiguity, 3–4, 10, 12, 14, 24, 50, 109–10, 114–15, 142–43, 207–8; hyperbole and sensationalism, 33–34, 69, 145–46, 148,

166, 172–73, 209; key literary influences, 11–12, 22–23, 29, 41–42, 44–45, 50–51, 71–72, 205, 206, 209 (*see also specific books and writers*); place in Thompson's work, 2, 75, 191, 205–6; prose style, 29, 69–70; San Francisco literary context and, 25–27; satire and humor, 33–34, 141, 143, 156, 167–68, 204, 209; "straight" journalism, 176–77, 209, 210; stylistic development, choices, and hallmarks, 36–37, 69–70, 103, 105–6, 132, 204, 205–8; teenage literary enthusiasms, 16–17; Thompson as cultural critic, 5, 6, 36, 201, 208, 209; Thompson as media critic, 37–38, 67–69, 89–90, 131, 166–67, 169, 173, 178, 194, 209; the work as participatory journalism, 36, 51, 69, 100, 105–6, 165; the work as performance art, 209–10. *See also* Gonzo journalism; —LITERARY REPUTATION AND LEGACY

—LITERARY REPUTATION AND LEGACY, 1, 4–6, 203–14; biographies and oral histories, 203–4; correspondence publication, 197–98, 203; importance of the Steadman collaboration, 3, 107–8, 143, 207, 214; in the last decade of his life, 203; Modern Library publications, 203; posthumous criticism, tributes, and editions, 203–5, 209–13

—PERSONAL CHARACTERISTICS AND BEHAVIOR: Barger on, 75; belligerence, 4, 31, 32–33, 73, 103–4, 157; drinking, 17, 18, 42, 46, 165, 175, 182, 199, 200; drug use, 42, 46, 59, 61, 62, 121, 144, 175, 181–82, 183–84, 208; the Gonzo persona's evolution and role, 1, 76, 114–15, 181–82, 186, 189–90, 191; and his work, 4–5, 212–13; independence and nonconformity, 8–9, 27; misogyny, 213; narcissism, 34; personal finances, 9, 75, 96, 184, 199–200; pessimism, 9; physical courage, 69; social behavior

and skills, 17, 181, 191; as a teenager, 17–18. *See also* —VIEWS, VALUES, AND PREOCCUPATIONS

—PROFESSIONAL RELATIONSHIPS AND BEHAVIOR: with agents, 96; authorial image construction and maintenance, 38–39, 45, 76, 77; with editors, 3, 184, 193, 200–201, 208, 214; editors' roles in his process, 3, 175, 208, 214; freelance ethic, 8–9; networking and self-promotion skills, 2–3, 17, 30, 37; the Steadman collaborations, 3, 13–14, 106–8, 143, 207, 214. *See also specific editors and media outlets*

—VIEWS, VALUES, AND PREOCCUPATIONS: American Samoa preoccupation, 151; on conformity and financial security, 17–18, 27, 45; the death/decline of the American Dream, 40, 57, 104, 194, 208; getting paid, 9, 96, 142, 186–87, 195; on his own work and literary status, 4, 77, 113–14; on his Southern heritage, 15–16; on homosexuality and gender nonconformity, 33, 76–77; independence and self-reliance, 8–9, 18, 22, 27, 95; musical enthusiasms, 59, 66, 95; personal heroes, 15, 23, 59, 135, 185; political views, education, and engagement, 8, 23–24, 99, 100–101, 119, 120–24, 159, 170–71, 205, 207; on race and racial politics, 16, 42–44; Thompson and guns, 2, 16, 30–31, 57, 103, 121, 191

—WORKS: bibliographic list, 246–48; film rights and adaptations, 152, 153–54, 190, 198–99, 203. *See also* —CORRESPONDENCE; Gonzo journalism; —LIFE AND CAREER; —LITERARY FORMATION, STYLE, AND METHODS; —LITERARY REPUTATION AND LEGACY; *specific topics, titles, and media outlets*

Thompson, Jim, 66, 76–77, 103–4

Thompson, Juan Fitzgerald, 41, 197, 199, 202, 204–5

Thompson, Sandra Conklin, 35, 36, 184; background, 20; in Big Sur, 27, 31, 34; contretemps over *Argosy* photo, 37–38; in Glen Ellen, 41; and the Merry Pranksters/Hell's Angels party, 61, 62; pregnancies, marriage, and divorce, 34, 39, 41, 190, 191; Thompson's relationship with/ behavior toward, 20, 31, 34, 39, 57, 103; and Thompson's work, 31, 55, 114, 209
Thompson, Virginia, 103
Time magazine, 68, 85, 86, 89, 177, 181; *Ramparts* critiques, 80, 81–82; Thompson at, 19; White and, 162
Torrey, Beef, 203
Trudeau, Garry, 189
Trump, Donald, 5–6, 71, 102, 105, 204
Truscott, Lucian K., IV, 139, 156
Twain, Mark, 21, 26, 51, 78, 192, 209, 211
"Twirling at Ole Miss" (Southern), 50

"Ultimate Free Lancer, The" (Thompson), 32
Under the Volcano (Lowry), 150
University of California: campus activism, 49, 53, 83–84, 91–92; Didion and, 85, 86; Reagan's budget cuts, 83; *Rolling Stone* and, 92, 93; Wenner at Berkeley, 91–92. *See also* Berkeley; Kerr, Clark
Unnatural Enemy, The (Bourjaily), 30–31
Us Weekly, 188

Vetter, Craig, 188–89
Vietnam War, 49, 113, 145, 147, 171, 193, 194; anti-war activism and sentiment, 49, 79, 100–101, 108–9, 140, 171; the Pentagon Papers, 102, 141; *Ramparts* photo essay on US bombing impacts, 79, 80; Thompson's Vietnam assignment, 185–87
Village Voice, 30, 139, 156, 161
violence and threatened violence: at Altamont, 117–18, 145, 149; in *Fear and Loathing in Las Vegas* (Thompson), 148, 149; in Mailer's *An American Dream*, 155; the Manson Family murders, 88, 116, 137; police violence, 101, 108, 130, 131, 168, 171; Thompson's Hell's Angels beating, 74; Thompson's potential for, 4, 31, 32–33, 57, 103. *See also* sexual violence
Von Hoffman, Nicholas, 121
Vonnegut, Kurt, 161
Voorhis, Jerry, 53

Walk on the Wild Side, A (Algren), 71–74
Wallace, George, 163
Wall Street Journal, 36–37, 39
Walsh, John, 199–200
Ware, Ned, 123
War News, 196
Warren, Earl, 86
Warren, Nina "Honey Bear," 86
Washington Post, 121, 160, 177, 188
Wasserman, Lew, 135
Watergate and its aftermath, 160–61, 163, 177–78, 188, 194
Watts Riots, 44, 63–64
Weir, David, 180, 211
Welch, Lew, 32
Welty, Eudora, 40
Wenner, Jann, 59, 91–92, 93–94, 121, 203, 205; and *Fear and Loathing in Las Vegas*, 137, 141, 142, 153, 156; first meeting with Thompson, 118–19; and Hearst, 195; as key Thompson ally and promoter, 3, 141, 156–57, 158, 179; and the Pulitzer divorce piece, 193; at *Ramparts*, 92, 93; and *Rolling Stone's* editorial formula, 93–94, 118, 179–80, 188; and *Rolling Stone's* founding, 92, 93–94; souring of the relationship with Thompson, 186–87; on Thompson's work and legacy, 209; at UC Berkeley, 91–92; on working with Thompson, 182. *See also* *Rolling Stone*
Westword, 212, 213

"What Lured Hemingway to Ketchum?" (Thompson), 45

Where the Buffalo Roam (film), 190

White, Curtis, 213

White, Hayden, 166–67

White, Theodore, 162–64, 176

"White Album, The" (Didion), 88, 89, 167

Who, The, 91

"Why Boys Will Be Girls" (Thompson), 76

Williams, Jay, 42

Wilson, Edmund, 21

Wolfe, Tom: background, 50; correspondence and friendship with Thompson, 49–51, 63; as influence on Thompson, 12, 51, 101, 206; and the Merry Pranksters, 62–63; parallels and comparisons between Wolfe's and Thompson's work, 50–51, 110, 155; on Thompson's legacy, 209

women: and the Hell's Angels, 62, 68, 70; Thompson's behavior toward, 31. *See also* sex; sexual violence; Thompson, Sandra Conklin

women writers: Thompson and, 21. *See also specific writers*

Wood, Michael, 81

Woods, Crawford, 156

Woodstock festival, 91, 94–95, 116

Woodward, Bob, 188

Woody Creek, Thompson in, 1, 39, 94–96, 139, 179, 191, 205; final years and death, 202; Pitkin County sheriff campaign, 14, 120–24; sexual assault arrest, 196. *See also* Aspen

World of Sex, The (Miller), 29, 34

Yeamon (character), 21–22, 198–99

Yorty, Sam, 63

Zaire, Thompson on assignment in, 184–85

Zevon, Warren, 201

Ziegler, Ronald, 160, 177

Zion, Sidney, 102, 130

Founded in 1893,
UNIVERSITY OF CALIFORNIA PRESS
publishes bold, progressive books and journals
on topics in the arts, humanities, social sciences,
and natural sciences—with a focus on social
justice issues—that inspire thought and action
among readers worldwide.

The UC PRESS FOUNDATION
raises funds to uphold the press's vital role
as an independent, nonprofit publisher, and
receives philanthropic support from a wide
range of individuals and institutions—and from
committed readers like you. To learn more, visit
ucpress.edu/supportus.